THE PUNIC WARS

THE PUNIC WARS

ADRIAN GOLDSWORTHY

CASSELL&CO

Cassell & Co
Wellington House, 125 Strand
London WC2R 0BB

A catalogue record for this book is available from the British Library

ISBN 0-304-35284-5

Typography Gwyn Lewis

Printed and bound in Great Britain by
MPG Books, Bodmin, Cornwall

Contents

PART THREE

THE THIRD PUNIC WAR 149–146 BC

List of Maps

Preface

O H YES, HANNIBAL and his elephants' was the almost universal reaction whenever I told someone that I was writing a book about the Punic Wars. The Alps were mentioned fairly often, and every now and again the Romans put in an appearance, but that seemed to be about the limit of most people's knowledge. Only a few had much idea of when and by whom this series of conflicts had been fought, and who eventually won. A small minority, most of whom had an interest in ancient or military history, knew much more, and their knowledge was often remarkably detailed and embraced the minor tactical details of particular battles or the peculiarities of Punic religion. Perhaps it should be more surprising that even these few remembered anything at all about wars fought twenty-two centuries ago, but it is only in the last few generations that the Punic Wars have disappeared from the wider consciousness in Europe and North America. Until well into the twentieth century Greek and Latin languages and literature lay at the heart of Western education, and the major events and personalities of the Graeco-Roman World, especially those described by one of the great ancient authors, were familiar and frequently alluded to in art and literature.

All this has now changed, as Latin and Greek are now rarely taught in schools, and the perception of the classical roots of modern culture steadily diminishes. The distant – and often bitter – memory of childhood acquaintance with Caesar's *Gallic Wars* and Passives, Subjunctives and Ablative Absolutes is now increasingly uncommon. I am probably one of a relatively small minority in my generation who attended a school where Latin was compulsory from the age of nine. I can still remember toiling my way through a passage in my first Latin textbook (and so using only a few simple tenses) which recounted the story of Regulus keeping his oath even though it meant death by horrible torture. Such things were rare in the late

1970s and have become rarer still, but moral tales like that of Regulus, or Cincinnatus and Horatius Cocles were long seen as highly appropriate for children. Very few even of the students who study Ancient History, Classics or Philosophy at university now have any prior knowledge of Greek or Latin. Amongst the population as a whole references to Hollywood epics such as *Spartacus* or *Ben-Hur* are far more likely to prompt a response than mention of Polybius, Livy or Tacitus. A reversal of this trend seems extremely unlikely, but it is clear that interest in the long-distant past remains, evidenced by the regular appearance of television documentaries featuring history and archaeology. There are several reasons for this continued attention. The classical world witnessed many intensely dramatic events and was peopled with remarkable personalities, charismatic individuals whose careers were often both heroic and tragic. It is, in short, the source of many good stories which still bear retelling. Its influence, along with that of Christianity, also did more than anything else to shape the culture of today.

This is a work of military history and is not primarily aimed at an academic audience. Its intention is to provide an accessible account and analysis of the three wars fought between Rome and Carthage in the third and second centuries BC, placing them firmly within the context of the struggle for dominance of these two cities and within the background of warfare in this period. I have not attempted to provide references to the entire literature dealing in some way with aspects of these wars, nor have I included every theory or interpretation advanced by scholars in the nineteenth and twentieth centuries AD. More care has been taken to mention the ancient accounts of each incident, nearly all of which are available in translation and are essential for any deeper study into the subject. The general reader may rightly choose to ignore all of the references to both ancient and modern works. Those whose interest takes them further should be able to gain access to the mass of books and articles devoted to aspects of the Punic Wars through the bibliographies contained in the modern works cited here. The best narrative accounts of the First and Second Wars, with detailed discussions of the primary sources, are J. Lazenby's *The First Punic War* (London, 1995) and *Hannibal's War* (Warminster, 1978, reprinted with new introduction Oklahoma, 1998). These works provide sound starting places for more detailed study into either conflict.

No one can attempt any serious study of this period without leaning heavily upon F. Walbank's *A Historical Commentary on Polybius, 3 volumes* (Oxford, 1970), which has been recently reissued. It would easily have been possible to place a reference to this remarkable work on nearly every page of this book. The starting place for any discussion of the locations of the major battles in this period still remains J. Kromayer & G. Veith, *Antike Schlahtfelder* (Berlin, 1903–31) and its accompanying *Schlahtenatlas* (Gotha, 1922). However, we must admit that it is impossible to locate many battlefields with any certainty. In the current work I have only expressed a firm opinion on such matters in the case of areas which I have actually visited. Even the finest maps cannot replace the impression gained by actually walking over the ground itself. The precise location of many of these actions does not greatly affect our understanding of the conflicts as a whole.

Many conversations over the years have contributed to the ideas expressed in this book. Especially useful was a series of seminars run by myself and Louis Rawlings as part of the Cardiff University MA programme in 1996-7 on the theme of the Second Punic War. I would also like to thank all the family and friends who read the early drafts of the text and contributed many helpful comments, and in particular Ian Hughes and Kevin Powell. Finally, I should thank Nick Chapman, formerly of Cassell, who suggested and commissioned this book in its current form.

Note Throught this book centuries and dates mentioned should be assumed to be BC unless the text specifically indicates otherwise.

Introduction

T HE STRUGGLE BETWEEN Rome and Carthage spanned over a century from the first clash in 265 down to the final destruction of Carthage in 146. The First and Second Wars were fought on a scale seldom rivalled until the modern era. Fleets of more than 300 oared warships, crewed by over 100,000 sailors, were employed by both sides in the First War, and in the Second War hundreds of thousands of men were recruited to fight in the rival armies. The cost of constructing so many galleys, and paying, equipping and feeding so many men consumed a great part of the resources of the two most powerful states in the western Mediterranean. The human cost was even higher. In one battle alone in 216 the Romans and their allies lost around 50,000 dead. During the Second Punic War a sizeable part of Rome's adult male population perished, mostly in the first few years of the conflict. Casualties were not restricted to soldiers. Many civilians were massacred when one of the armies stormed a town or city, others were killed by the raiding bands which ravaged the fields and villages controlled by the other side, and, although the evidence for this is poor, we must assume that many, many more died from disease or starvation. Others were captured and enslaved, living out the remainder of their lives in squalid drudgery.

By the end of the conflict Carthage was in ruins, its life as a state ended and its culture almost totally extinguished. Between 265 and 146 Rome rose from being a purely Italian power into a position of unrivalled dominance throughout the Mediterranean basin, and was well on her way to creating the Empire which would control Western Europe, North Africa and the Near East for more than five centuries. The intervention in Sicily which led to the confrontation with Carthage was the first occasion that a Roman army was sent outside Italy. Roman imperialism did not begin with the Punic Wars, since by 265 Rome had already absorbed all of the Italian

Peninsula south of the River Po, but it was greatly accelerated by the struggle with Carthage. The Punic Wars accustomed the Romans to waging war on an enormous scale, sending armies further and further afield to fight in several widely separated theatres simultaneously. The eventual victory over Carthage confirmed the deep-seated determination with which the Romans waged war and which was to make them so difficult to defeat. Had the Romans lost the Punic Wars then the history of the world would have been very different. At the very least such a defeat would have seriously retarded Roman expansion, and it might well have ended it for ever. The centuries of Roman rule had a profound effect on their Empire, especially in Western Europe, both directly and through the revival of the Renaissance. As Europeans colonized America and established great overseas empires, they spread their Latin-based languages, legal systems and culture throughout the rest of the globe. None of this need have happened if the Romans had lost in 241 or succumbed to Hannibal's onslaught.

The Punic Wars marked an important phase in the history of Rome and the rise of the Roman Empire. Probably the largest conflict of the ancient world, the century-long struggle is also one of the best documented, although even so there remain some significant gaps in our knowledge. The three wars fought between these two great cities were epic in their scale, intensity and drama, and were filled with remarkable characters. On the Roman side were such men as Fabius Maximus, the man who saved the Republic by avoiding battle, and Marcellus, his far more aggressive contemporary who had killed a Gallic king in single combat. Then there are the many members of the Scipio family, most notably Publius Scipio Africanus who won Spain and invaded Africa, and his grandson by adoption and namesake, Scipio Aemilianus, who presided over Carthage's destruction in 146, weeping as he wondered whether the same fate would one day overtake his own homeland. Set against these heroic figures are the buffoons and incompetents, men like Appius Claudius Pulcher and Caius Flaminius who ignored both auspices and common sense to lead their men on to disaster. Some figures so rapidly became surrounded by myth that it is difficult now to know the full truth of their actions. Marcus Regulus was captured by the enemy and tales told of how they sent him to urge the Roman Senate to make peace, first binding him with savage oaths to return to Carthage. Regulus advised the Senate to continue the fight until victory and then returned to Africa, where he suffered death by torture. On the Carthaginian side the most charismatic figures were all members of the Barcid family, notably the father, Hamilcar, who kept the First Punic War going in Sicily and avoided battlefield defeat, and most of all Hannibal.

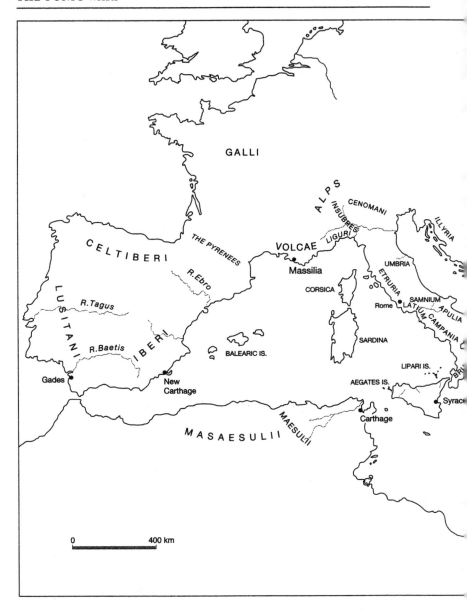

Hannibal has the sort of glamour which only surrounds those military geniuses who won stunning victories but ultimately lost the war, men such as Napoleon and Robert E. Lee. The march of his army from Spain via the Alps into Italy and the battles he won there were all epics in themselves. Not all the main figures of the conflict were either Carthaginian or Roman. There were Greeks too, like Hiero the wily ruler of the great Sicilian city of Syracuse, and his relative Archimedes, the geometrician who designed

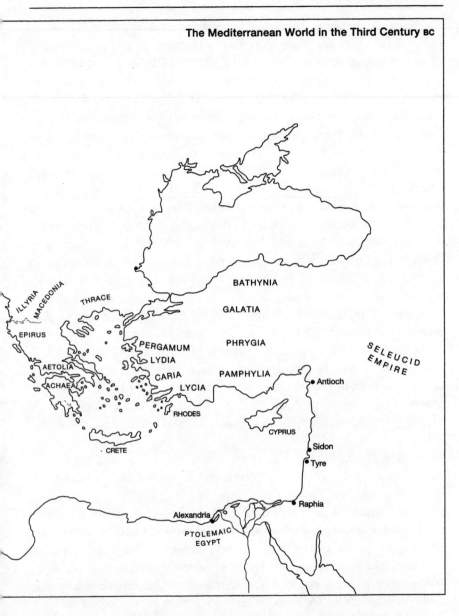

The Mediterranean World in the Third Century BC

ILLYRIA
MACEDONIA
THRACE
EPIRUS
BATHYNIA
GALATIA
PERGAMUM
PHRYGIA
SELEUCID EMPIRE
AETOLIA
LYDIA
ACHAEA
CARIA
PAMPHYLIA
LYCIA
• Antioch
RHODES
CYPRUS
CRETE
• Sidon
• Tyre
• Raphia
Alexandria
PTOLEMAIC EGYPT

fabulous war engines and is said to have been killed when he refused to be interrupted in the middle of a mathematical problem. Then there was Masinissa, the Numidian king who was still fathering children and riding into battle at the head of his men as he approached his ninetieth year.

It was the Punic Wars which first led the Romans to begin writing the history of their people, first in Greek and then in Latin. Others too realized the importance of this conflict and many Greek writers produced narratives of the struggle, trying to explain the Romans' rapid rise to power. These wars which began twenty-two centuries ago have continued to receive considerable attention to this day, and Cannae is one of the few battles before the eighteenth century AD to merit attention in modern military academies. Napoleon numbered Hannibal amongst the 'Great Captains' of the past whose campaigns could teach much to modern commanders. In the nineteenth century AD German academics and soldiers studied the Second Punic War in great, sometimes obsessive detail, and Von Schlieffen, the architect of the offensive which was launched into France in 1914, consciously attempted to reproduce the genius of Hannibal's battle tactics on a vast scale. Liddell Hart and Fuller, two of the leading British military theorists of the first half of the twentieth century AD, likewise commented upon and drew inspiration from the third century BC conflict. The First and Second Punic Wars seemed especially relevant in the twentieth century, with its World Wars fought on an unprecedented scale, the outbreak in 1939 growing directly from one side's dissatisfaction with the treaty ending the 1914–18 conflict, in the same way that Carthage had renewed the war with Rome in 218 apparently because of its resentment of the harsh Treaty of 241. As recently as the Gulf War in AD 1991, the UN commander claimed to have drawn inspiration for his swift and highly successful operation from Hannibal's campaigns. Experienced soldiers are still drawn to write about the Punic Wars, using their own practical knowledge to gain new insights and often seeking lessons for modern strategy and tactics. Others, both soldiers and civilians, remain fascinated by the route followed by Hannibal's army and elephants across the Alps and the debate on this subject still rages fiercely. New books appear and many of the older works are reprinted.[1]

Military history is no longer fashionable in the universities of the West, and relatively few studies of Roman warfare are produced by academics. The majority of the most influential works dealing with strategy, tactics or the locations of ancient battlefields were written in the late nineteenth or early twentieth centuries AD. In political, social and economic history the studies produced in that era have long since been supplemented or supplanted, sometimes several times, by more recent works. Yet even though little military history is now produced by ancient historians, it is rare when a year passes without the publication of a book or article dealing in some way or other with the Punic Wars. Some of this work is prompted by new archaeological evidence, but the vast majority consists of fresh interpretations of the existing evidence. There still seems to be a particular interest in Punic culture in France, a result in part of the exciting archaeological discoveries made on the site of Carthage itself which began when the area was under French rule and have continued to this day. For a while, the inhabitants of nineteenth-century France had the same sort of appetite for anything Carthaginian that they and many other countries developed for Ancient Egyptian culture. Gustave Flaubert's savage novel *Salammbô* was one product of this interest.

Much has been written about the Punic Wars, and it might well be asked what more can be added. Certainly some areas have been debated so thoroughly that it is very difficult to say anything new. Yet in some respects the wars have not been properly treated. Few studies have attempted to cover all three conflicts; most concentrate on just one of the wars, usually the Second Punic War. The First Punic War can perhaps with some justice be treated in isolation, although in fact it has received little attention and only recently has an up to date account in English appeared, but the Second and Third Wars arose directly from the earlier conflict. The three wars were episodes in the longer, ongoing struggle between Rome and Carthage and need to be understood in this context. The causes, each side's war aims and the course of both of the later wars were directly determined by the outcome of the previous encounters. A few accounts have dealt with all three wars, but none are entirely satisfactory. Many of their faults are shared with much of the literature dealing with aspects of the conflict, for instance viewing Roman politics as dominated by clearly defined factions, an interpretation no longer accepted by mainstream studies of the politics of this period. Even more importantly, they have tended to analyse the campaigns on the assumption that they were fought in obedience to essentially the same rules of strategy and tactics as more recent wars. This view has always been especially favoured by the experienced soldiers who have studied the wars of the past in order to understand how better to fight the wars of the present day. Such studies inevitably focus their attention on the aspects which the warfare of all periods has, or appears to have had, in common. Therefore it is assumed that army commanders in all periods of history do essentially the same job in much the same way, making it entirely valid to judge Roman or Punic generals by the standards of Frederick the Great, Napoleon or Rommel. The very title of Liddell Hart's book, *A Greater than Napoleon – Scipio Africanus* (1930), assumed the validity of such a comparison.[2]

There is no question that some aspects of warfare have changed little over the centuries. The practical problems of moving large numbers of troops, feeding and supplying them, conveying orders, and the restrictions imposed by natural obstacles and terrain remain the same as they did in the

Stone Age, and a soldier will often comment more practically on such issues than an academic whose life has been spent in universities. However, whilst the problems do not change, the solutions proposed for them vary enormously from one society to another and are not simply dictated by the restrictions of available technology. Peoples at the same technological level and with similar resources at their disposal do not necessarily wage war in the same way. Warfare is affected as much by culture as any other human pursuit. The Roman system of drawing commanders from men following a political career would make little sense in modern western democracies, who emphasize the professional training of their military leaders. The Romans would have not understood the clear distinction between military and political leadership maintained in these countries. A Roman senator was not either a politician or a soldier, but automatically both. Despite much modern criticism of this aspect of the Roman military system, it does seem to have worked very well for them. Not every society organizes its armed forces or fights in the precisely the same way. Even more importantly each culture tends to have its own concept of what war is, why and how wars are fought, how they are decided and what are the consequences of victory and defeat.[3]

This study will try to place the Punic Wars firmly within the context of the military theory and practice of the third to second centuries BC. It will examine the Roman and Carthaginian attitude to warfare, their military institutions and the political and social organizations which produced them, arguing that these shaped the conflict and that the differences between them ultimately decided its outcome. This is primarily a military history and will only touch briefly on the social and economic impact of the wars. It is not intended to provide a full year by year narrative of each campaign. In many cases the evidence is too poor to attempt this with any confidence, but even where it is, the account tends to become simply a catalogue of unfamiliar place names. Where campaigns occurred simultaneously in several different theatres, each will be dealt with in turn. Different types of fighting are examined separately, so that for instance the naval and land operations of the First Punic War each receive their own chapter. Certain episodes are examined in great detail, for instance Hannibal's campaigns from 218 to 216. These were important in their own right, but are also very well recorded and provide many insights into the formal battles of the period. The aim throughout is to examine how the armies and navies of the period operated, and how the different types of fighting had an impact on the wider war. The analysis is concerned with why a general made a decision and what consequences it had, and not with suggesting alternative and perhaps better courses of action. The armchair strategist who seeks to prove how Hannibal could easily have triumphed if only he had done things differently convinces only himself.

The Evidence

The study of any aspect of ancient history differs from that of more recent periods for the simple reason that the sources of information are far less plentiful and their interpretation uncertain. There is doubt as to whether some major events happened in one year or the next, whilst it is now difficult to say whether some incidents, including certain battles, occurred at all. We cannot say with any certainty how the quinquereme, the main warship of the Punic Wars, was designed and constructed, and there are numerous gaps in our knowledge of the equipment, organization, command structure and tactics of the opposing armies, most especially the Carthaginians. Sometimes it is a question of trying to work out a basic sequence of events before any attempt can be made at understanding it, a situation largely unparalleled by military history from the eighteenth century onwards. Nor is the evidence evenly distributed over the period. The Second Punic War is fairly well recorded by our surviving sources, but the Third and most of all the First War are more poorly covered. Overwhelmingly the evidence is drawn from the literary accounts of Greek and Roman authors. Archaeological excavation has told us much about the layout and defences of some cities, most notably Carthage and Syracuse, and provides information about Punic culture and settlement in Sicily and Spain. Yet archaeology is best at revealing long-term trends, and is too clumsy to tell us much about military operations. Direct archaeological evidence for warfare is very rare from the entire classical period.

History tends to be written by the winning side, but the situation is more extreme when the losers were utterly destroyed. No account exists describing any part of the conflict from the Punic perspective. Some Greek authors produced narratives favouring the Carthaginians, most notably those by the two historians who accompanied Hannibal on his Italian expedition, one of whom was his former tutor Sosylus.[4] None of these accounts have survived although it is clear that they were known to and used by some of the surviving sources. Even these lost accounts were written by Greeks in the Greek language and thus by outsiders, who may not fully have understood Punic institutions and culture. It is therefore inevitable that we see the Punic Wars from either a Greek or Roman perspective and in the accounts of authors who knew that Rome would eventually prevail. It is impossible to write a Punic version of the conflict, since it would be as unwise automatically to discount every story favourable to the Romans and credit every incident favourable to the Carthaginians as to accept all of the Roman propaganda about Punic treachery. Ultimately, this must remain the story of Rome's wars against a Punic enemy, as the name Punic Wars implies, since the Carthaginians would hardly have thought of the conflict as wars against themselves.

Greek and Roman historians did not aspire to the same ideals as their modern counterparts. History was a branch of literature intended to entertain – an idea which would be anathema to many academics today – as well as to inform and inspire. Convention permitted appropriate speeches to be invented and assigned to leading participants at major events, and encouraged the inclusion of familiar generic set-pieces, or *topoi*, in descriptions of such events as the sack of cities or the aftermath of a battle. Whether this meant that such incidents were invented or simply that these were the type of events which were automatically chosen by authors for inclusion is impossible to say. The ideal of ancient historiography was that it should be truthful as well as skilfully crafted, and it is probable that at the very least the bare narrative of their accounts conform closely to the actual events. There is anyway no real alternative to this view. If we reject the accounts of ancient authors altogether – an extreme view, but one which some scholars come close to – then there is nothing with which to replace them. Some authors are clearly more reliable than others and it is worth looking individually at the main sources for this period.

By far the most important was the Greek historian Polybius. An Achaean nobleman who fought against the Romans in the Third Macedonian War, he was one of a thousand hostages from the Achaean League taken to Rome at the formal end of the war in 167. There he became an intimate of a young Roman nobleman, Publius Cornelius Scipio Aemilianus who was later to destroy Carthage, and received preferential treatment. Polybius accompanied Scipio Aemilianus on campaign in Africa and Spain, as well as travelling widely in the western Mediterranean. It is uncertain precisely when he began to write his *History*, and what was its original scope, but it certainly came to include the Third Punic and Fourth Macedonian Wars which ended in 146. Its detailed narrative began with the Second Punic War and contemporary events in the Greek East, for Polybius aimed to write 'universal history' describing the events during the same period throughout the civilized world. The main theme was to explain to a Greek audience how the Romans had come to dominate the Mediterranean world in such a short time. The finished work consisted of forty Books, the first two covering the period before the Hannibalic war.

Book 1 as a result provides our most complete and reliable account of the First Punic War, despite the fact that Polybius covered this in far less detail than the Second and Third Wars. Sadly only a small part of the total work has survived. The narrative is complete down to 216, but exists only in fragments thereafter.

Polybius attempted to establish the truth of events and is scathing in his criticism of other authors who did not. He was able to speak to some surviving participants of the war against Hannibal, and was an eyewitness to the Fall of Carthage in 146. His association with one of Rome's great noble families placed him in a unique position to understand how the Roman political and military systems worked. Occasionally his theories of universal history may have led him to be over schematic in his interpretation of events, but on the whole he is sober and carefully analytical. Although a great admirer of the Romans, this does not prevent him from criticizing their behaviour on some occasions, or revealing them to have been sometimes duplicitous and incompetent. His association with Scipio Aemilianus did result in a very favourable depiction of the role played by his relatives in the conflict. Scipio Aemilianus had been adopted by the son of Scipio Africanus, the man who finally defeated Hannibal at Zama. He was the best Roman commander of the Second War and deserves at least the greater part of the praise which Polybius lavishes on him. Africanus' father played a far less distinguished role, but receives very favourable mention. Aemilius' actual father was Aemilius Paullus, son of the consul killed at Cannae. Polybius does much to exonerate the elder Paullus for responsibility for this disaster although, it should be noted, he does not go as far as other sources in this respect. Finally, Aemilianus' older brother was adopted by one of the descendants of Fabius Maximus, whose dictatorship in 217 and subsequent commands all seem to have received favourable treatment. Sadly we do not have Polybius' account of 205 when Fabius Maximus is supposed to have opposed Scipio's appointment to the African command.[5]

Polybius' account is usually to be preferred when it differs with any of our other accounts, but its fragmentary nature means that we are frequently reliant on other authors. The most important of these is Livy, who wrote in Rome during the reign of the first Emperor, Augustus, in the late first century BC and early first century AD. His *History of Rome* began with the mythical origins of that city and ended with Augustus. It was a fiercely patriotic account, intended to celebrate the virtues of former generations, explaining how all of Rome's problems were caused by declining morals and the actions of a few misguided, popularizing politicians. The mood was in keeping with the ethos of the Augustan regime which, despite its radical nature, claimed to have revived traditional piety and morality, and to be a proper successor to the strong Republic of the third century BC and before. Unlike Polybius, Livy had no direct experience of military or political life, and was far less discerning in his use of sources. His work originally consisted of 142 Books, but only Books 1–10, covering the period down to 293 BC, 20–30, dealing with the Second Punic War of 218–201, and 31–45, which continue the narrative down to 167, have survived. The other books, including those dealing with the First and Third Punic Wars, exist only in brief summaries of their contents.

Livy provides the longest and most complete account of the war with Hannibal and we must rely heavily on him for the war after 216 for which we have only a few fragments of Polybius. Livy's narrative is intensely dramatic and includes many of the most romantic stories associated with the war. He had access to the full version of Polybius' narrative and appears to have used it extensively in some sections. However, even with such a good source Livy could be guilty of fairly major mistakes. His narrative of the battle of Cynoscephalae in 197 BC reads in places almost like a translation of Polybius' account, which has survived intact. Yet where Polybius informs us that the Macedonian phalanx lowered its pikes from the marching position resting on the shoulder to the fighting position held level in both hands, Livy misunderstood the Greek text and informs us that the Macedonians dropped their pikes and drew their swords instead. Elsewhere Livy employed far less reliable sources, some heavily influenced by the traditions of Roman senatorial families which exaggerated the achievements of their own ancestors. Occasionally he lists different versions of a story given by various earlier authors, providing us with an impression of some of these lost works, but most often he presents us with a simple narrative. Livy provides more detail than Polybius concerning Roman politics, especially some of the controversial elections, and of Rome's state religion. All of his account, and the military narratives in particular, do need to be used with some caution.[6]

Most of our other sources are even later than Livy. Diodorus Siculus was roughly contemporary and produced a universal *Library of History* in the last decades of the first century BC. It consisted of at least forty Books, but survives only in fragmentary form for this period. A Sicilian Greek, Diodorus drew somewhat eclectically on various earlier, lost sources, such as the pro-Carthaginian account of the First Punic War written by Philinus. Appian was an Alexandrian Greek and a Roman citizen who produced a twenty-four-book Roman History. The sections dealing with the Punic

Wars are intact, but vary considerably in their style. His description of the battle of Zama reads like an extract from the *Iliad*. However, he produced by far the best account of the Third Punic War and appears to have drawn heavily on Polybius' lost narrative. In the early third century AD, Dio Cassius, a Roman senator of Greek extraction, wrote an eighty-book *History of Rome*. Only fragments of this survive, but an epitome of the work produced in the twelfth century AD by a Byzantine monk, Zonaras, still exists as a continuous narrative. In addition to these historical narratives, there are the biographies of notable Roman figures produced in the early second century AD by Plutarch, a Greek from Chaeronea. Plutarch was more interested in the character of his subjects than in providing a detailed narrative of their careers, but nevertheless includes much useful information. Brief biographies of Hamilcar and Hannibal were also produced in the later first century BC by Cornelius Nepos and preserve some information not included by any of our other sources.

Most of our sources were written long after the events that they describe. Polybius witnessed the Third Punic War and spoke to men who had fought in the Hannibalic War, but no participants in the First War were still alive by the time he arrived in Rome. How much information about these conflicts was available to our sources? Mention has already been made of some Greek accounts sympathetic to the Carthaginians, notably the Sicilian Philinus for the First War and the Spartan Sosylus for the Second. In the late third century BC the Romans themselves began to write history, largely because they realized the importance of their victories over Carthage. Quintus Fabius Pictor and Lucius Cincius Alimentus, both of them distinguished senators, wrote histories in Greek, and in the second century Marcus Porcius Cato wrote the first Latin prose history. Polybius noted that such accounts consistently tended to favour their own side and that sometimes they directly contradicted each other. In addition to the written accounts there were memories preserved by the great families in Rome, although these were often little more than propaganda, and far more reliable documents such as the Treaties between Rome and Carthage which Polybius consulted and inscriptions such as the Lacinian column set up by Hannibal. There was clearly far more documentation available for the Second Punic War than the more distant First Punic War. Polybius mentions that he was even able to read a letter in which Scipio Africanus described the planning of his Spanish campaign to the Macedonian King Philip V. No such direct sources existed for the earlier conflict.[7]

We can be fairly confident that our narratives of the Second War are on the whole reliable and that most of the detail in the better accounts was drawn from contemporary or near contemporary sources. The situation is less certain with the campaigns of 265–241 BC. The basic outline of events is likely to be correct, but many of the details remain questionable. Readers will note that our lesser sources are mentioned far more often in the discussions of this period than for the operations between 218–201 where the main emphasis is on Polybius and Livy. The Third Punic War is almost totally based upon Appian's account, supported by the few surviving fragments of Polybius. Where several parallel accounts exist of the same period it is possible to compare them and decide which author was most likely to have supplied the most reliable information. When only a single narrative exists there is little choice but to accept it as long as it seems reasonably plausible, since if it is rejected there is nothing with which to replace it. On many occasions in the following chapters it will be noted that doubt exists about some of the events described. The numbers supplied by even the most reliable sources need always to be treated with caution since numbers, especially Roman numerals, were one of the easiest things to be corrupted as manuscripts were copied and recopied by hand over the centuries. Even so, the modern historian must be very cautious before suggesting more 'plausible' alternatives.

CHAPTER 1

The Opposing Sides

EFORE LOOKING IN detail at the political organizations and military systems of Rome and Carthage on the eve of their first conflict, it is worth considering what the Mediterranean world was like in the third century BC. The death of Alexander the Great in 323 BC without a clear, adult successor had quickly torn his vast Empire apart. Eventually, three major dynasties emerged, the Ptolemies in Egypt, the Seleucids in Syria and much of Asia, and the Antigonid Kingdom of Macedonia. These bickered with each other and with the various smaller kingdoms, cities and leagues of cities which appeared in Greece and Asia Minor. The Greek communities which occupied most of Sicily and southern Italy – known as Magna Graecia – and were dotted around the coasts of Spain and southern Gaul, notably the great city of Massilia (Marseilles), were culturally part of the Hellenic world, but politically divided. Spain was occupied by the Iberians in the south, Celtiberians of mixed Spanish and Gallic stock in the north and the Lusitanians in the west. Gaul and northern Italy were populated by the people known to the Greeks as Celtoi and the Romans as Galli. All of these peoples were essentially tribal, although the level of unity within a tribe, the power of its leaders, and the strength of individual tribes fluctuated. Some peoples were developing settlements which already resembled classical city states. The Ligurians of north-western Italy were much more fragmented socially, with few leaders able to control more than the warriors of their own small village. In all of these peoples a leader's status depended primarily on his martial prowess. Raiding and small-scale warfare were endemic; battles less common, but by no means unknown.[1]

At the beginning of the third century Carthage was undisputedly the greatest power in the western Mediterranean. The Romans first really came to prominence, at least in the eyes of the literate Greek world, following their stubborn resistance to and eventual victory over Pyrrhus in 280–275. Yet they remained entirely an Italian power and it is fitting that we should look first at Carthage.

Carthage

Phoenician merchant ships, initially powered solely by oars, were a familiar sight throughout the Mediterranean world from the beginning of the last millennium BC. A Semitic people, whose great cities of Tyre and Sidon lay on the coast of what is now Lebanon, the Phoenicians established trading settlements throughout the Mediterranean. There is archaeological evidence for their presence in Spain from the eighth century BC, but it is probable that they were active in the area earlier than this, for this was clearly Tartessus, the Tarshish of the Old Testament, a source of great mineral wealth. Carthage was not the first Punic settlement in Africa – Utica was certainly older – but it seems from the beginning to have had a special importance. Myth later told of Elissa (Phoenician Elishat) or Dido who fled from Tyre after her brother, King Pygmalion, had killed her husband, and in 814 she founded Carthage. Granted as much land as an ox-hide could cover by the Libyans, Elissa cut the hide into thin strips and so was able to claim far more ground than anticipated, in an early display of that deviousness which the Romans and Greeks considered a Punic trait. Subsequently Elissa chose to burn herself on a funeral pyre rather than marry the Libyan King Hierbos, an act which protected her people and maintained faith with her dead husband.[2]

Whether there is any slight trace of the truth in this story is impossible to say, for foundation myths were common in the Graeco-Roman world and frequently fabricated. We do not know what the Carthaginians themselves said of the origins of their city. Excavation has yet to reveal any traces of occupation before the very end of the eighth century BC. It is clear that Carthage maintained a close link with Tyre throughout its history. Annually an expedition was sent to sacrifice at the Temple of Melquart ('The Lord of the City') at Tyre, a connection that was preserved even after Carthage grew in power and began to found colonies of its own. Culturally the city remained distinctively Phoenician in language and culture, the adoption of some Greek and Libyan customs not changing its essential nature. In at least one aspect of religious practice the Carthaginians were more conservative than the people of Tyre. They continued the ghastly Moloch sacrifices of infants which were killed and burned in honour of Ba'al Hammon and his consort Tanit, a practice which had been abandoned at Tyre by the time Carthage was established. The Tophet of Salammbô, the

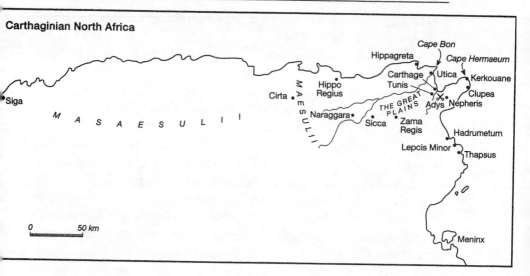

Carthaginian North Africa

cult site where this ritual occurred, is the oldest structure yet discovered by archaeology at Carthage and the excavations have shown that the practice continued until 146. Disturbingly, the proportion of sacrifices where a lamb or other animal was substituted for the child decreased rather than increased over the centuries. Similar tophets have been discovered at other Carthaginian foundations, but rarely if ever on sites founded directly by the Phoenicians. Religion was closely controlled by the state at Carthage and its senior magistrates combined a political and religious function.[3]

Carthaginian overseas foundations remained primarily trading centres, like their Phoenician predecessors, but from the sixth century onwards they came into direct competition with the Greek colonies which began to spring up. The main driving force behind Greek colonization was the shortage of good, cultivatable land to meet the demand of an expanding population. The colonies they established were replicas of the city states or *poleis* of Greece itself, communities in which status was normally dependent on ownership of land. Competition between rivals both eager to exploit territories for their own benefit developed into open conflict, primarily for the control of Sicily. Numbers favoured the Greek colonists, for Carthaginian settlements were always small in size, but the Greeks were handicapped by their political disunity. An especially ferocious tone was added to the conflict by the strong religious differences between the two sides, and it was common for shrines and temples to be desecrated. This attitude softened slightly as the Carthaginian state began to accept certain Greek deities. The worship of Demeter and Kore (Persephone) was formally introduced to Carthage in 396, an act of propitiation after the destruction of one of their temples in Sicily had been followed by a devastating plague amongst the Punic army there.

The fortunes of both sides fluctuated during the long contest for Sicily. In 480 the Greeks won a great victory at Himera, an achievement which happily coincided with the defeat of Xerxes' invasion of Greece at Salamis in the same year and Plataea in 479, and was a cause of much satisfaction throughout the Hellenic world. Despite such failures, the Carthaginians persevered and Greeks increasingly were forced to accept the leadership of tyrants, notably Dionysius and Agathocles, or mercenary captains, of whom Pyrrhus was one of the last, to continue the struggle. In 310, Agathocles, the tyrant of Syracuse, landed a force at Cape Bon in North Africa and posed a direct threat to the Carthaginian homeland. This produced a panic and political upheaval at Carthage. Agathocles defeated a much larger Carthaginian army, drawing troops away from the Punic expeditionary force. Ultimately, he was incapable of storming Carthage itself and could not raise enough of its Libyan subjects in revolt to weaken it fatally. Abandoning his army, Agathocles returned to Syracuse from which he dominated much of Sicily until his death in 289. Pyrrhus' intervention on the island initially checked the Carthage's reviving power, but failed to achieve any long-term results when his allies turned against him and the Carthaginians defeated his fleet in 276. By the time of the war with Rome, Carthage was clear master of all of the southern and western parts of Sicily.[4]

In the fifth century Carthagian power in Africa itself had steadily increased, perhaps in part encouraged by the failures in Sicily. The city had ceased to pay the subsidies levied by the local Libyan rulers and had come to control all the other Phoenician towns in the area, notably Hadrumentum and Utica. In the middle of the century Carthaginian fleets mounted great exploratory voyages along the North African coastline, passing the Straits of Gibraltar and pushing hundreds of miles along the western coastline. More permanently this led to the establishment of further trading posts in Africa, whilst the settlements in Spain continued to be developed. Control of all these outposts on the key coastal positions, for Carthaginian settlements were always based around good harbours, combined with the power of the Punic fleet, gave the city control of all the major trade routes in the western Mediterranean. Everywhere its merchants traded in the most favourable conditions, whilst those of other nationalities paid dues and tolls which further enriched the city's coffers. The enormous wealth of Carthage was reflected in the steady growth of the city and the splendour of its defences and buildings. Remains of the new areas of the city show evidence of having been laid out to a clearly organized plan, conforming to, although not as rigid as, the most advanced contemporary Hellenistic town-planning.[5]

Trade was not the only source of the city's prosperity. It is important not to forget that Carthage's wealth was also derived from a highly organized and effective agricultural base. The Agricultural Manual produced by a Carthaginian nobleman, Mago, probably dating to the late fourth century, was later to have a massive influence on the rest of the world when it was translated into both Greek and Latin after 146. Mago wrote about the methods of running a large estate worked at least in part by servile labour, supplemented by Libyan peasants. By 300 the Carthaginians directly controlled about half of the territory of modern-day Tunisia and the greater part of this was owned by the nobility. The nobles of Carthage were just as much a landowning aristocracy as the ruling élites of other cities, including Rome. The land was fertile (far more so than today), the climate favourable and their productivity foreshadowed the time when the African provinces would be the great granaries of the Roman Empire. These estates produced vast quantities of grain and especially the tree crops for which Africa was famous, such as grapes, figs, olives, almonds, and pomegranates. Agathocles' army is supposed to have been amazed by the fertility of the Carthaginian farms when they landed in Africa. Not only did this supply the city's needs, but it also provided a great surplus for export.[6]

In 300 the land controlled by Carthage was significantly greater than the *ager Romanus*, the lands owned by the Roman people, and rivalled the sum of these and the territories of Rome's allies. Its yield was probably significantly greater, for much of the land in Italy had poorer soil. Yet the benefits from this agricultural richness were not evenly shared and were enjoyed largely by the Carthaginians themselves, and most of all by their nobility. Carthage proved reluctant to extend citizenship and political rights to the peoples within the areas she came to control. The citizens of Carthaginian and Phoenician communities enjoyed a privileged position, as did the people of mixed race known to the Greeks as the Liby-Phoenicians, but others remained clearly subordinate allies or subjects. Therefore the extension of Punic hegemony over Africa, Spain, Sicily and Sardinia did not result in a great expansion of the Carthaginian citizen body. The Libyan population on the great estates seem to have been tied to the land and had little freedom. Libyan communities allied to Carthage enjoyed some internal autonomy, but were clearly subject to Punic will. Whilst waging the First Punic War, other Carthaginian soldiers were engaged in bitter fighting to conquer more Libyan communities. When after the peace with Rome the mercenary soldiers of Carthage mutinied and turned against her, they were swiftly supported by many Libyan communities. Other allied peoples, such as the Numidian kingdoms in Africa, enjoyed greater or lesser autonomy, but derived few benefits from being part of the Carthaginian empire to which they paid subsidies and for which they were often obliged to fight as soldiers.

Carthage had originally been a monarchy, its kingship possessing a strongly religious character, but by the third century the senior executive officers of the state were the two annually elected suffetes. It is unknown whether this office developed from or replaced the monarchy, but the Greek use of the word *basileus* (king) for this magistracy makes it possible that there was a connection. The nature of the Punic monarchy is fiercely debated by scholars, but it may be that it had been an elective office. Wealth as much as merit was important in the election of the suffetes, who held supreme civil and religious power but did not act as military commanders. A Council of Thirty Elders (or *gerousia*) acted in an advisory capacity and was supervised by and probably drawn from another tribunal, the Council of 104. If the suffetes and the Elders agreed on a course of action then they had the power to implement it. If they were unable to reach agreement then the proposals were taken to the Assembly of the People to decide the matter. At these meetings any citizen was permitted to make a counter-proposal. It is clear that a relatively small number of noble families dominated the council and probably monopolized the office of *suffes* (suffete). The details of the internal politics of the city are far less clear, and whilst we gain hints of disputes and factionalism, it is impossible to describe these with any precision. Greek philosophers, most notably Aristotle, praised Carthage for possessing a balanced constitution combining elements of monarchy, aristocracy and democracy, which allowed it to avoid the chronic instability which was the weakness of most Greek states. Certainly Carthage appears to have been very stable, although it is difficult to say whether or not the Greeks had understood the true reason for this, and its regime was one from which the citizens, and most of all the wealthy, benefited greatly.[7]

The Carthaginian Military System
The Hellenistic kingdoms of the eastern Mediterranean all fielded armies modelled closely on those of Philip and Alexander. They were composed of professional soldiers recruited from a relatively small pool of citizens settled in military colonies. The core of each army was the phalanx of highly drilled pikemen, supported by close-order shock cavalry, although few were able to field as many of the latter as Alexander had done. These well-trained

and disciplined soldiers were very effective, but it was difficult for the kingdoms to replace heavy casualties quickly. The frequency with which the kingdoms fought each other ensured that more often than not the armies operated against enemy forces composed of the same basic elements and fighting in a similar manner. It was no coincidence that these armies began to experiment with such unusual elements as cataphract cavalry, war elephants and scythed chariots, seeking in some way to gain an advantage over their similar enemy. Works of military theory, which had begun to appear in the fourth century, were produced in great profusion in the third. Pyrrhus himself wrote a work on Generalship, although sadly this has not survived. This theoretical literature dealt firmly with the expectation of war between similar Hellenistic armies. However, neither of the armies involved in the Punic Wars conformed closely to this model.[8]

Carthage had a very small citizen body and early on in its history abandoned the practice of relying on citizen soldiers for the bulk of its armies, being unwilling to risk heavy casualties amongst this group. Citizens were only obliged to undergo military service to face a direct threat to the city itself. When they took the field they did so as close order infantrymen, fighting in a phalanx and armed with shields and long spears, but their military effectiveness was poor, probably as a result of their inexperience. Agathocles defeated a far larger army including a large contingent of these citizen spearmen in 309, and their record in the first two conflicts with Rome was undistinguished.

More Carthaginian citizens appear to have served in the navy, although admittedly our evidence for the recruitment of sailors is very slight. Unlike the armies, which tended to be raised for a particular conflict and were disbanded at its end, the Carthaginian navy had a more permanent status, since there was always the need to protect the trade routes which brought the city so much wealth. The famous circular naval harbour at Carthage provided ramps to act as berths for about 180 ships and all the facilities for their maintenance. Excavations at the harbour dated it at the earliest to the second century, although the evidence was not certain and it is possible that this was a period of rebuilding. Even if the earlier naval harbour was not located on this site, it is likely that it was constructed on a similarly grand scale. The entire fleet is unlikely to have been crewed and in service except in wartime. However, an efficient fleet could only have been maintained if crews were regularly exercised at sea, so it is likely that sizeable squadrons were permanently maintained. It is distinctly possible that many of the poorest citizens of Carthage derived their livelihood from service as rowers in the fleet. If this is so, then it may well have contributed to the city's political stability, since the unemployed, debt-ridden poor in other cities were frequently inclined to support revolutionary leaders in the hope of improving their own desperate lot.[9]

The lack of citizen manpower ensured that Carthaginian armies were recruited from foreign soldiers. Libyans provided probably the steadiest and most disciplined element in most armies. Their close formation infantry were equipped with long spears and round or oval shields, and wore helmets and probably linen cuirasses. Libyan cavalry were also close order troops armed with thrusting spears, trained to deliver a controlled, shock charge. The Libyans may well also have provided some of the infantry skirmishers, the *lonchophoroi* of Polybius, each armed with a small shield and bundle of javelins. The Numidian kingdoms were renowned for their superb light cavalry, who rode their small mounts without either bridle or saddle and harassed the enemy with volleys of javelins, avoiding close combat unless conditions were absolutely in their favour. Numidian armies also included infantry skirmishers equipped with javelins and the same round shield borne by the cavalry and it is possible that contingents of these troops were also sent to Punic forces. From Spain came both light and heavy infantry, whose normal dress was a white tunic with a purple border. The heavy infantry (*scutati*) fought as a dense phalanx, carried a long body shield and were armed with a heavy throwing spear and a sword, either the short, thrusting weapon which provided the model for the Roman *gladius* or the curved, slashing *falcata*. The light infantry (*caetrati*) carried a small round shield and several javelins. Gallic infantry fought in massed formation and carried shields and javelins, but relied on their long, slashing swords. Both Spaniards and Gauls also provided contingents of well-mounted and brave, if undisciplined, cavalry, whose primary tactic was the all-out charge. Body armour was very unusual amongst the tribal peoples of Europe, helmets only a little less uncommon. The warriors of these nations were characterized by classical authors as ferocious in the first charge, but easily tired and inclined to lose heart if things did not quickly go their way. There was some truth in this statement, but on other occasions these troops proved far more stubborn than this stereotype would allow.[10]

Our sources primarily speak of the components of Carthaginian armies as national groups. Only a very small detachment from a field army was ever likely to be composed of a single nationality and some armies were very mixed. Usually an effort was made not to rely too heavily on the peoples indigenous to the theatre of operations for fear of defection or desertion. Before his Italian expedition Hannibal sent a large contingent of

Spanish troops to Africa, replacing them with units raised there. The Carthaginian high command provided the sole unifying force in each army.[11]

It is conventional to describe Punic armies as consisting of mercenaries, but this is a gross oversimplification, since these forces included soldiers raised in many different ways with a great variety of different motivations. Some contingents were not hired, but provided by allied kingdoms or states as part of their treaty obligations. This always seems to have been the case with the Numidian kingdoms, whose royal families enjoyed a fairly close relationship with the Carthaginian noble families, bonds that were sometimes strengthened by marriage alliances. Numidian contingents were usually led by their own princes. Similarly many of the tribes in Spain and Gaul were formally allied to Carthage and fielded contingents identical to their own tribal armies and commanded by their own chieftains. Again, there is some indication of Punic leaders forming strong connections with the native aristocracy, perhaps allowing them to exploit traditional patterns of loyalty. Hasdrubal certainly married a Spanish princess and it is possible that Hannibal also did so. It is clear that the Spanish tribes' loyalty focused on the Barcid family rather than the distant Carthage. Later, the tribes would similarly adhere to the Scipiones, rather than Rome, rebelling when it was rumoured that Scipio Africanus had left Spain.[12]

We do not know precisely how the Libyan units were raised. Some troops were probably provided by allied cities in a similar manner to the Numidians. Others may well have been formed by peasants conscripted from the great Carthaginian estates. This area was later to prove a very fertile recruiting area in the Roman Empire. Even the troops clearly hired as mercenaries were not all recruited in the same manner. In some cases these men were hired as a group, a leader or chieftain offering his own and his warband's services for hire. The leader received payment for his services and then supported, and distributed rewards amongst, his followers much as any chieftain would do. In the tribal societies of Europe there was a strong tradition of warriors seeking service with the leaders who could support and give them wealth and glory, for a martial reputation was highly valued wherever it was attained. The bond between such a chieftain and his followers was intensely personal. They fought for him and would just as happily fight with or against Carthage as their leader chose. We hear of one group of Gauls led by a chieftain who served several masters in succession and proved of dubious loyalty to each of them. The loyalty of such soldiers must have been significantly different from that of men who had been directly recruited and were directly paid by their Carthaginian leaders. Presumably some units in the army, especially those which included Roman and Italian deserters and escaped slaves, were of mixed nationality.[13]

Our sources rarely refer to the organization of the various contingents in Carthaginian armies, simply telling us where each nationality stood, so it is unclear whether any troops were organized into units of a set size. Livy makes reference to a unit of 500 Numidian cavalry, but this might simply have been one contingent and there is no indication that these horsemen fought in regular units. Another passage mentions 500 Libyan infantry at Saguntum in 218 and we also hear of 2,000 Gauls divided into three bands or units at the capture of Tarentum in 212, although it is uncertain whether these were permanent or temporary arrangements. Normally Gallic and sometimes Spanish troops fought in tribal contingents, each under their own leaders in much the same way that they would fight for their own people. However, at Cannae Hannibal's centre consisted of alternate units of Spaniards and Gauls, clearly breaking up any tribal structure they possessed. Polybius uses one of the terms he also employs for the Roman maniple of 120–160 men, and the same term was used by later authors for the cohort of 480 in the Late Republican and Imperial army. This makes it probable that these 'companies' consisted of a few hundred men, certainly less than a thousand.[14]

The mixture of contingents from different nationalities usually provided Carthaginian armies with a good balance of different troop types, with both close and loose order infantry and cavalry. Many of these contingents were of high quality, although their standard of discipline varied considerably. It was rare for troops whether serving as allies or for pay to fight without enthusiasm, and mutinies were uncommon. An additional element was provided by the fairly frequent use of war elephants who might well panic an enemy unused to them. The elephants employed were probably African Forest elephants, somewhat smaller than Indian elephants, but more amenable to training than today's African elephants. The elephant was the main weapon, using its bulk and strength to terrify or crush opposition, but Hellenistic armies also mounted towers on the animals' backs, from which crewmen hurled or fired missiles. There is no direct evidence indicating that Punic war elephants also carried towers, but Polybius' account of the Battle of Raphia in 217 BC implies that the African breed was capable of carrying the extra weight. The main danger with elephants was that they were inclined to panic and might then trample friend and foe indiscriminately. Hasdrubal is said to have equipped the drivers, or mahouts, with a hammer and a chisel-shaped blade, which they were supposed to drive into the animal's spine to kill it if threatened to stampede towards friendly troops.[15]

Carthaginian commanders usually had well-balanced forces at their disposal, but the difficulty lay in co-ordinating the movements of these
disparate elements. Orders issued in Punic had to be translated into various
languages in order to be conveyed to the soldiers. Carthaginian magistrates, such as the suffetes, did not hold military commands. Instead
generals were appointed, although it is not clear precisely by whom, and
usually held command on a semi-permanent basis until they were replaced
or for the duration of a conflict. Although not serving magistrates, it is
clear that the commanders were drawn from the same social class who filled these offices and there is no reason to believe that ability, more than
family connections and wealth, was the main reason for their selection. In
the First Punic War the Carthaginians continued their traditionally harsh
treatment of commanders who failed, several men being crucified for
incompetence. In several cases this penalty was inflicted on them when they
lost the confidence of the senior Punic officers under their command.

However, the long duration of the commands which they were given
did mean that many Carthaginian commanders became highly experienced. The longer a general held command over an army the more efficient
it tended to become. Gradually, the disparate elements composing it became
accustomed to operating together, their leaders and the higher commander became familiar with each other and, at least to some extent, their
languages. The army which Hannibal led into Italy in 218 was probably the
finest Carthaginian army ever to take the field. Its efficiency was in part the
result of its commander's ability as a leader, but was more the product of
long years of hard campaigning in Spain under the leadership of Hamilcar,
Hasdrubal and Hannibal himself. During this time its command structure
had developed to a high level, and this, as well as its march discipline and
ability to manoeuvre, was markedly superior to the Roman forces drawn up
against it. The high quality of this army, around which he could more easily
incorporate Gallic and subsequently Italian allies, allowed the genius of
Hannibal to dazzle his opponents in the opening campaigns.

Hannibal's army was not a typical Carthaginian army. Indeed, it is
doubtful whether there was such a thing, since each Punic force was
unique. There is no suggestion that all generals sought to control and lead
their forces in the same way. Their relationship with the different national
contingents varied. Each individual army gradually developed a means of
working together. Freshly raised contingents often failed to co-ordinate
their actions on the battlefield effectively. Similarly, even experienced
armies had problems when called upon to act in concert with each other.
At Zama Hannibal's army includeed troops raised by three different

commanders at different times. In the battle these were kept as clearly distinct bodies and failed to support each other well.[16]

Large numbers of mercenaries and allied contingents could be raised fairly quickly by the Carthaginians, whose economic resources were normally sufficient to do this. The quality of the individual soldiers and contingents hired in this way was usually good. However, it took some time and considerable care to turn such forces into efficient armies. This meant that an experienced army was a precious thing, difficult to replace, and so not to be lightly risked. Carthage was never able to field troops in anything like the quantities of the Romans. Also the difficulty of replacing a tried and tested army often encouraged a more tentative approach to campaigning on the part of Punic generals, who, with a few notable exceptions, tended to be far less aggressive than their Roman counterparts.

Rome

Later tradition held that Rome had been founded in 753. Many stories circulated concerning this event, but the most popular told of Romulus and Remus, the twin sons of Mars who were suckled by a she-wolf. Romulus founded the city, but killed his brother in a rage when the latter mocked his plans. A bandit chief whose followers were vagrants and outcasts forced to abduct women from the neighbouring Sabines when they wanted wives, Romulus was the first of Rome's seven kings, the last of whom was expelled in 509 when a Republic was founded. Whether there is any truth at all in these myths is impossible to say. Certainly Rome was at one stage a monarchy, and the Republic was probably created round about the traditional date. The archaeological record shows settlement in the area from the tenth century, but the villages in the area do not coalesce into something which could be termed a city until the sixth. The site was a good one, positioned at a natural crossing point of the River Tiber and with hilltops providing strong defensive positions. It also lay on several important trade routes, notably the *via Salaria*, or salt road, running from the coast into central Italy. Gradually Rome emerged as the dominant city in Latium, head of the Latin League. She managed to endure the onslaught of the Oscan-speaking peoples from the Apennines who swept through most of central Italy and overran Campania in the late fifth and early fourth centuries, and the Gallic tribes who simultaneously pressed down from the north. In 390 a Roman army was routed at the River Allia and the city sacked by a band of Gauls, but little permanent damage was inflicted and the check to Roman growth was only temporary.

In 338 the last great rebellion by the other Latin cities against Rome was

The Italian Peninsula

defeated after a hard struggle. The Roman settlement in the aftermath of this conflict set the pattern for and accelerated her absorption of the rest of Italy. Some territory was confiscated and used to establish colonies of Roman and Latin citizens. Many noble families from Campania, which had remained loyal to Rome, were given citizenship and incorporated into Rome's ruling élite. The Latin League was abolished and the Romans did not negotiate with the defeated cities collectively, but formed a separate alliance with each community. Each city was now tied directly to Rome and obliged to provide her with soldiers to serve with her armies. The status of these communities was clearly defined by law, so that some were given full Roman citizenship, others citizenship in every respect apart from the right to hold office or vote at Rome (*civites sine suffragio*), and others continued to be Latin citizens, but were allowed the rights of intermarriage and commerce with Roman citizens. Most of Campania received full citizenship and the fertile lands of this area added greatly to Rome's prosperity. In 312 construction began on the *via Appia*, the first great Roman road, which ran from Rome to Capua, providing a physical link with the new territory.[17]

The Roman willingness to extend its citizenship was something unique in the ancient world and a major factor in her eventual success. Unlike those in other cities, freed slaves at Rome received the full franchise and by the third century many members of the population, including some senatorial families, numbered freedmen amongst their ancestors. The Roman talent was to absorb others and make them loyal to her. For the first time, the settlement of 338 extended full citizenship to communities which were not native Latin-speakers. The allied cities lost their political independence, although they continued to manage their own internal affairs, but gained benefits from the bond with Rome. Their soldiers were called upon to fight Rome's wars, but they also profited from the spoils of the subsequent victories. Latin as well as Roman citizens were almost certainly included in the colonies established on captured lands. In the late fourth and early third centuries Roman expansion assumed great momentum. The Samnites, Etruscans and Gauls were all defeated, despite some Roman disasters, notably at the Caudine Forks in 321 when a Roman army surrendered to the Samnites. The cities of Magna Graecia – the 'Greater Greece' heavily colonized by Hellenic communities – were subdued, despite the intervention of King Pyrrhus of Epirus on behalf of the city of Tarentum. Pyrrhus' modern army with its pike phalanx of professional soldiers and its war elephants inflicted two heavy defeats on Roman armies, but was eventually beaten. What was especially notable about this conflict was the refusal of the Romans to negotiate with Pyrrhus after his victories. This was certainly a surprise to

the king of Epirus, who expected all wars to end in a negotiated peace settlement in the way that was normal in the Hellenistic world. Rome
continued to expand, turning defeated enemies into loyal, but clearly subordinate allies. As Rome expanded so too did her citizen population which,
combined with her allies, gave Rome vast resources of military manpower,
far greater than those of Carthage.[18]

The number of Roman citizens steadily increased, and by the third century BC many lived long distances away from Rome, but the political life of
the State was still entirely conducted in the city. Only when physically present in Rome could a citizen vote or stand for office. There were three
main Assemblies where the Roman People expressed its collective will. The
Comitia Centuriata voted to declare war or accept a peace treaty, and
elected the consuls, praetor and censors, the senior magistrates of the State.
The *Comitia Tributa* elected most of the more junior magistrates and
could pass legislation. The *Concilium Plebis* was very similar, but excluded
members of the numerically small patrician class. In these assemblies the
People could only vote for or against a proposal, and there was no opportunity for debate or for an ordinary citizen to present a counter proposal.
In all three the opinion of the wealthier citizens tended to predominate.
This was especially true of the *Comitia Centuriata*, where the voting structure was based upon archaic military organization. The more prosperous
citizens voted first and had fewer members in each voting-group or century, in the same way that they had once provided the cavalry and the most
heavily armed infantry, who had the most prominent role in wartime. The
senior class of the old heavy infantry, together with the even wealthier cavalrymen, totalled 88 out of the 193 centuries composing the assembly, not
far short of a majority. It is always important to remember that Popular
support, most of all in consular elections, always meant that a man had the
favour of the bulk of the prosperous citizens at Rome and not simply the
poor. The ten tribunes of the plebs had originally been created to defend
the plebeians against aristocratic and especially patrician oppression, but by
this time they were normally young senators at an early phase in their
career. Potentially the powers of this office were considerable, since they
presided over the *Concilium Plebis* and could present motions to it. Tribunes also possessed the right to veto any measure brought by another
magistrate, however senior.

The Assemblies did not debate issues and were summoned only when
required to vote. The Senate was the permanent council which discussed
affairs of State and advised the magistrates. It consisted of around 300
members who were enrolled in its ranks by the censors, two senior senators

elected every five years to oversee the census of citizens. Many were ex-magistrates and all had to possess substantial property, but the censors had considerable discretion in adding or removing names from the senatorial roll. The Senate's decrees did not carry the force of law and needed to be ratified by the people, but its very permanence ensured that it had the dominant role in foreign policy, receiving foreign embassies and choosing Roman ambassadors from its own ranks. Every year the Senate decided where the senior magistrates would be sent, allocating them 'provinces', which at this period were spheres of responsibility rather than primarily geographical areas. It also allocated military and financial resources to them, setting the size and composition of each army to take the field, and had the power to extend a magistrate's authority for an extra year, although this was a rare practice before the Punic Wars.

The Senate was permanent, its membership fairly stable, but the main executive officers of the State were all annually elected magistrates. The most senior of these were the two consuls, who were expected to cope with all the most important issues facing the State during their twelve months in office, whether this meant framing legislation or leading an army in battle. Their military role was especially important given the frequency of Roman war-making. The provinces allocated to the consuls were always an indication of current military priorities, since they expected to be given the most important enemies to fight. On the rare occasions that both consuls were sent against a single enemy it was a sign that a massive effort was to be made against an especially dangerous threat. Consuls and other magistrates received for the duration of their office *imperium*, the power to command Roman soldiers and to dispense justice. *Imperium* was symbolized by the magistrates' attendants or lictors, who carried the *fasces*, axes bound around with a bundle of rods indicating that their master could decree both capital and corporal punishment. A consul was attended by twelve lictors, more junior magistrates by fewer.

Although the consuls provided Rome's senior military commanders, they were not professional soldiers. A political career at Rome combined both military and civil posts. Before standing for office a man had to have served for ten campaigns with the army, perhaps as a cavalryman, but often as a military tribune or a member of a relative's staff. In his late twenties or early thirties a man might hope to be elected quaestor. The quaestors were primarily financial officials, but might also act as the consuls' second-in-command. The office of aedile was normally held in the mid thirties and had little role outside Rome itself, where it was primarily responsible for festivals and entertainments. Only one praetor was elected each year, and prior to the First Punic War the office had a purely judicial role. At least half of the consuls never held this post and some did so only after their consulship. Later the number of praetors and junior magistrates increased and their roles expanded as the victories in the first two conflicts with Carthage greatly expanded Rome's territory and responsibilities. The political career, or *cursus honorum*, as a result became much more highly regulated in the second century BC, with for instance the legal minimum ages for each post being much more tightly imposed.

Candidates for political office at Rome were not elected for membership of a particular political party (for such things did not exist), and only rarely for espousing a particular policy. Men were elected on the basis of their former achievements, or, since the young men standing for the junior offices had rarely had much chance to gain distinction, on the achievements of their family. The Romans believed very strongly that characteristics and ability were passed on from one generation to the next. If a man's father or grandfather had won the consulship and led Roman armies to victory in battle, then there was every reason to believe that he would prove equally competent. The noble families took care to advertise the achievements of former generations, placing their busts and symbols of office in the porches of their houses alongside the insignia of the current generation. Funerals of family members were staged in public and included speeches recounting not just the achievements of the deceased, but of all earlier generations, whose presence was represented by actors wearing masks and dressed in their respective insignia and robes of office. The Roman electorate knew what to expect from a Claudius or a Fabius and were more likely to vote for them than a man whose name and family were unfamiliar. In addition to this advantage, the established families possessed many clients, men for whom they had done favours in the past, who were expected to support them. If past favours were not enough, then they also had the wealth to win support and mount a campaign celebrating their qualities. It was very difficult for a man whose ancestors had never held office to have a distinguished career. If such a man did manage to rise to the consulship then he was known as a 'new man' (*novus homo*). In every generation a few 'new men' rose in this way, adding their families to the existing nobility, so that although difficult, such success was by no means impossible. The 'new men' themselves, including Cato the Elder and later Cicero, were apt themselves to exaggerate the obstacles they had overcome and thus to add to their own achievement.[19]

Roman senators competed fiercely for high office and the honour, glory and financial rewards which it brought. The majority of senators never achieved the consulship, which was largely monopolized by a small number of wealthy and influential families. In the early years of the Republic the office had only been open to the few patrician families, but by this time plebeians had been admitted and some of the older plebeian families were every bit as aristocratic and powerful as the patricians. By the third century BC it was normal for there to be one patrician and one plebeian consul in each year. These established families possessed great wealth, large networks of clients and the prestige of numerous ancestors who had distinguished themselves in the service of the Republic. In the narrative of the Punic Wars the same names crop up again and again as each new generation of a family attained high office. The consulship brought command in the most important wars, and military glory was the greatest ambition of a Roman aristocrat. A great victory might win the right to celebrate a triumph, an honour which the Senate voted to successful commanders. For this ceremony the general had his face painted terracotta red like the statues of Jupiter and wore the regalia of the god, as he rode through the heart of the city, the spoils of his victory on display and his soldiers marching in parade. The only higher honour was the right to dedicate *spolia opima* on the Capitol, which only generals who had killed the enemy leader in single combat could win. Only two men, one of them Romulus, had performed this ritual before 265. Former consuls and men who had triumphed were chief amongst the elder statesmen in the Senate, the men with the reputation (*auctoritas*) which demanded that they be called upon in its debates. These men competed with each other to outshine their peers in glory and reputation. Their triumphal monuments were rich in superlatives, as everyone sought to be best and greatest, to conquer the most peoples, storm the most cities, win the most battles and lead the most captives into slavery. Rivalry amongst senators encouraged them to strive to serve the State more effectively as magistrates, but at this period it was closely controlled and aided the stability of the State. A Roman aristocrat did not want to overturn the Republic, but to be successful on its terms. The Senate and the Republic needed to be preserved if he was to be acknowledged as its pre-eminent member by his peers. A Roman senator would never dream of defecting to an enemy in the hope of rising to power in a future, defeated Rome.

It used to be believed that the Roman Senate was divided into clear political groupings or factions based around some of the dominant families. These were perceived as having consistent policies so that, for instance, it was suggested that the faction based around the Fabii, one of the old patrician lines, favoured expansion into southern Italy, whilst the Aemilii were more eager to expand overseas. It was an attractive idea since whenever a consul appeared who was connected by blood, marriage or association with such a family, historians could automatically assume that he favoured a particular policy, even when little was known about the individual and what he actually did. In this way patterns seemed to appear in Roman foreign policy, which could be explained by the changing fortunes of particular family groups. None of this is supported by our ancient sources, who never attribute particular political views, instead of character traits, to specific families. The Roman Senate, and especially the small number of dominant families, was a very small community which freely intermarried, so that most of the prominent figures in any period had some familial tie, however distant. It was not unusual for cousins to oppose each other politically. Faction was a negative term for the Romans, invariably applied to political opponents. Senators naturally sought as many friends and allies within the Senate as possible, but since all were ultimately in competition for the same offices and honours these groups were inevitably very fluid. When it conformed with their mutual interests, senators might combine to aid each other in their election campaigns or when involved in a legal dispute. Such a connection was not permanent, and might be abandoned if it no longer served a useful purpose. Only the members of the immediate family could invariably be relied upon. Roman politics was about gaining personal and familial success, not about the formulation of long-term policy. Its rhythm was the political year, with annual elections and allocation of provinces.[20]

Aristocratic competition at Rome was ardent but closely controlled and the Republic, like Carthage, proved far more stable than most Greek city states. The Greek historian Polybius believed that this was because it possessed a mixed constitution, that ideal of Greek political theory which combined the three main types of government believed to be the natural conditions for a civilized state, monarchy, aristocracy and democracy. At Rome the magistrates, and especially the consuls, possessed tremendous power and represented the monarchic element, whilst the more permanent advisory role of the Senate suggested an aristocracy. Democracy was provided by the Popular Assemblies who declared war, elected magistrates and passed legislation, and the ten tribunes of the plebs. The power of each group balanced the others, so that no one section of the State had overwhelming power. Few modern commentators have accepted the perfection of Polybius' version, most believing that the oligarchic element represented by the Senate was the dominant force in the State. However, it was certainly a fundamental principle of Roman politics that no one individual should gain unrivalled power. Therefore there were two consuls, each with equal *imperium*, who held office for twelve months and then returned to private life, since it was illegal to hold the same office in consecutive years and in theory a decade was supposed to pass before the same post could be held again. The competition between senators for the senior office made it unusual for it to be held more than once, highly exceptional more than twice. Only at times of great crisis was the normal order suspended and a single dictator appointed with supreme power overriding even that of the consuls. Yet this post was no basis for lasting dominance of the State, since it only lasted for six months. Most often it was used as a way of holding elections for the next year's magistracies in the absence of the current consuls and the dictator resigned after a matter of days.[21]

Rome's political structures do not fully explain the strong sense of community which bound all classes in the State together. To a modern eye Roman society may seem grossly unfair. The more prosperous classes had a disproportionate political influence and a small élite monopolized the important offices. There is no evidence to suggest that poorer citizens felt themselves to be unfairly disadvantaged. Although poorer citizens do seem to have been fairly deferential in their attitude to the wealthy, they still felt free to voice their opinion of their leaders in certain circumstances, as when soldiers marching in a triumph customarily sang ribald songs about their commander. Patronage pervaded Roman society, connecting all classes together in an intimate bond of mutual dependence. Patrons expected support and respect from their clients, senators for instance would demand their political and electoral support, but in return clients expected to receive aid in their own affairs. However indirectly, whether through the patron of their patron's patron or even further removed, most poorer citizens had some form of access to those at the centre of power. Social advancement was also possible, and perhaps far easier than is often imagined. Roman citizens identified themselves very strongly with the Republic and felt a part of it. When the State went to war all classes participated, each according to their level of prosperity, and all shared both the danger and the prizes of victory, even if the wealthier benefited more from the latter.

The Roman Army
Like the Greek city states Rome had originally possessed a hoplite army, composed of citizens wealthy enough to equip themselves with the panoply of a heavy infantryman. Most hoplites were farmers and could afford to spend only a few weeks on campaign before they needed to return to their

fields. As a result a conflict between the hoplite armies of two city states was of short duration, usually decided by a single clash between the rival phalanxes. The principle of a citizen militia was retained at Rome, long after other states had come to rely on professional soldiers. However, the Romans modified the system to cope with demands of wars which were being fought further and further away from the city, and the intimate link between hoplite warfare and the agricultural year was broken. From the beginning of the fourth century the Roman State paid its soldiers for the duration of their service. The wage was not high and certainly did not make the army a career, but it supported the soldier during his service. Men now served in the army until they were discharged, usually at the end of a campaign which might last more than one year. Some effort was made to distribute the burden of military service evenly throughout the population, since it was rare that more than a small minority of citizens were required for the army in a single year. Legislation required a man to serve for no more than sixteen campaigns and it was unlikely that many men reached this maximum before the Punic Wars. Effectively the Roman army had changed from a citizen militia into something resembling a conscript army similar to those which flourished in Europe after the French Revolution. The State could call upon citizens to serve in the army and for the duration of their service it provided them with food and pay, but also required them to be subject to military law and a harsh system of discipline. The willingness of Roman citizens to submit to these conditions allowed the Romans to develop an army that was larger, better trained and more complex than the citizen armies of any other city state.[22]

Our most detailed picture of the Roman army is provided by Polybius, but it is difficult to know whether all the practices he describes were followed throughout the period of the Punic Wars. His description of the army appears to be set in the Second Punic War, although it has sometimes been argued that it refers to the mid second century. We do not know whether or not the armies fielded in the First Punic War were significantly different to this in structure and tactics, but the admittedly brief descriptions of the battles in this conflict do not suggest this.[23]

Originally the word *legio* (legion) had simply meant army or levy and referred to the entire force raised by the Roman people in one year. However, as the number of citizens regularly enrolled for military service increased, the legion became the most important subdivision of the army. By the third century the legion consisted of five elements. Its main strength consisted of the three lines of heavy infantry. All of these men had the same basic property qualification and they were divided according to age and experience. The youngest men formed the front line and were known as the *hastati*. In the second line were men in their late twenties to early thirties, considered by the Romans to be the prime of life, and were called the *principes*. The third, rear line of heavy infantry were the *triarii*, consisting of the oldest and most experienced soldiers.

Each of the three lines of heavy infantry was divided into ten maniples. Maniples of the *hastati* and *principes* consisted of about 120 men, although in times of crisis when larger legions were raised this might be increased to as many as 160. The maniples of the *triarii* always consisted of sixty men. All maniples were divided into two centuries each commanded by a centurion, but these did not fight independently and the maniple was the basic tactical unit of the legion. If both centurions were present then the commander of the right-hand century was senior and led the maniple. Centurions were chosen usually from experienced and proven soldiers, steady rather than especially bold men, but had to be literate, since even at this time the army had developed a considerable bureaucracy. The second in command to the centurion was the *optio* who probably stood at the rear of the formation and helped to keep the ranks dressed. Other officers in the maniple were the *signifer* who carried the standard, and the *tesserarius* who supervised the posting of sentries at night and distributed the day's password on a clay *tessera*. Polybius twice mentions in his narrative a legionary cohort, telling us that this is what the Romans call a unit of three maniples, although the Greek is slightly ambiguous. In the late Republic the cohort consisting of one maniple from each of the *hastati, principes*, and *triarii* replaced the maniple as the legion's basic tactical unit. It is probable that when other authors mention legionary cohorts during the Punic Wars they are guilty of anachronism. There is no indication that it was a permanent subdivision of the legion in the third century BC and most probably 'cohort' was simply the term used to describe any *ad hoc* formation larger than a maniple, although perhaps detachments of three maniples were particularly common.[24]

The defensive equipment was the same for all three lines. The most important item was the oval, semi-cylindrical body shield, conventionally known as the *scutum*, about 4 feet (1.2m) long and 2 feet 6 inches (76cm) at its widest point. It was constructed of up to three layers of plywood glued together and covered with calf-skin, a combination which made it both flexible and resilient. The top and bottom edges were protected by brass strips to defend against sword cuts, whilst the layers of wood were thicker around the centre. The shield was held by a horizontal hand grip behind the central boss, which was usually bronze or iron, but sometimes perhaps of wood. Judging from reconstructions based on a surviving first-century example found in Egypt, the Roman shield was very heavy, weighing around 22 lb (10 kg). During lulls in the fighting its weight could be rested on the ground, but during combat it was held rigidly in front of the legionary and offered good protection for his body down to his knees. In addition to his shield, a legionary wore a bronze helmet, bronze greaves and some form of body armour. Wealthier men sported a mail cuirass of linked iron rings which, although heavy, was flexible and offered good protection. Poorer legionaries made do with a circular or square pectoral, a bronze plate suspended by leather straps which covered only their chest. Unlike the Greek design made of flexible bronze which clipped onto the leg, Roman greaves were tied into place. In some cases a man wore only one greave, usually on the left leg which was held nearer to the enemy in the classic Roman fighting posture, as a man turned his left side towards the enemy, protecting as much of his body as possible behind his shield. The most common Roman helmets seem to have been the Montefortino and Etruco-Corinthian designs, both of which offered good protection to the top of the head. Both were topped by a tall crest, of two black and one purple feather according to Polybius. The crest made the soldier seem taller and more intimidating to an opponent.[25]

All legionaries were primarily swordsmen and it was most likely during or after the First Punic War that the Romans adopted what they called the 'Spanish sword', the short, cut-and-thrust *gladius*, which was to be their standard side arm until the third century AD. Probably copied from Spanish mercenaries in Carthaginian service, the *gladius* had a blade of around 20–24 inches (51–61 cm) ending in a long triangular point designed to puncture armour. Most examples reveal high quality workmanship and confirm that the sword was able to retain a wickedly sharp edge. The *triarii* retained the old hoplite thrusting spear, but both the *hastati* and *principes* were equipped with the *pilum*, the famous Roman heavy javelin. The origins of this weapon are as unclear as the date of its introduction, but it was certainly in use by the last quarter of the third century and there is no good reason to believe that it was not also in use in the First Punic War. Polybius tells us that each legionary carried two *pila*, one heavier than the other, although it has not proved possible to categorize the surviving examples so neatly. In each case a wooden shaft about 4 feet (1.2m) in length was attached to a narrow iron shank 24–30 inches (61–76 cm) long topped by a small pyramidal point. All the considerable weight of a thrown *pilum* was concentrated behind this point, giving it the momentum to punch through an enemy's shield and still allow the narrow head to go on and strike the target's body. Even if it did not wound an enemy the *pilum* was difficult to dislodge from a shield, often forcing an enemy to drop it and fight unprotected.[26]

Poorer citizens, and those not yet considered old enough to join the *hastati*, served as light infantrymen or *velites*. Although it has sometimes been suggested that the *velites* were only introduced in 211 and replaced the less well armed and efficient *rorarii*, this has been based on a dubious interpretation of a single passage in Livy. It is more likely that the two terms were synonymous, although perhaps *velites* came into common usage at a later period. Polybius describes the *velites* as armed with a *gladius* and a bundle of light javelins. They were protected by a circular shield 3 feet (40 cm) in diameter and many wore helmets which they covered with pieces of animal skin – often wolfskin , to make themselves more conspicuous to their own officers. It is unclear how the *velites* were organized as they certainly did not form maniples of their own. Probably they were attached, at least for administrative purposes, to the heavy infantry maniples. In battle they fought as skirmishers in open order, supporting either the three infantry lines or the cavalry. There were normally 1,200 *velites* to support the 3,000 heavy infantry of the legion, but at times of crisis their numbers might be increased.[27]

Like the *triarii* the numbers of the cavalry component of a legion never changed. There were always 300 horsemen divided into ten *turmae* of thirty, each led by three decurions. The cavalry was recruited from the wealthiest citizens in the State, including the top eighteen centuries of the voting assembly, the *Comitia Centuriata*, who were rated *equo publico*, obliging the State to provide them with the cost of a remount should their horse be killed on active service. Cato was later to boast that his grandfather had had five horses killed under him in battle and replaced by the State. This class included the sons of senators and it was as cavalrymen that many served out some of the ten campaigns which were needed to make a man eligible for political office. Cavalry service offered a chance for a man to make a name for himself which would aid a subsequent career. As a result Roman cavalry were normally brave and inclined to indulge in displays of bravado and fight single combats. Their chief tactic was the headlong charge in battle, but they showed little skill as scouts during a campaign. Annoyingly Polybius mentions the equipment of the Roman cavalry before they adopted Greek-style equipment, but does not bother to describe the latter in detail, assuming that his audience would already be familiar with it. However, Roman horsemen seem to have carried a round shield, worn a bronze helmet and mail or scale cuirass, and been armed with a spear and sword, possibly a longer weapon than the *gladius*. It is probable that they already employed the four-horned saddle which gave later Roman horsemen a firm seat and meant that they were not hindered by the absence of stirrups, perhaps having copied the saddle from the Gauls who may have invented it.[28]

Each legion was commanded by six elected military tribunes, who were often young aspiring politicians but sometimes included experienced former magistrates. Pairs of tribunes exercised overall command in turn. When a legion took the field it was normally supported by an *ala* of allies which fielded about the same number of infantry and around 900 cavalry. As far as we can tell their equipment and tactics were essentially the same as those of the legion, but it must be confessed that our sources rarely provide much detail concerning allied troops. The individual Latin colonies contributed a cohort of infantry and a *turma* of cavalry. It is not clear whether cohorts were of a standard size, and we hear of units varying in strength from around 400 to 600 men. The pick of the allied infantry were formed into the cohorts of *extraordinarii* who camped near the general's tent and were at his immediate disposal. These troops headed the column during an advance and brought up the rear during a retreat. The *ala* was commanded by three prefects of the allies (*praefecti sociorum*), who were Roman citizens. It is immediately noticeable that no unit of the Roman army had a single commander. There were six tribunes to a legion, three prefects to an *ala*, two centurions to a maniple and three decurions to a *turma* of cavalry. Only in the case of centurions are we told that one man in each maniple was senior. In every other case the Romans seem to have extended to the army their deep-seated dislike of entrusting sole political power to one man and preference for colleges of magistrates. To modern eyes the system seems flawed, and it would eventually be abandoned by the later professional Roman army, but it proved adequate for the relatively simple tactics employed by the legions in this period.

The very high number of officers certainly made it easier to control a Roman army. Centurions were chosen from the bravest soldiers, although Polybius emphasizes that it was normal to promote the men who were gifted leaders rather than individual fighters. A centurion was supposed to stay with his men, whom he led from the front and by personal example. Stubbornness and the refusal to give any ground were considered to be amongst their greatest virtues. In general the Roman army also placed great emphasis on individual bravery, having a complex system of military decorations and rewards. A soldier who saved the life of a fellow citizen received highest decoration of all, the *corona civica*, a laurel crown which

49

was worn at every public festival in Rome and commanded great respect. Roman commanders held formal parades after a battle or at the end of a campaign, when conspicuous gallantry was rewarded, the achievements of each man being read out and admired by the serried ranks of the army. The greatest rewards were reserved for acts of individual boldness, such as fighting a single combat when there had been no need to do so. Aggression was encouraged in all ranks of the Roman army. The army made it clear what standards of behaviour were expected from its men, and was as willing to punish as to reward. A unit which failed badly in combat and fled without putting up a fight could suffer decimation, one in ten of its members being beaten to death. The remainder as a symbolic humiliation were issued barley instead of wheat and pitched their tents outside the ramparts. We hear at one point of defeated legionaries who were ordered to eat their meals standing up instead of reclining in the usual Roman style. The standards of discipline to which Roman citizens were willing to submit themselves during their military service were extremely harsh and much like those of a professional army. Sentries discovered asleep, usually propped up on their long shields, suffered the death penalty, as did men who stole from their comrades, and practising homosexuals.[29]

The discipline of the Roman army in this period was often very tight, citizens losing most of the protection offered by the law to civilians. Even at this early date, Roman armies generated large amounts of bureaucracy and had a rigid daily routine. This was emphasized by the marching camp, the highly organized, neatly laid out structure built every night by an army on the march. Always built to recognizably the same pattern, a camp had four gateways and two main roads running at 90 degrees to each other and meeting in front of the main concentration of command tents. Everything was regulated, from the positioning of each unit's tents and baggage to the duties carried out by various contingents, so that for instance the *triarii* always provided guards for the horse lines. The responsibility of various officers to supervise the sentries and pickets around the camp and to transmit orders for the next day's march were all clearly allocated.

In most years the Roman Republic fielded four legions. Each consul was given an army of two legions and two *alae*. In battle the legions formed the centre of the line with one *ala* on either flank. For this reason the *alae* were often known as the Left and Right *ala*. Legions were usually numbered, one consul commanding the First and Third Legions, the other the Second and Fourth. It appears that all the legions in existence were renumbered every year so few of these units developed a lasting sense of esprit de corps or identity. It was rare before 264 for a praetor to be given a military command, but during the Punic Wars this was to become common. A Praetorian army usually consisted of only one legion and *ala*. Each year the consuls were first allocated the most important and largest scale operations, and then praetors were put in charge of smaller campaigns. Usually a Roman legion mustered 4,200 infantry and 300 cavalry on formation, but this was not a fixed size, rigidly imposed. According to the Senate's judgement of the strength of the opposition, the size of the legion could be increased to 5,000, 5,200, or even 6,000. This was done by enlarging the maniples of the *hastati* and *principes* and increasing the number of *velites*. This did not require any significant change in the legion's organization or tactical system. In exactly the same way the size of the *ala* could be increased, which may in part explain the variation in the recorded size of Latin cohorts. In times of extreme crisis, each consul might be given four instead of two legions.[30]

The Roman army of this period operated most efficiently at the level of the consular army of two legions and two *alae*. This force of at least 20,000 men was well balanced, perhaps ten per cent of the total consisting of cavalry, and had a clear command structure leading up to the unchallenged authority of the consul. It was sufficient for most tasks, but there was no clear mechanism for providing the command structure of an army composed of the forces of more than one consul. The temporary office of dictator, whose authority superseded that of all other magistrates, was exceedingly rare. When two consuls joined forces then each man held command on alternate days. The system was not ideal and was used by later authors to explain some of the early disasters of the Second Punic War. However, earlier in the third century both consuls had occasionally joined forces and seem to have operated without major problems. Both consular armies also participated in the victory at Telamon in 225; but in this case the actions of the two armies were not concerted but the result of a happy chance, since both consuls had been unaware of the other's presence before the battle. The system of shared command was not ideal, but it may have taken a commander of Hannibal's great ability to exploit the opportunities it offered to an opponent.[31]

It took time to form a Roman army and then train and drill it to a reasonable standard. Throughout their history, the Romans' concept of the ideal commander was always a man who carefully trained and prepared his army before risking them in battle. The longer legions and *alae* remained in service the more opportunity they had to drill and the more experience they gained, so that steadily their efficiency increased. The armies which served for much of the Second Punic War were eventually indistinguishable from professional soldiers. The weakness of the Roman system was that every time the legions were discharged and a new army raised, the whole process had to start again from scratch. Most levies of citizens included men with prior service, but although this aided the process of making an army battle-worthy it did not render it unnecessary. Such men would not have served together in the same units and under the same officers. There is a little evidence from the second century BC for a class of semi-professional junior officers and centurions who viewed the army as a career. It is unclear how numerous these were and we have no idea whether or not such men existed in the third century.[32]

Roman generals were amateurs in a modern sense, in that they received no formal training for command. The twelve-month political cycle ensured that very few ever enjoyed the long periods of command common with their Punic opponents. In the event, only Hamilcar Barca and Hannibal were to show themselves to be markedly more skilled than their Roman opponents. During the later stages of the First Punic War, the Roman electorate seems to have favoured re-electing experienced men, something that became even more common in the Second War, when the Senate also made extensive use of its power to prorogue the *imperium* of a magistrate for an additional year or years. In this way many able leaders were retained, some commanding the same army for years on end. However, as with success in elections, whether or not a man's command was extended sometimes had more to do with his political influence than his ability. The Roman system produced some incompetents who led their armies to disaster, but it also produced men of exceptional talent, most notably Scipio Africanus. The average Roman commander appears to have been at least as good as his average Punic counterpart. He was certainly likely to be far more aggressive and, whilst this carried the risk of rashness, it produced more spectacular victories. It used to be claimed that the Roman army won its victories in spite of the shortcomings of its amateur officers, whose inexperience was compensated for by the skill of more junior men, especially the centurions. Yet Roman commanders needed to make many important decisions before a battle, and were highly active during the fighting, paying attention to the small detail of the action. It was a style of command which demanded considerable skill. Although they received no formal training, we should not forget that most Roman senior officers did have extensive military experience before they achieved high rank. They were also the products of a class which valued military glory above all else and had clear ideas about how its members should face the danger of battle. A senator was expected to embody the characteristics implied by the Latin word *virtus*, which embraced not only physical courage, but also technical and tactical ability.[33]

The standard Roman battle formation was the *triplex acies*, based around the three lines of legionary heavy infantry. The maniples of the *hastati* deployed perhaps six to eight ranks deep, with an interval equivalent to the frontage of the unit between each maniple. The formation of the *principes* was the same, but the maniples were stationed behind the gaps in the line of *hastati*. In the same way the smaller maniples of *triarii* covered the gaps between the units of the second line. This created a checkerboard of maniples, like the *quincunx* or number five on a gaming dice. Polybius tells us that each Roman legionary occupied a frontage and depth of 6 feet (1.8 m), although a later source makes it more likely that the frontage was in fact only 3 feet (90 cm) and the depth 6–7 feet, (*c.* 2 m). The distance between the ranks was necessary to allow the legionaries to throw their *pila*. Assuming a frontage of a yard (90 cm) per man and a depth of six ranks for the unit, then a maniple of *hastati* or *principes* would have occupied a frontage of 20 yards (*c.* 18 m) and a depth of just over 12 yards (11 m). The entire legion would have formed up on a front of around 400 yards (*c.* 365 m), allowing for the intervals between the maniples, and the infantry of a consular army occupied something like a mile, assuming, as seems probable, that the *alae* deployed in a similar formation. We have no direct evidence for the distance between the three lines, and the above calculations must remain to a great extent conjectural, but do provide a rough idea of scale.[34]

Our sources clearly state that the legion deployed for battle with wide intervals between the maniples in each line. The advantages of such an open formation for moving across country are obvious, since it allowed the sections of a line to flow around any obstacles without losing their order, in a way that would have been impossible for a solid formation. However, the vast majority of scholars have refused to believe that the legion would actually have fought with gaps in the line, since surely this would have allowed a charging enemy to stream through the intervals in the Roman line, surrounding and overwhelming each separate maniple. They have therefore proposed various schemes allowing the legion to alter its formation and create a solid, unbroken line before it made contact with the enemy. Connected with this problem is the question of how the three lines of the *triplex acies* interacted with each other. Clearly the Roman tactical system was based upon the principle that the lines ought to be able to support each other. The *principes* and *triarii* were able to join the combat in some way, and it is claimed that they might even advance and replace the

53

troops in the front line, but it is not easy to understand how this was achieved. The problem is particularly complex if it is accepted that when in contact with the enemy the maniples were packed together in a solid line. In fact, it is far more likely that they were not and that the gaps in the line remained during combat, but in order to understand the Roman tactical system we must first look at the nature of warfare and battle in this period.

Warfare in the Third Century BC

The main developments in military theory and practice before the Punic Wars had all occurred in the Greek world. Greek city states had first developed the hoplite phalanx, a dense mass of heavily armoured infantrymen which advanced and fought their way through anything in their path. On level ground such Greek spearmen had proved superior to any other type of soldier down to the earlier fourth century. It was a system of fighting ideally suited to the Greek soldier-farmers, who wished to resolve a campaign quickly so that they could return to working their farms. It required little technical skill or training, for which Greek citizens apart from the Spartans had little time, but needed considerable courage and group solidarity, things which the hoplites of the city states possessed in abundance. Tactics were simple, especially when two similar phalanxes confronted each other in a war between rival cities, and such subtleties as reserves were virtually unknown. Many wars lasted a matter of weeks and were resolved by a single day's clash on one of the few level plains in the Greek Peninsula. Greek warfare developed as society changed and in the late fifth and fourth centuries professional soldiers appeared in increasing numbers, campaigns tended to last much longer and not be so closely tied to the agricultural year, whilst generalship and tactics grew in importance. Philip II and Alexander the Great of Macedon led well-trained and drilled professional soldiers, forming armies that included heavy and light cavalry, and light infantry as well as the heavy infantry of the phalanx, who were now armed with two-handed pikes instead of the spears. It was with such an army that Alexander swept across the Near East and on into India in little more than a decade. The Hellenistic military system had proved itself superior to anything else in the world at that time, but after Alexander's death and the break-up of his empire into a number of bickering Successor Kingdoms Macedonian style armies most often found themselves facing another similar force. Where both sides employed the same tactical system and equipment, a decisive victory was much harder to achieve. As a result armies began to experiment with all sorts of unusual weapons, such as scythed chariots, war elephants and heavily armoured cataphract cavalry, in an effort to gain some advantage over the enemy. More emphasis was also placed on the role of the commander, who tried to force a battle on terms most favourable to his own army and avoid contact if the odds were against him.

Neither the Romans nor the Carthaginians possessed a modern army based on the Hellenistic model, but the campaigns between them were to be fought largely in the manner of contemporary Hellenistic warfare. The most important and decisive element in warfare remained the pitched battle, although raiding and sieges now played a far more significant role than had ever been the case with hoplite warfare. A clear victory in a massed battle was the best way of putting pressure on the enemy, but there was always the possibility of defeat and a battle was not something to be risked lightly. Heavy casualties were difficult to replace quickly, since both Carthaginian mercenaries and Roman levies needed time to be turned into a battle-worthy force. Even if the majority of a defeated army survived an engagement, their morale was severely reduced and made it unlikely that they could face the same enemy again with any prospect of success until some time had passed. Battles were rarely if ever fought for any strategic purpose greater than destroying the enemy field army. Therefore a good commander sought battle when he felt that there was a good chance of victory and avoided a confrontation if there was not.

The area covered by the campaigns of the Punic Wars was very large, whilst the armies involved were relatively small. With long-range strategic intelligence usually poor and sometimes non-existent, it was rare for either side to have a clear idea of the enemy's location until the two armies neared each other. Armies in this period tended to march carelessly, moving as quickly as possible towards the anticipated campaigning area, only becoming cautious when the opposing army was located within a few days' march. The march of a large army was difficult to conceal from scouting parties, the cloud of dust thrown up by tens of thousands of feet and hoofs being visible for many miles. It was normally expected that the presence of a hostile army would be recognized before it came close enough to pose a direct threat. Roman armies in particular tended to have a casual attitude towards reconnaissance, in part because their aristocratic cavalry had little taste for the rigours of patrolling. In the third and second century BC Roman columns managed to get themselves ambushed with monotonous regularity. Even with more experienced and professional armies it was not unknown for either or both sides to lose track of an enemy, and accidental encounters, some of which resulted in battle, were not unknown. A good commander took care to seek as much information about the enemy's location, strength and intentions as possible before planning his own actions.[35]

Once close to the enemy, the movements of the rival armies became extremely tentative and hesitant. The rate of march slowed, until the armies camped within a few miles of each other. It was not uncommon for them to remain in these positions, perhaps as little as half a mile apart for days or even weeks before a battle occurred. Skirmishing and single combats between the cavalry and light infantry of the two sides occupied much of the time, and either one or both commanders might march out and deploy their army for battle. There was a strong element of ritual about this posturing. How far forward a side chose to advance its battle line towards the enemy army or camp displayed how confident it was of victory. Camps were usually pitched on high ground so that a force which deployed close to its camp was in a strong uphill position which no enemy was likely to attack. If an enemy army stayed too close to their camp when the other side advanced towards them, or remained behind the ramparts and refused to deploy at all, then this allowed a general to tell his men that the enemy were afraid of them. This was one way of raising their morale, and during the days of delay before battle this was what a commander attempted to do, encouraging his army and trying to give it as many advantages as possible. Cumulatively, even very slight advantages, such as manoeuvring so that the enemy fought with the wind blowing towards them or the sun in their eyes, could contribute to victory. Sometimes though, after spending weeks facing each other, the two armies parted without fighting a battle, one or both sides unwilling to risk forcing a fight. Disengaging when so close to the enemy was a difficult and dangerous operation, but could be preferable to fighting in unfavourable conditions. There was a strong degree of mutual consent about the battles of this period. It proved very difficult even for highly skilled commanders to force an unwilling opponent to fight.[36]

If and when a battle finally occurred, both sides marched out from their camps to deploy into battle order just as they had when challenging the enemy to battle in earlier days. There was of course always the danger that when they did this, perhaps merely with the intention of displaying their confidence, the enemy would rise to the challenge and join battle. The normal procedure was for an army to form into a column with each unit in the order it was to take up in the fighting line. This column would march out of the camp to a point roughly on the left flank of the planned battle line, then wheel to the right and march along parallel to the enemy until the head of the column reached the extreme right of the line. Then the unit at the head of the column formed up as the right flank unit of the army and each unit took its place beside it. In the case of the Romans, it was normal to form three such columns, one each for the *triplex acies*, and if there was a possibility of encountering the enemy during a march a Roman army might march for some distance in this formation. It took a considerable time to form up an army in this way and by the time that the process was complete many units may have marched several miles, apart from having the frustration of stopping and waiting for each unit ahead of them to contract from looser marching order into battle formation. It required considerable supervision on the part of senior officers to ensure that this process ran smoothly and that the army ended up in the right order and in the right place. There is some evidence to suggest that in the Roman army this task was a particular concern of the tribunes. In most cases while this process was going on the enemy was engaged in a similarly laborious process, but it was normal to send out cavalry and light troops to protect the vulnerable columns as they deployed.[37]

The majority of soldiers in both Roman and Punic armies carried some sort of missile weapon, either a throwing spear or javelin, or a longer-ranged sling or bow. Even these weapons could not harm an enemy more than a few hundred yards away. The missile exchanges in ancient battles probably occupied more time than hand-to-hand combat, but it was the latter which was usually decisive. Ultimately victory went to the side most willing to close and attack the enemy with spear and sword. Massed hand-to-hand combat is very difficult for us to picture, in part because it has been exceptionally rare in the warfare of the last two centuries, even in battles involving armies armed primarily with close combat weapons. We have no detailed description of the fighting in a single battle from the Punic Wars, but it is possible to create a composite picture of what infantry combat was like, drawing from all accounts and those of other battles in the same period. These give the impression that close combat was often far more tentative than our imagination, or cinematic representations, may suggest.

The opposing battle lines might begin an action as much as a mile or as little as a few hundred yards apart. Unless holding a strong position, it was normal for both sides to advance, since moving forward gave the men confidence. As they came towards each other, both sides attempted to intimidate the opposition, by trying to look as confident and frightening as possible. They yelled their war cries, blew trumpets and clashed weapons against shields, hoping to make more noise than the enemy. Individual appearance, such as tall plumes, brightly painted shields and highly polished armour, helped to make a man feel more confident and dismay the opposition. Ideally the advance of such an impressive and noisy body of troops was enough to break the morale of the enemy and cause them to retreat or break and run, but such easy victories only occurred when one army had a massive advantage in morale over its opponents. Normally both sides closed to within missile range, perhaps 30 yards or so, and began to throw whatever missiles they possessed. It is probable that the advance checked whilst they did so. Each Roman legionary carried two *pila*, neither with a range of more than 100 feet (30.5 m) and with an effective range of half that. There was insufficient time to throw both of these missiles whilst running towards an advancing enemy, and it was impossible for a man to hold one of the heavy javelins in his left hand and still use his heavy shield effectively.

It is unclear how long such an exchange of missiles normally lasted, but at some point one or both sides built up enough confidence to surge forward and close the last short distance to contact the enemy. Again, the confidence of the enemy onslaught, the sound of his battle cries and trumpets, or perhaps the casualties caused by thrown missiles might just have been enough to crack the opposing unit's spirit and cause them to rout. Otherwise the two lines met and fought in a cacophony of yells and clashing blades. Only the men in the front rank of each formation could actually strike at the enemy, although in a spear-armed unit some of the second rank might have been able to thrust over the shoulders of the men in front. Relatively few wounds were instantly fatal, and cuts to the right arm or lower legs (especially the left leg nearest to the enemy) most common. The head, unprotected by the shield, was vulnerable to a serious or incapacitating wound and for this reason a helmet was the single most desirable piece of defensive armour after a shield. The objective was to knock down, kill or force back an opponent in the enemy front rank, and then step into his place to begin making inroads into the opposing formation, although this was a dangerous thing to do. A unit's confidence relied very heavily on coherence of its formation, since men were more inclined to remain where they were if they believed themselves to be surrounded by trusted comrades. If the enemy penetrated the front rank of a unit then its members became nervous and were highly inclined to panic and run. It was then, as one side turned to flee, that the greatest casualties were always suffered, the winning side frenziedly striking at the backs of the running men. Those who were too slow in joining the flight, and the injured, especially those with leg wounds, were usually caught and cut down.

Hand-to-hand fighting with sword and spear was hard physical effort combined with massive emotional stress. Such combats could not last for long before the participants in the opposing front ranks were physically exhausted and unable to continue. It is extremely unlikely that such combats ever lasted for more than fifteen minutes, and most were probably far shorter. Many such conflicts, perhaps the vast majority, did not end with one side fighting its way into the enemy formation and routing them, but were indecisive. In these cases the two sides seem to have separated, a gap of a few yards opening up between the lines, one or both units taking a few paces back. There was then a lull as the rival fighting lines faced each other, recovering their strength and confidence, perhaps yelling or throwing any remaining missiles at the foe. Eventually one or the other side was able to surge forward again in a fresh charge and renew the combat.

With each time that the opposing lines came into actual contact and parted without a decisive result, it must have become harder after the next lull to urge the weary men forward once more. Both sides steadily became exhausted, the front rank men from the physical effort of fighting, the men in the rear ranks from the strain of waiting, unable to see much of what was going on and knowing that at any moment their formation might collapse and a vengeful enemy appear to slaughter anyone who did not run quickly enough. Casualties were comparatively few – judging from Greek battles probably less than 5 per cent until one side fled – but fell most heavily on the boldest men, the ones who tried to cut their way into the enemy ranks. Less confident men were inclined to drift to the rear. Greek military theory recommended putting the bravest men in the front and rear ranks of a unit. The ones in front did the actual fighting, whilst the ones in the rear prevented everyone else from running away. The Romans stationed their *optiones* behind the line to push the men back into place if they tried to flee. The number of leaders, both formally recognized officers or chieftains and those particularly bold individuals willing to go forward and lead a new onslaught, was vitally important. This highlights the importance of the large number of junior leaders in the Roman legion and its encouragement of boldness, especially individual boldness, in its soldiers. The confrontation between two lines of infantry may well have lasted for an hour or more, since we hear of battles lasting at least two to four hours altogether. Sometimes we hear of one line being forced back without breaking for several hundred yards. In the end these contests were decided by two major factors, stamina and aggression. A fighting line needed stamina to endure such a long slogging match. Discipline and experience added to a unit's endurance, as did the depth of its formation, since the men in front could not flee until the ranks behind collapsed. Aggression was needed to persuade the men to advance one more time and close to contact with the enemy, since this was the most likely way of causing his eventual collapse.[38]

This is a rather different picture of ancient combat, but makes the tactics of the period, and especially those of the Roman legion, far more intelligible. In the context of such tentative fighting, the presence of gaps between the units forming a line becomes less important. In fact it is clear from our sources that all armies maintained intervals separating their units. We hear of light infantry moving forward to skirmish and then retiring through the gaps in the main lines of Roman and Carthaginian heavy infantry at Trebia in 218. It would in fact have been impossible to move an army across even the flattest country without significant breaks in the line, since otherwise the units would inevitably collide, merging into one and becoming very difficult to control. The main difference between the Roman and other systems was that the intervals between maniples were especially large, not that the gaps existed at all. Charging enemies, even 'wild barbarians', did not sweep through these gaps and swamp the maniples in the first line because the charges delivered in reality appear to have been far less concerted and rapid than those of popular imagination. Such charges were themselves not delivered by an enemy line that was solid anyway, but one made up of distinct units or groups with small gaps between them. Far more importantly the intervals in the Roman line were covered by the maniples of the next line.[39]

All armies apart from the Romans tended to concentrate the vast majority of their infantry strength in a single line. Hellenistic armies, for instance, preferred to deepen their phalanx rather than form troops into a second line and made little or no use of reserves. This was in part because their commanders, usually monarchs, were obliged by tradition to fight in person at the head of their Guards and were in no position to send orders to reserve formations. The deepening of the phalanx also gave it great stamina in combat. In every battle over half of the Roman infantry were initially kept uncommitted in the second and third lines. Deeper lines had more stamina, but even the men in the rear ranks were affected by the exhaustion of prolonged combat. The Roman system allowed fresh men to be fed into the fighting line, renewing its impetus and leading a surge forward which might well have been enough to break the wearying enemy. The wide intervals between maniples made it easier to reinforce a combat in this way. Committing the reserve lines required careful judgement on the part of a Roman commander. Too early and the fresh troops risked being absorbed by the front line and sharing their exhaustion. Too late and the fighting line might collapse, perhaps even sweeping the second and third lines away in its rout. A good commander kept a tight rein of his reserve lines and restrained them from joining the combat on their own initiative, as excitable and nervous men and centurions were eager to join the fight. The *triarii* traditionally squatted or kneeled down in the third line. The posture made it easier for them to brace their spear-butts on the ground and present a hedge of point to the front, but it may also have been intended to discourage them from moving forward prematurely. The *triarii* numbered fewer than half of either of the first lines and traditionally offered a refuge for these to retire behind, hence the expression 'the affair came down to the *triarii*' which applied to any desperate situation.[40]

The Roman military system was directed to the single end of applying massive, steadily renewed pressure to an enemy in front. The second and third lines were not true reserves in the modern sense, and only in the most experienced legions were they capable of any form of manoeuvre. The legion's drill and tactics were ideally suited to the formal, almost ritualized battles of the period. The marching camp with its formal layout and the wide lanes between the tent lines and behind the rampart allowed the troops to form up in the columns used to deploy into battle order and then each march out through one of the gateways. The large number of officers with the army helped to regulate and control this process. Indeed the system placed considerable responsibility in the hands of the general and senior officers, which in itself belies the old view that these men were inexperienced and scarcely necessary for the army to function. With much of the army kept in reserve at the beginning of an action, it was important that someone, usually the commander himself, took the decision to commit these fresh troops. Roman commanders did not charge spear in hand at the head of their Guard cavalry like Alexander the Great or the Successor Kings. On some occasions, especially in a desperate situation, a Roman general might choose to lead a charge, but he did not expect to spend the entire battle this way. Roman generals tended to stay near to the fighting without actually joining it, riding around just behind the fighting line. From this position they were able to encourage their men and also, through the noise made by and appearance of the men in combat, judge how well the action was going and issue orders to commit their reserves accordingly. The general needed to guess where the most important fighting would occur and move to that point in the line, although all along the line tribunes, allied prefects and the general's immediate subordinates or *legati* were usually stationed to cover each section of the front. It was a style of command which made great demands on senior officers and put them at considerable risk, for their close proximity to the fighting line put them at risk from missiles and the attacks of lone enemies. Roman commanders needed to be mobile, moving from one crisis point to the next or riding back to fetch reserves in person when these were required quickly and there was not time to send a message. For this reason it was normal for Roman commanders to lead their armies on horseback, and even the dictator, who was banned from riding by archaic taboo, by this period automatically sought permission to ride. Roman soldiers fought better when they believed that their general was with them, able to observe and either reward or punish their behaviour.[41]

The Roman army was well suited to formal pitched battles, where it could form up against an enemy to its front and attack straight forward, throwing in men from the reserve lines to reinforce the main attack, to plug a breakthrough in their own line or exploit a penetration of the enemy's. Until well into the war with Hannibal Roman commanders were indeed inclined to seek such a confrontation as swiftly as possible. Hannibal in particular was to prove far more skilful in the careful manoeuvring before a battle, exploiting the instinctive desire of his Roman opponents to meet him as soon as possible to ensure that the battle was in fact fought in a situation and place of his own choosing. Yet it was a striking feature of the Romans, especially in their military enterprises, that they were willing and able to learn from their opponents and adapt.

PART ONE

THE FIRST PUNIC WAR
264–241 BC

CHAPTER 2

The Outbreak of War

T HE LONG-TERM CAUSES of great wars have fascinated historians
since Thucydides attempted to explain the outbreak of the Pelo-
ponnesian War by tracing Athenian ambition in the years after the
victory over Persia, but they are seldom easy to isolate.[1] This is especially
true of conflicts in the ancient world, when we rarely know when, by whom
and acting under what information and preconceptions the decisions were
taken which eventually led to war. It is tempting but highly dangerous to
employ hindsight and attempt to reconstruct the causes of a war from its
course. No Roman or Carthaginian could have dreamed in 264 that their
states were about to embark on a twenty-four-year struggle which would
involve huge casualties, still less that it would be the first of three wars
between the two peoples. It is extremely unlikely in the case of the First
Punic War that either side believed that they were even about to begin a
full-scale conflict with the other. Prior to 264 relations between Rome and
Carthage had generally been good.

However difficult it may be to trace the deeper causes of a conflict, the
incidents which provide the sparks to ignite the greater conflagration are
usually more obvious, as with Princip's assassination of Archduke Ferdi-
nand in Sarajevo in AD 1914 which plunged Europe into a World War. In
the case of the war between Carthage and Rome these events occurred at
Messana (modern-day Messina) in Sicily and had their origins in the career
of the Syracusan tyrant Agathocles, who had captured the city sometime
around 315–312. Agathocles had relied heavily on mercenary soldiers to
fight his long conflict with the Carthaginians and in his efforts to expand
his city's dominion. Amongst his forces was a band of soldiers recruited
from Campanians, Oscan-speaking descendants of the hill tribesmen who
had overrun that fertile plain in the last quarter of the fifth century. After
Agathocles' death in 289 this group failed to find an employer in the

65

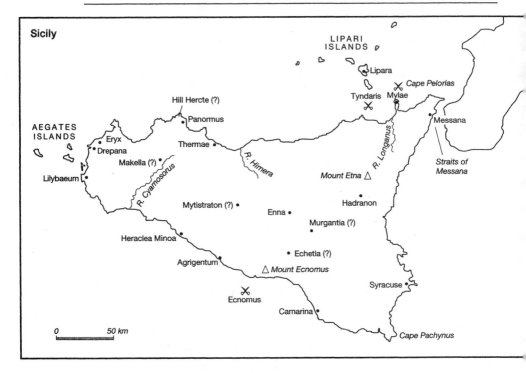

confused political situation at Syracuse. At some point in the next few years the Mamertines were admitted freely into the city of Messana, but treacherously massacred the citizens, taking their wives and property for their own.[2] Using the city as base they raided the neighbouring territories, forcing other communities to pay them tribute and exploiting the confused situation on the island. Emphasizing their martial strength, the mercenaries styled themselves Mamertines, followers of Mamers the Italian war god whom the Romans worshipped as Mars.

Messana lay on the north-eastern coast of Sicily, commanding one side of the narrow Straits between the island and Italy. On the Italian shore lay Rhegium, a Roman ally which had requested a Roman garrison to defend it against Pyrrhus.[3] The Romans duly despatched 4,000 men led by one Decius, an officer of uncertain rank. Although Roman citizens in every respect save that they lacked the right to vote at Rome (*civites sine suffragio*), these soldiers were also Oscan-speaking Campanians. Inspired by their kindred at Messana, they too turned upon the city they were supposed to protect, killing or expelling its male citizens and stealing their possessions. At the time, the Romans were occupied by the wars with Pyrrhus and Tarentum, and were unable to avenge this breach of their faith, so that it was not until 271 that an army went south and began the siege of Rhegium.

The defeat of Tarentum had confirmed Roman control over the predominantly Greek southern Italy, making it all the more important to demonstrate to their new allies that such abuses of Rome's *fides* (faith) would not escape punishment. Rhegium was captured after a long siege and the 300 Campanians taken alive were sent to Rome for public punishment. There, as befitted citizens who had turned against the State, they were flogged and beheaded in the Forum. One source claims that Decius, who had lost his sight, was negligently guarded and managed to commit suicide before enduring this punishment.[4] As yet the Romans had no connection or contact with Messana.

The Mamertines had not joined Pyrrhus' campaign against Carthage when he answered the call of Syracuse to defend the Greeks cities on the island and made his short, spectacular, but ultimately unsuccessful foray into Sicily. However, deprived of their allies across the Straits they came under increasing pressure as a new leader emerged at Syracuse. Hiero was a skilled soldier and a shrewd politician whose popularity was based upon his campaigns against the Italian raiders. Initially elected to power by the army, Hiero made his position more stable by marrying the daughter of one of the city's leading politicians. The precise chronology of Hiero's campaigns against the Mamertines is very uncertain, but need not concern us here. In an initial battle at the River Cyamosorus he seems to have checked them, as well as allegedly taking the opportunity to sacrifice a contingent of unreliable mercenaries. Later, probably sometime between 268 and 265, Hiero won a decisive victory at the River Longanus, an action in which a body of the original citizens of Messana and a picked unit from Syracuse were concealed in ambush behind the enemy line.[5]

The power of the Mamertines was broken, and seeing no prospect of salvation without external aid, their leaders, or different factions within the leadership according to Polybius, sent embassies appealing for assistance to both Carthage and Rome in 265. Once again the precise chronology of these events is unclear. What we do know is that the Carthaginians were the first to respond, one of their commanders in Sicily dispatching a token force to occupy Messana's citadel. In one version of the story, this officer, Hannibal, happened to be with a naval squadron off the nearby Lipari Islands. He rushed to Hiero's camp, ostensibly to congratulate him on his victory, but in fact to delay his advance for long enough to persuade the Mamertines to accept an alliance and insert a Carthaginian garrison. Hiero was not willing to commence open hostilities with the Carthaginians, so returned to Syracuse. This may be just another tale of Punic cunning and is not mentioned by Polybius, although it is not necessarily incompatible with his version. That intervention in this dispute was attractive to the Carthaginians is unsurprising. Throughout the Carthaginians' centuries-long struggle to control Sicily the chief opposition from the Greek cities had always been led by Syracuse, the wealthiest and most powerful of them all. Allowing another strong tyrant to emerge there, his power based on the glory of having destroyed one group of foreigners who had attacked the Greeks of Sicily, was clearly undesirable. Controlling Messana, and with it the most direct route to Italy, increased Punic power. Whether it would inevitably have led to their eventual subjugation of Syracuse and complete conquest of all Sicily, as was claimed by some later sources, is more questionable.[6]

The intervention at Messana was no great initiative on the part of the Carthaginians, for they had long been active in Sicily. It was a very different matter for the Romans. Whilst their dominion had been steadily expanding for over a century, until this time they had never fought outside the Italian Peninsula. Polybius tells us that the Senate was divided over how to respond to the appeal from the Mamertines, and although it may be questioned whether he or his sources knew precisely what was said in the subsequent debate, the arguments he presents are plausible enough. The similarity between the actions of the Mamertines at Messana and Decius' troops at Rhegium must have been obvious and the hypocrisy of punishing the latter and making an alliance with the former blatant. The opposing argument was that it would prove advantageous for Rome to intervene, and dangerous for her not to. Carthage already controlled North Africa, parts of Spain, Sardinia and the lesser islands of the western Mediterranean. Control of Messana might well lead to the conquest of all Sicily and gave them command of an easy route to Italy. Rome's recently acquired dominion of southern Italy may have appeared especially vulnerable, for the Hellenic cities there and the Greeks of Sicily had always enjoyed close links.[7]

Polybius claims that the Senate was unable to make up its mind, but that the consuls for 264 were eager to seize the opportunity for intervention and persuaded the People to vote in favour of sending an expedition to Sicily, winning them over with the promise of rich booty in addition to the arguments already rehearsed in the Senate. One of the consuls, Appius Claudius Caudex, was appointed to the command and it is distinctly possible that he was the driving force behind this move, for his colleague Marcus Fulvius Flaccus may already have been in Etruria suppressing a disturbance amongst the Volsinii, an operation for which he received a triumph in the following year. For Claudius the Mamertines' appeal offered an opportunity to achieve ın his year of office the glory which all senators craved, made especially attractive because he would be the first man to lead a Roman army across the sea. Although Polybius presents the People as more interested than the Senate in plunder and profit, it is important to remember that when the Roman people were called upon to vote they did so in Assemblies heavily favouring the wealthiest citizens. This was especially true of the *Comitia Centuriata,* where this particular vote probably occurred. The motion could not have been passed unless a good proportion of the more prosperous citizens, including the equestrian order, were in favour. These men would profit more from receiving the State contracts to supply and equip the army, or from handling the massed sale as slaves of prisoners captured during the war, than from plunder picked up on the battlefield.[8]

It is highly unlikely that the People voted for a formal declaration of war with Carthage. The potential for confrontation with the Carthaginians clearly existed, and a clash with Syracuse was almost certain, but the Romans may have felt that their military power was strong enough to deter, if not swiftly defeat, any opposition in Sicily. Polybius criticized the pro-Carthaginian historian, Philinus, for maintaining that the Roman decision to send an expedition to Sicily violated a treaty between the two states which recognized Roman sovereignty in Italy and Carthaginian control of Sicily. Polybius lists the three treaties made between Rome and Carthage before 264, which he had seen still preserved on bronze tablets in the Treasury of the Quaestors beside the Temple of Jupiter Capitolinus at Rome. The numerous scholarly disputes over the details of these treaties and their reliability need not concern us here, for no good evidence has been put forward to make us reject them. The earliest, dated to the first year of the Roman Republic (508–507) and written in archaic Latin, placed heavy restrictions on Roman traders in Libya and Sardinia, granted Romans equal trading rights in the Carthaginian territories in Sicily, and offered protection to Rome's power and allies in Latium. A second treaty, undated by Polybius, but probably the one mentioned by Livy and Diodorus for 348, extends the area allied to Carthage in Libya, repeats the restrictions on the Romans trading there and in Sardinia and the clauses protecting Roman interests in Latium, and confirms their trading status in Sicily. Polybius does not mention the treaty listed by Livy for 306, and his final treaty is dated to 279–278 and was mainly concerned with mutual support during the wars of both states against Pyrrhus, although it seems that nothing practical actually came of this. (It is difficult to discern the truth behind the stories of the intervention of a Punic fleet in the latter stages of the Roman siege of Tarentum in 272, for the narratives are clearly distorted by later propaganda.) There is no good reason for rejecting Polybius' judgement and accepting Philinus' treaty. However, it is possible that one or both sides, either at the time of the treaties or with hindsight, felt that each state recognized the other's sphere of influence. What the treaties do appear to confirm is the long tradition of relatively friendly relations between the two, and the apparently widespread trade taking place, something which was to be renewed after hostilities in the First and Second Wars ended.[9]

Polybius represents the Roman decision to go to Sicily as shamelessly opportunistic, their awareness of the hypocrisy of assisting the Mamertines overcome by greed for plunder and glory, backed by a concern about the potential threat posed by a Carthage fully in control of Sicily and with easy access to Italy. Dio felt that the real reason for the First Punic War was the mutual fear in both Carthage and Rome of the other's growing power, now that the Roman conquest of southern Italy had brought their empires face to face. Each believed that their only long-term security lay in weakening the other's power.[10] For much of the nineteenth and twentieth centuries AD it was believed that Rome had never really been an aggressive power, but that her empire was the result of a long series of primarily defensive wars. Time after time she had gone to war to protect her interests and defend her allies (causes which were considered unimpeachably just), only conquering her enemies to ensure future peace. Therefore Roman expansion appeared haphazard and spasmodic with little sense of forward planning, the rule of the many provinces of this accidentally acquired empire a burden and a problem to which the Republic only slowly began to adapt. It was an appealing idea for German scholars, notably the great Theodore Mommsen, for whom the creation of the Roman empire was a distraction from the far more important absorption of Italy into a single culture, a trend foreshadowing the union of German peoples into a single state in his own day. It was even more attractive to the many scholars working in those countries such as Britain which themselves controlled vast colonial empires. These scholars were produced by a society which believed that the rule of civilized peoples of the world over the uncivilized was beneficial, almost as much to the conquered as the conqueror. Given that the great empires were an improving force, spreading education, the rule of law, and Christianity to the dark corners of the world, it was unappealing to believe that they had been created out of aggression or greed. The idea that the British Empire had been created 'out of a fit of absentmindedness' was readily extended to the Roman, especially since its culture, once allied to the best of the Greek civilization, was so clearly superior to the rest of the world at that time.[11]

The rapid demise of the European empires following the end of the Second World War led to an almost equally rapid condemnation of all that they had stood for amongst the new generations of historians, an unquestioned assumption that empires were, by their very nature, wrong. These scholars emphasized the greed and brutality of the imperial powers, the oppression of indigenous peoples and the destruction of their rich cultures. Eventually ancient historians began to examine Roman imperialism from a similarly critical standpoint. The assumption that Roman war-making was primarily defensive had always lacked plausibility in view of the eventual conquest of most of the known world. Some emphasized the economic motivation for conquest, in particular the acquisition of large numbers of slaves to work the great estates purchased by the noble families from the profits of successful wars. Others concentrated on the elements within Roman society which made them prone to expansion, focusing in particular on the senatorial quest for glory which could best be won by leading the armies of the state in a successful foreign war, so that each year a new set of magistrates were installed who were eager to wage war. There were also advantages and profits to be gained by all classes in Roman society through military service. Rome's network of alliances throughout Italy, for almost all of whom the chief bond was the obligation to provide soldiers to serve the Romans in war, has also been seen as encouraging further expansion. According to this theory the only means for the Romans to confirm the loyalty of their allies was to fight constant wars. That the Romans were frequently willing to fight wars and extend their power, even if not the physical extent of their territory, is undeniable, but the emphasis on Roman aggression can be taken too far. Too often this is studied in isolation with little account being taken of the targets of imperialism, many of whom were themselves highly aggressive. It has recently been pointed out that Roman expansion did not occur at a steady, constant rate. Its intensity varied immensely, with bursts of expansion being followed by relative lulls, when fewer wars were fought and only a small proportion of citizens enrolled to serve in the legions. Nor can the fear of strong neighbours entirely be dismissed as a motive for some of Rome's wars, even if with hindsight we may suggest that a people or state were not a genuine rival to Rome's power. If the Romans were as aggressive as some scholars have suggested, it would be unsurprising if they in turn expected other peoples to behave in a similar way and treated them accordingly.[12]

The desire for glory on the part of a Roman consul was the main reason why he incited the people with promises of profit and persuaded them to vote in favour of aiding the Mamertines. This is a clear case where the

71

factors within the Roman political system seen as favouring expansion did come into play and were the prime cause of a war. However, at least one scholar has gone further and argued that a clash between Rome and Carthage became inevitable after the Roman conquest of southern Italy, citing the establishment of colonies in Paestum and Cola in 273, the alliance with Ptolemy II Philadelphus of Egypt and the acquisition of a supply of timber ideal for shipbuilding when much of the Sila forest was confiscated from the Bruttians. Yet, as supporters of this theory admit, there were also opportunities for potential Roman expansion in northern Italy. It is dangerous to imply too high a level of forward planning on the part of the Roman Senate. Perhaps we might fairly say that after the defeat of Tarentum the potential for a clash between Rome and Carthage existed, but not claim inevitability. Once again it is worth recalling that it is highly unlikely that anyone at Rome expected more than a brief confrontation with the Carthaginians in 264.[13]

Once the Romans had made the decision to send an expedition to Sicily there was a long delay before they could actually move. It took time to enrol and muster a consular army and in addition to this, triremes and pentekonters to carry them across the Straits of Messina from Rhegium had to be requested from Rome's naval allies at Locri, Tarentum, Elea and Naples. In the meantime the Carthaginians moved a squadron of their galleys to a position near Cape Pelorias, from where they could observe the Straits and oppose any ships trying to cross. The precise chronology is once again unclear, but at some stage the small Carthaginian garrison of Messana was evicted from the city by the Mamertines. Their commander Hanno was subsequently crucified by his own side for this failure. Dio tells the story of how an advance party of Romans led by the tribune Gaius Claudius preceded the main force to Rhegium. Attempts to cross the sea in daylight were intercepted by the Carthaginian ships and repulsed. However, eager to avoid open conflict and perhaps confident that a display of naval power would deter the Romans from the folly of campaigning on an island without the support of a fleet, the Carthaginians returned the ships and prisoners they had taken. Claudius twice crossed at night in a small boat and began negotiations with the Mamertines, encouraging them with the direct promise of Roman support to evict the Carthaginian garrison. Finally Claudius was able to bring his main force over under cover of darkness.[14]

Polybius mentions none of this, and it may all be a later Annalistic invention or a confused version of the actions of Appius Claudius, for the coincidence of the tribune's name is highly suspicious. Appius Claudius also had difficulty in crossing the Straits in the face of the Punic ships. At a later point in the narrative Polybius mentions that one Carthaginian quinquereme ran aground and was captured when it too recklessly attempted to head off the Roman ships. Finally, Appius Claudius also managed to bring most of his force across to Messana at night. All sources attest to a good deal of negotiation between the various parties during these early stages. Dio records the famous threat made by Hanno to Gaius Claudius following the return of the prisoners and captured ships, urging them to seek peace rather than confront Carthaginian naval might and claiming that he would not allow them even 'to bathe their hands in the sea'. In Diodorus' version, Appius Claudius sent envoys to Hiero and the Carthaginians stressing the Romans' need to fulfil their *fides* (faith) to their allies the Mamertines. The Romans were understandably condemned as self-seeking, the need to maintain an obligation to the criminal Mamertines dismissed. The only concrete result of these rounds of negotiation was the alliance between Hiero's Syracuse and the Carthaginians to capture Messana and, presumably, oppose Roman intervention. The ease with which Hiero agreed to co-operate with the Carthaginians who had so recently duped him over Messana emphasized the degree to which all parties were acting out of self-interest.[15]

Hiero led an army from Syracuse which camped near a Carthaginian force and began the blockade of Messana. When negotiations had failed, the Romans made the next move, Appius Claudius attacking Hiero's camp. A sharp encounter ensued before the Romans were victorious, remaining in command of the field and despoiling the dead, an important mark of success in the ancient world. Hiero abandoned the siege and withdrew back to Syracuse. Polybius rightly demonstrated the implausibility of Philinus' claim that it was Hiero and not the Romans who won this action, but Zonaras does claim that the Syracusan cavalry initially defeated their Roman counterparts and that the day was only saved by the legionary infantry. Given the difficulties of transporting horses by sea and the specific problems encountered by Claudius in running the Punic blockade, it is quite possible that the Roman horse was not numerous, but it is also worth recalling that historically the Syracusan cavalry had a good reputation, unlike the city's hoplites. On the next day Claudius attacked the Carthaginians at dawn and drove them off. Zonaras says that after an initial repulse the Carthaginians pursued carelessly and were in turn routed by the Romans. It is highly unlikely that either of these actions was anything more than a large skirmish, but through them the Romans had broken the league around Messana.[16]

Claudius followed up his success by making a foray down towards Syracuse, raiding and devastating its territory. It is unlikely that this was anything more than a demonstration of force, since he had neither time nor resources to contemplate the siege of, or assault on, the city. Zonaras claims that several skirmishes were fought with Hiero's soldiers, before Claudius withdrew, his term of office having expired. It is notable that despite his successes, Claudius was not awarded a triumph on his return to Rome. It is possible that this was a result of personal unpopularity in the Senate, but more likely that it is confirmation of the small scale of the actions he had fought. In 263 the Romans decided to send both consuls, Marcus Valerius Maximus and Manius Otacilius Crassus, to Sicily, each at the head of the standard consular army of two legions and two *alae*, so that something like 40,000 Roman soldiers would campaign in the area. This display of force persuaded many Sicilian cities to defect from Carthaginian or Syracusan control and others were captured by surprise assaults. The attitude of most cities throughout the war was to be openly pragmatic, seeking to ally themselves with the strongest power as the only way to prevent the devastation of their fields and homes. There is little sign of much affection for any of the sides in the conflict. Marcus Valerius Maximus gained the most credit for ending the war with Hiero and celebrated a triumph in the next year. It is possible that he received the cognomen Messala as a result of winning a victory on behalf of Messana.[17]

Syracuse was the main target for the Roman offensive and clearly perceived as the prime enemy. Faced with the overwhelming force of both consuls, Hiero decided to make peace. His approach was readily accepted by the Romans, whose large army was already facing major supply problems. In part this was a result of the continued Carthaginian blockade of the Straits, their only active participation in this phase of the campaign, but also a product of the Romans' unpreparedness for fighting a campaign so far away. A direct assault on a large and well-defended city was always dangerous and the army could not have fed itself for the duration of a long siege, even if they could have preserved a blockade and prevented supplies from reaching the city, which was probably impossible without a Roman fleet to seal off the harbour. By the terms of the subsequent treaty Hiero became a friend and ally of Rome, returned without ransom all the Roman prisoners in his hands, presumably taken in the skirmishes with Claudius, and paid them 100 talents. The alliance, confirmed in perpetuity in 248, allowed Hiero to control an independent Syracuse and extensive territories, ruling in a way that earned praise from Polybius which, he claims, was reflected by Hiero's Greek subjects. Hiero's loyalty to Rome was to remain staunch even at the lowest ebb of their fortunes and without his aid, in particular in ensuring the supply of provisions to the Roman armies, the campaigns in Sicily would not have been possible.[18]

Syracuse was the weakest of the three states, which explains Hiero's easy shift in alliance from Carthage to Rome. In this way he achieved his original objective of removing the threat of raiding by the Mamertines, even if he could not conquer the city. The short-lived alliance between Syracuse and Carthage had always been a strange one, given the fact that they were natural rivals and the recent Carthaginian insertion of a garrison into Messana. It is interesting to speculate, but impossible to know, what they expected to happen if they had taken Messana together. The Carthaginians' actions were merely a continuation of their long-term attempt to dominate Sicily. They disliked the prospect of a reinvigorated Syracuse capturing Messana, but were even less willing to see the Romans establish themselves on the island. In the past the Carthaginians had endured the onslaught of various foreign armies which had come to Sicily to fight them on behalf of the Greek cities, the most recent example being Pyrrhus. Though such leaders had achieved notable successes the Carthaginians had always weathered the storm and eventually repulsed them. Whatever the details of earlier treaties, the Roman landing in Sicily was a direct challenge to Carthaginian power in an area where they had long had a presence. The contrast between Carthage's great naval power and Rome's lack of a fleet can only have encouraged them in their belief that the Romans would have extreme difficulty in maintaining a presence in Sicily. There seemed no reason for them to admit the Romans to the island in the first place, or to believe that the initial reverse was anything other than temporary.

Syracuse, Carthage and Rome all acted out of self-interest, but it is important not to judge their actions by modern standards. It was considered proper in the Graeco-Roman world for states to seek to increase their hegemony over others, a view which did not conflict with the importance of freedom as a political ideal. Yet Rome had no tradition of a presence in Sicily to mitigate their opportunistic actions and the Mamertines were clearly undeserving allies. Both Rome and Carthage were supremely self-confident, probably rather naively inclined to assume that their strength was great enough to overawe any opposition, or swiftly overcome it if force proved necessary. It was in this light mood that they were to enter upon twenty-three years of war.

CHAPTER 3

The Land War

THE OPERATIONS OF armies and fleets were intimately related in the ancient world, especially in a conflict like the First Punic War when much of the fighting occurred on or around islands or near coast-lines. However, it is easier to understand the events of the war if we deal separately with the actions of the navies and armies involved, and concentrate in turn on the activity in each theatre of operations. This chapter will describe the campaigns fought on land.

Sicily, 262–258 BC

Syracuse provided the Roman armies with a secure base for their operations, where grain, fodder and other supplies could be massed. Messana was now secure and the ostensible objectives for Rome's going to war had been achieved, but our sources do not suggest that either side attempted to begin peace negotiations. The Carthaginians saw no reason why their initial reverses should force them to accept a permanent Roman presence in Sicily and began to build up a powerful army for use there. Large numbers of mercenaries were enlisted in Spain, whilst other contingents were provided by the Gauls and Ligurians. For the Romans, hostilities could not end until the Carthaginians admitted defeat and were willing to come to terms favourable to Rome, as Hiero had done. The prospects of glory and plunder from the rich Sicilian cities which had first attracted the Romans to the area provided a further incentive for continuing the struggle. Polybius claims that after the capitulation of Hiero the Romans had reduced their forces from four to two legions, trusting to the king's aid to ease their supply problems. Subsequently, in reaction to the Carthaginians' preparations, both consuls and four legions were dispatched to Sicily in 262.[1]

The Carthaginians intended to use Agrigentum (also known by the Greek name Acragas), roughly midway along the coast of Sicily nearest to Africa, as their main base. However, by the summer of 262 when the Romans moved against the city few, if any, of the newly raised troops had arrived. The consuls, Lucius Postumius Megellus and Quintus Mamilius Vitulus, marched together, their combined armies theoretically giving them around 40,000 men, and arrived outside the city at harvest time (probably in about June). Hannibal, son of Gisgo, the commander at Agrigentum, had gathered many people from the surrounding area within the city walls, so that Polybius tells us that its population had swollen to 50,000, but his garrison appears to have been relatively small. His refusal to contest the area outside the city walls may well have been interpreted by the Roman consuls as weakness, for, at least in the western Mediterranean, it was normal for a confident defender to fight for some time outside his fortifications even against a numerically superior attacking force. Once the Romans had built their camp about a mile from the city, a large proportion of the army dispersed to harvest the ripened crops in the surrounding fields. For an army recruited mainly from small farmers and agricultural labourers, the task must have been a familiar one. Nevertheless it is striking that once again the logistical arrangements of a Roman army seem to have been inadequate. Roth, in his excellent study of the army's logistics, argues that the army at this time was simply unprepared to feed large forces campaigning so far afield for long periods of time.[2] It had been very rare for four legions to take the field together in the past. Only the small picket placed outside the camp, following a practice which was to remain standard in the Roman army for several centuries to come, was composed of formed and equipped troops. These men were oath-bound not to leave their position and the Roman army's harsh discipline punished with death any man who did so.[3]

Hannibal seized the opportunity and launched a vigorous sally. The foragers, scattered and probably largely unarmed, could offer no effective resistance and fled. A major Roman disaster appeared likely as Carthaginian troops advanced on the Roman camp. The only resistance came from the picket guarding the Roman camp and these men, despite being heavily outnumbered, put up a fierce fight. The Roman losses were heavy, but in the end they routed the attacking troops, defeated another group which had begun to penetrate the camp and pursued them all back to the city. Both sides were chastened by this experience, and their behaviour was subsequently more circumspect. Hannibal could not risk further losses to his garrison and became reluctant to risk further attacks, whilst the Romans ceased to underestimate their enemy and in future took care to forage in a more organized way, posting larger numbers to troops as a covering force.

The easiest way to take a city in this period was by surprise or stealth, attacking at night or from an unexpected direction. Such sudden attacks were most likely to succeed if aided by treachery amongst the defenders. The frequently bitter internal politics of the city state often provided disaffected elements willing to open a gate and admit an enemy force, which could then seize key points before the defenders were aware of their presence. Almost as many cities fell to treachery as to conventional means during the Punic Wars, but it was difficult for an attacker to plan for this, and he could merely act on the opportunity if it was offered. Treachery was even harder for the defender to guard against, although considerable efforts were made to do so and this was the main theme of the fourth century BC Manual on Siegecraft written by Aeneas Tacticus. No opportunity occurred at Agrigentum for the Romans to take the city through treachery or surprise, which left them with a choice between the other two options for a besieging force, assault or blockade.

Assault was the one aspect of ancient warfare most affected by technological advances. It involved the attacker finding a way over, through or under the defender's fortifications. The simplest method was escalade, when the attacking infantry carried ladders up to the walls and attempted to scale them, but this invariably involved heavy casualties and was rarely successful unless the walls were denuded of defenders. Mobile siege towers which dropped a drawbridge onto a rampart and allowed men to cross, whilst providing covering fire from archers or artillery on top, were essentially an extension of this same basic idea. The main alternative was to create a breach in the walls by battering ram or tunnelling underneath to undermine them. This required extensive preparation, scientific knowledge and labour to create siegeworks allowing engines such as a battering ram to pass over any defensive ditches and reach the wall. All the time the defender would be employing artillery to hinder this activity, countermining to thwart the attacker's tunnelling, and launching sallies to burn his engines. The ingenuity of both sides was severely tested as they struggled to find measures to counter the moves of the enemy. Once the defences had been breached then ingenuity and technical skill counted for little as the assaulting infantry had to storm their way inside. Casualties might still be heavy, and failure was a real possibility. Such was the massive effort and the uncertainty of the outcome that assaults on major cities were not contemplated lightly. Convention decreed that a defender would normally only be permitted to surrender on terms if he did so before the first battering ram touched the wall, otherwise the city would be subject to a sack. At this period the Roman army lacked the technical skill to undertake such a project on a city as large as Agrigentum with any real prospect of success.[4]

This meant that the only viable option available to the consuls in 262 was blockade, cutting off the city from the outside world until its food supplies ran out and starvation forced a surrender. If the enemy had had time to prepare for the siege by massing stocks of essentials, then this might well take a very long time. However, the Romans had a large enough army to blockade Agrigentum effectively, and began by throwing up a system of ditches and small forts which completely surrounded the city. Each of the consular armies constructed its own camp to support this line of circumvallation and a second line facing outwards, or line of contravallation, was built to prevent supply columns from trying to break in. Unlike many Carthaginian strongholds, Agrigentum did not have its own port and was situated on a plateau several miles inland. The Romans would have found it virtually impossible to seal off a harbour without ships of their own. The long duration of a blockade imposed severe burdens on the logistic arrangements of the besiegers, since a large army which remained stationary swiftly consumed all the food available locally. Rome's allies provided grain and cattle, which were massed at the supply dump created at an unidentified place called Herbesus a short distance away.[5]

After five months of siege, Hannibal began to become concerned about the city's resources of food and began to make urgent appeals for aid. The Carthaginians shipped the bulk of their recently raised forces over to Sicily, concentrating them at Heraclea Minoa, about 20 miles up the coast from Agrigentum, where they were placed under the command of Hanno. Polybius does not give a figure for the strength of this force, although he subsequently mentions that it included around fifty elephants. Diodorus, explicitly citing Philinus, gives their total as sixty elephants, 6,000 cavalry and 50,000 infantry. This gave Hanno at least parity, and possibly a slight advantage, in numbers over the two consular armies and any allies besieging Agrigentum. His first move was to mount a surprise attack on Herbesus, capturing the Roman supply dump and severing their lines of communication. The legions outside Agrigentum soon began to suffer from food shortages. In their weakened state the men became prone to disease which spread rapidly through the crowded camps. Confidently the Carthaginian advanced his main force from Heraclea Minoa, sending his Numidian light horsemen on ahead, with orders to engage the Roman cavalry and then feign retreat. The Roman cavalry took the bait and too rashly pursued the Numidians when they turned to flee. Reaching the main Carthaginian column, they rallied and turned on the blown and disorganized Roman horse, routing them and chasing them back to the Roman lines with heavy loss. It was with similar tactics that these superb light cavalry would play such a prominent role in the Second War with Rome.[6]

After this success, Hanno moved his army to within a mile and a quarter (10 stades) of the Romans and built a fortified camp on a hill known as Torus. Zonaras says that Hanno deployed his army and challenged the Romans to battle, but that they declined, chastened by the defeat of their cavalry. As time passed and their food shortage became more severe, the Roman consuls decided to march out and offer to fight, but their sudden apparent rise in confidence deterred Hanno from a direct encounter. The tentative nature of this manoeuvring and the reluctance of generals to risk a battle unless convinced that they held every possible advantage, as well as the difficulty of forcing an enemy to fight even when he was camped only a mile or so away, are typical of the warfare of this period. Polybius does not discuss this period in detail, merely saying that for two months the armies were camped close together without any direct conflict apart from periodic exchanges of missiles. Ultimately, it was only because of a constant flow of messages and fire-signals from Hannibal, stressing the desperate food shortages in the town and the growing rate of desertion to the enemy, that Hanno was forced to fight. The Romans, themselves close to starvation, readily accepted and deployed in the plain between the camps.[7]

Polybius gives few details of this battle, but it seems that the Carthaginian army was deployed in more than one line, with a front line of infantry supported by a second containing more infantry and the elephants. It is possible that the intention was to tire out the Roman infantry, weakening their formation and destroying the impetus of their advance, but this is no more than conjecture. Presumably the cavalry formed the wings and the Romans were in their usual *triplex acies*. After a long struggle it was the Romans who drove back and routed the Carthaginian first line. As these mercenaries retreated, the panic spread to the reserve formations and these fled. The Romans captured the Punic camp and most of the elephants. Diodorus claims that Hanno lost 3,000 infantry and 200 cavalry killed, and 4,000 men captured, whilst eight elephants were killed outright and thirty-three disabled, but includes in this total the losses of the earlier cavalry victory. However, he also says that Roman losses in the siege and battle amounted to 30,000 foot and 540 horse, but this is from the total of 100,000 which he claims the besiegers mustered. Both the size of the army and the casualties seem too high, although the latter may well have been substantial.[8]

Zonaras provides a different version of the battle in which Hanno hoped to co-ordinate his attack with a sally by Hannibal's garrison, but was thwarted when the Romans learned of the plan and ambushed the main force, whilst easily defeating the garrison's raid with the outposts guarding the camp and siege lines. Zonaras implies that the battle began late in the day, and the same thing is claimed by Frontinus who attributes to the consul Postumius the strategem of refusing battle and remaining close to the camp as he had done for several days. When the Carthaginians decided that the Romans were unwilling to fight and began to withdraw, satisfied that they had demonstrated their greater fighting spirit, the Romans suddenly attacked and defeated them. It is impossible to know how accurate these traditions are, but all our sources at least agree that the battle ended in a clear Roman victory. Hanno's use of his elephants has often been criticized, given their failure to support the first line. It has been suggested that the Carthaginians were still unused to employing elephants and unaware of correct tactics, this being the first recorded instance of their use by a Punic army.[9] However, lacking a more detailed narrative we cannot be certain what Hanno's battle plan was, or precisely what went wrong. The failure of the different elements in his army to support each other effectively may be a reflection of its composition. Most of the troops were recently raised and had not had much time to learn to manoeuvre as an army or become familiar with their commanders.[10]

Aware that relief was no longer possible, Hannibal led the garrison in a daring breakout during the night, filling the Romans' ditch with baskets of earth and evading the vigilance of an army which was resting or celebrating after its victory. A pursuit the next morning failed to catch many of his men, but the Romans were able to enter Agrigentum unopposed after a siege lasting about seven months. The city was plundered and its inhabitants sold into slavery. It was a significant Roman victory, but the campaign had come close to disaster on several occasions, especially once the besieger's supply lines were cut, when the army had only survived because Hiero with great resourcefulness had been able to ensure that the barest minimum of supplies got through to them. The escape of the garrison also detracted from the success and it is notable that neither of the Roman consuls received a triumph. However, according to Polybius the fall of Agrigentum did encourage the Senate to extend their war aims to include the total expulsion of the Carthaginians from Sicily. As a result they made the critical decision to construct a fleet. Walbank criticizes Polybius' portrayal of events as being too schematic, but it is at the very least highly likely that the capture of the main Punic stronghold greatly encouraged the Romans.[11]

The defeat of Hanno outside Agrigentum was one of only four massed battles fought on land throughout the twenty-three years of war, a marked contrast with the Second Punic War where pitched battles were far more common. Two of these battles occurred in the relatively brief African campaign of Regulus, and only two in Sicily, despite the deployment of large numbers of soldiers there by both sides for much of the war. Part of the reason is topographic, for the rugged terrain of most of central Sicily does not favour the movements of large armies. With so many good defensive positions, it was difficult for a commander to force a battle on an unwilling adversary. More importantly, the bulk of the island's population lived in the numerous walled cities or their dependent villages. These were the key to Sicily and only through controlling these communities could the island be secured. The territories controlled by Syracuse and Carthage had little unity, being composed of a patchwork of these small city states, most of whom still enjoyed local autonomy. From the earliest actions to break the blockade around Messana, the operations of the armies were dominated by the need to secure each individual town and city. The outcome of a pitched battle was always uncertain and a defeat might well involve very high casualties and the demoralization of the rest of the army. Even a victory merely left the successful army to pursue its main task of subduing cities more freely. Under normal circumstances the potential gains were insufficient for both sides to be willing to risk joining battle. It is significant that both the major battles to occur in Sicily were fought outside, and for the control of, cities. A high proportion of the troops deployed in Sicily were probably dispersed in small garrisons to hold the various cities.

As we have seen, the advantage in siege warfare lay with the defender. The Romans began the war lacking the technical experience required to take a strong city by direct assault. The Carthaginians lacked the manpower both to provide the labour force such operations required and to risk the heavy losses that were likely to be entailed. Sometimes a city might be forced to surrender by repeated raiding of its territory, and it was common for other cities in the locality to defect after a major success by one side. Diodorus claims that sixty-seven cities went over to the Romans after their successes in 263, a factor which contributed to Hiero's willingness to seek peace. Blockade was the most common and successful means of taking a city employed by both sides, but it was still a difficult task, requiring a sizeable force to remain in one area for a long period of time. Nor was success guaranteed. In 263 Appius Claudius failed to take Echetla and, following the peace with Syracuse, the Romans failed to achieve anything after long sieges of Macella and Hadranon, the latter described as only a village by Diodorus. In 261 a seven-month siege of Mytistratus also ended in the Romans being forced to abandon the enterprise. More spectacular successes could be achieved by treachery and, according again to Diodorus, it was by this means that Hanno had so easily taken Herbesus. His successor

Hamilcar recaptured Camarina and Enna, which had probably defected to Rome in 263, when they were betrayed to him by a faction in the population in 259. The Romans were readmitted to Enna in the next year by rival groups within the city, although some of the garrison escaped. Camarina also fell to the Romans in 258 after a full-scale siege aided by siege engines – and perhaps experts – provided by Hiero. As the war progressed, the Roman armies steadily began to show more proficiency at siegecraft, but neither side ever rivalled the professional Hellenistic armies in these skills.[12]

Reliance on traitors within a community produced some startling successes, but was inevitably dangerous. The first commander of Rome's newly constructed fleet, the consul Cnaeus Cornelius Scipio, was captured in 260 when he recklessly led an expedition to Lipara, acting on the promise of the city's betrayal. Our sources conflict as to whether or not this was a deliberate Carthaginian trap. The planning and implementation of attacks to exploit offers of betrayal were also fraught with difficulties. Diodorus claims that in 253 a Roman column was secretly admitted to Thermae by a traitor, but that the small assault party closed the gate behind them, eager to keep the booty for themselves. They were massacred when the defenders realized how small their attackers' numbers were. Either Hanno or his successor Hamilcar is supposed to have disposed of a group of mutinous Gallic mercenaries by sending them to take possession of a Roman-held city under promise that it was to be betrayed to them. The Gauls, given permission to plunder freely once they were inside the place, departed enthusiastically. However, the Punic general sent men pretending to desert to reveal the plan to the Romans. The latter prepared an ambush and the Gauls were massacred. Plunder figures very heavily in the accounts of the First Punic War.[13]

It is both very difficult and unprofitable to attempt to provide a detailed, chronological narrative of the campaigns in Sicily, given the poor quality of our sources. Polybius concentrates more on the naval operations after 261 and other sources are fragmentary, consisting of anecdotes, many of which seem implausible. The very nature of the war made it difficult for them to provide a coherent account. Sieges, surprise attacks and acts of treachery were interspersed with frequent raiding, much of it probably very small-scale. Our sources tend only to mention the spectacular successes, such as Hamilcar's surprise attack on Rome's Syracusan allies when they were camped alone at Thermae in 260, in which 4,000 were killed. The Carthaginians enjoyed several advantages from the relative permanence of their commanders and armies. Once the mercenary forces were recruited and shipped to Sicily they served for long periods under the same officers and acquired considerable experience of the type of fighting there. It is exceptionally difficult to trace the deployment of Roman legions during the war. It is uncertain whether every new consul brought newly raised troops with him and what proportion of the army returned to Italy when each magistrate left. Yet overall the Romans deployed far more troops in the area and continually replaced their losses, whereas Carthaginian commanders received few reinforcements. However, the annual replacement of commanders may well have made Roman operations less concerted and led to minor setbacks as Zonaras claimed.[14]

Africa 256–255 BC

The development of the Roman navy and the string of remarkable successes which the Romans enjoyed at sea will be discussed in the next chapter. Carthaginian ships had raided the Italian coast as early as 261, but in 256, whilst the war continued in Sicily, the Romans mounted not just a raid, but a full-scale invasion of Africa. After a brief pause to regroup and rest following their great victory over the Carthaginian fleet at Ecnomus, the Roman consuls, Lucius Manlius Vulso and Marcus Atilius Regulus, sailed to Cape Bon, and landed near the city of Aspis, later known to the Romans as Clupea – both words mean 'shield'. The ships were drawn up onto the beach and surrounded with a rampart and ditch and Aspis besieged. Once the city had fallen and a garrison was installed, the consuls despatched a report to Rome and then sent the troops out on a series of plundering expeditions throughout this highly fertile region. Cattle were rounded up, the farmhouses of wealthy Carthaginians put to the torch and over 20,000 slaves were captured or defected, including numbers of Romans and Italians taken prisoner earlier in the war according to Zonaras. It was quite probably during these operations that the excavated settlement at Kerkouane on the coast was taken, and its defences destroyed. The Senate replied to the report, instructing one consul to return to Italy with the fleet and the other to remain in Africa with an army. Vulso took the bulk of the ships, along with the prisoners, back, leaving a squadron of forty to support Regulus' land forces.[15]

Many myths came to surround Regulus and, as with all the other important figures of the First Punic War including Hiero and Hamilcar Barca, it is now impossible to know what sort of man he was. He was clearly an able commander, and if he was perhaps over-aggressive this was a common trait in Roman commanders and not considered a vice. One tradition claimed that Regulus was impoverished by senatorial standards, and that it was only reluctantly, following an assurance by the Senate that they would provide for his wife and children at state expense, that he accepted the African command. However, the moralizing tone of this anecdote strongly suggests a later invention as part of the Regulus myth. Regulus' army in Africa consisted of 15,000 infantry and 500 cavalry. It was probably a standard consular army, if an understrength one, since Polybius later mentions a 'First Legion' which implies that he had at least two. The disproportionately low number of cavalry was a result of the difficulty of transporting horses by sea.[16]

Once the Carthaginians had realized that they were incapable of preventing the Romans from landing in Africa, they began to look to the immediate defence of Carthage itself. Two generals were elected, Hasdrubal, son of Hanno, and Bostar, whilst Hamilcar, the current commander in Sicily, was recalled from Heraclea Minoa with 5,000 foot and 500 horse. The three seem to have held a joint command, but the size of their united forces is not clear, although these evidently included a sizeable contingent of elephants and numerous cavalry. It is unlikely that they significantly outnumbered the Romans in overall numbers, since our sources do not imply a major disparity between the strengths of the two sides. In late 256 Regulus began to advance, plundering the countryside. Reaching the town of Adys (possibly Roman Uthina, modern Oudna), he began to besiege it. The Carthaginians had already decided that they must make some effort to prevent the Romans from devastating their territory with impunity, and moved their army to its relief. Arriving near Adys, they followed a similar policy to Hanno outside Agrigentum and built a fortified camp on a hill overlooking the town and the Roman siegeworks. Clearly their commanders were reluctant to commit themselves to a battle too hastily, before they had gained some advantage. [17]

Polybius is highly critical of the Carthaginian leaders for taking up a position on high, broken ground, where cavalry and elephants would be less effective, and thus denying themselves their greatest advantages over the Romans. He claims that the Roman commanders realized that this was a mistake as a result of their past experience of warfare. It is rather unclear which officers he means by this, the Greek term used being vague, but it was decided to mount an immediate attack on the Carthaginian camp. It was a very bold plan and the contrast with the tentative posturings of the rival armies outside Agrigentum is most striking. There, when first Hanno and then the Romans offered battle, they made no effort to force an encounter when the other side declined, being content with the moral victory of seeing their enemy refuse a direct challenge. However, the situation was very different in 256. In Sicily the war was fought for the control of cities, each side attempting to maintain or establish as permanent a presence as possible. Both were contesting a region which had no natural ties to either side. Regulus' army was far too small, and lacked a secure base of allied support, for him to consider attempting to subjugate the cities of Carthaginian Africa one by one. Agathocles had spent years in the same region and ultimately failed to achieve very much. The Roman invasion was a means of placing pressure on Carthage as part of the wider struggle. Its aim was to bring about Carthage's defeat, not conquer territory for a new province. The defeat of the main Punic army in the field was the best means of placing pressure on the élite of the city and encouraging them to seek peace. Therefore, the Roman plundering operations and capture of towns and villages had as its prime objective the provoking of the Carthaginians to open battle, though it also provided the Roman army with food and the plunder which all classes at Rome expected to gain from warfare. This main aim was achieved when the Carthaginians marched to Adys, but this does not explain why Regulus risked a surprise assault on the camp rather than simply waiting for the opportunity to give battle. It may be that the recent experience of the campaigns in Sicily, although not by Regulus himself, had accustomed the Romans to rapid raids and surprise assaults on towns and encouraged them to attempt this sort of action. If so, then it is surprising that Hamilcar was unprepared for this move.[18]

Polybius tells us that the Romans attacked the hilltop camp at dawn, but Zonaras says the assault occurred at night, although his claim that many Carthaginians were killed in their beds seems unlikely. It is possible that a night-time approach march was followed by a dawn attack, for it seems that the Carthaginians did not have sufficient warning to deploy more than a part of their army. Two Roman columns assaulted from opposite sides of the camp. A group of mercenaries did manage to form up and drove back the First Legion in considerable disorder, but pursued too rashly. They were attacked from the rear by the other Roman force and themselves routed. Their defeat seems to have marked the end of effective resistance and the rest of the army abandoned the camp in a panicked flight, although the cavalry and elephants escaped with few casualties once they reached the level ground. The bold attack had been an outstanding success, but the repulse of the First Legion emphasized the risks involved. The twin attack does not appear to have occurred simultaneously, perhaps as a result of the night-time approach march, although in the event this resulted in the fortuitous appearance of the second Roman force in the mercenaries' rear. Had the Romans been detected during their approach they risked having to fight a deployed Carthaginian army attacking down from the high ground. However, it is worth noting once again that a recently created Carthaginian force, (even Hamilcar's mercenaries were fighting along-side unfamiliar troops and leaders), failed to co-ordinate its different elements effectively, and the successful mercenary counter-attack was not supported.[19]

The Romans followed up their success by taking Tunis, using it as a base to mount raids on the area around Carthage itself. The Carthaginians were utterly despondent. In the last year their proud navy, which had put to sea with more ships than ever before, had been decisively defeated at Ecnomus, and now the army tasked with defending the capital itself had been beaten with consummate ease by Regulus. At the same time they were involved in bitter fighting with the Numidian kingdoms, resulting from attempts to expand Carthaginian territory in Africa, a policy which had been pursued alongside the struggle with Rome. Refugees from the areas raided by the Numidians as well as the Romans flooded into Carthage itself, spreading panic and creating some food shortages. According to Polybius it was at this point that Regulus guessed that the enemy might be willing to nego-tiate to end the war and sent peace envoys, which were welcomed by the Carthaginians. He was said to be nervous that his year of office had nearly expired and that he might not have finished the war before a successor arrived to gain an easy victory. Similar motivation clearly did influence the behaviour of other Roman magistrates. All our other sources agree that it was the Carthaginians who actually began the negotiations after their recent defeats.[20]

Only Dio claims to preserve the details of the terms dictated by Regu-lus, but their absence from all the earlier sources can only make their authenticity dubious. For what they are worth, these were that the Carthaginians should give up both Sicily and Sardinia, release all Roman prisoners freely whilst ransoming their own, pay the Romans an indemnity and annual tribute, only make war and peace on the approval of Rome, and only retain one warship for their own use, but provide 50 to serve under the Romans whenever requested. In several respects, notably the inclusion of Sardinia, these terms are harsher than the treaty which actually con-cluded the war in 241. Whatever the precise details, it is clear that Regulus sought to impose a treaty which forced the Carthaginians to admit total defeat in their war with Rome. All our sources state that the Carthaginians felt that the terms were far harsher than their actual fortunes in the war warranted. Despite its recent setbacks, the city was by no means at the end of its resources. Faced with a Roman refusal to grant any concession, the talks failed.[21]

During the winter of 255 the Carthaginians reformed their field army, adding drafts recruited from Greece – either 100 or 50 soldiers according to Diodorus. Amongst these was the Spartan-trained Xanthippus, a mercenary leader of some experience and ability. Polybius takes obvious pride in recounting the achievements of this Greek soldier, whose actions confirmed the deeply held Hellenic admiration for the Spartan military system, and it may be that Philinus described these incidents in a similar tone. Some of the stories about Xanthippus are probably later inventions, and Polybius himself was sceptical about the conflicting tales of his subsequent assassination by jealous Carthaginians, but there is no reason not to accept the basic narrative of this episode. Xanthippus was openly critical of the Carthaginian commanders who had let their army fight a battle on unfavourable ground when their advantages in cavalry and elephants could easily have been employed to defeat the Romans in the open plains. After explaining his views he was appointed as some sort of senior military adviser to the army and heavily involved in training the men. Polybius stresses his use of proper military commands and manoeuvres as he drilled the army beneath the walls of Carthage. The soldiers' confidence was renewed and the Punic generals gave them an encouraging speech and then moved out to confront Regulus. Their forces mustered 12,000 infantry, 4,000 cavalry and nearly 100 elephants. The infantry included the survivors of Hamilcar's mercenaries from the Sicilian army, presumably some of the newly recruited Greeks, and a contingent of Carthaginian citizens fighting as a phalanx of spearmen. Although the army was not huge, it probably enjoyed at least parity with Regulus' forces. The scene was set for the one battle which most resembled the formal clashes of the Second War. It was also to prove the only Carthaginian victory in a land battle.[22]

The Romans were surprised by their opponents' renewed confidence, but, now that the first round of negotiations had failed, eager to inflict another defeat. They advanced and camped just over a mile (10 stades) away from the Punic camp and eagerly accepted battle when the next day the enemy marched out and deployed. Precisely where the battle occurred is unknown, beyond Polybius' vague assertion that it occurred in level plains, but it is often referred to as the Battle of Tunis, since this was the place he mentioned that the Roman army had occupied. Xanthippus is given credit for the Carthaginian formation which placed the Citizen phalanx in the main line, with a body of mercenaries on their right. The cavalry were divided between the two wings, supported by more mercenaries, some of whom may have been skirmishers. The elephants were formed in a single line a 'suitable distance' in front of the infantry, although it seems that they did not fully cover the mercenaries on the right.[23]

The Romans were clearly concerned about the danger posed by the massed elephants and Regulus adapted his formation accordingly. *Velites* ran out ahead of the main line to skirmish, for elephants were vulnerable to missiles which might cause them to panic even if they did not inflict serious wounds. As usual the cavalry formed the wings and the legions the centre, but the latter were formed especially deep, or 'many maniples deep' in Polybius' description. It is unclear precisely what this means, but Polybius certainly believed that it was an appropriate formation for meeting elephants. Normally the legions deployed in the *triplex acies* with three lines of maniples, and it is possible that on this occasion Regulus formed the maniples into a larger number of lines. Lazenby suggested that they formed six lines, and probably closed the gaps normally kept between the maniples in each line, but contrasts this compact formation with Scipio's successful creation of lanes through his centre to channel the elephant attack at Zama. However, there are no other clear examples of a Roman legion forming in more than three lines until the first century BC when the maniple had ceased to be its main tactical unit. In the early second century BC, and possibly during the Hannibalic War, there were cases of an entire legion formed in the *triplex acies* being kept as a reserve behind the main line, but this usually occurred in actions which developed unexpectedly or when the enemy were significantly outnumbered. A more likely interpretation of Polybius is that Regulus' legions were formed in the usual three lines, but that each individual maniple took up position in a greater number of ranks than usual. The great danger in an elephant charge was that the terrifying appearance of the beasts would cause the waiting infantry to panic and run. A deeper formation made it harder for the men in the front ranks to do so, as those in the rear had to flee before they were able to go anywhere but forward. If a unit stood its ground when attacked by elephants there was a greater chance that its missiles would drive the beast off. It also seems likely that at least some intervals remained between the maniples, for the Roman infantry clearly covered a frontage at least as wide as the Carthaginian foot, since the Roman left wing managed to avoid the brunt of the elephant attack. This interpretation of the Roman deployment involves a slightly less natural reading of the Greek, but does seem to make better sense of the rest of his narrative. The main weakness of the Roman formation was that, as Polybius noted, it failed to protect their already grossly outnumbered cavalry. Perhaps Regulus hoped to defeat the enemy centre with his infantry before the Carthaginians could exploit their advantage on the wings.[24]

After a delay of the type so common before battles, Xanthippus ordered the elephants to attack and the Romans moved forward to meet them, raising their battle cry and rhythmically banging their weapons against their shields in what Polybius describes as their usual custom. The Roman horse, facing odds of at least four to one, were swiftly routed. The 2,000 men on the left flank of the Roman infantry line, who would normally have been allied troops, achieved considerable success. Eager to avoid the elephants and contemptuous of the mercenaries who had been defeated in the previous battle, they charged the units on the enemy right flank and routed them, chasing them back to their camp. Elsewhere, the Roman infantry reeled under the onslaught of the mass of elephants, but despite taking casualties, the depth of their formation prevented them from breaking. A few maniples and small groups fought their way past the animals, and after reforming moved against the Carthaginian phalanx. Weary, their *pila* almost certainly gone, and greatly outnumbered, they were easily defeated. In the meantime the Punic horse had swept in against the flanks of the Roman infantry. Their attacks robbed the Roman formation of what forward impetus it had left, as flanking maniples had to turn to face the new threat. Struck by missiles from the cavalry or trampled by the elephants the Romans were destroyed whether they stood their ground or turned to flee. Regulus and 500 men initially made their escape, but were quickly captured. Only the 2,000 men who had broken through the mercenaries were able to retire in good order, eventually making their way back to Aspis which, with the troops left there, they successfully defended until evacuated by the Roman fleet later in the year. This was the only substantial part of the Roman army to escape. Polybius records losses of 800 men amongst the routed mercenaries, but does not give a figure for the casualties suffered by the rest of the army.[25]

This was the most striking success achieved by elephants throughout the course of the Punic Wars and had a great moral effect on the Roman armies in Sicily, who for the next few years did not dare contest control of the open ground with the Carthaginians for fear of these beasts. However, it is important to note that the victory had not been achieved by the elephants alone and owed a great deal to the successful cavalry actions which had allowed the envelopment of the Roman infantry. If Regulus' plan had been to use his superior infantry to break the enemy's main line before their numerically superior cavalry could come into play, it had failed because of the effectiveness of the elephants. At Trebia in 218 a substantial part of another Roman army which had been defeated on both wings was able to burst through the Carthaginian line and escape. Regulus' army was about one third of the size of that later force, which made it easier for the Punic cavalry to envelop the infantry centre, even more so as its deeper formation can only have reduced its frontage.

Xanthippus departed after his success, aware according to Polybius of the jealousy of the Carthaginian nobility, and may subsequently have served under the Ptolemies. Later a deeply romantic tradition developed around Regulus, claiming that the Carthaginians sent him as an ambassador to Rome to negotiate for the ransom of Roman prisoners, but that he advised the Romans against making the agreement. Bound with an oath to return to Carthage, Regulus nobly kept faith and refused to stay in Rome, in spite of the fact that he knew that going back would mean a cruel death by torture. One source says that first his eyelids were cut off and then he was finally trampled to death by an enraged elephant. Another tradition told how his wife was given two eminent Carthaginian captives and in vengeance for her husband had them brutally maltreated until one died. Sometimes scholars have been tempted to accept this part of the account and claim that the Regulus story was invented to excuse his family's cruelty, but it is probably safer to reject the entire tradition, especially since none of these events are mentioned by Polybius.[26]

The African campaign of 256–255 remains one of the most dramatic episodes of the war, even without these almost certainly mythical embellishments. The Carthaginians' victory restored their confidence, which had reached such a low ebb after Ecnomus and Adys, and began an upsurge in their fortunes. In the following year they gained some ascendancy in Sicily, whilst a brutal campaign suppressed the Numidian princes. The Romans made no attempt throughout the remainder of the conflict to land another invasion force in Africa, although several large raids were sent against the coastal areas.[27]

Why had the invasion been mounted in the first place? It is clear that the Romans saw this expedition as a way of putting further pressure on Carthage. At least since the fall of Agrigentum and the Roman decision to attempt the expulsion of the Carthaginians from the whole of Sicily, the war had become an open struggle between Rome and Carthage. The limited objectives of the early phases of the war, assistance to the Mamertines and gaining control of the Straits of Messina, had passed into the background. The Carthaginians might eventually have been driven from Sicily by the piecemeal capture of each of their strongholds, but this was an enterprise which would take many years to achieve, and considerable effort could be wasted when captured cities were retaken or betrayed to the enemy. Once the conflict had become an open war between Rome and

Carthage, then it would only end when one or the other side conceded defeat. The Roman invasion of North Africa was an attempt to apply sufficient pressure to force Carthage to do just that, and it is notable that it was the Romans who decided to escalate the conflict in this way. Our sources are apt to blame Regulus for excessive pride in offering terms that were too harsh to be acceptable to the Carthaginians, but it is unlikely that any other Roman commander would have been markedly more lenient. The Romans demanded that their enemies admit that they had been utterly defeated and accept terms reflecting this. It is the first clear reflection we have of the Roman attitude to warfare discussed in an earlier chapter. Roman wars ended only when the enemy ceased to be a threat by admitting total defeat and accepting their future as a subordinate ally. The only alternative was for the Romans themselves to suffer such a defeat. The Carthaginians' attitude to warfare was far less determined, for they, in accordance with Hellenistic practices, expected a war to be ended with a negotiated treaty which reflected the actual balance of power. They did not anticipate the total destruction of an enemy's capacity to do future harm to them, still less that such terms would be imposed on them. Whether they or Regulus in fact initiated the negotiations, it is notable that the Carthaginians were willing to seek peace terms when the enemy had the upper hand in the conflict. The contrast to the Roman attitude when Pyrrhus had defeated them in two battles, or Hannibal had inflicted a string of disasters, is most striking. Both generals sent ambassadors to Rome and could not understand when the Senate refused even to speak to them unless they, the victors, conceded defeat. The relentless Roman attitude to warfare was one of their greatest assets in the wars with Carthage.

Sicily 258–241 BC

The Carthaginian cause was resurgent in the late 250s, but the territory they controlled in Sicily had been steadily reduced to little more than an enclave in the north-western corner of the island. In 254 the combined Roman army and fleet took Panormus, one of the largest of the cities still loyal to Carthage. Polybius tells us that, whilst the two sides were frequently camped less than a mile apart for months on end, the Romans refused to risk battle or leave the high ground, such was their terror of the elephants. However, the Carthaginians made no attempt to copy Regulus' daring assault on the enemy army in its camp. The Romans took a few more cities, notably Lipara and Thermae, the latter having been lost when Hamilcar surprised their Sicilian allies, but this was a fairly poor return for the efforts of the two consular armies which were sent to Sicily most years.

The pace of their conquest of Sicily had certainly slowed. When one of the consular armies withdrew late in 250, the current Carthaginian commander, Hasdrubal, advanced from Lilybaeum against the other which was occupying the city of Panormus. The Romans were there to protect the local population against raids whilst they harvested their crops, since an inability to defend allies would swiftly lead to defections to the enemy. This was especially true given the fairly recent capture of the city. Yet the Roman commander, Lucius Caecilius Metellus, deliberately kept his troops within the fortifications, feigning a reluctance to fight in an attempt to lure the Carthaginians into an unfavourable position. Hasdrubal readily took the bait, since the recent campaigns in Sicily can only have led him to despise the Romans' lack of spirit, and in an effort to demonstrate to Rome's allies the impotence of her soldiers, advanced right up to the city walls.[28]

It was a bad position, for Hasdrubal had to cross a river to approach the city and this severely restricted his ability to manoeuvre and would make it difficult to retreat. Metellus had made careful preparations. The inhabitants of the city had been tasked with stockpiling missiles by the city walls, and part of the Roman light infantry were stationed on the walls ready to employ this ammunition. The main body of *velites* were sent out to harass the advance elements of the Punic army as they crossed the river, forcing them to deploy into battle formation. A ditch had been dug close to the walls, and the *velites* were ordered to withdraw and shelter in this if hard pressed. They were given specific orders to concentrate their missiles on the elephants if the opportunity arose. Metellus kept his maniples of heavy infantry waiting inside a gate facing the left of the Punic army, ready to sally out. The Roman commander was also careful to provide a steady stream of reinforcements to the skirmishers fighting outside, and it is probable that some maniples were used in this way to provide a semblance of a fighting line outside the city. The Carthaginians were still not faced with serious opposition to their entire army and Hasdrubal let himself be drawn further into an escalating action, which he was not controlling, as his main line advanced against the thin Roman one. The elephant crews, eager to live up to their high reputation, charged and easily punched through the weak Roman forces, pursuing them back towards the city. The *velites* followed their orders and withdrew to the trench, still bombarding with missiles the elephants, who also came under a barrage from the walls. Wounded elephants panicked and began a stampede back towards their own army, creating widespread disorder. Metellus saw the opportunity and gave the order for the waiting column to charge out of the gate. Struck unexpectedly by a flank attack, the Carthaginian disorder turned into a rout. Heavy casualties were inflicted, although no reliable figures have been preserved and the claims of 20,000 or 30,000 dead in later sources do not seem plausible. The elephants suffered especially badly, ten being captured immediately and the rest subsequently, but it is unclear whether all 140 which he tells us were landed in Sicily after the defeat of Regulus were present. Diodorus claimed that a total of sixty were killed or taken, but Zonaras says 120 were taken and Pliny the Elder, writing in the first century AD, gives the far larger figures of 140–142. One story claims that Metellus offered the captured drivers their freedom if they would control the beasts, which were later shipped to Rome to be killed in celebratory games. Diodorus tells us that drunkenness amongst the Carthaginians' Gallic mercenaries was a major factor in the rout, but this is probably no more than a stereotypical tale of barbarian intemperance.[29]

This was the last massed land action of the war, although it scarcely warrants being classed as a pitched battle and it may be that our accounts exaggerate its scale. Its importance was undoubted, for the victory restored confidence to the Roman armies in Sicily and to the Senate. A major effort was planned for the next campaigning season in 250. Cities remained the key to Sicily, and the war continued to be dominated by sieges. Two strong cities with good port facilities remained in Carthaginian hands, Lilybaeum and Drepana which lay about 15 miles apart (120 stades). The Romans decided to attack Lilybaeum with both consular armies supported by a large fleet, a total of around 110,000 men according to Diodorus. The technical skills of the Roman forces had greatly improved since Agrigentum, for from the beginning they planned the construction of siegeworks to carry battering rams up against the walls of Lilybaeum and open breaches through which the assaulting infantry could charge. Again one suspects that much of this knowledge may have been provided and learned from experts provided by Hiero. This was the first siege to rival the complex affairs of the wars of the Hellenistic world, with attacker and defender each thinking up counter-measures, responding in turn to the other's initiative. The garrison commander, Himilco, mounted a very active defence, his 10,000 mercenaries tunnelling under the attacker's works to undermine them, and launching vigorous sallies in an effort to put them to the torch. Roman casualties were heavy both from enemy action and privation. Carthaginian forces, including the cavalry from Lilybaeum which had been evacuated by sea early in the siege as unnecessary mouths to feed, raided the Roman lines of communication. The Roman fleet experienced great difficulty in maintaining a blockade around the harbour as we shall see in the next chapter. Finally, the labour of many weeks was destroyed by fire when a strong wind aided the incendiary efforts of a group of Greek mercenaries in the garrison. An earlier attempt by some mercenary officers to betray the city had been thwarted by another officer, the Greek Alexon, leaving the Romans no other option but to starve the defenders into submission. Despite staggering naval disasters in 249 and the small chance of success when they lacked control of the sea, the Romans persevered with the blockade throughout the remainder of the war. The Carthaginians lacked sufficient land forces to break the siege.[30]

It is in the last years of the war in Sicily that the most famous of all the Carthaginian generals of this conflict appeared on the scene, Hamilcar Barca. His name was a suitably dramatic one, probably derived from the Semitic word for lightning-, or perhaps sword-, flash, but his greatest achievements were to come after the war with Rome and it is doubtful whether he would have received so much attention had he not been the father of Hannibal. Nevertheless, Polybius considered him the ablest commander on either side throughout the first conflict. By the time that he landed in Sicily in 247 the Carthaginians had been hemmed into a small enclave. He established himself on a hill called Hercte not far from Panormus, a secure base with command of a good anchorage. For three years he skirmished with the Roman forces near the city, winning minor victories, but not achieving anything in the longer term. Then in 244 he withdrew at night and sailed to Eryx near Drepana. The Romans had captured the abandoned town in 248, installing a garrison there and on the mountain's summit. Hamilcar captured the town in a surprise attack, cutting off the force on the summit, which was occupying the Temple of Venus, from the main Roman forces at the foot of the mountain. He managed to maintain this position and besiege this force for the remaining years of the war, again winning minor successes in the frequent raiding and skirmishing pursued by both sides.[31]

Hamilcar achieved little during his operations in Sicily, but it is probable that he lacked the resources to do much more and certainly did not have enough troops to defeat the Romans in open battle. It is distinctly possible that by this time the Carthaginians were directing more resources to their campaigns against the indigenous peoples of North Africa. With a power other than Rome, the prolongation of the struggle in Sicily and the avoidance of defeat may eventually have persuaded them to negotiate a peace acceptable to Carthage. In the end the land operations in Sicily became almost an irrelevance and the war was decided at sea. It is to the naval side of the First Punic War that we must now turn.

CHAPTER 4

The War at Sea

THE FIRST PUNIC WAR was the greatest naval conflict of antiquity. The resources both sides lavished on their fleets were truly enormous, and their losses in men and material were staggeringly huge. If our sources are correct, then the battle of Ecnomus in 256 may have involved more people than any other sea battle in history. Sea battles were more common than major land actions during the war and ultimately proved decisive. Polybius marvelled at the scale of the naval war, but even more at the speed with which the Romans, who, he claims, had never before built a warship, adapted to the sea and created a navy able to defeat Carthage with its long maritime tradition. The early years of the naval conflict witnessed a spectacular, and almost unbroken, string of Roman successes over an enemy whose ships were better constructed and crews far more skilful. When the war ended in 241, Rome had replaced Carthage as the unchallenged seapower in the western Mediterranean. The navies created during the war made possible the later victories over Carthage and the Hellenistic kingdoms.[1]

It was not true that the Romans had no experience at all of constructing and manning warships before 260, but Polybius' exaggeration was pardonable. There had been little need for warships of any size during Rome's steady conquest of Italy, for even those enemies who possessed a navy could be reached and defeated on land by the legions. In 311 the Romans created a board of two officials, the *duoviri navales classis ornandae reficiendaeque causa* with responsibility for construction and maintenance of warships. Each *duumvir* seems to have commanded a squadron of ten ships, which were probably triremes. Little is recorded of their activities, although one squadron was defeated with dismissive ease by Tarentine ships in 282. Although certainty is impossible in this poorly documented period, it seems that the fledgling Roman navy was disbanded after the defeat of Tarentum. Instead the Romans chose to rely on ships supplied and crewed by those of her allies with a maritime tradition, notably the Greek cities of southern Italy. As we have seen it was in ships provided by the allies, notably Tarentum, Naples and Locri, that Appius Claudius crossed to Sicily in 264. This was essentially an extension of the traditional Roman reliance on allied military support, save that these cities, known as the *socii navales*, provided ships rather than soldiers. It is worth recalling that the 278 treaty with Carthage had provided for the possibility of Punic ships providing support for the legions. In 267 the number of quaestors was doubled from four to eight, the new magistrates being known as the *quaestores classici*. It is possible that one of the responsibilities of these men was the regulation of the naval allies, and each may have been responsible for the communities in a particular region of Italy. It is impossible to know just how many ships Rome's allies were capable of providing, but it is unlikely that either in overall numbers or in ship size they would have been capable of challenging Punic mastery of the sea. Allied ships had difficulty both in transporting the Roman armies to Sicily and in supplying them there during the early years of the war in the face of Carthaginian naval activity. The role of the naval allies remained strictly subordinate to the land armies, which still formed the main effort in any Roman campaign.[2]

Therefore, the Senate's decision to construct and man a fleet of 100 quinqueremes and twenty triremes, with the intention of directly confronting the Carthaginian fleet, marked a major change in Roman practice. Polybius claims that the decision was made after the fall of Agrigentum encouraged the Romans to extend their war aims beyond the protection of the Mamertines and attempt to expel the Carthaginians entirely from Sicily. It is possible that there had been some advocates of constructing a fleet before 261. A very late source credits Valerius Messala, the consul of 263, with first realizing that a fleet was essential for ultimate victory in the war, but it is uncertain whether this tradition is accurate, or simply a later invention by a family eager to glorify its ancestors. A strong naval capability was clearly essential for the total subjugation of Sicily. Despite the acquisition of Syracuse as a base, it was still difficult for the Romans to supply, maintain, and reinforce their armies in Sicily when the sea routes were dominated by the Punic fleet. Ships were also essential if the Romans were to blockade cities with their own ports into submission, since otherwise the garrisons would be easily re-supplied by sea. Finally, it must have been clear that the Carthaginians' main strength was, and always had been, their fleet. The defeat of this fleet would inevitably be a major blow to Carthage, more so than the destruction of its mercenary armies, and would therefore be a major contribution towards forcing her to submit. This appears to be another example of a Roman decision to escalate the conflict in an effort to achieve a decisive result.[3]

Naval Warfare in the Third Century BC

In general the ancient sources are far less informative about operations at sea than on land. The problem is made worse by the essentially alien nature of oared warships to us. Maritime archaeology has started to provide some information, although wrecks of warships rather than merchantmen are exceptionally uncommon, and much has been learnt by reconstruction. Nevertheless there remain numerous gaps in our understanding of the construction and maintenance of classical galleys, and the strategic and tactical uses of fleets. An indication of this is our uncertainty as to the precise design of the quinquereme, the standard warship of the Punic Wars.

The great naval battles of the fifth century, when the Greeks had defeated the Persian invaders, and Athens and Sparta had vied for dominance, were fought and won by fleets of triremes. The evidence for this type of ship is relatively good, much of it coming from the literature and epigraphy of classical Athens and the excavations of the shipyards in the Piraeus harbour. The full-scale reconstruction of an Athenian trireme in the 1980s AD and its extensive sea trials vastly increased our knowledge. The trireme, or 'three', derived its name from the basic rowing group of three men. Each man sat at a different level and operated an oar 14 feet (*c.* 4 m) or so in length, those of the upper row projecting from an outrigger. Considerable skill was required in each oarsman for the successful functioning of the ship. Long and sleek, the Athenian trireme was about 120 feet (36.5 m) in length and just under 20 feet (6 m) across at its widest. It carried a crew of about 200, around 30 of whom were deck crew, officers and marines, and the remainder rowers. In trials the reconstructed version reached speeds of 8 knots and could maintain a steady 4 knots for hours on end, with half the rowers resting at any one time. Turns through 180 degrees were completed in a distance equivalent to two and a half ship lengths. These speeds were achieved despite the comparative inexperience of the modern crew and their use of oars which were probably heavier than the originals. Under sail the trireme was able to achieve 8 knots in a favourable breeze. All in all the performance of the reconstructed trireme was remarkably good and challenged many past assumptions about ancient naval warfare.[4]

In the fourth century several states began to construct larger warships than the trireme. The Carthaginians were the first to build 'fours' or quadriremes, whilst Dionysius I, the tyrant of Syracuse in the early fourth century, was responsible for the design of the 'five' – pentereis in Greek and quinquereme in Latin. The kingdoms which emerged in the Hellenistic world in the late fourth century were able to lavish huge resources on the construction of their fleets. Some of the largest ships were built by the Ptolemaic kingdom of Egypt, including such monsters as Ptolemy II's 'thirties' and 'forty', but there is no record of anything larger than a 'ten' seeing actual combat. The realization that, although the trireme had three banks of oars, its name derived in fact from the number of each team of rowers goes some way towards understanding the design of these ships. Clearly, galleys with four or five banks of oars would have been absurdly impractical and ones with ten or more utterly impossible. In fact, there is no evidence for any warship in the classical world ever having more than three banks of oars. Therefore in 'fours' and larger ships at least some of the oars must have been operated by more than one rower.[5]

The quinquereme had a basic team of five rowers, but how were they arranged? Did it have one level of oars rowed by five men each, two levels, one rowed by three and the other by two, or three levels with two oars operated by a pair of rowers and one by a single man? The navies of the Mediterranean powers in the late Middle Ages included many galleys, all of which had a single bank of oars, regardless of how many rowers operated each one. Two men can sit side by side and operate an oar effectively, but if there are more than two rowers per oar, then it is necessary for them to rise to their feet to dip the blade and then hurl themselves back onto the bench when they deliver the stroke. This was the method employed in the Middle Ages and must also have been used in the larger galleys in the classical world. Of necessity, this design required a somewhat broader and heavier hull to accommodate the rowers, which probably made them slower and less manoeuvrable than the sleeker types. It has been suggested by Casson that this had the advantage of reducing the requirement for skilled rowers, since it was only essential for one man per oar to be highly trained. This might seem an attractive prospect for the Romans who were undertaking the creation and manning of a fleet on an unprecedented scale. On this basis Casson argued that the Romans used quinqueremes with a single bank of oars, each rowed by five men, unlike the Carthaginians who used more slender, three-banked 'fives'. This, he felt, explained why our sources emphasized that the Punic ships were individually faster and more manoeuvrable than their Roman counterparts. However, Polybius tells us explicitly that the Roman ships were copied from a captured

Carthaginian 'five' and there seems no good reason to reject this evidence.[6]

The superior performance of Carthaginian ships for most of the war was a reflection of their more highly trained crews, and, at the very beginning, better construction, not a result of a fundamentally different design. On the whole, it is more likely that the quinqueremes of this period had more than one bank of oars. Two levels of oars, with three and two rowers respectively, would have meant an uneasy combination of the two different designs, and it is more probable that the quinquereme had three levels, the lowest with a single rower and the others with a pair. This would make the quinquereme a more logical development from the trireme. The upper level of oars in a trireme were mounted in an outrigger and this has sometimes been perceived as a weakness. Even if this was so and would have remained a failing in similarly designed 'fives', it is distinctly possible that the quinqueremes of the Punic Wars were constructed differently. Morrison and Coates have recently argued from the iconographic evidence that the Carthaginian 'five' differed markedly in its layout from Greek ships of the same size, suggesting that this distinction had its origins in Phoenician building methods. The Punic 'five' had all three levels of oars emerging from a single, deep oar-panel, the oarports being arranged in a chequerboard pattern. This they interpreted as an oarbox containing all the rowers and constructed separately to, and projecting from, the main hull. This would have produced a somewhat wider ship, but may have allowed the hull to be strengthened against ramming and possibly increased storage space in the main hull. This pattern of ship was, they argued, copied by the Romans, offering confirmation of Polybius' account, and continued in use with the Roman navy until well into the Principate. This system offered limited possibilities for development of higher ranked ships, since only a 'six', putting two crew on each oar, was really feasible within the confined space. As they point out, the Romans are not recorded as having floated anything larger than a six during the war, although whether these were of Punic or Greek pattern is unknown.[7]

Morrison and Coates' interpretation of the evidence is an attractive one, especially as it appears to confirm the literary tradition, but the evidence is too poor to reach a final conclusion. Ultimately there must remain some doubt about the precise nature of the quinquereme. However, certain reasonably confident assertions can be made about its capabilities and general characteristics. The crew of a Roman quinquereme consisted of 300 men, of whom about twenty were deck crew and the remainder rowers. At Ecnomus, Roman ships carried 120 marines, but this was because a major encounter was anticipated, and the normal complement was probably fewer, perhaps around forty. Athenian quadriremes were accommodated on the same slipways originally constructed for triremes and cannot have been much larger than these. 'Fives' were markedly higher than these earlier ships and were probably longer and a little broader as well. They were certainly slower and less manoeuvrable than threes and fours, although their greater mass allowed them to make better headway in rougher seas, and increased the effect when they rammed another ship.

There were two main tactical options open to ancient galleys, ramming and boarding. The amount of missile fire which could be delivered by a ship's marines, and the artillery mounted on the larger ships, was insufficient to inflict serious or incapacitating damage on an enemy vessel. At best such fire served to suppress an enemy crew preparatory to boarding. Shooting remained an adjunct to the main methods of attack and for this reason the wind was too uncertain a means of propulsion to be relied upon during a battle. Therefore all decisive combats necessitated physical contact between the opposing ships.

The earliest rams mounted on oared warships had been pointed in shape, but by the fifth century these had been replaced with much blunter devices. As ships became more powerful, there was a real danger that a narrow-headed ram would become deeply fixed into the enemy hull that it could not easily be extricated, immobilizing the ramming vessel as surely as the victim. For the same reason, it was normally inadvisable to ram from an angle higher than 60 degrees, since this also ran the risk of too deep a penetration. A third-century ram found off the coast of Athlit in Israel and now in the National Maritime Museum at Haifa is blunt-headed, broadens towards its tip and has wider projections on either side. It is 7 feet 6 inches (2.2 m) long, 30 inches (76 cm) at its widest point and 37.75 inches (96 cm) at its highest and weighs 1,023 lb (464 kg) The ram is probably from a Ptolemaic warship; Casson suggested that it may have come from a 'four' or 'five'. The ram found on the wreck of a small Punic warship discovered near Lilybaeum (Marsala in Sicily) was formed of timber encased on either side with a metal tusk, the whole ram curving upwards, presumably intended to puncture the enemy hull beneath the waterline. Rams were fixed to the ship's keel, but never formed a part of it, since this would have transferred too much of the force of a successful ram to the ramming ship's own hull. The other advantage of this design was that if the ram did become fixed in an enemy vessel, then it would probably break off and allow the ramming ship to withdraw.[8]

Ramming the bow of an enemy ship was dangerous and usually avoided, since this was the strongest part of a vessel and the resultant collision was likely to inflict serious damage to both ships. Instead, captains would manoeuvre their ships to ram the enemy's side. The ideal position was to attack from astern at a narrow angle, the ram not breaking through at one single point but rupturing a wide section of the enemy's hull, causing its seams to split and take on water. Sea battles therefore consisted of a series of individual duels as ships carefully tried to out-turn the opposition and strike from the flank, whilst trying to avoid making themselves vulnerable to another enemy, a type of combat sometimes compared to the aerial dog-fights of the First World War. A highly skilled crew might choose to strike an opponent at such an angle that the ram ran along the enemy's side slicing off the ship's oarbanks and rendering them helpless, but this was difficult to achieve without damage to the attacker's own oars. Manoeuvres such as the *periplus*, which involved outflanking the enemy line, and the *diekplus*, which involved penetrating the enemy line to deliver rams from astern, cannot now be reconstructed precisely, but it is probable that they were tactics for squadrons rather than individual ships.[9]

The alternative to ramming was boarding, grappling the enemy vessel and overrunning it with a swarm of attackers. Success in the resultant hand-to-hand combat depended on the numbers, enthusiasm and fighting skill of the boarders compared to those of the defending marines and deck crew. As a result this method favoured the largest ships, which were able to carry more marines and also had a height advantage. Boarding placed far less demand upon the seamanship of a ship's crew whose main task was simply to bring their vessel into contact with an enemy ship and grapple it securely. Ramming required a far more highly skilled crew to perform successfully, since it relied upon speed and manoeuvrability. In the fifth century the Athenian navy had been brilliant exponents of ramming tactics, making use of their light, un-decked or *aphract* triremes, crewed by highly skilled rowers drawn from their poorest citizens. Few states other than the radical democracy of classical Athens were willing to pay huge numbers of rowers the regular wage needed to keep them in constant training. The Hellenistic kingdoms which emerged after Alexander were in general shorter of available manpower to provide crews than they were of the funds to construct fleets of increasingly large ships. The new emphasis on larger and larger warships diminished the importance of the ram, since such vessels were slower and less manoeuvrable and their main advantage was that they could carry greater numbers of marines. In addition to this, the hulls of the bigger ships were more strongly constructed and so perhaps less vulnerable to enemy rams, although a ram delivered by another large and heavy ship was likely to cause great damage. By the third century the ram had become in effect a secondary weapon, although the well-trained Carthaginian navy were still to prove highly skilled in its use.

The crew of a quinquereme, like other galleys in the ancient world, was exceptionally large in proportion to its size, especially in comparison to the sailing ships of more recent history. The rowers who formed the majority of the crew were confined for most of a journey to their benches, since their bodily weight made up a significant part of the ship's ballast, making it undesirable for them to be allowed to move about. Galleys had very little space for the storage of food and, most important of all for rowers labouring in the heat of the Mediterranean summer, fresh water. This imposed a severe limitation on their strategic range, making journeys of more than a few days impossible for a properly crewed fleet. Ideally, ships would be drawn up on land at the end of each day to allow the rowers to rest, but beached squadrons were intensely vulnerable to attack by land or sea and this practice was unwise unless the landing could be protected by land forces. Fleets were therefore very dependent on secure bases where they could be re-supplied. Sicily and its offshore islands, and to a lesser extent Sardinia and Corsica, were ideally placed between North Africa and Italy to provide suitable staging points for each side's navies. The range of fleets was subject to further significant reduction if a major encounter with the enemy navy was anticipated, especially for fleets who relied primarily on boarding tactics. When a battle was expected it was normal to increase the number of marines carried on each ship, perhaps doubling or trebling the complement. This resulted in a much more rapid consumption of whatever supplies of food and water were carried. Even more importantly, it represented a great increase in the weight carried by a ship, drastically reducing both its speed and handling capability, problems only exacerbated if the marines were not evenly distributed and kept stationary as far as possible. Therefore, it was normal practice only to take on board the majority of marines immediately before a battle. This was not always possible and on several occasions fleets were placed at a severe disadvantage because they had failed to make contact with friendly land forces and draw marines from their ranks.

The Early Rounds

The Romans' decision to include twenty triremes in their fleet of quinqueremes has been plausibly interpreted as a revival of the old duumviral squadrons, perhaps a sign of the Romans' innate conservatism. Triremes were no longer large enough to play a significant part in a massed battle, but any fleet needed a number of faster vessels to support its heavier warships. Polybius is inclined to imply that later fleets consisted entirely of 'fives' and they were clearly the majority type, but he does mention the presence of smaller 'fours' and 'threes' as well as occasional larger vessels, and it is clear that he uses 'five' as a shorthand for 'warship'. Polybius tells us that the model for the Roman quinqueremes was a Punic 'five' which had been captured after running aground near Rhegium in an attempt to prevent the crossing of Claudius' forces. It is unclear where the construction work was undertaken. Presumably the skills of the shipwrights from the naval allies was drawn upon, but it is distinctly likely that the work was undertaken at a central point under the direct supervision of Roman magistrates, perhaps at Ostia. Many of the skills involved were those of carpentry and woodworking used in many other day-to-day activities with which Roman craftsmen would have been familiar. Although inexperience may have lowered the quality of the first ships produced, the production of so many vessels makes it highly likely that the standard of workmanship steadily improved. Whilst the ships were being built crews of rowers began their training on benches erected to represent their positions in a ship. Pliny tells us that the ships were completed in only sixty days.[10]

The story is a typical instance of the Romans' pride in their ability to copy the technology and tactics of their enemies and eventually surpass them, but there is no good reason to disbelieve it, nor to doubt Polybius' explicit statement that quinqueremes had not been manufactured in Italy before this time (Polybius 1. 20. 10). Syracuse had constructed large ships in the past, but if Morrison and Coates are right then the Carthaginian 'five' may anyway have been of a different design to Greek patterns and perhaps believed to be superior. The speed of the construction has recently been given added credibility by the analysis of the Marsala wreck. This small Punic warship revealed traces of many markings on its timbers clearly indicating the stages of construction. For instance the outlines of tenons had been painted onto the planks showing the workmen where to cut. The Punic alphabet, used as numerals, had been painted along the keel at intervals which corresponded to the positions of the ribs. Unlike more modern techniques, the shell of the hull was made before the skeleton of ribs was put into it. Since this meant that the men working inside the hull to fit the timbers of the floor would therefore have been unable to see this series of marks on the keel, the same sequence had been repeated on one of the strakes inside the hull. Another word of instruction had been painted upside down, since this was the direction from which a workman would have looked at it during construction. Interestingly, the shipwrights had not followed the more modern practice of trying to employ suitably shaped pieces of wood to make each component, but had been quite happy to join several bits of timber to form the requisite shape. Such joints could be stronger than the natural wood. The use of a pre-marked template conforming to a standard design must have greatly speeded construction. For a long time it was believed that such techniques of mass production had been unknown before the Industrial Revolution.[11]

Before describing the first operations of the newly created Roman fleet, we must consider who provided its crews, in particular the over 30,000 rowers required. Clearly some were drawn from the *socii navales*, who probably also provided a good number of the skilled captains and deck crew, but it is doubtful that these cities could have provided such a large number of rowers and certain that they could not have mustered the bulk of the huge crews required for the Roman fleets later in the war. Some of the other Italian peoples seem to have provided some men, notably the Samnites who are mentioned in this respect purely because they attempted a mutiny in 259. There is no reason to suppose that it was only the Samnites who supplied sailors. However, despite the dismissive comments of some historians regarding the seafaring aptitude of the Roman people, it is distinctly probable that a good proportion of the crews were from the class of citizens known as *proletarii*, the very poor who lacked the qualification for service in the legions, as well as freedmen from the urban population. This seems to be confirmed by the, admittedly problematic, census figures recorded by Livy, as well as the colourful anecdote told of the sister of Claudius Pulcher which we shall encounter later in our narrative.[12]

As the ships of the completed Roman fleet put to sea, their crews spent a short time training before moving along the Italian coast to the Straits. Of the two consuls in 260, the patrician Cnaeus Cornelius Scipio was appointed to command the fleet, whilst his colleague, the *novus homo* Caius Duilius, was given command of the land forces in Sicily. Scipio went on ahead with the first seventeen ships to be ready and crossed to Messana, to prepare the logistical support for the fleet's arrival. Whilst there, he received the offer to betray Lipara to the Romans already mentioned in the last chapter. Lipara was the most important port in the small group of islands lying off the north-eastern tip of Sicily, ideally placed to threaten the direct route to Italy. Denying the Carthaginians this base was clearly highly desirable and Scipio readily seized this opportunity for an early success. Taking his seventeen ships he travelled the short distance to Lipara and occupied the harbour. Whether or not this was a deliberate trap, the Carthaginian response was swift. The Punic fleet was currently at Panormus, a short distance away on the northern coast of Sicily, under the command of Hannibal, the man who had led the defence of Agrigentum. As soon as he was aware of Scipio's movements, Hannibal sent twenty of his own ships to the city. Led by Boödes, a Carthaginian nobleman, this squadron arrived at night and boxed the Romans into the harbour. The Roman ships failed to put up any serious resistance; some of the inexperienced crews panicked and fled inland. One tradition maintained that Scipio and his officers were treacherously seized whilst negotiating with Boödes, although this may simply be a stock tale of Punic perfidy. Scipio was later to acquire the nickname Asina or 'donkey' as a result of this disaster, the feminine form perhaps intended to add to the insult; but it did not have too great an effect on his career, for he achieved the consulship for the second time in 254. Presumably he had been released from captivity either by ransom or exchange at some stage before this.[13]

Soon after this success, the Carthaginians themselves suffered a similar small-scale setback when Hannibal himself stumbled upon the main Roman fleet, whilst he was carrying out a reconnaissance or perhaps mounting a raid on Italy. Rounding a place Polybius calls the Cape of Italy, Hannibal lost the majority of his fifty ships before making his escape. This encounter highlighted the difficulty ancient fleets encountered in trying to keep track of each other's movements and there is no reason to accept suggestions that Polybius has created a garbled account of a mythical action through misunderstanding Philinus' account of the later battle of Mylae. Despite these initial setbacks, both sides remained eager for a major confrontation with the enemy fleet and the Romans were already preparing for this at Messana when Caius Duilius arrived to take charge.[14]

The Romans realized that their ships were neither as fast nor as manoeuvrable as their Punic counterparts. The Romans had copied the method of construction, but as yet could not duplicate the skill of Carthaginian shipwrights, and even more importantly the Roman crews were far more poorly trained. It was clear that they could anticipate little success if they relied on ramming to defeat the enemy and that therefore they must depend on getting close and boarding. To this end someone put forward the idea of a new type of boarding bridge, known to modern historians by the Latin word *corvus* (raven), although no ancient author employs the term and Polybius uses the equivalent Greek word *corax*. The name of its inventor has not been recorded, so that some have suggested that the man was a Sicilian Greek, a foreigner with whom the Romans had no wish to share the glory of their subsequent success, or even that the inventor may have been the young Archimedes, but these can never be more than conjectures.

Later sources viewed the *corvus* as some sort of grapnel, which encouraged some historians to doubt Polybius' description, but the reliability of his account was finally confirmed when Wallinga constructed a viable working model of the engine. The *corvus* was a boarding bridge 4 feet (1.2 m) wide and 36 feet (10.9 m) long with a knee-high parapet on either side. The last third of its length formed two prongs separated by a long groove which slotted around a 24 foot (7.3 m) high pole erected on the deck of a ship. Pulleys allowed the bridge to be raised at an angle against the pole. Underneath the raised end of the bridge was a heavy, pointed spike resembling a bird's beak, from which the device probably derived its name. When released, the *corvus* fell onto the deck of an enemy ship, the spike embedding itself into its planking. The groove allowed the bridge to be swung around in a wide arc to fall ahead or to either side of the ship's bow, depending on the direction of the approaching enemy. Once the bridge was securely fixed in the other vessel, the Roman marines could swarm across and overwhelm the enemy crew with their skill as swordsmen, their ferocity and their numbers. It was a simple, practical device allowing the Romans to extend their advantages in land fighting to naval battles, and was to enjoy spectacular success during its brief career.[15]

Soon after his arrival with the fleet, Duilius received a report that the Carthaginian fleet had been raiding the area around Mylae, a city situated on a peninsula on the northern coast of Sicily, not far from the Lipari Islands. The entire Roman fleet put to sea and moved around the coast towards Mylae, and as soon as this was reported to Hannibal he prepared his fleet to meet them. Polybius tells us that the Carthaginians mustered 130 ships, which seems more likely than Diodorus' figure of 200. Hannibal himself led the action from a *hepteres* or 'seven' which had been captured from Pyrrhus in 276. The Romans presumably had what was left of their original 120, minus the seventeen lost with Scipio, plus however many Punic ships captured in the earlier engagement they had been able to salvage and man, as well as any vessels provided by the naval allies. The bulk of ships on both sides were presumably quinqueremes and it is improbable that either fleet was markedly bigger than the other.[16]

Polybius tells us that the Carthaginians were confused by the strange appearance of the tall *corvus* near the prow of each Roman ship, but remained supremely confident of their own superiority over their inexperienced enemy. It was difficult for the commander of an ancient fleet to exercise much control over his squadrons during a battle, but Hannibal seems to have allowed his fleet to get out of hand almost immediately. The Punic ships surged towards the enemy, the great 'seven' in the van. Some of the Romans ships were rammed, but each dropped its *corvus*, whose beak speared through the deck of the enemy vessel and held them fast. Thirty Punic warships, all those who had first engaged, were grappled and held fast. Amongst them was Hannibal's flagship, attacked by a trireme according to Zonaras, although he tends to use the word as a generic term for a warship and it is more likely that the Roman ship was in fact a 'five', since the difference in height between a seven and three must have been considerable. In each case the Roman marines poured across their boarding bridges and swiftly defeated the enemy crews. Hannibal abandoned his flagship and escaped in a small rowing boat. The remainder of the Carthaginian fleet then took advantage of the superior speed of their vessels and swung around, outflanking the Roman line and attacked from astern, hoping in this way to avoid the *corvi*. Somehow the Romans were able to manoeuvre to meet this onslaught, and once again any Punic ship which came within range was pinned and held by the 'ravens'. Polybius describes how the boarding bridges 'swung around and plunged down in all directions', but it is not quite clear what he means by this (1. 23. 9–10). A *corvus* mounted near the prow of a ship would have been able to be dropped ahead and for a short distance to port or starboard, but clearly could not have reached nearer the stern. Evidently a Roman ship seeing an enemy vessel approaching would have tried to turn to bring the enemy within this arc. Thiel suggested that the Roman ships may have been formed into two lines and that it was the second line which turned to face the second Punic attack, but, whilst this suggestion is plausible enough, our sources are too brief to confirm or deny it. He may well have assumed that it was more difficult to turn a quinquereme than was in fact the case, even one rowed by an inexperienced crew and overloaded with a *corvus* and, probably, marines.[17]

The ease with which the Carthaginians were able to disengage and retreat again confirmed the superior speed of their ships, but they had failed to achieve anything positive through this advantage. It was a spectacular success for the fledgling Roman fleet, owed almost exclusively to the ingenuity of whoever had designed the *corvus*. According to Polybius fifty Punic ships were lost, although our later sources give thirty-thirty-one captured and thirteen-fourteen sunk, figures which may derive from the inscription erected by Duilius himself in commemoration of his victory, the *columna rostrata*, although this has survived in fragmentary form so that only the first X of a numeral can be read. The tone of the surviving text is typical of the Roman aristocracy's self-promotion, with its emphasis on having been the first Roman ever to defeat a Punic navy, and claiming that in his land operations Duilius defeated all the greatest of the Carthaginian forces. The extant texts mentions triremes and has been reconstructed as also mentioning quinqueremes, which may offer additional confirmation for our suspicion that the fleets of this conflict were not exclusively composed of 'fives'.[18]

The new man celebrated Rome's first naval triumph, decorating the speaker's platform in the Forum with prows (or *rostrata*) cut off captured ships, from which it later derived its name. When Duilius went out to dine at Rome he was accompanied to and from his host's by a procession of musicians. However, in spite of these great honours, his subsequent political career was not especially distinguished.[19]

The Carthaginians were chastened by this defeat and although Hannibal avoided punishment for his incompetence on this occaision, he was executed by his own officers not long afterwards for allowing his ships to be blockaded in a Sardinian port by the Romans. Sardinia offered a good base for raids against Italy and its conquest rapidly became a Roman objective. Otherwise in the next years the Roman fleet mainly acted in support of the army in Sicily and it was not until 257 that another major clash occurred at sea. Like many naval battles in this period it was brought on by a chance encounter. Caius Atilius Regulus (brother of Marcus), one of the consuls in 258–257, was with the Roman fleet off Tyndaris, a short distance to the west of Mylae, when the Carthaginian fleet was observed sailing past. It is probable that neither side had been aware of the other's presence until they came into view, and certainly neither fleet was formed and prepared for battle. Nevertheless Regulus decided to attack and headed straight towards the enemy with the first ten ships ready to move, the remainder of the fleet trailing far behind. The Carthaginians reacted quickly and turned on the small squadron led by the consul with overwhelming force. Nine ships were rammed and sunk, only the consul escaping in his fast and well-manned ship. However, as the main body of the Roman fleet managed to get itself into formation and finally reached the enemy the odds began to swing back in their favour. Ten Punic ships were captured and eight sunk, although it is unclear whether this included any of the Roman vessels taken earlier in the fight. Unwilling to bring on a full-scale action, the Punic fleet withdrew to the nearby Lipari Islands. It is probable that the Roman fleet was in the area in the first place to raid the well-placed Punic base there.[20]

Ecnomus

The Roman fleet had steadily improved in efficiency and training, although judging from the ease with which the Carthaginian ships disengaged at Tyndaris their ships were probably still slower and less manoeuvrable than

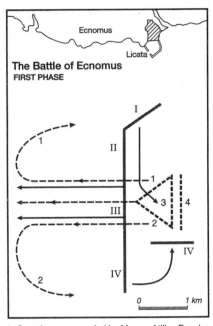

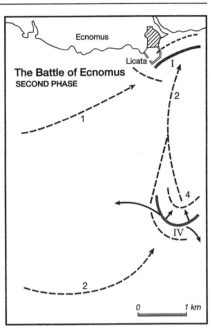

1 Squadron commanded by Marcus Atilius Regulus
2 Squadron commanded by Lucius Manlius Vulso
3 Squadron towing transports
4 The 'triarii' or reserve squadron

I   Punic left squadron
II &III Main body of Punic Fleet with Hamilcar
IV   Hanno's squadron
1,2,3,4. Roman Fleet I,II,III, IV. Carthaginian fleet

the enemy's. A measure of equality in strength had developed between the two fleets and both sides threw massive resources into ship construction in an effort to gain a decisive advantage. In 256 the Romans made their bold, but characteristic, decision to escalate the conflict by mounting an invasion of North Africa. To this end they amassed an enormous fleet of 330 vessels which moved along the Italian coast and crossed to Messana, before sailing south along the Sicilian shore past Syracuse, round Cape Pachynus where they linked up with the main army in Sicily. The pick of the Roman infantry were taken on board to serve as marines and provide an invasion force, so that each quinquereme now had a complement of 120 marines. Polybius claimed that the combined total of the crews and marines in the Roman fleet was about 140,000. The Carthaginians had managed to put together a grand total of 350 ships which sailed from Africa to Lilybaeum, before moving round to Heraclea Minoa. Polybius gives their strength in men as more than 150,000, presumably calculated on the assumption that their crews were roughly the same size as those of the Romans.[21]

Many eminent scholars have refused to accept the numbers Polybius gives for the fleets in this and other battles of the war. In particular Tarn and Thiel tried to analyse the narratives of the war and establish the real size of the navies involved. In the case of Ecnomus, they have tended to reduce the total of each side by about 100 ships. It may be that the numbers preserved in our sources are not always accurate, and, as has been pointed out, there has always been an understandable tendency for victors to inflate the size of the defeated enemy forces to add to the glory of their achievements. Yet acknowledging that this may be so does not provide any guidance as to what the actual figures may have been. Analysis of fleet numbers has tended to be very rigid in its methods, assuming that only when specifically mentioned by our sources were ships constructed, manned, lost or captured, when it is very unlikely given the brevity of the accounts of this twenty-three-year war that we can expect such a full coverage of these small details. Ultimately, we cannot know whether or not Polybius' figures are accurate, but do best to assume that they are broadly so. In the narrative of the action he mentions that the Roman flagships were two 'sixes', and we may assume as mentioned earlier that the Roman fleet was not exclusively composed of 'fives' even if these were the majority type. Some of the Roman ships may have been smaller and thus the overall total for Roman crews slightly reduced. It is also not at all clear that the Carthaginian ships carried as many marines as the Roman 'fives', and certainly they did not do well in the boarding actions brought on by the Roman use of the *corvus*.[22]

The Romans put to sea ready either to fight a fleet action or to continue the journey to the African coast and stage a landing, since they could not yet know the likely Carthaginian reaction to their move. Amongst the fleet were a number of horse transports, although precisely how many is unknown. They were later to land horses for the 500 cavalry left with Regulus, presumably as well as the mounts required by the senior officers. The transports did not travel under their own power, but were towed behind war galleys, allowing them to keep station with the rest of the fleet. In fact, the Punic commanders had already resolved to fight a fleet action off the coast of Sicily, judging this to be the best way of protecting Carthage itself. In addition, if their fleet was as strong as Polybius suggests, then it may well have been the largest naval force ever assembled by the city and this, with their continued belief in their superior skill to the enemy, may well have encouraged the belief that that they had the opportunity to win a major success over the Romans. The two fleets moved towards each other, within sight of the coast of Sicily.

Such was the importance of this venture that both of the year's consuls, Lucius Manlius Vulso and Marcus Atilius Regulus, were present. They had divided the fleet into four divisions, numbered one to four and known either as 'squadrons' or 'Legions'. This was simply a nickname and bore no relation to their actual size, and it seems that the four divisions were not equal in numbers. The first two groups were led by the consuls themselves, whose two 'sixes' headed the Roman formation. The other ships from these squadrons took station from the flagships, in line echeloned back to either side, so that each ship's prow lay behind and to the side of the ship in front. In effect these squadrons formed the apex of a triangle, the base being composed of the third squadron, arrayed in line abreast, each ship towing one of the horse transports. The fourth squadron was arrayed in line behind this group and was probably more numerous than the third, for its ships overlapped its line on either flank. Protecting the rear of the formation and acting as an ultimate reserve, this squadron was also nick-named the *triarii*. The Roman formation was praised by Polybius for its practicality, being relatively dense and keeping the fleet together, but also permitting it to turn and face a threat from any direction. It was a sign of the improved quality of the Roman crews and the greater experience of their commanders that they were able to adopt such a plan, and there is no good reason to doubt Polybius' account or assume that he had misunder-stood what was no more than an accidental formation.[23]

The Carthaginians made some changes to their deployment once the Roman fleet came into view, having apparently advanced in the normal battle formation of line abreast. The Carthaginian line was formed with the coast of Sicily to its left. The left wing, one quarter of the fleet's ships, reached forward towards the shore. Angled away from this was the remain-der of the fleet; the extreme right wing, commanded by Hanno (the general who had failed to relieve Agrigentum in 261), was made up of the fastest ships and extended beyond the flank of the Roman formation. The centre was led by the overall commander in Sicily, Hamilcar, who had instructed the captains of his division to begin by withdrawing in the face of a Roman attack. Hamilcar's plan appears to have been to break up the compact Roman formation, so that his divisions on the right and left could sweep in and attack the enemy from the flank or rear. This would produce a series of smaller encounters between parts of each fleet in which the Carthaginians might hopefully exploit their skill in ramming tactics and avoid frontal attacks on the *corvus*-equipped Roman ships. Attempts to suggest a far more complex Carthaginian plan are not convincing.[24]

At first the battle seemed to be developing as Hamilcar had hoped. The Roman consuls had judged that the centre of the Punic line was weak – Polybius describes it as 'thinner' which may suggest that there were wider intervals between the ships than elsewhere. The flagships led the charge of the first and second divisions straight at this apparently vulnerable spot, and Hamilcar's ships withdrew in haste, so that a large gap swiftly developed between the consuls' ships and the third squadron, still towing the transports. Deciding that the Romans had been lured far enough forward to isolate the rear of their fleet, Hamilcar gave a signal to his ships to turn and engage. A fierce fight developed as the Romans surged forward and tried to grapple the enemy vessels, inspired by the presence of both consuls who played an active role in the fighting. The Carthaginian ships' greater speed produced some successes and some may even have passed through the Roman line and turned to deliver rams from the stern.[25]

In the meantime, Hanno's right wing had enveloped the Roman fleet and mounted a fierce attack on the *triarii*, whilst the left wing had changed its alignment to face the Romans and closed with the third squadron. The horse transports were cast adrift and the Roman galleys surged forward to meet the enemy. Thus, as Polybius comments, in effect the battle developed into three separate and widely spaced actions. Although this was probably the situation that the Carthaginians had hoped to achieve, in the event they failed to gain a lasting advantage from it. The Roman sailors were no longer as poorly trained as they had been in 260. More importantly, the great expansion in the Carthaginian fleet can only have reduced the average quality of its crews, so that their superiority over the enemy was no longer as marked. The sheer number of ships involved in each action added to the confusion and made it far harder for Punic ships to attack and ram a victim and then escape without encountering another Roman ship. Finally, as Lazenby rightly emphasizes, the Carthaginians had failed to discover an effective remedy to the *corvus*. An army or navy with a long tradition of success may well have difficulty in adapting to a novel tactic employed by an enemy, as seen for instance in the radically varying attitude to aircraft carriers of the navies in the Second World War.[26]

The clash between the Carthaginian centre and the first two Roman squadrons was decided first, when Hamilcar's ships gave up the struggle and fled. Despite initial successes, several Punic vessels had been caught by the ravens' beaks and boarded. As the Carthaginians fled, Manlius Vulso supervised the securing of the captured prizes, whilst Regulus led as many ships as he could back to the aid of the rest of the Roman fleet. The *triarii* had been given a hard time by Hanno's squadron until the Roman ships came up behind him; together the Roman forces drove the Carthaginians off. The Punic left had driven the Roman third squadron up against the shore, but when the Roman ships had bunched up and formed a line with their prows facing towards the enemy, the Carthaginians had been reluctant to close for fear of the *corvi*. Their ships had done little more than hem the Romans in and were finally driven off when Manlius Vulso came to their aid from one direction and Regulus from the other. Fifty Carthaginian ships were captured in this final phase of the action, for it was difficult to escape, trapped as they were between the shore and the Roman third squadron and the converging forces led by the consuls. Another fourteen Punic ships were captured, probably mainly in the centre, and thirty were sunk. Roman losses were twenty-four sunk and none taken.[27]

The largest clash of the war, and possibly the biggest naval battle in history, had ended in a clear Roman victory. Once again the *corvus* had proved its worth, most markedly when the beleaguered third squadron had still been able to hold the enemy at bay despite its bad position. The achievement of the Roman consuls also deserves mention. It was difficult at the best of times to control a fleet in this period, with only the simplest signals and plans standing much chance of success. The speed with which, following the defeat of Hamilcar, Regulus and then Manlius Vulso gathered enough ships to make a difference and led them to the aid of the rest of the Roman fleet was truly remarkable. It was in these last phases of the action that the most damage was inflicted on the Carthaginian squadrons. Carthage's greatest ever fleet had not performed well and its commanders had failed to have much influence on the fighting after the initial clash. The Carthaginians did not take advantage of their success in dividing the Roman fleet up. There is no evidence for their successfully boarding and taking a Roman ship, which may suggest that they carried significantly fewer marines. The sheer size of the fleets may have made them clumsy and been better suited to the simpler boarding tactics favoured by the Romans.

At the end of the battle the three divisions of the Punic fleet had retreated in different directions and were in no position to renew the fight. The Romans returned to Sicily to rest their men, repair their ships and salvage as many of the captured warships as possible. This action has caused needless surprise amongst some scholars and led them to doubt that the fleet had intended to cross to Africa in the first place, which would then render the presence of the horse transports somewhat curious. Yet it is important to remember that the battle had been fought close to Sicily and the bulk of the journey still lay before them. The exertion required of crews during a battle was far greater than that of normal travel and it was sensible to allow the rowers to rest and to renew each ship's supply of water before continuing the voyage. Probably the majority of Roman marines were transferred to transport ships to ease the burden on the warships. In addition some of the Roman ships may well have been badly damaged in the fighting and the fleet had certainly become scattered and needed to be reorganized. The Carthaginian fleet still retained a large number of serviceable ships and crews, but its morale must have been very low after its decisive defeat. There was no reason to expect it to risk a second encounter soon after Ecnomus, but in fact this proved to be the case when the Roman fleet sailed to Africa shortly afterwards.[28]

Sieges and Storms

The African campaign and Regulus' ultimate defeat have already been described. As soon as the outcome of this was reported to the Romans they mustered a large fleet to rescue the survivors from Aspis. The expedition was led by the consuls for 255, Servius Fulvius Paetinus Nobilior and Marcus Aemilius Paullus, who led 350 ships. The Carthaginians were only able to provide crews for 200 vessels to oppose them and were defeated off Cape Hermaeum north of Aspis, a success which may have been aided by a fortuitous attack by the forty ships from the besieged Roman garrison of that city. However, both numbers and morale may anyway have made a Roman success likely. Polybius claims that 114 of the Punic ships were taken along with their crews. The survivors at Aspis were then taken on board and the Roman fleet returned to Sicilian waters. Polybius tells us that the consuls wished to take advantage of their recent victory and the great size of their fleet by cruising along the Carthaginian held south-western coast of Sicily, hoping to overawe the cities there and persuade some to defect. This was against the advice of the experienced ships' captains, who knew that this shore was hostile and possessed few safe harbours, and that there was a strong risk of bad weather at this time of year, between the rising of Orion and that of Sirius (roughly mid July). Off Camarina the fleet was caught in a violent storm and many ships floundered or were driven against the shore and wrecked with huge loss of life.[29]

Polybius says that only eighty ships survived out of the 364 in the Roman fleet, although other sources provide a wide range of alternative figures. Again the numbers have been doubted. If the Romans had begun the expedition with 350 ships and captured 114 at Hermaeum then they should have had at least 464, apart from the surviving ships from the squadron originally left to support Regulus in Africa. Many ingenious, and often plausible, solutions have been proposed for this problem, but once again we are forced to admit that we cannot establish a precise figure. Clearly it was a major Roman disaster with more men and ships being lost than had previously fallen to enemy action. An attractive suggestion is that the fitting of the *corvus* to the Roman ships made them dangerously unseaworthy in bad conditions and contributed to the catastrophe. The sensitivity of the reconstructed trireme to shifts in weight caused even by movements amongst the crew would tend to support this view. The *corvus* was mounted near the bow of the ship and its weight may well have made the galley bow-heavy, which would clearly be a major problem in a rough sea. If the Romans had captured so many ships at Hermaeum then this would suggest that the *corvus* was still in use, and indeed there seems no reason for the abandonment of such a successful device, although it is not mentioned in our sources after Ecnomus. It is in this section that Polybius famously comments on the Roman reliance on brute force (*bia*) in all their activities, throwing massive resources into a project and expecting success through effort alone. This attitude, he says, has usually been a source of frequent victories on land, but at sea, when opposed by the power of nature, it has produced some spectacular failures. The narrative of the Punic Wars on the whole supports this judgement on the Roman character. Nevertheless, although the consuls may have been blamed for this disaster, it does not seem to have outweighed the credit they had gained by their earlier victory, for both men survived and went on to celebrate a naval triumph.[30]

An indication of the Romans' capacity for massive effort came in their swift rebuilding of their naval power. In 254, 220 ships were built and floated in three months, a remarkable but not unprecedented building programme. Sailing to Messana and gathering the eighty ships which had survived the storm (which may imply that this figure included only those ships which were still felt to be seaworthy), the fleet attacked Panormus. The two consuls for 254, Cnaeus Cornelius Scipio, the man who had been captured at Lipara in 260, and Aulus Atilius Caiatinus, who had been consul in 258, besieged the city by land and sea. The election of two experienced former consuls, even if Scipio's reputation may not have been entirely creditable, may suggest a Roman feeling about the seriousness of the situation after the disasters in 255. Panormus' defences were breached nearest the sea and the city was successfully stormed.[31]

In late 253 the bulk of the Roman fleet crossed to Africa and made extensive raids along the coast, collecting a large amount of booty, but achieving little. Near the island of Menix (modern Djerba) much of the Roman fleet became grounded on a shoal when caught by the unexpectedly low local tide. At high tide they managed to float the ships, but only after ditching all of their heavier and non-essential equipment. Sailing round the western tip of Sicily to the recently captured Panormus, they then attempted to return directly to Italy, but were caught in another storm, probably near Cape Palinurus in Italy, and lost 150 ships . However, once again the consul in command survived to celebrate a triumph for the dubious successes of his African expedition.[32]

This string of heavy losses seems to have reduced the aggressiveness of the Roman commanders in the next years, and in particular deterred them from major efforts at sea. However, in 252 they did capture Lipara, denying the Carthaginians the control of these well-placed islands. In 251 the consuls chose to man a mere sixty ships, simply to protect the supply routes to Italy. A greater effort was made in the next year when fifty new ships were constructed. The victory at Panormus in 250 encouraged a major effort against the Carthaginian stronghold at Lilybaeum, a fleet of 200 ships supporting the combined armies of both consuls. The navy's primary role was to seal off the city's harbour and prevent any reinforcements or supply reaching the active garrison. The approaches to the harbour were difficult, only a narrow passage running between the shoals, and this may have encouraged some complacency amongst the Roman fleet. Early in the siege fifty warships had been specially prepared at Carthage to carry supplies and a force of 10,000 mercenaries to the city. Commanded by Hannibal, the son of Hamilcar, this squadron travelled to the Aegates Islands west of Sicily and from there waited for a favourable wind. With a strong wind behind their stern, the Punic ships sailed straight into the harbour of Lilybaeum in broad daylight, surprising the Romans, who failed to make any move to stop them, in part because of a reluctance to risk being blown into the harbour. Hannibal's arrival gave a major boost to the garrison's morale as well as adding to its strength. However, he took care to leave the city at night, carrying out the useless cavalry from the fortress, and sailed undetected by the Romans to Drepana further up the coast.[33]

No more attempts at re-supply were carried out on such a large scale, since without the benefit of surprise the chances of success were slight, but Carthage was eager to keep in communication with Himilco, the commander at Lilybaeum. Another Hannibal, called 'the Rhodian' – perhaps a name intended to celebrate his skill as a sailor, for the Rhodians were famously skilled seamen – volunteered to take his ship into the city and report on the status of the defenders. Hannibal's crew was clearly highly trained and experienced and he took great care in preparing for the voyage, before adopting a similar plan to the other Hannibal, sailing to the Aegates Islands and there awaiting a favourable breeze. Then, when conditions were right, he used his knowledge of the waters to sail straight into Lilybaeum's harbour in mid morning, in open sight of the Roman fleet. Eager to avenge this humiliation, the Romans stationed ten fast ships to catch him on the way out. Hannibal declined to make the attempt under cover of darkness, and rowed out on the next day. Again his intimate knowledge of the shoals and the superb training of his crew allowed the Carthaginian ship to avoid its pursuers and escape. Disdainfully, Hannibal halted in sight of the Romans and waited without setting sail, challenging any Roman ship to fight. The enemy were so impressed by the speed and manoeuvrability of his ship that they declined the offer. Hannibal was to repeat this exploit on several later occasions and his success encouraged a number of other Carthaginian captains to run the blockade, so that the garrison remained in full communication with Carthage and was kept well supplied.[34]

Failing to intercept the blockade runners, the Romans attempted to block the passage leading to the harbour by dumping boulders and spoil into the sea. Most of this material was swept away by the current, but in one place enough of an obstacle was created to cause a Punic 'four' to run aground whilst attempting a night-time escape from the port. The Romans discovered this to be an exceptionally well-made and speedy ship, so they gave it a picked crew and crammed it full of boarders, and then set it to patrol in an effort to catch their swift opponents. By chance, Hannibal the Rhodian once again sailed openly into the harbour that night and left just as confidently. The captured quadrireme gave chase and managed to overhaul him. Unable to escape, the Punic vessel turned to fight, but was grappled by the Romans and then swiftly overrun by the flood of marines. Hannibal's ship was then also equipped with a chosen crew and a strong force of marines and set to patrol the approach to the harbour. In this way, the Roman fleet was finally able to seal off Lilybaeum from the sea. This episode was the main occasion where the superiority of Carthaginian seamanship was demonstrated. Yet throughout the war it proved exceptionally difficult for them to turn this skill to any tangible advantage in battle, although, unlike the Romans, they avoided any serious losses to the elements. It is notable that the differences in skill were most marked in actions involving only a small number of ships. The massed naval battles offered slight opportunity for subtlety, perhaps the most important factor explaining the Romans' early successes.[35]

Apart from blockading the city by sea, the Roman fleet played an active part in the progress of the siegeworks on land, since the job of rowing a warship produced large numbers of strong men who were an ideal labour force. As a result of this role, heavy casualties were suffered by the fleet during this siege, probably more from disease spread in the crowded camps than from enemy action. Therefore the Senate collected a draft of 10,000 rowers and dispatched them to Sicily, where they marched overland to

Lilybaeum. Guessing that the Carthaginians would be unaware of this accession of strength and so doubt the readiness of the Roman fleet, one of the consuls for 249, Publius Claudius Pulcher, decided to mount a surprise attack on the main base of the Punic fleet at nearby Drepana. It was a bold action but, as we have seen, a surprise attack if successful was probably the easiest, quickest and least costly means of taking a stronghold. The capture of this supporting base would certainly have added to the pressure on the defenders of Lilybaeum. The prospects seemed good, and there were plenty of volunteers from the army to serve as marines, everyone anticipating a good haul of booty.

Claudius went down in Roman history as a reckless incompetent, famously falling into a rage when favourable omens for the attack were not forthcoming. When the sacred chickens refused to eat and so signify that the gods favoured the enterprise, Claudius picked them up and hurled them into the sea, proclaiming that if they would not eat, then let them drink. However, despite his reputation for Claudian arrogance, his initial preparations were careful enough. He put to sea at night to avoid being spotted and news of his departure being carried by land to Drepana, and sailed along the coast. However, in the darkness it was difficult for the Roman ships to remain in close formation, especially since they were

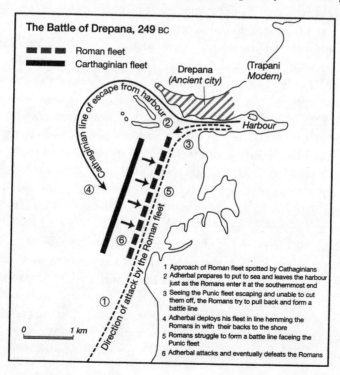

The Battle of Drepana, 249 BC

Roman fleet
Carthaginian fleet

Drepana (Ancient city)
(Trapani Modern)

Carthaginian line of escape from harbour

Harbour

Direction of attack by the Roman fleet

0   1 km

1 Approach of Roman fleet spotted by Cathaginians
2 Adherbal prepares to put to sea and leaves the harbour just as the Romans enter it at the southernmost end
3 Seeing the Punic fleet escaping and unable to cut them off, the Romans try to pull back and form a battle line
4 Adherbal deploys his fleet in line hemming the Romans in with their backs to the shore
5 Romans struggle to form a battle line faceing the Punic fleet
6 Adherbal attacks and eventually defeats the Romans

crewed by a mixture of the experienced rowers and the new, unabsorbed draft. The route was simple to follow, since it hugged the coast, but throughout the night the Roman fleet straggled and by morning it was in a long, scattered line as it approached the enemy base. Claudius' flagship was somewhere near the rear. The Romans were spotted and word brought to Adherbal, the Punic admiral, who then took the bold decision to put to sea and confront the enemy, rather than permit himself to be blockaded in the harbour. He gathered his crews and collected large numbers of merce-naries to act as marines. It now became a matter of time as to whether or not the Carthaginian fleet could escape from the harbour and gain sea room before the Roman ships were able to block the entrance.[36]

The disordered and scattered formation of the Roman fleet and the poorer quality of their crews proved decisive, but only by the narrowest of margins. The entrance to the harbour at Drepana was wide and as the first Roman ships were entering at its southernmost edge, Adherbal's flagship was rowing out past the long spit of land which formed its northern edge. He had signalled the rest of the fleet to follow him, so the Carthaginian ships proceeded in line astern, rounded the two small islands opposite the harbour mouth and ran southwards parallel to the coast, but further out to sea than the Roman fleet. Claudius saw that he had just missed his chance and sought by signal to bring some sort of order to his fleet which was spread over a wide area. Dreadful confusion resulted as the ships which had entered the harbour tried to turn around and escape back into the open sea. Collisions occurred and ships had oars sheared off by friendly vessels. Eventually, the Romans managed to form a rough line of ships close in to the shore, with their rams facing out to sea. The flagship was on the extreme left. In the meantime Adherbal had outflanked the left of the Roman line with five ships, angled forward, and placed his own ship facing the Roman line. As the rest of the fleet came up, he ordered them to form line on his vessel, subordinate officers regulating the deployment, presum-ably in small boats. After this delay as the two fleets formed up, Adherbal signalled his ships to attack. It would prove the only significant defeat suffered by the Roman navy throughout the war.

The size of the opposing fleets is not certain. Polybius mentions that about thirty Roman ships survived and that ninety-three were captured, but does not make clear whether this figure includes any ships that were sunk. The Carthaginian fleet has been variously estimated as between 100 and 130 and on the whole there is no suggestion of a marked disparity between the two sides. On this occasion the Carthaginian ships carried large contingents of marines and were evenly matched with their Roman counterparts. The Punic crews were undoubtedly better than their opponents, making their ships faster and more manoeuvrable. This might not have mattered had the Romans not been in such a bad position, with their sterns close to the shore. If hard pressed a Carthaginian vessel could back water and pull out of the fighting, but the Romans lacked room to do this. Polybius does not tell us explicitly, but it seems clear that the Roman ships were no longer equipped with the *corvus*, that major deterrent against attacking them from the front. For the first time in a significant action, the Carthaginians were able to display their skill in ramming, striking the enemy and then pulling back without being grappled. The Roman ships lacked the room to manoeuvre to avoid rams or move to each other's aid, and their crews simply did not have the skill to drive through the enemy line and try to ram them from the rear. They may also have felt that it was better to stay in as close a formation as possible for mutual security. The battle was not over quickly, but steadily the Carthaginian advantage became overwhelming. Many Roman ships were sunk, others ran aground and were abandoned, whilst only the thirty ships including Claudius' flagship were able to break out and escape. Claudius was later brought to trial for treason (*perduellio*) at Rome and only narrowly escaped with his life.[37]

The victory at Drepana heralded a series of further Roman disasters at sea. Claudius' consular colleague Lucius Junius Pullus was with another Roman fleet of 120 warships escorting a convoy of 800 transports, carrying grain to supply the besiegers of Lilybaeum. This got into some disorder crossing to Sicily, so Pullus halted with half the ships in Syracuse to allow the stragglers to catch up. The remainder were sent ahead under the command of the quaestors who were given a small number of warships to protect them. The Carthaginian fleet had also divided, Adherbal adding thirty more vessels to the seventy recently brought to Sicily by Carthalo and sending them to attack the Roman naval support at Lilybaeum. After creating some havoc there and burning several ships, Carthalo sailed around the coast towards Heraclea Minoa, hoping to intercept any Roman supply convoys. The quaestors were warned of his approach by the small ships (*lemboi*), which Polybius tells us in an aside normally preceded a fleet, but lacked the strength to face him at sea or the speed to escape. Instead they put in to the shore near a Roman-held town and drew their ships out of the water. Getting *ballistae* from the town's fortifications, the quaestors managed to establish a rudimentary fortified line protecting the ships, which proved enough to deter the Punic squadron, who only managed to capture a few ships. Pullus had by this time brought on the remainder of the convoy, and rounded Cape Pachynus south of Syracuse, heading towards Lilybaeum. Unaware of the recent Roman defeats, he unexpectedly sighted Carthalo's fleet. Pullus was unwilling to risk a fight so led his warships and transports close in to this rugged part of the Sicilian coast. Carthalo did not follow, but merely observed from a distance. At this point, once again the weather took a hand. A heavy gale blew up and the signs of this impending gale were spotted by Carthaginian captains who knew this coast, and who promptly advised Carthalo to sail immediately around the Cape. Again the skill of the Punic sailors was displayed as they battled to bring the fleet successfully round the headland where they were sheltered from the wind. The Romans were exposed to the full force of the gale and so close inshore that they stood no chance of escape. The entire fleet was dashed to pieces on the rugged shore, but numbers of the crew escaped, including the consul, although he seems to have been captured soon afterwards.[38]

The disaster suffered by the Roman fleet was probably more total than the earlier losses to the weather and, unlike them, came in the aftermath of naval defeat and not victory. Polybius tells us that the Romans for the moment abandoned all efforts to fight the war at sea and it is unlikely that the State could have afforded to construct another fleet. A few private citizens were given licence to equip ships at their own expense and act as privateers raiding Carthaginian territory, but this was never going to contribute anything significant to the outcome of the war. Some idea of the scale of Roman losses may come from the census figures preserved for this period, although the reliability of these figures for the period before 225 is uncertain.[39] These give the total number of male Roman citizens registered by the censors as 292,234 in 265–264, 297,797 in 252–251, but only 241,712 in 247–246. The drop of more than 50,000 in the last figure may well indicate the losses suffered at sea, although the absence of any noticeable fall after the storms in 255 and 254 may make the second figure doubtful. However, it is important to remember that even if these figures provide a guide it is only to citizen losses. Many men in the fleet were drawn from the allies. It was in these years that Claudia, the sister of Claudius Pulcher, was prosecuted. Whilst travelling through the streets of Rome, the progress of her carriage had been blocked by the crowd. In a display of aristocratic arrogance she was heard to wish that her brother would lose another battle and drown some more of the poorer citizens.

The End: The Battle of the Aegates Islands
Although the Romans had abandoned their maritime ambitions, they continued to prosecute the war on land with no apparent doubt about their

eventual success. The Carthaginians made little use of their naval superiority, the few raids mounted against Italy achieving very little, whilst the war continued sporadically in Sicily. It was not until late 243 that the Romans decided once again to rebuild their fleet and push the war to a decisive conclusion. Even so, the State was not able to afford this project from its own resources and the money was provided by private citizens, one man, or two or three banding together, agreeing to provide the cost of building and equipping a quinquereme. The money was a loan to be paid back after the victory when the State's finances had recovered, but it appears to have been interest free and should be interpreted as a gesture of genuine patriotism. The Roman élite clearly identified themselves very strongly with the state in a way which modern cynicism should not make us doubt.[40]

In this way 200 quinqueremes were constructed, and once again a Carthaginian design was copied, for all were modelled on Hannibal the Rhodian's captured ship. Morrison and Coates have suggested that both this ship and the new Roman fleet were in fact 'fours'. They claim that a quinquereme was significantly higher than a quadrireme and that Hannibal's ship could not have been successfully boarded by the captured 'four', citing an incident in the Second Punic War when the smaller ships proved unable to capture a disabled 'five'. Yet in that case the encounter was unexpected, whereas the Romans had planned to waylay Hannibal's vessel with their swift 'four' and had prepared accordingly. It may well have been because their marines were outnumbered rather than unable to reach the enemy deck that the 'fours' in the later incident were unable to take the 'five'. There seems no good reason to doubt Polybius' statement that the new Roman fleet were quinqueremes.[41]

One of the consuls for 242, Aulus Postumius Albinus, held the priesthood known as the *flamen Martialis* and was forbidden by religious taboo from leaving the city, so the fleet was entrusted to the command of his colleague, Caius Lutatius Catulus, backed by the senior praetor, Quintus Valerius Falto. The Romans immediately renewed the pressure on their enemy's last major strongholds in Sicily, moving to capture the harbour at Drepana and cutting off Lilybaeum from the sea. Hamilcar Barca's forces were now cut off from re-supply by sea. Polybius states explicitly that the main Roman objective in these operations was to provoke a major encounter with the Carthaginian fleet, since they felt that its defeat would be a greater blow than any successes that might be achieved in Sicily. To this end Catulus took great care to exercise his ships at sea each day, training the crews to a high level of efficiency. His sailors were not allowed to waste away in the heavy labour and privations of siegework, but were kept healthy and provided with a good diet of food and drink. By 241 the Roman fleet was in superb condition, its crews experienced and skilled, its ships built to a far better design than in the past. The number of ships constructed in the preceding twenty years and the Romans' practical experience of naval operations can only have refined the skills of their shipbuilders.[42]

The Carthaginians were far less well prepared for the upcoming encounter, for they had made little use of the naval superiority which they had achieved after Drepana and the Roman losses to weather. The Punic navy had done little in the years since then, and it appears that relatively few ships had been kept in commission. It took them some time to muster the crews for the fleet of 250 or so ships which they gathered to send to Sicily. For probably the first time in the war, the average Carthaginian crew was to prove less well trained than their Roman counterparts. It is also possible that many crews were under strength, although certainty is impossible. Their objective was twofold. In the first instance the priority was to load the ships with supplies of grain for Hamilcar's army and the remaining Punic garrisons in Sicily. The Roman pressure on these troops must have made it difficult for them to survive by foraging. Once the supplies had been offloaded, the fleet was to take on board the pick of Hamilcar's soldiers to serve as marines and seek out and destroy the Roman fleet. Command in this operation was given to one Hanno, who may or may not have been the same man who had presided over the defeats at Agrigentum in 261 and Ecnomus in 256.[43]

The Carthaginians followed the same route as the fifty ships carrying reinforcements and supplies which Hannibal, son of Hamilcar, had sailed into Lilybaeum in 250. Crossing to the Aegates Islands just to the west of Sicily, they stopped at the westernmost of these, known as 'the Holy Island', and waited for a favourable breeze to carry them into Eryx before the Romans were aware of their presence and could react. However, Catulus received a report of their arrival and immediately took on board extra marines drawn from the army and crossed to another of the islands in the group. The next day, 10 March 241, the wind blew strongly from the west in just the direction that Hanno had hoped for. The Punic ships raised their sails and began the run in to link up with their land forces. Catulus was faced with a difficult decision. The heavy swell was against the Romans, since their rowers would have to battle hard against it if they were to move and intercept the Punic fleet. In the past, Roman commanders who had treated the elements in a cavalier fashion had presided over spectacular disasters. Yet if Catulus delayed, then he was unlikely to stop the Carthaginians joining Hamilcar and taking on board large numbers of experienced soldiers. Catulus took the risk and put to sea.

The carefully trained and prepared Roman crews then proved their worth, coping well with the high seas and forming a line to intercept the enemy before they reached Sicily. In response the Carthaginians lowered their sails and took down their masts to prepare for battle. Polybius says that the Punic crews yelled out encouragement to each other as they bore down on the enemy, but they were at a serious disadvantage. Their ships were overburdened with the supplies they carried, they had few marines and their crews were poorly trained. Not only would the Romans have the advantage in boarding actions, but their ships were for once faster, more manoeuvrable and better prepared for ramming. The difference in the two sides was quickly apparent, as the Romans sank fifty ships and captured another seventy. Polybius does not mention Roman losses, but Diodorus implies that the battle was less of a foregone conclusion, and that for the 117 Punic ships lost, twenty of these sunk with all hands, the Romans had thirty vessels sunk and fifty crippled. However, he also claims that the Roman fleet numbered 300 rather than 200 ships. Both authors provide relatively low figures for the number of Punic prisoners, given their heavy losses in ships; Polybius saying 10,000, whilst Diodorus tell us that Philinus made it 6,000, but other sources 4,040. This has been used to support the suggestion that the Punic ships were undermanned, but it may be that more men were drowned when their ships were rammed and floundered than was normal for a sea battle in this period because conditions were rougher.[44]

Fortunately for the Carthaginians the wind changed during the battle, shifting to an easterly, which allowed many of their ships to raise masts and sails once again and escape. The Romans, who had been deliberately prepared for battle, were probably not carrying masts and were unable to pursue very far. However, the excavators of the Marsala wrecks conjectured that these light Punic warships may have been sunk in the aftermath of this defeat, so the Roman pursuit may have been a little more effective than our sources suggest. Catulus returned to Lilybaeum to continue the blockade and deal with the spoils of success, both the captured ships and prisoners. Soon, the consul and the praetor began to bicker over who deserved credit for the victory. The praetor Falto was later to claim that Catulus had been incapacitated on the day of battle as the result of a wound to the thigh suffered in a skirmish outside Lilybaeum. Both men were allowed to celebrate a triumph.[45]

The battle of the Aegates Islands decided the war. Hamilcar Barca's army and the few strongholds left in Sicily were now utterly isolated. Carthage lacked either the will or, according to Polybius, resources to build another fleet and try once more to wrest naval dominance back from Rome. The Punic aristocracy seems to have made no attempt to follow the example of the Roman élite and put their private wealth at the disposal of the state. However, given the difficulty encountered in crewing the last fleet, it may have been shortage of manpower rather than resources to construct ships that prevented the rebuilding of the navy. For whatever reason, the Carthaginians conceded defeat and resolved to make peace.[46]

The resources expended in the naval campaigns of the war had been massive, Polybius claiming that the Romans had lost about 700 warships and the Carthaginians nearer 500, although the accuracy of these figures has been doubted. The heaviest Roman losses all occurred in storms and this ensured that the casualties suffered by the crews were disproportionately high. Many of the crews of these Punic ships were saved, although this sometimes meant going into captivity. It was the victors who suffered the greatest losses at sea. Ultimately the Romans won because their ruthless determination and pursuit of victory made them willing to accept its high price in men and ships. The initial decision to create a Roman fleet may have been at least in part motivated by a desire to defend the Italian coast from the depredations of the Punic navy, but the Romans were to use their naval power in a consistently aggressive manner. The support of the navy allowed the Roman land forces in Sicily to press on more successfully with the task of subduing the Punic strongholds there. The fleet's first action was the bold if unsuccessful attempt to seize Lipara. The ingenuity which produced the *corvus* allowed the Roman ships to face and defeat the superior Carthaginian ships in battle, and encouraged the increasing Roman willingness to seek encounters at sea. The direct attack on North Africa again showed the Roman willingness to escalate the fighting in an effort to achieve a decisive result. Roman confidence was curbed by the heavy losses in the storms in 255–254, and again by the defeat at Drepana and the catastrophic storm in 249, but each check was only temporary. On each occasion the Romans eventually rebuilt their fleet and resolved to make another effort. Had the new fleet been badly defeated in 241 – a real possibility if the Carthaginians had been able to unload their ships and cram them with Hamilcar's veteran mercenaries – then at the very least the delay before the Romans were able to contest the sea again must surely have been even longer.

Throughout the war the Carthaginians failed to make much use of their initially superior fleet, and let it decline after they had regained naval dominance in 249. The Carthaginian approach to war on land and sea was markedly less aggressive and determined than their opponents'. The objective seemed always to be to endure and continue the struggle, rather than to force it to a conclusion. Fleets of galleys were heavily dependent on land bases because of the comparatively short range of their warships. This meant that control of the sea was ultimately based on control of the bases in the area, adding to the importance of Sicily's, and to a lesser extent Sardinia's, coastal cities. The war in Sicily saw the steady reduction of Carthage's strongholds which, despite the temporary checks and the recapture of some strongholds, was never halted. The Carthaginian commanders, despite the length of time they remained in their posts, never managed to maintain a concerted offensive to win back lost ground and drive the Romans from the island. Their successes on land tended to have no more than local significance and were often small-scale. The achievements of the Punic navy were similarly minor and it never was able to derive a wider advantage from its greater skill and experience. Drepana, the only battle won by the Carthaginians, was notably smaller in scale than most of the other clashes, involving fewer than 150 ships on either side. As the size of fleets grew larger, so the superiority of the Punic navy declined. Its spectacular successes, such as the blockade running at Lilybaeum, were always small-scale, and even these were eventually checked by Rome.[47]

CHAPTER 5

The End

FTER THE DISASTROUS defeat at the Aegates Islands, the Carthaginians gave Hamilcar Barca full authority to negotiate a peace
with Rome. In fact, Hamilcar, eager to disassociate himself from any
admission of defeat, acted through one of his subordinate officers, Gesgo.
The consul Catulus' year of office had almost expired and the desire to gain
credit for completing such a major war before his successors arrived to steal
the glory may well have made him more conciliatory. An initial Roman
demand that Hamilcar's Sicilian army should immediately surrender its
weapons and hand over for punishment all the Roman and Italian deserters in its ranks was swiftly rejected. The mercenaries would leave the island
as an army, their arms and honour both intact.[1] Yet this seems to have been
the only concession that the Carthaginians were able to gain, for in other
respects the peace terms made it clear that they had been defeated and that
Rome was not negotiating with an equal. Peace was declared between
Rome and Carthage providing that the following conditions were met:

a The Carthaginians were to evacuate all of Sicily.

b Neither side was to make war on the other's allies, nor seek to subvert their
allegiance by allying with them directly or becoming involved in their internal
affairs. They were not to recruit soldiers or raise money for the construction of
public buildings in the territory of the other.

c The Carthaginians were to give up all Roman prisoners freely, whilst paying
a ransom for their own.

d The Carthaginians were to pay an indemnity to the Roman State of 2,200
Euboean talents over a twenty-year period.

A Roman consul did not have the authority to conclude a final peace himself, since a treaty could only be ratified by the Roman People voting in the

Comitia Centuriata, the same assembly which had the power to declare war. Therefore Catulus referred the terms back to Rome for approval. Not uncharacteristically, the Roman People decided that the terms were too lenient and a senatorial commission was sent to Sicily to modify the treaty. The indemnity was increased to 3,200 talents, 1,000 payable immediately and the remainder over ten years, which was perhaps a reflection of the desire for the State to repay the loans made for the construction of Rome's last fleet. The Romans had traditionally expected defeated enemies to contribute to the costs of their war effort.[2] The only other change was the addition of a clause requiring Carthage to evacuate all of the small islands between Sicily and Africa.[3]

It is clear that the complete expulsion of the Carthaginians from Sicily had become the Romans' main war aim, whether or not we should follow Polybius and date this ambition to the fall of Agrigentum in 261. The invasion of Africa in 256 had never been intended to establish a permanent Roman presence, but was a means of applying further pressure on the Carthaginians in the hope of forcing their submission. This primary objective had been fully achieved. In addition to this, Punic naval power had been broken and no longer dominated the western Mediterranean, more as a result of the loss of its island bases than the losses in ships which it had suffered, since in time the latter could be replaced. Yet Carthage had lost none of its power in Africa or Spain, and, for the moment, held on to Sardinia. There was no attempt to absorb Carthage into Rome's network of allies in the way that she had come to conclude most of her wars fought in Italy. In part this was a reflection of the reality of the situation. At the end of the twenty-three-year struggle both sides were exhausted and eager to settle. A continuation of the war until one or the other side was destroyed as an independent political entity was simply not feasible. Carthage in its sheer size, territories and economic prosperity was on an utterly different scale to the states of Italy with whom Rome had dealt in the past. In addition the Romans seem to have acknowledged the differences between the Italian Peninsula and lands separated from their own by sea. Sicily was not to be absorbed in the same way as the communities of mainland Italy and was not settled with colonies of citizens. Initially much of the island was administered by Hiero's Syracuse, but at some point a Roman governor, usually a praetor, was appointed to govern the western part of the island, creating Rome's first province, as we would understand the term. It is unclear precisely when this occurred, but it may have been as late as *c.* 227, when the number of praetors annually elected was increased to four, quite probably to provide governors for Sicily and

Sardinia where permanent Roman garrisons appear to have been established.[4] Unlike the Italian allies, the communities within the Roman province had a different bond to the Roman State, their main obligation being to pay tax, rather than supply soldiers to fight with the Roman army. Grain from Sicily rapidly became a major source of food for Rome itself, and many Romans, especially equestrians, probably became wealthy from its exploitation.[5]

With hindsight it is difficult to see any occasion during the course of the war when the Carthaginians came close to victory. The most serious Roman losses were due to bad weather and not to enemy action. Perhaps in the earliest phases, if they had been able to prevent the Roman expedition from crossing the Straits of Messina or had defeated Claudius' army after it had landed, then they might have dissuaded the Romans from further overseas adventures, at least in the short term, but that in effect would have been to prevent the crisis developing into a war in the first place. Yet it was extremely difficult for squadrons of galleys to block a stretch of water and the Punic forces in Sicily in 264 were utterly inadequate to achieve such a quick victory over a Roman consular army. Apart from the decision to continue the struggle and send a large army to Sicily after Rome's defeat of Syracuse, the Carthaginian war effort was essentially passive, a series of reactions to Roman moves, all intended to protect their position in Sicily.[6] Even when they sought to harass the enemy by raiding the Italian coast, the main objective was to draw Roman forces away from Sicily. On the island itself their strategy followed the traditional Carthaginian pattern of enduring the enemy onslaught and trying to maintain control of as many strongholds as possible, waiting for the enemy to weaken so that eventually the lost ground could be regained. Carthage had been involved in sporadic conflict in Sicily for centuries before the Romans arrived, and if she had never gained full control of the island, neither had she been completely expelled.

The Romans were not like Pyrrhus, who would abandon his offensive when he failed to gain widespread support from the Greek communities of Sicily, nor was their power as precarious as that of the successive tyrants of Syracuse. Roman persistence was at least the equal of Punic, but was married to an extremely aggressive mode of war-making, applying continuous pressure on the enemy in an effort to force a decision. Throughout the conflict they consistently assumed the offensive, methodically expanding the territory which they controlled in Sicily, continuing to do so even when their armies' morale reached a low ebb after the defeat of Regulus. More importantly they were willing to escalate the conflict in an effort to defeat the enemy, invading Africa and, most of all, deciding to create a fleet and pursue the war at sea in spite of their colossal losses. Rome's huge reserves of manpower made it possible to absorb appalling losses, but this in itself does not explain the willingness with which the population continued to be ready to serve in the war.

The annual replacement of Roman commanders may have meant that they were usually less experienced than their opponents, but it is hard to find clear examples of Zonaras' claim that this was the cause of numerous Roman defeats.[7] All but two of the major battles fought on land and sea were Roman victories and it seems likely that most of their defeats were very small-scale affairs. Hamilcar Barca, whom Polybius considered the ablest commander on either side, displayed his talent in relatively low-level raiding and skirmishing. In one respect the annual arrival of new Roman commanders may have proved an asset, for it ensured that the army and navy were commanded very aggressively, by men hoping to gain distinction in their short term of office. Roman strategy remained continuously aggressive, even if it sometimes lacked consistency. If this produced acts of great boldness or even recklessness, such as the failed surprise attacks on Lipara in 260 and Drepana in 249, it also produced some notable successes, such as Regulus' victory at Adys. On the whole Roman commanders performed fairly well.

As the war progressed the number of men holding office for the second time increased, which may have provided more experienced commanders, although in the case of Scipio Asina, consul in 260 and 254, this was experience of defeat and capture. Of the forty-seven consuls elected during the twenty-three years of war – the odd number a result of the death of Quintus Caecidius soon after taking office in 256 and his replacement by Regulus – eleven had held the office before, all but two during the war itself. Two others would go on to second consulships after 241. The proportion of multiple consulships was much the same in the decades before the war and may well be more a reflection of the politics of the day and the dominance of a few aristocratic families than a desire on the part of the electorate to choose experienced commanders during a hard war. A shift in the political balance may explain the slight decline in the number of multiple consulships in the years between the First and Second Punic Wars. Following the disaster at Drepana in 249, the Senate certainly did select a commander on the basis of experience as well as his political influence, when it took the very rare step of appointing a military dictator to take charge of the operations in Sicily. The man chosen was Aulus Atilius Caiatinus, who had been praetor in 257, and as consul in 258 and 254 had already commanded in two Sicilian campaigns earlier in the conflict.[8] However, the Senate made little use of its power to prorogue a magistrate's *imperium* (the prolonging of the command of those of proven ability), something which became common in the Second Punic War. This was partly due to the more restricted theatre of operations in the First War, but also a reflection of the low casualty rate amongst Roman senior officers compared to the Hannibalic war. The campaigns of the First War involved both consuls serving together more often than had been the case in the past. Disagreements between men of equal rank sharing command of an army were to figure prominently in the explanations for the Roman disasters of the Second War, but there is no trace of this in the earlier conflict, perhaps because there were fewer defeats to excuse. The bickering between Catulus and Falto occurred after their victory and had not apparently been reflected by any difficulties during the actual conduct of the campaign. Both of the major defeats of the war occurred when only one consul was in command and Agrigentum, the only land battle where command was shared, was a clear Roman success. However, pitched land battles were rare during the conflict and it was the subtle manoeuvring in the days before these which offered most opportunity for a divided command to lead to confusion.

Carthaginian commanders may have been more 'professional' than their Roman counterparts, and certainly remained in their posts for much longer periods, but few would have had much experience of commanding such large forces as were frequently employed during the war. This was especially true of the admirals appointed to control the operations of the unprecedentedly large fleets which were formed on several occasions. Their inexperience of command at this level added to the already major practical difficulties in co-ordinating the movements of hundreds of oared warships and was perhaps another factor in denying the Carthaginian navy the advantages it ought to have derived from the superior skill of its crews. Several Punic generals were crucified in the aftermath of military failures during the war, usually, it seems, by order of their own immediate subordinates. Yet other defeated leaders escaped punishment and went on to hold further commands which suggests that political influence as much as actual responsibility determined their fate.[9] The Romans were considerably more lenient towards their magistrates who had presided over disasters, awarding triumphs to successive admirals who had lost most of their fleets to bad weather. Only Claudius was prosecuted on the charge of *perduellio* (in a sense 'bringing the state into disrepute') for his behaviour at Drepana, but narrowly escaped condemnation and was instead found guilty of a lesser charge and fined.[10] However, the subsequent arraignment of his sister suggests that the family was perceived to be politically vulnerable in the years immediately afterwards.

The Mercenary War

Within months of the end of the war, Carthage was plunged into a conflict which, if shorter than the struggle with Rome, seemed to pose a far greater threat to her very existence. It took over three years to suppress the rebellion of former mercenaries and African subjects, who for this time ravaged the territory up to the walls of Carthage itself. It was a bitter campaign, punctuated by acts of extreme barbarity on both sides. It was also completely unnecessary, if the Punic authorities had not consistently mishandled all their dealings with Hamilcar's veterans from the Sicilian campaign.[11]

Hamilcar Barca had led his army to Lilybaeum following the conclusion of the war with Rome, but had then surrendered his command and sailed back to Africa, full of contempt for what he believed to be an unnecessary peace. He left the task of demobilizing his mercenaries to the same Gesgo who had conducted the negotiations with Catulus. This officer performed the new role with great competence, dividing the 20,000 strong army into smaller detachments which he then dispatched one at a time to Carthage. Once there, each contingent should ideally have received their arrears of several years' backpay and been returned to their country of origin before the next group arrived, spreading the burden placed on the state treasury and preventing any problems arising from the presence of so many unruly foreign soldiers in Carthage at one time. However, the Carthaginians chose to ignore these sensible arrangements and refused to pay anyone until the whole force had been shipped to Africa, convinced that the mercenaries could be persuaded to accept a lower settlement, in the light of the unsuccessful outcome of the war and Carthage's difficult financial position. It was a small-minded decision they were soon to regret.

After numerous disturbances on the streets of Carthage, the mercenaries were sent to the town of Sicca, where they encamped without a commander and with no duties to maintain their discipline. Understandably, the mercenaries who had fought loyally and well for their masters according to their contracts were reluctant to accept payment of less than their due and felt betrayed. They were especially bitter towards Hamilcar, who had made lavish promises of future reward during the operations in Sicily, only to abandon them to the whims of a government and generals they did not know. The Carthaginians soon realized that the negotiations were not succeeding and, aware that they would have difficulty in controlling 20,000 well-equipped veteran soldiers, agreed to pay the full amounts the men were due, but it was too late. The disgruntled mercenaries had become aware of their own strength and steadily increased their demands, forcing one concession after another out of their former masters. Resentment at their unfair treatment gradually turned into deep hostility towards the Carthaginians. Like all Punic armies, the veterans from Sicily were a mixture of many races, Libyans, Gauls, Spaniards, Ligurians, Sicilian Greeks and half-breeds, runaway slaves and deserters. Lacking a common language and without the unifying force of a Carthaginian command structure, the mercenaries at Sicca had fragmented into groups along ethnic lines. The Libyans were the largest group and it was they who finally turned mutiny into open revolt when they seized and imprisoned the unfortunate Gesgo, the man the mercenaries themselves had chosen to deal with as the only Punic officer they trusted.

It was the presence of this Libyan element within the army which was to make the rebellion so serious, for they were swiftly able to rally most of their countrymen to their cause. Carthaginian rule had always been harsh and unpopular for the Libyan peasantry, but during the war with Rome the burdens of taxation and conscription had grown far worse. With very few exceptions the Libyan communities declared for the rebels and swelled the size of their forces. They were joined by many of the Numidian princes whom the Carthaginians had been fighting to control in the last decade and who now saw an opportunity for revenge and booty. Soon an army many times the size of the one Regulus had led began the blockade of Carthage. The main rebel leaders were Mathos, a Libyan, and Spendius, an escaped Campanian slave who feared being returned to his former master for execution, supported by the Gaul Autariatus, the chieftain of a remarkably unreliable band of warriors. Some of his followers had deserted to the Romans during the war and later went on to betray successive employers.[12] Though veteran soldiers (Spendius had an especially distinguished record during the war with Rome) none of these men had experience of high command and the movements of the rebel armies were clumsy and poorly co-ordinated.

This was one of the very few advantages the Carthaginians enjoyed in the conflict. It was always difficult for them to raise large armies quickly, but the situation was worsened when their own mercenaries turned against them. In addition the rebellion in Libya denied them access to the revenue and resources of manpower on which they could normally rely. The forces which they were able to raise, composed of still loyal mercenaries who felt no particular bond with the unfamiliar Sicilian veterans, and newly raised citizen soldiers, were heavily outnumbered by their enemies. Further problems were caused by a divided command, similar to the appointment of three generals to lead the operations in 256–255. Hamilcar Barca and Hanno, who was a better organizer than commander, did not get along with each other and the operations of their armies were hindered by the sort of disputes which are normally held to be more typical of the Roman than Punic military systems. Hanno was later forced to resign by vote of the army, or perhaps the senior officers, and replaced by the more amenable Hannibal. It is in these campaigns far more than the war in Sicily that we see evidence of Hamilcar's skill as a general, consistently out-manoeuvring the larger rebel forces. Force was combined with diplomacy, for instance when Navaras, a Numidian prince, offered to defect with his followers and was rewarded by marriage to Hamilcar's daughter. Both sides made extensive and escalating use of horror and atrocity, Barca ordering captured mercenaries to be trampled to death by his elephants. Mathos and Spendius were both eventually crucified, but so was Hannibal who had been captured in a night raid on his camp, whilst Gesgo and the other hostages were dismembered and tossed into a ditch where they bled to death. Eventually, by 237, the rebel armies had all been defeated, the Libyan communities surrendered and the revolt collapsed.

The Roman attitude towards her recently defeated enemy at this time of crisis was at first scrupulously correct. Early in the war the Senate sent a Commission to Carthage following reports that Roman traders dealing with the rebels had been arrested or killed.[13] In fact, the merchants had merely been imprisoned and when the Carthaginians readily agreed to their repatriation the Romans responded warmly. Italian traders were in future banned from supplying the mercenaries and actively encouraged to trade in Carthage itself. In addition, all Punic prisoners not yet ransomed according to the treaty of 241 were immediately returned without charge. Hiero's Syracuse also made every effort to sell Carthage the supplies it needed for its war effort, although Polybius believed that in part this was to ensure that the city continued to exist as a balance to Roman power.[14] Around 240–239 the Punic mercenaries in Sardinia mutinied and murdered their officers, and persuaded the punitive expedition sent by Carthage against them to repeat the mutiny and join them. Together the mercenaries seized the island and tried to make an alliance with Rome, rather as the Mamertines had once done. The Senate refused to countenance such an alliance, a decision all the more striking if Polybius correctly judged that the acquisition of Sardinia had become a Roman ambition as soon as they constructed their first fleet. Nor, subsequently, did it accept approaches from Utica for similar protection when this Libyan city finally abandoned its loyalty to Carthage and joined the rebels.[15] Instead it respected the protection offered to each sides' allies set down in the treaty of 241.

Eventually, probably in 237, the mutinous soldiers in Sardinia were expelled from the island by the native population and fled to Italy where they once again approached the Senate. This time the Romans decided to send an expedition to occupy the island and, when the Carthaginians objected, threatened them with a war which they were in no position to fight. Carthage had no choice but to surrender to Rome a second time, accepting their seizure of Sardinia, and paying a further indemnity of 1,200 talents. It was an act as shamelessly opportunistic as the initial intervention in Sicily in 265, an injustice which highlighted Carthage's weakness and was to create a far greater legacy of bitterness and resentment towards Rome than the initial defeat of 241. Our sources do not explain why the Romans chose to act in this way after their earlier refusal. However, it is important to remember that the Senate consisted of a collection of individuals, all competing to win glory in the service of the state and with differing views on how best to conduct its affairs. The groups based around the stronger families were loose and rarely espoused a consistent policy on anything, whilst the influence of individual senators fluctuated greatly from year to year. It may simply have been that the consul of 238, Tiberius Sempronius Gracchus, who was to lead the expedition, was eager to command in a war and had enough influence at the time to persuade the Senate to answer the mercenaries' appeal. Alternatively the anarchy in Sardinia may have been seen as a potential threat to Italy's maritime trade, but our sources lack any detailed discussion of the reasons for the Roman change of heart.[16] However, most, and especially Polybius, agreed that the action was morally indefensible.[17]

Sardinia did not prove an easy conquest and for much of the 230s fierce campaigning continued there, with both of the year's consuls active there in 232 and 231.[18] Whether or not there was truth in the accusation, the Romans certainly seem to have believed that Carthaginian agents actively encouraged Sardinian resistance to Rome and the island remained a continued source of friction between the two states during these years.[19]

The Barcids in Spain
Sicily and Sardinia were lost, and, in the aftermath of the Mercenary Rebellion, Africa was too unstable for further expansion to be contemplated there, so Carthage turned her attention increasingly to her Spanish territo-

ries. In 238–237 Hamilcar Barca was sent at the head of an army to take charge of the province there, and the choice of such an experienced and aggressive commander for a region which does not appear to have faced a major threat can only mean that the objective was expansion. For the next nine years Hamilcar fought almost continuously, securing Punic control of the coastal strip of southern Spain and pushing up to the valley of the Guadalquivir, until he was killed in an ambush by a Celtiberian tribe known as the Oretani in 229, one tradition claiming that he deliberately sacrificed himself to save his young sons.[20] He was succeeded in the command by his son-in-law and second-in-command, Hasdrubal, who continued the programme of expansion, achieving more through diplomacy than war, even marrying a Spanish princess to cement one alliance. The succession seems to have been first voted for by the army in Spain and subsequently approved by the authorities at Carthage. This was certainly the case when Hasdrubal was assassinated in 221 and the army, or at least its officers, gave the command to Hamilcar's eldest son, the 26-year-old Hannibal, a decision later ratified by the Popular Assembly in Carthage.[21]

The basic narrative of Punic expansion in Spain under the leadership of the Barcid family is straightforward and uncontroversial, even if our sources sometimes contradict each other on minor points, but many important questions remain unanswered. It is unclear how and why Hamilcar was given the Spanish command in the first place and to what extent his activities once there were supervised. One extreme view is to see this period as the triumph of the Popular Party in Carthage, Hamilcar the demagogue winning the support of the ordinary citizens wearied by the incompetence displayed by the old aristocracy during the war with Rome and the Mercenary Rebellion. This allowed him to secure an unlimited command in Spain with the freedom to wage war and enrich himself for his own purposes. There may be a few indications of political change at Carthage, since the Council of 104 seems far less prominent after this period, and the importance of the two annually elected suffetes may have increased.[22] However, it must always be remembered that our evidence for the constitution and internal politics of Carthage is exceptionally poor. Most of our sources do portray the Barcid family as facing strong opposition from rivals who feared their growing power and from those who objected to their policies, but it is unclear how strong and consistent such opposition was.[23] In one tradition Hamilcar used the booty from his Spanish campaigns both to secure the loyalty of his soldiers and to buy himself political support at home.[24] It is equally possible to interpret the same evidence as showing Hamilcar as nothing more than a servant of the state, appointed with the general approval of the élite at Carthage.[25] The truth may lie anywhere between the two extremes.

The Second Punic War began in Spain, making the activity of the Barcid family there in the years after the First War especially important, but our sources' awareness of this only makes it more difficult to understand what sort of regime they created, and how significant it was that the command was held exclusively by members of the family. It is not entirely clear whether the Carthaginians ratified the army's choice of leader because they felt that they were powerless to change this or because they approved of the decision. There may have been a practical benefit from this, since it was far easier for Spanish tribes and leaders to focus their loyalty on an individual general and his family than on a distant Carthage, emotions which the Romans would also later exploit. The activities of the Barcids in Spain may simply be seen as an effective way for the Carthaginian state to expand its territory there, allowing them more easily to exploit the resources of mineral wealth and military manpower. For other historians these years saw the creation of what was in effect a semi-independent principality ruled by the family for their own ends, the Barcid perhaps assuming the trappings of Hellenistic monarchs. Again, our evidence is utterly inadequate to resolve this debate. The same series of coins produced by mints in Punic Spain in this period have been interpreted as showing Hamilcar and Hasdrubal depicted as Hellenistic kings with divine associations, or simply as being images of deities.[26] Hasdrubal certainly founded a major city called New Carthage (modern Cartagena), but whether this should be seen as the seat of provincial government or the capital of a semi-independent kingdom depends on the view taken of Barcid ambitions.

Rome 241–218 BC

The Romans certainly kept a wary eye on the Carthaginian activity in Spain, although as yet they had no direct involvement in the area. In 231 a delegation of senators went to Hamilcar to question him about the motives for his aggressive campaigns and was told that these were necessary if Carthage was to pay her indemnity to Rome. Later, sometime around 226, another set of envoys went to Hasdrubal, who formally agreed not to expand beyond the River Ebro. It is possible that Rome's interest in Spain was encouraged by her long-time ally, Massilia, but the concern over growing Carthaginian power may well have been genuine. As yet Rome had no direct connection with the Spanish Peninsula, although Latin traders were certainly active there by the second half of the third century.[27]

Rome's world was gradually expanding beyond the Italian Peninsula, with her newly acquired overseas provinces and the powerful navy created during the war with Carthage. In 228 and 219, Roman consuls at the head of fleets of warships fought two wars in Illyria on the other side of the Adriatic, allegedly provoked by the piracy routinely practised by the Illyrian kingdom. Nevertheless it was with an Italian problem, the Gallic tribes of northern Italy, that the Senate was most concerned between the wars. Latin colonies established on land captured from the tribes, notably Ariminum which was founded in 268, were a continual source of friction with the Gauls. Yet as Rome's population increased and her web of alliances expanded the need to find land for the poorer Roman and Latin citizens steadily grew and the fertile plains of Cisalpine Gaul proved especially attractive. In 232 one of the tribunes of the plebs, Caius Flaminius, carried a law to distribute much of the captured *ager Gallicus* to poorer citizens. These were not to be concentrated in new colonies, but each plot of land allocated individually to create a large number of small farms. There was much opposition to this move, in part because other senators resented the prestige that Flaminius would gain and the money that he would doubtless make in the process, but also because it was seen as a provocative gesture.[28]

In 238 the Boii had rallied other tribes and some warriors from beyond the Alps to attack Ariminum, but the war had fizzled out when bickering amongst the Gauls turned to open fighting and they were forced to make peace. By 225 resentment against the flood of settlers sparked another, far larger war. This time the Boii united with the Insubres, and were joined by a large contingent of semi-professional warriors from Transalpine Gaul, known as the Gaesatae. When the Gallic army invaded Etruria, it is said to have mustered around 70,000 men. The Gauls were undefeated when they decided to withdraw in front of the consul Lucius Aemilius Papus' army and carry away their substantial booty. The two Roman armies were completely unaware of each other's presence and by a stroke of luck the other consul, Caius Atilius Regulus, who had been recalled from Sardinia, found himself directly blocking the Gauls' line of march. Trapped between the two Roman armies, the tribes were forced to fight at Telamon, forming up in two lines back to back in order to face the enemy armies coming on from opposite directions. Despite this disadvantage the battle was a desperate one. Regulus fell in the early stages and his severed head was carried in triumph to one of the Gallic kings, and it was only after a long struggle that the Romans prevailed, inflicting appalling casualties on the enemy.

In 224 both consuls led armies north and forced the Boii to accept peace. The next year's consuls, the same Flaminius who as tribune had passed the bill to distribute the *ager Gallicus,* and Publius Furius also invaded the tribal lands. Flaminius won a great victory over the Insubres and another tribe, the Cenomani, although a hostile tradition gave the credit for this victory to the army's tribunes. According to Polybius it was these officers who ordered the *hastati* to be re-equipped with the spears of the *triarii* instead of their *pila.* The first line of the legions was then formed into a dense, defensive formation, standing fast until the fury and enthusiasm of the initial Gallic charge had exhausted itself. In 222 the Gauls sued for peace, but the new consuls, eager for glory or perhaps in the genuine belief that the enemy were undefeated, persuaded the Senate to reject these approaches and both took armies against them. One of the consuls, Marcus Claudius Marcellus, relieved the siege of Clastidium, fighting an action in which he single-handedly killed a Gallic King, Britomarus, and stripped him of his armour, winning the highest honour available to a Roman aristocrat, the right to dedicate the *spolia opima.*[29] His colleague Cnaeus Cornelius Scipio stormed Mediolanum (modern Milan), the tribal capital of the Insubres. After these continued defeats, the tribes all surrendered to Rome, yielding up more of their land. In 218 two new colonies were established, one on either side of the Po at Cremona and Placentia, 6,000 settlers going to each. The provocative presence of a new wave of settlers further north than before, and occupying prime land, only added to the bitterness and resentment of the defeated tribes, ensuring that peace would prove short-lived.

Spain and northern Italy would see much activity when war was finally renewed between Rome and Carthage. In addition, many of the individuals on both sides who were prominent in the campaigns in the 220s would later play a significant role in the Hannibalic war. For the generation of Roman commanders who grew up between the wars with Carthage, their military experiences in Sardinia, Illyria and, most of all, Cisalpine Gaul accustomed them to warfare against armies which were tactically unsophisticated, however individually brave and skilled the warriors composing them might have been. It was to prove poor preparation for confronting a general as skilled as Hannibal at the head of a well-trained army.

PART TWO

THE SECOND PUNIC WAR
218–201 BC

CHAPTER 6

Causes of the Second Punic War

T HERE WERE CERTAINLY moments of tension after the First Punic War, but relations between Rome and Carthage were not entirely unfriendly. Trade was renewed, and Punic merchants were as familiar a sight in Rome as Italians seem to have been in Carthage. It may well have been during these years that the ties of guest friendship, so common a feature of international relations in the ancient world, linking Roman and Punic aristocratic families were created or perhaps ones from before 265 revived. The peace concluded in 241 lasted twenty-three years, assuming that we ignore the Roman threat to reopen hostilities over Sardinia in 238, and ended when Hannibal Barca, the Carthaginian commander in Spain, attacked the Iberian city of Saguntum, which was under Roman protection. Neither side showed much reluctance to go to war, in spite of the memory of the earlier hard-fought and costly struggle. Why they did so has been the subject of intense debate ever since, more often than not concerned with apportioning blame to one side or the other. Equally often historians have fallen into the trap of judging events by modern standards, forgetting that even the most politically advanced ancient states went to war frequently and with enthusiasm, especially when they expected to win and eagerly anticipated the benefits victory would bring. Before discussing these issues it is helpful to review the chain of events which led to the declaration of open war by Rome.[1]

Probably in 226 Hasdrubal had accepted the demands of the Roman envoys and agreed that the Carthaginians would not cross the River Ebro. The idea of setting a physical boundary to a nation's power was a familiar concept to both cultures.[2] In this case it was no great restriction, since at that time the heartland of the Punic province still lay a long way from the river. Attempts to suggest that the treaty in fact involved a boundary much further south have been unconvincing. Similarly, there is even less foundation for the common assumption that the Romans bound themselves not to intervene south of the Ebro. In fact, at this date the Roman State had no direct connection with Spain, save in the sense that her ally, Massilia, had dependent communities there at Emporion and Rhode.

At some point after 226, Rome formed an association with the city of Saguntum (modern Sagunto, not far from Valencia). Polybius tells us that this was 'some years' before Hannibal's time, but it seems plausible that it would have been mentioned in the Ebro treaty had the link existed at that time, since the city stood a long way south of the river. The debate over whether or not there was a formal treaty granting Saguntum allied status, or whether the city simply requested Rome's protection, as Utica had tried to do during the Mercenary War, does not matter for our present purpose. At some point the Roman Senate was asked to arbitrate in an internal dispute at the city, quite possibly between rival factions favouring Rome and Carthage respectively, and the representatives sent ordered the execution of several Saguntine noblemen. The attractions of a Roman alliance to the Spanish town seem obvious. A city state of local importance, Saguntum can only have watched nervously as the Carthaginian province expanded towards them. Roman support offered the greatest possible security against their stronger neighbour. Why the Romans accepted the alliance is less clear and intimately bound up with the cause of the war, so will be discussed below.[3]

In 221 the 26-year-old Hannibal succeeded his brother-in-law and continued the aggressive Carthaginian policy in Spain, ranging far more widely than his predecessors. He led his army against the tribes of central Spain, reaching as far north as modern-day Salamanca. Around 220–219 a dispute broke out between Saguntum and a neighbouring tribe accused of raiding its territory. Details are obscure and even the name of the people involved is uncertain, but the tribe was allied to Carthage and received Hannibal's support. Over the winter, a Roman embassy went to Hannibal at New Carthage and reminded him of the earlier Ebro treaty, as well as warning him not to attack Saguntum. The embassy received a frosty reception and proceeded to Carthage to repeat the demands. The young general also referred to Carthage for instructions and in the spring led his army against the city. Saguntum lay on a strong hilltop position, about a mile from the sea. (In the autumn of AD 1811, the Spanish defenders of a fortress improvised amongst its Iberian, Roman, and Moorish ruins would repulse several attacks launched by one of Napoleon's ablest subordinates, Suchet.) It took Hannibal eight months to capture the town, but from the beginning it was clear that his intention was to take it by storm, rather than starve it into submission. His tactics were far more openly aggressive than those adopted by the Carthaginians in any of the sieges of the First War, and as a result his casualties were higher. Livy even claims that Hannibal himself was wounded whilst directing an attack from very close to the fighting.[4]

The Romans did nothing to aid the Saguntines once the siege had begun. Livy claims that they sent another embassy to Hannibal, but his chronology at this point is hopelessly confused and, since Polybius does not mention such a move, it is probably best to reject this. Saguntum fell at the end of 219 or in the first weeks of 218, and news of this may have arrived in Rome within a month. An embassy was sent to Carthage in the latter part of the winter, including both of the outgoing consuls of 219, Lucius Aemilius Paullus and Marcus Livius Salinator. Livy tells us that it was headed by Quintus Fabius Maximus, thus completing the trio of men who would play prominent roles in the approaching war, but it seems more likely that the leader was the experienced former censor, Marcus Fabius Buteo, who had fought in Sicily as consul in 245. The embassy protested Hannibal's actions and demanded to know whether he had been acting with the approval of the Carthaginian Senate. The Carthaginians were faced with the choice of condemning Hannibal and handing him and his senior officers over to the Romans for punishment, or going to war with Rome. The style of diplomacy practised by Roman embassies seems seldom to have been very subtle, but in this case they were clearly obliged to seek revenge for an attack on an ally. In one tradition which depicted a strong party opposed to the Barcids, a certain Hanno is supposed to have condemned Hannibal's actions, but on the whole the Carthaginians responded angrily to the brusque Roman demands. They refused to recognize the Ebro treaty, saying that they had never ratified it and citing Catulus' referral of the peace terms in 241 to Rome, and disputed their need to recognize any relationship between Rome and Saguntum. Fabius is supposed to have stood in the middle of the chamber and announced that he carried in the folds of his toga both peace and war, and could let fall from it whichever the Carthaginians chose. Tempers ran high amongst the assembled Punic senators and the presiding suffete shouted out for him to choose. When Fabius responded by declaring that he let fall war, a great shout of 'We accept it!' filled the hall. In this way war was declared, although it may have become inevitable earlier than this. Hannibal certainly began preparations for his invasion of Italy once he returned to winter quarters after the fall of Saguntum. It is also quite possible that the *Comitia Centuriata* had already voted for war if the ambassadors failed to gain a satisfactory response at Carthage.[5]

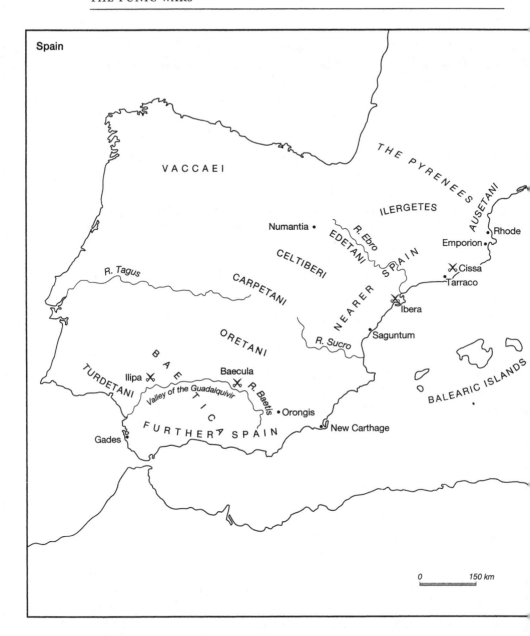

Spain

Polybius discussed the underlying causes of the renewal of hostilities in some detail and concluded that there were three main factors. The first was the bitterness or anger of Hamilcar Barca at the end of the First War when he was forced to surrender despite remaining undefeated in Sicily. The second, and most important, factor was the unprincipled Roman seizure of Sardinia in 238, whilst Carthage was still reeling from the turmoil of the

Mercenary Rebellion. Not only did this humiliation increase Hamilcar's resentment, but it spread a similar hatred of Rome throughout the Punic population. It was with the aim of building up a power base to use against Rome that Hamilcar went to Spain, throwing himself wholeheartedly into a programme of expansion. The successes of his family in the Spanish Peninsula formed the third cause, since the growth in Carthaginian power encouraged them to believe that they were now strong enough to defeat their old rival.[6]

Polybius supported his view of Hamilcar's motivation by recounting an anecdote which Hannibal had told whilst he was at the court of the Seleucid King Antiochus III in the 190s. Just before leaving to take up his new command in Spain Hamilcar Barca had sacrificed at the altar of a deity, who is called Zeus by Polybius and Jupiter by Livy, but was probably Ba'al Shamin. Receiving favourable omens, he called his 9-year-old son Hannibal to his side and asked the boy whether he would like to accompany him on the expedition. The lad, who had probably seen little of his father during his early life, responded enthusiastically, begging permission to go. Hamilcar placed the boy's hand on the sacrificial victim and made him swear a solemn oath 'never to be a friend to the Romans'.[7] Hannibal told this story to convince Antiochus that he was not consorting with the king's Roman enemies, and as Polybius received it at best third-hand, its accuracy is now impossible to assess. In the later Roman tradition the oath's wording becomes stronger, the child swearing to be always an enemy of Rome.[8]

In Polybius' version of events Hannibal inherited the war with Rome from his father, in much the same way that Alexander the Great would actually undertake the Persian expedition planned by his father Philip II. For a long time many modern historians accepted this interpretation, and a few went further, claiming that the plan to invade Italy across the Alps and even Hannibal's battle tactics may have been first devised by his father. More recently the idea that the war was the premeditated project of the Barcid family has fallen from favour, in part because historians are generally reluctant to attribute important events to the moods and actions of individual leaders, preferring to seek explanation in more general trends. Most often the argument has revolved around the precise details and chronology of the events leading up to the war, since Polybius is vague about much of this, whilst our other sources are of questionable reliability.[9]

Of fundamental importance is the question of what the Carthaginians led by the Barcid family were hoping to achieve in Spain, and once again we must lament the absence of sources from the Punic perspective. It has often been assumed that the loss of profitable territories in Sicily and Sardinia forced Carthage to seek revenue from elsewhere, and frequently the Spanish silver mines are cited in this context. Certainly, Hamilcar did bring many of these directly under Punic rule, and although it took several years to begin their effective exploitation, this did allow his family to mint several series of coins with an especially high silver content. In other respects it is difficult to see that expansion in Spain allowed any more profitable exploitation of its resources than had been possible through the Punic communities already there. In the short term there was certainly considerable income from the booty of successful campaigns, at least some of which may have come into State hands. Thus Hamilcar's reply to the Roman embassy's demand to know why he was fighting so many wars of conquest was that he needed to annex land to make a profit and so be able to pay off the Punic war debt to Rome. Much of the profit from successful campaigns went to pay for and expand the army in Spain. Punic recruiting officers had long been hiring Spanish soldiers, but the Barcid province brought a large part of this massive pool of military manpower directly under their control. The communities of Spain produced an excess of young males who could not be supported off the land and so frequently turned bandit or mercenary. On at least one occasion Hamilcar recruited captured enemy warriors directly into his own army, since removing this element from society made any conquest more secure. The armies of the First War had been predominantly African, but whilst large numbers of these soldiers still served, they were to be far outnumbered by Spaniards in the Second War. Most of these Spanish warriors would now serve not as mercenaries for pay, but as allied soldiers.[10]

Spain gave the Barcids and, depending on the view taken of the independence of their power, Carthage a formidable military force and the wealth to support it. Though it was this resource that would allow Hannibal to prosecute the war so effectively, this does not necessarily mean that this was the reason for its creation. It could be argued that the increase of Punic military might was essentially defensive, giving her some protection against such arbitrary Roman actions as the theft of Sardinia. Clearly the loss of the war with Rome and its aftermath had been a major blow to the pride of a strong Empire. The Spanish enterprise might simply have been an attempt to reassert her independence. Yet to maintain this view it would be necessary to believe that Hannibal's attack on Saguntum was merely a statement of the revival of Punic power, not expected to provoke war with Rome. The rapidity with which Hannibal began the colossal preparations for the Italian expedition make this extremely unlikely. The Romans seem always to have been nervous about the Barcids' activity in Spain, as evidenced by the number of embassies sent there.

The Second War was clearly a legacy of the First, which had ended suddenly with both sides almost equally exhausted. The Romans expected their wars to end in their own complete victory, the former enemy ceasing to present any threat usually through being absorbed as a subordinate ally. Whatever internal autonomy they preserved, they were not allowed an independent foreign policy, still less one which did not agree with Rome's interests. In 241 Carthage was too large and too distant to be absorbed by Rome in the same way that she had taken much of Italy, but even so the Romans refused to treat her as anything like an equal in the decades after the war. Sardinia was a blatant example of this attitude, forcing the Carthaginians to back down to an unjust demand, but the repeated interventions in Spain were another symptom. Whilst the Ebro treaty may not have imposed a major limit on Carthaginian expansion in Spain, it nevertheless made it clear that the Romans felt at liberty to impose such restrictions on Punic activity far from their own territory. The acceptance of some form of alliance with Saguntum reminded the Carthaginians that the Romans placed no such limits on themselves. The annual payment of the indemnity served as a continual reminder of Carthage's defeat, but this was probably completed by the mid 220s and it may have been at this time that Rome began to take an even closer interest in the Spanish Peninsula. A former enemy who appeared to be becoming an independent, rival power once again would have been perceived as a clear threat by the Romans, whatever the reality of the military situation. The interventions of Roman embassies served as a reminder to Carthage of her proper status. Until 219 the Carthaginians had always backed down in the face of Roman demands. It is highly probable that the Senate expected them to do so once again when the legation told Hannibal not to attack Saguntum, and their surprise that he disregarded this prohibition partly explains the failure of the Romans to send any aid to the city.

From the Carthaginian perspective, there was no reason for them to behave as a subordinate ally to Rome. Their military culture was different to Rome's and did not expect the results of wars to be so final. Added to this, their actual power had not been as seriously weakened by their defeat in 241 as the Roman attitude suggested, especially once it had had time to recover from the cost of the war and the disturbances of the Mercenary Rebellion. Carthage was still a large and wealthy state, with extensive territories in Africa and a growing realm in Spain. There was no good reason for Punic citizens to think of their city as anything less than Rome's equal, and their resentment at the Romans' refusal to acknowledge this is understandable. Both states had ample resources for making war and were mutually suspicious. In those circumstances the renewal of hostilities seems less surprising.

The Carthaginians' desire to reassert themselves as an independent power was as natural to them as it seemed threatening to the Romans. Some individuals may have consciously desired and planned for war. Hannibal was a young nobleman at the head of a powerful army and already assured of his own ability to command it. Ancient authors continually explain major wars as inspired by the lust for glory of kings, emperors and princes, and we would be rash wholly to ignore this view. It is possible that Hannibal had sought a war, and certain that he accepted it readily and prosecuted it with considerable enthusiasm. There may well have been some at Carthage who opposed the young general and who hoped for peace, but there was certainly a majority amongst the élite who saw no reason for the renewed Punic state to submit to such arrogant Roman demands. Whether or not they had acquiesced in, or had even ordered, Hannibal's activity which had provoked the crisis is impossible now to answer.[11]

Preparations and Plans

The Romans reacted very slowly to the attack on Saguntum, probably, as we have seen, in part because they expected the Carthaginians to submit to diplomatic pressure. Roman war-making was also still tied very closely to the consular year. By the time that the Senate heard that Saguntum was under siege, both of the consuls of that year were already abroad, commanding the fleet and army campaigning in Illyria. That war was as yet incomplete and even if one consul had been recalled, it would have taken some time for him to recruit a new army. It would therefore have been very late in the campaigning season before a Roman army arrived in Spain and difficult for it to achieve anything before winter halted operations. It was both more sensible and, by Roman standards, proper for the Senate to wait and allocate the major war with Carthage as the special responsibility of the consuls of 218, who would take up office in March. This was of course little comfort to the Saguntines who were left to fight to the end against an overwhelming enemy, but it is doubtful that any effective aid could have been sent.[12]

The Senate's plan for the conduct of the war was simple and direct in a characteristically Roman way. The consuls were to operate separately, one going to Spain to face Hannibal, whilst the other went to Sicily from where he would launch an invasion of North Africa. In this way the enemy commander who had provoked the war was to be defeated in battle, whilst the

Carthaginian authorities which had supported him were faced with a direct attack on their city. Direct confrontation of the enemy at their strongest points brought heavy pressure to bear on the mainstays of their opposition. Carthage had come close to folding under such pressure in 256–255 and there was no reason to believe that she would not do so again. Indeed, given the willingness of Carthage to give in to Roman threats in the decades between the wars, the Romans may even have expected her to be less resilient to actual war.

Of the two consuls of 218, Publius Cornelius Scipio was given Spain as his province and Tiberius Sempronius Longus received Sicily and Africa. Six Roman legions were raised for the year, each consisting of 4,000 infantry and 300 cavalry. Both consuls were given the standard consular army of two of these legions supported by two Latin *alae*. In total Scipio received 14,000 allied foot and 1,600 horse, whilst Longus had 16,000 and 1,800 respectively. The remaining legions along with 10,000 allied infantry and 1,000 cavalry were sent to Cisalpine Gaul under the command of a praetor, Lucius Manlius Vulso. The willingness to alter the size of allied contingents to cope with the scale of the problem once again emphasizes that the Roman military system was not as rigid as is sometimes assumed. The Senate's appreciation of the task in hand was also reflected in the allocation of naval resources. Longus, who was to mount an invasion of Africa possibly in the face of opposition from a large Punic fleet, received 160 quinqueremes and twenty lighter ships. Scipio was far less likely to encounter a powerful enemy fleet whilst moving his army to Spain, and so was given command of sixty 'fives'. The recent war in Illyria will have ensured that the Roman navy was in good condition.[13]

Before any move could be made against Carthage, a rebellion broke out in Cisalpine Gaul, provoked once again by the tribes' resentment of the incursions of Roman colonists. The Boii and Insubres drove the settlers from the as yet unfortified colonies of Placentia and Cremona, chasing them to the city of Mutina. The Gauls then sat down outside the city walls and began a blockade. Three Senatorial commissioners sent to organize the distribution of land in the new colonies were taken prisoner when they attempted to negotiate. A relief column set out under the command of the praetor Manlius Vulso, marching rapidly and taking little care to reconnoitre. It was ambushed when moving along a narrow path in heavily wooded country and suffered heavily, Livy claiming that 500 men were lost in one ambush and 700 along with six standards in a second. The battered army managed to reach a small town called Tannetum, where it too found itself under a loose siege.[14]

The situation was serious and the trouble in Cisalpine Gaul was too close to Rome for the Senate to ignore until the Carthaginian war had been completed. Scipio's army had been mustering in northern Italy, preparatory to sailing to Spain, so the Senate ordered another praetor, Caius Atilius Serranus, to take one of the legions and 5,000 allied troops and relieve Manlius, an objective he achieved quickly and without opposition. Scipio was instructed to levy a new legion and fresh allied troops to replace these, but it is not altogether clear whether or not Livy's total of six legions for the year includes this unit. The resultant delay meant the postponement of the move to Spain. In the meantime, Longus had gone ahead to Lilybaeum where he threw himself into major preparations for the African expedition.[15] However, the war was not to be fought in the manner the Senate had anticipated.

In the First War the Carthaginians had invariably responded to Roman moves rather than attempting to dictate the course of the war themselves. It had always been their opponents who escalated the conflict and pushed for a decisive result. From the beginning the Second War was to be very different and the main reason for this was the influence of one man, Hannibal Barca. In our sources Hannibal is represented as making all the key decisions to organize the initial Punic war effort in 219–218, not only in Spain but also in Africa. The Carthaginians habitually interfered very little with commanders once they had been appointed to a task, indeed often to the extent of failing to support them in subsequent operations, but the resources at the young general's immediate disposal were huge. It is at this time more than any other that Hannibal appears most like the ruler of the semi-independent principality in Spain depicted by some scholars.

The war had begun with a local dispute in Spain, the Carthaginians refusing to acknowledge any longer the restrictions the Romans had imposed upon their power there. The Romans clearly expected them to remain there and fight a defensive war to protect their territory, much like the one they had fought in Sicily. With the forces at his disposal Hannibal was in a strong position to meet any invasion. He would in fact have greatly outnumbered the single consular army which Scipio was to lead into the Peninsula and ought easily to have defeated it if it could be forced into a battle. Yet the experience of the First War had shown that destroying a Roman fleet or army simply meant that another was raised to replace it. The dogged persistence which Rome had shown in the face of horrendous losses made it unlikely that they would quickly give up. The longer that a war continued in Spain the less solid the Barcid conquests would seem. Many of the tribes had been overawed by Punic military might, but their loyalty might not last when another army remained in the area, its leaders doubtless making every effort to seduce the Spanish chieftains. The more traditional Carthaginian mode of war-making, enduring an enemy's on-slaught till its power began to dissipate, offered at best the prospect of a prolonged stalemate and at worst defeat when the opponent was Rome. Hannibal rejected the defensive option from the beginning and resolved that every effort should be made actively to defeat Rome. Since heavy losses abroad had in the past done little to weaken her power, Rome must be confronted and beaten on her own territory, in Italy.

In many ways, the invasion of Italy was a markedly 'Roman' enterprise, bringing heavy force to bear directly against an enemy's strength. In that sense the Romans perhaps should have been less surprised than they were when Hannibal chose this option, but the past record of Punic war-making did not suggest such a bold venture likely, especially in view of the practical difficulties involved. A seaborne invasion was scarcely feasible in 218. Without bases in Sicily, even southern Italy was at the very limit of operational range for a fleet of galleys operating from North Africa, and Punic naval power in Spain was not great. In either case a landing on a hostile shore, probably in the face of opposition from the powerful Roman navy, was a highly risky venture and it is doubtful that a large enough army could have been landed to operate with any effectiveness.[16] This left the option of a land invasion from Spain, but the difficulties were formidable. Such an expedition involved a march of hundreds of miles through tribes which were at best neutral and potentially hostile, and the crossing of the major obstacle formed by the Alps. Once in Italy the Punic army would have no base, no supplies and be faced by steadily increasing numbers of enemies. It was a bold venture and our familiarity with the story should not blind us to the shock which the Romans must have received when they learned that this was precisely what Hannibal had done.

After the fall of Saguntum Hannibal withdrew to New Carthage for the winter, lavishly rewarding his soldiers with a proportion of the spoils from the city. His Spanish troops were allowed to disperse to their homes and families, having orders to reassemble by the beginning of spring. Correctly anticipating the Romans' course of action, Hannibal took measures to bolster the defences of both Africa and Spain. The figures for the forces involved are unusually precise by ancient standards and Polybius tells us that they came from an inscription erected by order of Hannibal himself during his time in Italy. Africa received a force of 1,200 Iberian horse and 13,850 foot, supported by 870 of the wild slingers from the Balearic Islands. A small detachment of these troops were stationed in Carthage itself, along with 4,000 Libyan foot, who in addition provided hostages for the good behaviour of their home communities. The bulk of the force was garrisoned in the area of Libya known as Metagonia. Hannibal's brother Hasdrubal was given command of the Spanish province, continuing the tradition of government by the Barcid family. Hasdrubal seems to have been an able man and certainly held the trust of his brother, but the personal nature of loyalty amongst the Spanish tribes may well have been another reason for this decision. In addition to the allies which could be levied in the province, Hasdrubal received a strong force of African soldiers. Altogether he had twenty-one elephants, 2,550 cavalry (consisting of 450 Liby-Phoenicians and Libyans, 300 Spanish Ilergetes, and 1,800 Numidians from four different tribes), and 12,650 infantry, mostly Libyans, but including 300 Ligurians and 500 Balearic slingers. Naval support was provided by a small fleet of fifty 'fives', two 'fours' and five 'threes', but only a proportion of these, thirty-two quinqueremes and all the triremes, were properly manned and ready. The exchange of soldiers levied in Spain and Africa was considered a good way of ensuring their loyalty, making it harder for them to desert and return to their homes.[17]

The bulk of preparations were concerned with the Italian expedition, massing a huge total of 12,000 cavalry and 90,000 infantry according to Polybius. Sadly he does not go into any detail about their composition, although it is likely that most of the nationalities and troop types in the other forces were represented. The bulk were evidently from the Spanish Peninsula and later events make it clear that they included representatives from all the main peoples of the region, Iberians, Lusitanians and Celtiberians. These tribal peoples provided good close order cavalry and both close order and open order foot. Then there was a strong contingent of African regular infantry, well drilled and disciplined, Numidian light horse and perhaps some foot, and a corps of war elephants, thirty-seven in number according to Appian.[18] This army was far larger than any force recorded for the Carthaginians during the century and it is likely that many of the soldiers, and particularly the Spanish, had been raised relatively recently. The core of the army were the troops who had won the many wars of conquest in Spain under Hannibal, his father and his brother-in-law. They were led by a staff of senior officers whom they knew and trusted. Together these men had welded the warriors of many disparate races into a highly efficient fighting force which, for its numbers, was probably better than anything else in existence in the Mediterranean world at that time.

This huge force of troops by the standards of the day required massive logistic support to feed, clothe and equip itself. This must have occupied

Hannibal and his officers throughout the winter and probably for many months or even years before. It has been suggested that Hannibal's Spanish campaigns from 221 had as one of their main aims the capture of some of the more fertile regions of the Peninsula to ensure a grain supply for his planned Italian expedition.[19] There were many other arrangements which also could not have been completed swiftly. Men were sent to gather as much information as possible about the proposed route for the march to Italy and in particular such major obstacles as the Alps. Representatives went amongst the tribes along the route and especially those of Cisalpine Gaul, seeking their support against Rome once the army arrived in Italy. The recent memory of heavy defeats inflicted by the Romans since 225 ensured that such approaches met a with warm reception. Having allies beyond the Alps, Hannibal could anticipate securing supplies of food as well as adding many warriors to his army. Polybius tells us that the emissaries had returned by the end of the winter assuring him of the welcome he would receive. This means that at the very latest these must have left as soon as Saguntum fell and it is distinctly possible that they went before. All of these arrangements suggest that the Italian expedition, and thus the war with Rome, had long been pondered and perhaps actively prepared by the young Punic general. The expectation of Gallic assistance as part of the plan has been seen by some as proving that the concept cannot have been devised before 225 and therefore at the earliest was created by Hasdrubal rather than Hamilcar. However, perhaps all this meant was that an earlier plan became more practical from that date. Once again without accounts from the Carthaginian perspective we can only speculate about all of this. Hannibal undertook one other preparation during the winter, perhaps as important by ancient, if not modern, standards as all the others: travelling to Gades to sacrifice at the Temple of Melquart – Herakles, a deity associated with his family and depicted on some of the coins they issued.[20] There he fulfilled vows taken earlier and made fresh ones for the success of his expedition.

What was Hannibal's objective in invading Italy? This topic has long been the subject of fierce debate, often revolving around his decision not to march on the city of Rome itself when he apparently had the opportunity in 217 and 216. The most commonly held view now is that Hannibal's plan was never to capture the city of Rome itself, but to weaken her power by persuading as many of her Italian and Latin allies as possible to defect. Therefore, when Hannibal negotiated an alliance against Rome with Philip II of Macedon, the terms clearly anticipated that Rome would still exist in a weakened state after their joint victory. Similarly, Livy tells us that after

155

Cannae in 216, Hannibal addressed his Roman prisoners and claimed that he was not fighting to destroy them, but 'for honour and power'.[21] The answer is a good deal simpler than the controversy over this would suggest. Hannibal attacked Italy to win the war. It was rarely possible in this period for one side to destroy its enemy utterly in war, unless the states involved were very small and one had an overwhelmingly advantage. Later, in 146, Rome possessed such an advantage over Carthage and was able after a hard struggle to destroy her as a political entity. Normally wars, particularly wars between states as large as Carthage or Rome, ended when one side lost the willingness to fight on, not the ability to do so. Then, as Carthage had nearly done in 255 and had actually done in 241, they acknowledged defeat and accepted peace terms which reflected this. The objective of any war was to force the enemy into a position where they would give in. The method was perhaps to win one or several pitched battles, to capture enemy cities, ravage their fields and burn their villages, or most often a combination of all these things. All the more powerful states had absorbed many smaller communities as subordinate allies of varying willingness. A demonstration of the weakness of their masters at the hands of an invader was likely to prompt defections, each group hoping to side with the eventual winners in any conflict. Most city states and tribes were riven by factional divides, who were often willing to side with an external power willing to give them control of their own people. In this way the Sicilian cities had flocked to join Rome after her initial successes in 264, whilst in 240 the Libyans had rapidly sided with the rebellious mercenaries. During the course of this war the tribes of Spain proved ever ready to abandon their alliance and join the side which appeared to be winning. A state seeing its allies and subjects breaking away would be under even more pressure to compromise and accept defeat. Therefore, it was not unreasonable to believe that, if Hannibal could reach Italy and begin winning victories there, Rome's allies would begin to waver. Hannibal was not adopting a novel strategy, and there is no need to claim that he appreciated that Rome's real strength lay in her network of allies. He was simply fighting a war in the normal way. What was unusual about his plans, at least in comparison to recent Carthaginian warfare, was the willingness to act so aggressively and attempt to force a decision in the war.[22]

Before following the Carthaginian army on their epic march to Italy, it is worth pausing to consider what sort of man their commander was. Hannibal was about 28-years-old when he left New Carthage in the spring of 218. It is not clear whether he had remained in Spain since his father took him there at the age of 9,[23] but he certainly had served on many campaigns there and was already an experienced soldier. His education seems to have included a strong Greek element and he was to take Greek historians with him on his expedition. Our sources are unanimous in admiring his military virtues. For Polybius he personified in every respect the ideal of Hellenistic generalship, planning operations carefully and acting with caution, but willing to be very bold when the situation required it. Livy depicts him more in accordance with literary clichés of his day. Therefore, like the best Roman commanders he was as proficient with his personal weapons as he was in directing the movements of an entire army. On campaign he shared the physical hardships of his men, sleeping in the open wrapped only in a military cloak, and wearing the same clothes as the ordinary soldiers, although Livy does note that his equipment and horses were of such high quality as to make him conspicuous. Physically brave and inclined to lead from close to the fighting, he had the moral courage to take decisions and adhere to them.[24]

Even his enemies acknowledged his military genius, though they were inclined to accuse him of Punic perfidiousness, perhaps because he had so often outwitted them. They also believed him to be cruel, although a similar charge could be laid against most of the 'Great Captains' of antiquity and Polybius suggested that some of the more brutal acts attributed to him may in fact have been committed by one of his subordinates, another Hannibal, nicknamed Monomachus, which means 'fighter of single combats' or 'duellist'. This man is supposed to have shocked a meeting of senior officers called by Hannibal to plan the invasion of Italy by suggesting that they solve their supply problems by training the soldiers to eat human flesh. Polybius also believed that men may be forced to commit acts of great cruelty in spite of an otherwise good nature, if a difficult military or political situation made such actions necessary. Polybius seemed to accept the charge repeated by most of our sources that Hannibal was overly avaricious. However, the sources he gives for this, namely a conversation with King Masinissa, the Numidian leader who defected to the Romans later in the war and had little love for his former Punic masters, and the opinion of Hannibal's political rivals who forced him into exile from Carthage in the years after the war, do not inspire confidence. Hannibal's apparent thirst for money may well have been necessary throughout the Italian campaign to support his army and pay his soldiers.[25]

The true character of Hannibal eludes us. None of our sources provide the equivalent of the anecdotes told about the childhood and family life of the important Greek and Roman politicians of the era, many of whom were the subject of detailed biographies. We can say a good deal about what

Hannibal did during his career, and often understand how he did it, but we can say virtually nothing with any certainty about what sort of man he was. As with so much else about Carthage and its leaders, there are so many things that we simply do not know, that even our sources probably did not understand. Was Hannibal for instance a Hellenized aristocrat who dreamed of copying and surpassing the great expeditions of Alexander or Pyrrhus, or did he remain very much the Punic nobleman with a very different set of beliefs and ambitions? Much as we try to understand Hannibal, he will always remain an enigma.

The March to Italy

The actual route Hannibal's army followed on its march to Italy has long fascinated historians. Even in Livy's day, there was a fierce dispute over which pass the Carthaginians had taken over the Alps. For many people, tracing the route has become a passion, and academics and ex-soldiers, including no less a figure than Napoleon, who himself campaigned in the area, have indulged in endless speculation, often spending many days travelling over the land itself. Their conclusions have varied enormously and unfortunately the nature of our sources makes it impossible to resolve these disputes. I do not intend to discuss this topic since it would be impossible to do it justice in the framework of a treatment of all three Punic Wars, in addition to which I do not possess the intimate knowledge of the ground of the best contributors in this field. In this section we shall simply trace the major events of Hannibal's march, mentioning only in passing the most favoured theories concerning the location of these episodes.[26]

Hannibal set out from New Carthage in late spring 218 and moved towards the River Ebro, a distance of about 325 miles (2,600 stades). His huge army probably advanced in several smaller groupings to relieve congestion on the main routes and ease the supply situation, for they crossed the river in three separate columns at different places. Although the Ebro treaty had earlier been of great significance, war between Rome and Carthage was already certain by this point, and the crossing merely confirmed this. Hannibal led his troops in a series of lightning expeditions against the tribes between the Ebro and the Pyrenees. Speed was essential if he was to reach Italy before the end of the year, so Hannibal drove his soldiers hard and was willing to accept a high casualty rate, taking fortified towns by direct assault and fighting a number of actions. After perhaps a month of intense fighting, at least four tribes had been overawed by this display of Punic military might and the violence of the onslaught. Yet the area was certainly not conquered and, like many other parts of Spain subdued by the

Barcids, would remain peaceful only so long as the Carthaginians were perceived to be strong. To control the region Hannibal left an officer named Hanno, giving him a force of 1,000 cavalry and 10,000 infantry.[27]

Although it has sometimes been suggested that Hannibal originally planned to remain west of the mountains to await the anticipated Roman invasion of Spain and only pushed on towards Italy when the Romans were delayed by the Gallic rebellion, this is not supported by our sources.[28] Instead he made a few quick alterations to his force and pushed on through the Pyrenees. All his heavy baggage was to be left behind with Hanno to allow the unencumbered army to move faster. It was now late summer and the harvest was due or already gathered in the lands the army was to pass through, allowing Hannibal to reduce the amount of food and forage carried in his pack train and instead live off the land. The great size of the army had been useful in the rapid campaign beyond the Ebro, but such numbers would prove hard to feed and difficult to control on the longer march to Italy, so Hannibal planned to take only the best soldiers. About 10,000 Spanish warriors were released from service and sent back to their homes. Some of these, and perhaps many others, had deserted of their own accord; one contingent of 3,000 Carpetani are mentioned as doing so during the crossing of the Pyrenees. By the time Hannibal crossed into Gaul he had an army of 9,000 cavalry and around 50,000 infantrymen, still large by the standards of the day, but more manageable and highly experienced. Even with the other detachments mentioned by our sources, the army's numbers had shrunk by some 20,000 men. Some of these were doubtless casualties in the operations beyond the Ebro, but the majority were probably stragglers and deserters. If, as seems likely, much of the army consisted of recently raised and inexperienced troops, many of these may well have lacked both the enthusiasm and the stamina to undertake the long marches Hannibal expected from his soldiers.[29]

After the Pyrenees, which were crossed without major difficulties, the next important obstacle was the River Rhone. Earlier diplomatic activity and the reception of chieftains with lavish gifts had proved highly successful and it was not until the river that Hannibal faced his first military opposition from the Gallic tribes. Polybius tells us that he reached the river at a point about four days' march from the sea, but the precise location is disputed. The people to the west of the river were generally friendly, especially when the Carthaginians began to pay them for the use of their boats and other material needed for the crossing, but on the far bank a sizeable tribal army had mustered to contest his crossing. Livy says that the tribe was the Volcae, the same people who lived on both sides of the river, but that most had fled to the far bank as the Carthaginians approached. The river was a formidable obstacle, and Hannibal was reluctant to force a crossing in the face of such strong opposition, so camped beside it and waited whilst his men constructed rafts. The Gauls may well have hoped that a display of force and the width of the river might have deterred the invader from attacking at all, for it seems to have been common amongst many tribes to use physical boundaries to mark the point at which they would defend their territory. In tribal warfare a show of determination may often have been enough to persuade an enemy to withdraw.[30]

Three nights after his arrival, Hannibal sent a detachment of men under cover of darkness to seek a crossing point upstream, giving the command to another Hanno, this one known as 'the son of Bomilcar the Suffete'. Led by local guides this party, which consisted mainly of Spaniards, marched about 25 miles to reach a point where the river forked and formed an island. Building rafts, and with some of the Spaniards swimming with the aid of inflated animal skins, they crossed and camped; Hanno then allowed his weary men a day's rest. The next night, the second after they left the main army, this detachment pushed south, arriving near the Gallic army by dawn. Using a prearranged signal, they lit a beacon to inform Hannibal of their presence. At once he ordered his army to cross the river, some of the horses being towed behind rafts or boats. The Gauls mustered to oppose them, but began to panic when Hanno's troops made a sudden attack on their camp, setting it on fire. Hannibal seems to have crossed amongst the leading troops, for he swiftly began forming up his army on the east bank and advanced to meet the reeling enemy. The Gauls never recovered from their surprise and, perhaps dismayed to see the enemy making light of the supposedly strong obstacle, soon broke into flight.[31]

After this victory, Hannibal's main concern was to bring the remainder of his army across the river, using the craft he had purchased or constructed on the spot. Men were detailed to prepare for the major task of carrying the elephants across the river. There are several different versions of how this was achieved, but the earliest and most likely is that engineers constructed several rafts, 50 feet (15 m) in width, two of which were fastened to the western bank of the Rhone. Additional rafts were lashed into place at the end of these, creating a bridge 200 feet (61 m) in length. At the end of this roadway were two smaller rafts which could be cut free and towed across the river by small boats to ferry the animals across. To persuade the nervous animals to step onto the raft in the first place, earth was spread over the planking to make it appear like dry land, and two cow elephants driven on first to persuade the majority of male animals to follow. When the ferry was cut loose from the bridge many of the elephants panicked at the unfamiliar motion of the water and, despite the attempts of their mahouts to calm them, a few jumped into the river. Several mahouts were drowned, although all the elephants were able to make their way across.[32]

Hannibal used the delays imposed by ferrying men and animal across the Rhone to rest his army. He held parades where he brought before them representatives from Cisalpine Gaul, notably the chieftain Magilus, who encouraged the men with promises of the aid they would receive and the plunder to be gained once the army reached Italy. It was during this halt that the news arrived that a Roman fleet had anchored off the mouth of the Rhone near Massilia. Hannibal immediately despatched 500 Numidian light horsemen to reconnoitre the enemy presence and report on their activity.[33]

The Roman fleet carried the army of Publius Scipio, who, after a long delay, had at last begun his move to confront Hannibal in Spain. The Romans had left Pisa and sailed along the coast of Liguria, reaching Massilia in five days, although it is probable that at least one, and probably several, landfalls were made before this to rest the crews. Apart from the limited range of ancient fleets, it made considerable sense for the Romans to confer with the Massiliotes before proceeding on to Spain, since this Greek city and faithful ally had a far greater knowledge of the area. It is most probable that it was only after arriving at Massilia that Scipio learned of Hannibal's crossing of the Pyrenees, since only reports of his march across the Ebro seem so far to have reached Italy. The news caused an immediate change of plan. Scipio's main objective was to confront the Carthaginian general who had initiated the war and there was no point in continuing to Spain when Hannibal was in southern Gaul. The Roman troops disembarked from their transports and spent several days recuperating from their sea voyage, preparing for the anticipated battle with the enemy. It is unclear how much of Scipio's army was present, but their commander's willingness to offer battle suggests that he had the vast bulk of the consular army allocated to him. Scipio still believed that Hannibal was many days' march away, but was swiftly disabused of this idea when a report arrived that the Carthaginians had reached the Rhone. Amazed at the speed of the enemy advance, the Roman general organized a reconnaisance, sending his 300 best horsemen, led by local guides and supported by a force of Gallic mercenary cavalry provided by the Massiliotes.[34]

The rival scouting parties bumped into each other and fought a short and bloody skirmish. Our sources claim that 200 out of 300 Numidians were killed, whilst the Romans and their allies lost 140 men. If these figures are correct then they would represent exceptionally high losses in proportion to the forces involved, but it may well be that both sides made exaggerated claims for the casualties they had inflicted on the enemy. The Roman force chased the Numidians back to Hannibal's camp and certainly believed that they had won a great victory, although it is possible that the enemy light horsemen withdrew deliberately because they were there to look and not to fight. The Romans then hurried back to Scipio to inform him that they had located Hannibal and his army. The consul did not hesitate, but loaded all his heavy baggage back onto his ships and led his army as fast as possible towards the enemy with the intention of bringing him to battle. They were too late. By the time the Romans reached Hannibal's camp, they discovered that the Carthaginian army had marched on up the Rhone three days before. Scipio was in no position to follow them. His heavy baggage had been left behind and he had not had sufficient time to arrange with the Massiliotes to gather enough food to supply his army, or the pack and draught animals needed to transport it overland. At best his soldiers had food for a few more days. Foraging for provisions would have been difficult in autumn and would anyway have slowed the Romans down, making it even less likely that they would be able to intercept the enemy. Even if he had possessed better logistic support, following the enemy would have taken the Romans into unfamiliar land, peopled by probably hostile tribes, and there was no assurance that he could catch up with the enemy.

The Roman army turned around and headed back to the coast, where they re-embarked. Scipio then made a critical decision which was to have a major impact on the outcome of the war, far more so than any of his other deeds. Giving command to his elder brother Cnaeus, the former consul who was now serving as Publius' deputy or *legatus*, Scipio sent the main body of his army on to Spain to attack the Barcids' bases. Publius himself hastened by sea back to northern Italy, planning to take charge of the forces there and confront Hannibal if he was foolhardy enough to try and cross the Alps. In this way he combined an adherence to the Senate's original instructions with a reaction to cope with a changing situation. He was aware that two legions were in Cisalpine Gaul under the command of the praetors to face what appeared to be the main enemy threat. These troops would now be commanded by one of the State's most senior magistrates, who would then gain the massive glory derived from the anticipated victory.[35]

We shall discuss the activities of Cnaeus Scipio and their great importance in a later chapter. The whole encounter on the Rhone, the surprise both armies felt when they realized each other's proximity, the ease with which they broke contact and lost all awareness of each other's current position or movements, emphasizes the poor strategic intelligence available to commanders in this period. This factor must always be borne in mind by modern historians attempting to analyse their decisions.[36]

Livy tells us that Hannibal considered fighting Scipio on the Rhone. This is possible, since he had a clear numerical advantage, especially in cavalry, and was likely to have been confident of his ability to win any encounter. On the other hand, Polybius tells us that he moved straight on and, whether or not he considered other alternatives, he seems to have led his army further north along the line of the river to ensure that he was not interfered with by the Romans he had encountered operating from Massilia. The first march was covered by a screen of cavalry deployed to the south. A victory won in southern Gaul would have less impact than one fought in Italy and any delay would mean that he arrived later at the Alps and would have to cross the passes in worse weather. It is also important to remember that Hannibal too had left the bulk of his baggage train behind and was relying to a great extent on foraging to feed his men and horses. He simply could not afford to keep his army in any one place for more than a few days.[37]

Hannibal followed the Rhone for four days until he reached an area known as 'The Island', whose location is again fiercely contested, where he allowed his soldiers a short rest. Here he encountered a Gallic tribe in which two brothers were engaged in a struggle for power. Hannibal aided the elder brother, Braneus, who gratefully provided his army with supplies of food, particularly grain, as well as replacement weaponry and boots and warm clothing suitable for their passage across the mountains. The army was about to move through the territory of another Gallic tribe, the Allobroges, who had so far not responded to any attempts to negotiate safe passage. As far as the approach to the pass over the Alps, Hannibal's column was shadowed by Braneus' warriors, who protected its rear from any attack.[38]

It was probably around the beginning of November 218 when the Carthaginians began the ascent of the pass, although which pass is perhaps more fiercely debated than any other aspect of his route. In the flat country the Punic cavalry and Braneus' men had deterred any hostile moves, but as the long column began to snake its way up the pass, Allobrogian chieftains began to muster their forces along the route. Hannibal discovered that a large group had massed on high ground overlooking the path. Moving his army ostentatiously to the foot of the pass, he camped there, sending some of his Gallic guides to observe the enemy. Like many other tribesmen throughout history, the Allobroges clearly despised enemies unfamiliar with their rugged homeland and trusted too much to the protection of their high position. Hannibal's scouts discovered that at night the tribesmen, for whom predatory attacks on travellers or soldiers passing through their land were a normal supplement to the meagre livelihood of agriculture, did not bother to keep watch, but returned to their nearby settlement to sleep, mustering again the next morning. Hannibal moved his army a little nearer the next day, but camped a little short of the ambush point, making a great play of lighting many campfires. That night he led out a picked body of men carrying only their weapons and, following the narrow path, took them up to occupy the ambush position. The next day the Gauls were amazed to see their plan foiled, and for a while allowed the main column to move unhindered through the pass. In time, the temptation of seeing so many vulnerable men and animals stretched out beneath them proved too much and Allobrogian tribesmen, at first as individuals or small groups, began to make sudden attacks on the Carthaginians. In the nineteenth and twentieth centuries AD it was usually enough to 'crown the heights' on the North-west Frontier of India to ensure passage for a column moving through the valley bottom, but Hannibal's picked force were not armed with any missile weapons with sufficient range to allow them to dominate all the ground below them. At first he was forced to watch as short raids were made on vulnerable parts of the column, creating local havoc, especially amongst the animals who panicked and added to the disorder or stumbled and fell off the steep slope beside the road. Hannibal led the picked force downhill, charging against the enemy who were trying to block the head of the column, driving them off with heavy loss. Following up on this success he stormed the Gallic settlement which was largely deserted. This success showed the neighbouring tribesmen that their homes were not secure from enemy reprisals and, more practically, the settlement was found to contain many men and animals captured during the day of attacks. In addition to this, the town's grain stores provided enough food to last the whole army two or three days. Wearily the rest of the column followed on and reached this sanctuary by the end of the day.[39]

Hannibal gave his soldiers a day's rest before pushing on, encountering few problems for the next three days. At this point he was met by a group of Gallic chieftains offering peace, claiming that his capture of the Allobrogian settlement had convinced them of his might. Hannibal did not fully trust these approaches, but considered that it was better to appear to accept them and receive the guides and livestock offered by the tribesmen. His suspicion appeared to have been proved right when two days later a force of warriors made a strong attack on the rear of his column as it was travelling through a difficult and narrow pass. Fortunately he had prepared for just such an eventuality, sending his baggage train with the cavalry, who were exceedingly vulnerable in this terrain, near the front of the column and forming a strong rearguard of heavy infantry – Polybius calls them 'hoplites'. These men, probably Libyan foot, bore the brunt of the Gallic assault, defeating it with heavy loss. Even so, small groups of tribesmen, knowing the ground, made darting attacks up and down the column, going chiefly for the baggage train. In some places they rolled boulders down onto the narrow path, crushing man and beast and spreading confusion. The advance guard pushed on to the main pass, Hannibal leading them in person. They seized it, but spent an uneasy night waiting for the baggage and cavalry to catch up. The Gauls, perhaps deterred by the fierceness of the Punic reaction, or maybe because they had already acquired satisfactory amounts of booty, withdrew in the night and returned to their homes.[40]

This was the end of the major fighting during the passage over Alps, only the occasional small raid on the column occurring in the remainder of the journey. The Carthaginian war elephants proved very useful in defending against these forays, since the unfamiliar appearance of the creatures ensured that the Gauls avoided whichever parts of the column included them. Hannibal's soldiers now found that their main enemies were the elements and the terrain itself. It took nine days to reach the summit of the pass and the army stopped there for two more days, allowing many stragglers to catch up. We are even told that many of the animals who had bolted in panic during the fighting wandered into the Punic camp during this time. Morale was not good amongst the men, most of them unfamiliar with both mountains and cold, for snow, already on the heights, was now beginning to build up on the path itself. Hannibal is supposed to have made a rousing speech to the assembled troops, pointing towards the Lombard plain, assuring them of the great opportunities for loot and glory awaiting them on arrival. The ability to view the northern Italian plain is one of the many criteria used by scholars to decide which Alpine pass Hannibal actually used, although we cannot be sure whether such a view was literally visible, or conjured in the men's minds by their general's words.

The path down was difficult, slippery from snow and ice and proved especially hard for the animals with the army – horses, mules and most of all, the elephants. At one point a landslide had completely blocked the path for several hundred yards, and the deep snow made it impossible for the animals to go round. Under the direction of his engineers, Hannibal set his

Numidian horsemen to building a new path through the obstacle. It took a day to make a path suitable for the pack animals, another three to make it viable for the elephants. Livy tells the story of how Hannibal's ingenuity found a way to break up the larger boulders blocking the path. His men piled faggots of wood around the rocks, setting them on fire and keeping the pyres going until a great temperature was reached. Then they poured onto them the sour wine, which was certainly the standard ration in the later Roman army and may also have been normal with the Carthaginians, causing the rocks to crack and allowing them to be broken into pieces. This is typical of the stories told of many ancient commanders, celebrating their intelligence and adaptability as well as reinforcing the belief that a good commander needed to be a highly educated man, as knowledgeable about weather, engineering and the natural sciences as he was about the technical aspects of warfare. Polybius does not mention the incident, and it may be a later invention, although it certainly became firmly embedded in the Hannibal myth, but there is nothing inherently impossible about it.[41]

The army suffered badly from the elements during the delay imposed by this obstacle, forced as they were to camp on the bare mountain sides. All were weary and weak by the time they moved down into the lower valleys, where the snow had not yet settled and there was grass for the animals. Three days after clearing the landslide, the army reached the flatter country. Polybius tells us that the army took fifteen days to cross the Alps, but it is not certain if this includes the entire journey or only the passage of the last, highest pass. It may be that three to four weeks elapsed between the beginning of the ascent in the territory of the Allobroges and the arrival on the plain to the south of the mountains. The entire march from New Carthage had taken five months. It had been an epic journey, leading in ancient minds to an obvious comparison with the hero and demigod Herakles, who had also crossed the Alps in the mythical past. Not for the first or last time, Hannibal had done what the Romans had not expected or believed impossible. He had ensured that this war would be fought on Italian soil. It now remained to seen what his invading army could achieve now that it had reached its destination.[42]

CHAPTER 7

Invasion

HANNIBAL WAS ACROSS the Alps, but all the effort up to this point had done no more than to place him in a position to begin the assault on his real enemy. The cost of getting this far had been enormous. For the moment his soldiers were exhausted by their privations, incapable of effective operations until they had been rested and fed. Very few of them were left: only 6,000 cavalry and 20,000 infantry – 12,000 Libyans and 8,000 Spanish – were still with the colours when the army came down from the mountains. Hannibal had been followed into Gaul by 9,000 horse and 50,000 foot; 8,000 and 38,000 respectively had crossed the Rhone, so in the course of a few months he had lost more than half of his army. Only a small minority of these losses were battle casualties. It has sometimes been claimed that large detachments were left behind to control the Gallic tribes and ensure the safe passage of future reinforcements and supplies from Punic Spain, but there is no good evidence for this and our sources never mention such garrisons in later narratives of the war. Nothing in Hannibal's later behaviour suggests that he expected to remain in constant communication with his base in Spain. When his brother Hasdrubal attempted to bring a reinforcing army into Italy in 215 and 207, he marched it in an expedition reminiscent of Hannibal's original invasion. It is possible that the large numbers for the earlier phases of the campaign are exaggerated, and certainly Polybius does not seem to attribute them to the same impeccable authority of the Lacinian inscription, but all our sources were convinced that Hannibal's losses before he arrived in Italy were substantial, especially during the crossing of the Alps, so it is probably best to accept them. Once again, the vast majority were probably deserters or young recruits unable to keep up on the long marches. (During Napoleon's invasion of Russia in AD 1812, it was the young conscripts who were first to give way under the strain of the rapid advance, quickly thinning the ranks of his massive army.) We should note that only 40 per cent of the infantry to reach Italy were Spanish, when these had probably formed the vast majority of the force which mustered in New Carthage earlier that spring. It is also interesting that the army's cavalry did not suffer as high a rate of attrition as the infantry, since as a rule horses break down before men. Hannibal's victories were to owe much to his numerically superior and well-disciplined cavalry and it is clear that they formed something of an élite. Perhaps they were more highly paid than the foot, and probably they were better motivated, but it is certain that Hannibal had taken great care to cosset his cavalry on the march. However, their horses must have been in a poor state and needed to be rested and properly fed. Hannibal may have lost the bulk of his soldiers in reaching Italy, but the ones he had left were the pick of the army, doubtless mainly the veterans of his family's Spanish campaigns.[1]

Hannibal had reached the northern Italian plain, descending in the tribal territory of the Taurini, roughly around modern Turin. He had two immediate priorities. The first, and most pressing, was to secure supplies of food for his men. The pack animals of the baggage train had suffered especially badly during the passage of the mountains, and it is extremely unlikely that the army was still carrying any significant reserves of food. His second concern was to recruit contingents of allied soldiers, for at present his forces were barely equivalent in size to a single consular army. Both needs could be supplied by the Gallic tribes of the area, but at first their response to his approaches was disappointing. Hannibal does not seem to have had any prior contact with the Taurini and the tribesmen were currently too busy fighting their neighbours the Insubres to be interested in joining a Punic war against Rome. The Carthaginian army surrounded the main *oppidum* or hill town of the tribe, storming it after a three-day siege. The inhabitants were massacred in a calculated display of ruthlessness intended to overawe the tribes, and the winter reserves of food usually gathered in such settlements seized to be devoured by the army.[2]

At this point the surprising news reached Hannibal that Publius Scipio, whom he had not long ago encountered on the Rhone, was operating at the head of an army in the Po valley. It was not common for Roman consuls to abandon their own army to take charge of another and Hannibal had no way of knowing that in fact Scipio's troops had continued on to Spain, so it was natural to assume that somehow the Romans had achieved the unlikely feat of transporting their army back to Italy faster than he could march there. As far as he knew, this meant that an entire consular army had already been added to whatever troops he must have assumed the

Romans already had in the area and in due course these might be augmented by further reinforcements. This made Hannibal's need to gain more troops and supplies from the Gallic tribes even more imperative. The Gauls would not rally to an invader who did not seem confident and anyway some of the tribes most likely to join him, the Insubres and Boii, lived further to the east, in the direction of the Roman army. As soon as he considered his troops sufficiently rested, Hannibal advanced down the Po. Scipio displayed the same confidence he had shown in his earlier brief encounter with the enemy and led his troops out from Placentia to confront the invader. At this stage the advance of a strong Roman force was enough to deter the nearer tribes from joining Hannibal.[3]

Both commanders are said by our sources to have assembled their soldiers and given them an encouraging speech. Such addresses were a well-established feature of ancient historiography, a rhetorical device adding drama to the narrative as the author created an elegant version of what he felt a general should have said on such an occasion. It is unlikely, though not entirely impossible, that such speeches preserve anything actually said by the commanders. However, Hannibal is said to have employed one rather unusual means to inspire his men, which may well be accurate. The Allobrogian prisoners captured during the fighting in the Alps were asked whether any would be willing to fight each other to the death, with the promise that the victor would go free and take a horse and weapons with him. The Gauls, products of a warlike society where single combats were a common means of settling disputes and frequently occurred during feasting and other celebrations, all jumped at the chance of gaining not only freedom, but glory in the process. Polybius says that a pair of warriors were chosen by lot, Livy that many pairs were selected, and both agree that they were the envy of the remaining prisoners. The Carthaginian army watched the fight and saw the victor (or victors) riding away to freedom. Hannibal is supposed to have used this to illustrate their own situation, where they were faced with a simple choice between death and fighting hard and so gaining great rewards. If Livy is to be believed he promised his soldiers land and even Punic citizenship when the war was won.[4]

The Battle of Ticinus, November 218 BC

The two armies marched towards each other along the north bank of the River Po. Probably somewhere near modern Pavia, Scipio bridged its tributary, the Ticinus, constructing a roadway across a line of moored boats, the ancient equivalent of a pontoon bridge. The Romans were now marching through the territory of the Insubres. Two days later, each army's scouts reported the enemy's presence, the first solid information which either army received about the other's whereabouts. The armies halted and camped, immediately becoming more cautious in their movements now that the enemy was close. On the next day both commanders led out a strong force and went in person to reconnoitre. Hannibal had the bulk of his 6,000 horsemen with him, and Scipio was significantly outnumbered despite having all of his cavalry, including Romans, Latins and Gallic allies, but did have the support of some of his *velites*. The first indication that either group had of the other's approach were the clouds of dust thrown up by their hoofs. Both sides were confident and deployed ready to fight. Scipio placed his *velites* in front supported by his Gallic allies and kept the Italian cavalry as a reserve. Hannibal formed a centre from his close order horse, which was mostly Spanish, and formed the Numidians into two groups, one behind each end of his line, ready to flow around the enemy flanks.

Skirmishing between the cavalry and light troops was a common preliminary to battles in this period, often occupying a number of days and tending to be very tentative. Scipio's initial deployment suggests that he expected the fight to begin with a long exchange of missiles, the cavalry units advancing rapidly to throw javelins and then retiring just as quickly. Such fluid engagements, where the fortunes ebbed and flowed as fresh, formed squadrons were committed, were considered typical of cavalry actions in the ancient world. However, any such plans were rapidly abandoned as both commanders decided that this was an opportunity to gain an early victory, which would inspire the rest of their soldiers in the anticipated battle. Hannibal must have seen that his own horsemen significantly outnumbered the enemy, whilst Scipio may well have unwisely despised the enemy whom his cavalry had so recently beaten in the skirmish on the Rhone. Before the *velites* had come close enough to throw a single javelin, both sides' close order cavalry surged forward in a full-blooded charge. The surprised *velites* fled back through the intervals between the Roman squadrons as these advanced through them. The heavy cavalry met in the centre, where a fierce standing mêlée developed, unlike the usual flowing cavalry battle. Not for the first time we hear of some horsemen dismounting to fight on foot. Contrary to popular belief, the lack of stirrups was not a major handicap to ancient cavalry, since the Romans and probably the Spanish and Gallic cavalry of this time were already using the four-horned saddle which provides an admirably firm seat. Yet men on horseback were not suited to standing fast and fighting stationary mass against stationary mass, since, apart from sacrificing their main advantages of speed and momentum, the horses are always inclined to shy or bolt. A closely formed group of men on foot were better able to endure a long combat and hold their position. Such groups provided highly effective support for their mounted colleagues, providing secure protection to rally and reform behind before charging again. This is most probably what we should understand occurred at Ticinus. The poor state of many of the Carthaginians' horses after their long and arduous march may have further encouraged this combat to be less fluid and mobile than was usual.[5]

For a while the fight was indecisive, but then the Numidians flowed around the Roman flanks. The *velites*, already nervous, panicked and were ridden down as they fled, for scattered infantry have always been intensely vulnerable to enemy cavalry. Other Numidians charged into the rear of the Roman cavalry, putting them to flight. Probably in this later stage of the fighting, Scipio himself was badly wounded. Family tradition held that the consul was saved by his 17-year-old son, also called Publius, although one early version held that a Ligurian slave was responsible. In the more popular version, the youth had been given command of a troop of cavalry stationed in the rear, and charged alone to rescue his father, shaming his reluctant men into following him. The young Publius would later prove to be Rome's greatest general of the war, the man who would conquer Spain, invade Africa and finally win the only pitched battle Hannibal ever lost as a commander, so it is unsurprising that this version of the story has been preferred by most ancient and modern authors. A small group of cavalry clustered together around the consul and made their way safely back to the Roman camp.[6]

Hannibal still expected there to be a full-scale battle in the next few days, but Scipio was clearly overwhelmed by his defeat and resolved on an immediate flight. Polybius tells us that the defeat of his cavalry showed him that it was unwise to fight on the open ground north of the River Po. His men began to withdraw during the night and the Roman army hastened back to the Ticinus. Hannibal pursued them and captured 600 men from the party left behind to destroy the bridge of boats, but only after they had completed their task. Unable to cross, the Carthaginians turned around and marched for two days westwards along the Po, until they discovered a place where the engineers could build a bridge, allowing them to cross to the south bank.[7]

Scipio pulled back as far as his base at the colony of Placentia, where he rested his soldiers and cared for the wounded. The Roman army seems to have camped to the west of the River Trebia, on the opposite bank to the city. Two days after crossing the Po, Hannibal's army arrived and formed up for battle on the flat land in front of the Roman camp. They refused the challenge, so, with his men encouraged by the enemy's timidness, Hannibal set up his own camp about 5 or 6 miles away from them. This demonstration of Roman weakness had an effect on some of the Gallic allies in the camp. In the night a group of Gauls massacred the Roman soldiers sleeping near to them in the camp, beheaded them, and then deserted to Hannibal. The Carthaginian welcomed the 200 Gallic cavalry and 2,000 infantry who came across in this way, promising them rich rewards and sending them back to their tribes to raise further support. It was at this time that his expectations for aid from the tribes began to become a reality. Chieftains from the Boii arrived bringing the Roman commissioners they had captured in their attack on the colonies earlier in the year. Hannibal made a formal alliance with the tribe, returning the prisoners to them to use as bargaining counters to regain their own hostages held by the Romans.

Scipio's position was becoming more untenable as the enemy's strength grew. The day after the Gauls had deserted, the Roman army prepared to move under cover of darkness, setting out before dawn and crossing the Trebia. Scipio moved to the high ground which rises suddenly up from the otherwise flat plain either side of the river. Withdrawing when in close contact with the enemy has always been a hazardous operation and as soon as reports came in of the Romans' departure, Hannibal launched his Numidian horsemen in pursuit. The other cavalry were despatched to support them, followed by the remainder of the army under his personal charge. Luckily for the Romans, the North African tribesmen paused to loot and burn the abandoned camp. This may be a sign of indiscipline or an indication that food was still scarce in the Punic army. The delay allowed the Roman army and most of its baggage to get across the river in safety, but even so numbers of stragglers were rounded up or killed by the enemy when the pursuit resumed. Scipio probably camped near the modern village of Rivergaro and there waited for reinforcements.[8]

Ticinus was one of the smaller actions of the war, little more than a large skirmish, but had a special importance as the first encounter between the two sides on Italian soil. The effectiveness of Hannibal's numerically superior cavalry was amply demonstrated, as was the high degree of control he and his subordinates exercised over them. This victory and the precipitate Roman flight it caused ensured his army would be able to fight in Italy, since it confirmed the decision of several of the Gallic tribes to join him. Scipio's behaviour had been typically Roman in its straightforward aggressiveness. He had marched to confront Hannibal's army as soon as possible, before he had any precise figures for its size and strength. His behaviour before the cavalry flight makes it clear that he anticipated a battle which he expected to win. The shock of his defeat, and perhaps of his own wounding, shattered his confidence. Scipio may have been right in that the open land west of the Ticinus favoured Hannibal's cavalry, but in other regards it is improbable that the Romans were significantly outnumbered by the enemy infantry and they may even have had a slight advantage. Soon the enemy numbers were to grow as more and more Gallic warriors joined them. The speed with which the Romans fled destroyed whatever façade of strength they had presented to the tribesmen.

The Battle of Trebia, late December 218 BC

The news of Hannibal's arrival in Italy had shocked the Senate, which immediately despatched an order to the other consul, Sempronius Longus, recalling him and his army from Sicily. Longus had carried out some minor operations around Sicily, but had spent most of his time preparing for the invasion of Africa at his base in Lilybaeum. It is normally assumed that the bulk of his two legions and allies were also in or near the city, but our sources are vague on this point. What is clear is the speed with which Longus was able to transport his troops to northern Italy. Our sources give slightly different versions of how the move was achieved, but it is distinctly possible that they travelled a fair distance by sea. Polybius tells us that the consul dismissed his men and put them under oath to assemble at Ariminum in northern Italy by a set date, which would imply that they travelled as individuals or in small groups. However, he also claims that the consul marched through, or more probably past Rome and outside the *pomerium* (the sacred boundary of the city, since armed men were never allowed inside the city save in triumph), fairly soon after the Senate had received reports of Ticinus, which suggests that at least part of the army moved as a formed body. The sight of the legionaries on the march proved a fillip to morale in the city, and added to the belief that at Ticinus only their cavalry had been beaten and that perhaps because of unreliable Gallic allies; Hannibal had yet to face the vaunted Roman infantry. Polybius maintained that the whole movement from Lilybaeum to Ariminum was achieved in forty days, a low but not impossible figure. Shortly afterwards, Longus marched to join his colleague.[9]

Scipio had remained unmolested by the Carthaginian army camping only a few miles away. Once again this illustrates the unwillingness of commanders in this period to force a battle with an enemy occupying a strong position, although in this case Hannibal may have been more interested in

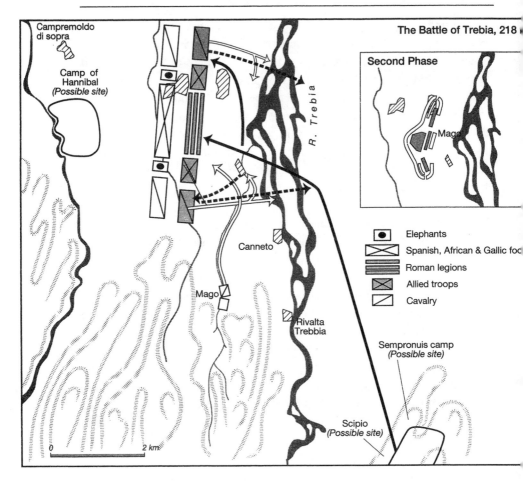

The Battle of Trebia, 218

Camp of Hannibal (Possible site)

Campremoldo di sopra

R. Trebia

Second Phase

Mago

Canneto

Mago

Rivalta Trebbia

Sempronuis camp (Possible site)

Scipio (Possible site)

Elephants	
Spanish, African & Gallic foot	
Roman legions	
Allied troops	
Cavalry	

0   2 km

raising Gallic allies. Another blow was struck to the Roman cause when their depot at Clastidium (modern Casteggio), where supplies of grain had been massed, was betrayed to the enemy. The captured food helped to ease Hannibal's continuing supply problems. The garrison commander, a native of Brundisium called Dasius, had turned traitor for the relatively modest sum of 400 gold coins. His troops, who were most likely Latin allies as the Romans did not normally give command of their own soldiers to a non-citizen, were treated well by Hannibal, who was eager to create a reputation for clemency. The Carthaginian army was not wholly inactive whilst it observed the Romans. Shortly after Longus' arrival Hannibal became suspicious that the Gallic tribesmen on the west bank of the Trebia, who had initially welcomed him, were now negotiating with the Romans. Perhaps the Gauls were genuinely duplicitous, but it may simply be that with their loose political structures, different leaders had approached each side. A force of 2,000 infantry and 1,000 Gallic and Numidian cavalry left the camp and began to ravage the area, gathering large amounts of plunder. Some of the tribesmen now did appeal for Roman aid and Longus sent a strong cavalry force with 1,000 *velites* across the river to attack the enemy raiders. The Carthaginians were scattered and encumbered with loot and the Roman attack met with rapid success, chasing the enemy in disorder back to their camp. The pickets on outpost duty outside Hannibal's camp moved out to support them and in turn the pursuing Romans were driven back. The fighting rapidly escalated as each side committed more and more troops as reinforcements, all the Roman cavalry and *velites* eventually becoming engaged. It was a fluid fight, spreading over a large part of the open plain and not one which either general could control. Hannibal decided that he did not want to feed more troops into the action and perhaps risk it developing into a full-scale battle which he had not planned and could do little to influence. Rallying the fugitives in person, he formed a fighting line only just outside his own camp, which was most likely on the high ground west of the river. He restrained any of the reformed troops from advancing again and the Romans refused to attack an enemy who was protected by missile fire from the camp, easily reinforced by the troops within it, and probably uphill. In this way the battle ended, with the Romans inflicting higher casualties and claiming a victory. Polybius praises Hannibal for the tight control he exercised over his men and his unwillingness to let a battle occur by chance, which Polybius believed demonstrated his wisdom as a commander.[10]

Longus, depicted by our sources as of an aggressive temperament, was confirmed by this success in his desire to fight a battle as soon as possible. His wounded colleague is supposed to have argued against this, predicting the disaster which did in fact occur. We must be very cautious in accepting this. This tradition may well have been spread by the Scipionic family from the immediate aftermath of the battle onwards, but it was reinforced by Polybius who was, and is, by far the most influential source for the period. It must always be remembered that the Greek historian's close association with Scipio Aemilianus led him to a favourable depiction of the latter's ancestors in his work. In this version, Scipio is supposed to have pointed out that the Roman legions had only been raised earlier in the year and would benefit from spending the winter months training, whilst Hannibal's Gallic allies might well begin to waver in their allegiance if he remained inactive, consuming their food, but winning no victories. Polybius skilfully reinforces the wisdom of these arguments by repeating them when he explains Hannibal's desire for an immediate battle. Longus did not wish to delay, for in three months' time the new consuls would take office, and before that Scipio might recover and he would have to share the glory of his anticipated victory with his colleague. Longus' boldness was typically Roman, and it is doubtful that any other Roman magistrate would have behaved differently in the circumstances. Scipio, who had led an army half the size of the force now mustered, had been just as aggressive in his pursuit of a pitched battle on the Rhone and before Ticinus, just as elated by the success of his cavalry outside Massilia, as Longus was now. It is possible that his defeat at Ticinus, and perhaps especially his own wound, had so depressed him that Scipio now doubted the likelihood of Roman victory, and probable that he hoped to postpone the battle until he could both take an active role in it and share the credit.[11]

Longus' decision to seek a battle as soon as possible reflects the deep-seated confidence in their own military prowess which pervaded all classes in Roman society and contributed so much to the formidable morale of Roman armies. The Romans enjoyed a numerical superiority over the enemy, even with the addition of their new Gallic allies, and were defending their own territory. If the Roman legionaries were still inexperienced and only partly trained, then it was also true that Hannibal's best soldiers were still weary from their arduous march to reach Italy. Refusing battle when the invader was so close was an admission of weakness and it would also be difficult to maintain both consular armies concentrated in such an advanced position throughout the winter. Defeating Hannibal decisively, so soon after his arrival, would cause his new allies to defect far more quickly than a winter of inactivity and could well end all the Carthaginian's hopes. On balance the Roman willingness to seek a battle is entirely reasonable. Equally, Hannibal's invasion needed a swift major victory if it was to gather momentum. Both commanders were surely right to risk the uncertainties of battle given the potential gains, but what distinguished the two men was that Hannibal made sure that the battle would be fought on his own terms.

In the days before the battle Hannibal and his commanders had ridden across the plain west of the Trebia, studying the ground over which he expected the battle to be fought. (The scene was paralleled when Napoleon and his Marshals examined the Pratzen Heights a few days before the Battle of Austerlitz in AD 1805; perhaps consciously so, as the Emperor was always aware of parallels from classical history.)[12] The plain west of the Trebia is wide, and as flat as any land ever is naturally, until it rises sharply at its southern and south-western edges. Hannibal located a watercourse crossing the plain and running between two steep and heavily overgrown banks, in which he decided to set an ambush under the command of his brother Mago. The day before the battle a picked force of 1,000 infantry and 1,000 cavalry, apparently mostly Numidians, was formed for this task. During the night Mago led his men secretly to the ambush position, where they concealed themselves. The watercourse presumably lay behind, but to the south of where Hannibal expected the Roman army to deploy, far enough away from their line of advance to minimize the risk of premature discovery. Polybius notes that the Romans were wary of wooded terrain, where they had often in the past been ambushed by the Gauls, but did not believe an ambush possible in an open plain.

At dawn – Polybius tells us that the day was near the winter solstice – Hannibal sent his Numidian cavalry across the River Trebia to attack the outposts stationed outside the Romans' camps and draw them into a missile fight. The Numidians had strict orders to involve the Romans in a skirmish and then steadily withdraw, luring the enemy across the river. In the meantime, Hannibal gathered his senior officers and explained his plans, encouraging them and telling them to return and prepare their soldiers for battle. The Carthaginian troops would enter the battle well fed, and physically and mentally ready for the fight.

Longus responded just as Hannibal had hoped, sending all his cavalry out against the Numidians, closely followed by 6,000 *velites*. The consul then gave orders for his entire army to muster and march out against the enemy. The Numidian light horsemen continued to skirmish, but did not become closely engaged and gradually pulled back, the Romans eagerly pursuing. The heavy infantry followed more slowly, but just as enthusiastically, almost certainly formed into three columns, each probably at least 2½ miles long. In this way they forded the River Trebia, the normally shallow waters swollen by recent rain, and processed onto the flat plain beyond it, where at a given point the columns wheeled to the right and marched along what would become the main battle line, the lead unit taking up its position at the extreme right. This was a laborious process, each column halting whilst the tribunes fixed the position of the next maniple in the line and deployed it from marching into battle formation. Eventually the Roman and allied heavy infantry occupied a frontage of some 2 miles in length. It was a long-drawn-out technical process, requiring much activity on the part of each legion's officers. This was especially so as the army was uncommonly large and relatively inexperienced, and the two elements composing it had had little time to practice manoeuvring with each other. Under these circumstances the open country west of the Trebia was ideal terrain on which to marshal such a Roman army, as suited to its tactics and drills as it favoured Hannibal's cavalry. It must have taken several hours for the army to march the 4 or 5 miles from their camps and then deploy into battle order. By the time they had done so, the men were tired and cold, still wet from fording the river and from the sleet which fell in sporadic showers. Most were also hungry, for they had been hurried out of camp without warning and had not had time to cook a meal. Yet Longus may well have been pleased with the day so far. His cavalry appeared to be winning another victory and his strong army was formed and ready facing the enemy. Either he would get the battle he desired, or his opponent would refuse to let the action escalate into a battle, in which case the consul could assure his men that the enemy were afraid of them and know that this would make them more confident when the battle did at last occur.

Hannibal continued his careful preparations for the battle. When the Roman heavy infantry began crossing the river and their army was fully committed, he sent out 8,000 light infantry to support the Numidians and form a screen behind which his army could deploy. Then, and only then, his main body left the camp and advanced a mile, where they formed into a battle line. The centre was formed by a single line of close order infantry, 20,000 strong. The Gallic allies, who were probably numbered about 8,000 men, seem to have formed the centre, with the Spanish and Libyan foot on the flanks. The close order Gallic and Spanish cavalry were placed on the wings, where they were soon joined by the retiring Numidians, so that about 5,000 horsemen mustered on each flank. Hannibal also divided his elephants into two bodies and seems to have placed them with the wings of the heavy infantry, although our sources disagree and are a little confused on this point.

Longus now recalled his cavalry and formed them onto the main line. Men and horses were tired after a fruitless morning chasing agile Numidians who never stayed to meet a charge, but fled, only to rally and return to plague the Romans with a renewed shower of javelins. The Roman army had deployed in its standard formation, with the legions in the centre, the allies on their flanks and the cavalry on the wings. Longus' four legions mustered 16,000 men according to Polybius, although Livy gives the higher figure of 18,000. In both cases they have clearly assumed an average size for each unit and multiplied this by four, so that at best this provides a rough guide to the actual number of troops. If one of the legions was the one which had been commanded by the praetor Vulso and ambushed by the Boii earlier in the year, then it is likely still to have been heavily under strength. There were 20,000 allied infantry including, according to Livy, a contingent of the last Gallic tribe to remain loyal, the

Cenomani. It is not clear whether this total of 38,000 infantry includes the skirmishers of the legions and *alae* or only the heavy infantry. It is usually assumed that the 6,000 light infantrymen mentioned earlier composed the entire skirmishing element of Longus' army, but our sources are not clear on this. Whether or not the skirmishers were included in the total, it is clear that the Romans enjoyed a significant numerical superiority in infantry. However, Longus had only 4,000 horsemen to divide between his two wings, less than half the number deployed by the enemy.

Longus remained full of confidence and advanced his whole line, carrying this out in the proper manner of a Roman general, so that the army came on slowly and in good order. Hannibal seems to have remained where he was and let them come on, perhaps wanting to ensure that the enemy moved ahead of Mago's concealed troops. Soon the skirmishers of both armies met in front of the main lines and began to exchange missiles. The Romans fared badly in this encounter, for they were tired and had used up many of their javelins whilst supporting the cavalry against the Numidians. They may also have been outnumbered if there were only 6,000 of them, and were neither as well trained nor as experienced as their opponents. Hannibal's men included the famous Balearic slingers, and the combination of their range with the shorter-distance thrown spears of the *lonchophoroi* or javelinmen probably gave the Punic skirmishers greater flexibility. As the main lines closed, the skirmishers retired through the intervals between the units of close order foot, although according to Livy it was only the advance of the *hastati* which forced the Carthaginian light infantry to pull back, after which they moved to the flanks to support their cavalry.

The Roman cavalry, weary and outnumbered, seems to have put up a feeble resistance as Hannibal at last ordered his horsemen forward. Livy claims that they were further weakened by sniping from the Balearic slingers now supporting the Punic horse, and also that the elephants frightened the Roman horses, but his account of the elephants' role in the battle is hopelessly confused. As the Roman cavalry broke, the Numidians and light infantry surged forward to lap around the flanks of the main Roman line, shooting at the allied soldiers. Polybius notes that they outstripped the close order cavalry, which may again be an indication that the mounts of these troops were not in good condition, although in this case they had begun the battle fresher than the Romans'. In spite of this support, the clash between the two main lines of close order foot was long and hard, its outcome uncertain. The *hastati* and *principes* alone outnumbered the enemy foot by a large margin and were also more heavily armoured. It must also be remembered that the Roman line was long and that it took a while for a reverse on the wings to affect the centre. Even when Mago's force emerged from ambush and attacked the rear of the Roman army, spreading confusion throughout the whole army, the legionaries maintained the struggle. Beset by the elephants and Punic foot to their front and skirmishers and Numidians to the rear, the wings of the Roman infantry eventually gave way. In the centre the legions managed to rout the Gauls and a unit of Libyans facing them, breaking right through the enemy line.

Hannibal had no reserves with which to oppose this breakthrough, for his infantry had formed in a single line. Fortunately, by this time it was clear that the Roman defeat was irredeemable, with the army degenerating into a mob of fugitives. The 10,000 legionaries who had broken through the enemy line made no attempt to rejoin the fighting, but keeping in formation, they marched north, swinging round the Punic army and recrossing the Trebia opposite Placentia, where they took refuge. Hannibal made no attempt to stop them. His men were weary and his victory was already clear. The rest of the Roman army suffered heavily in the rout, but numbers of soldiers made their way as individuals or small groups back to the camps or joined the force in the colony. We do not have a figure for the Roman losses, but these must have been heavy. Our sources are similarly vague for Hannibal's casualties, although Polybius tells us that the heaviest losses were suffered by the Celts in the centre. However, in the cold spell of weather which followed the battle, many of his men and horses and all but one of the elephants died.[13]

Longus at first attempted to portray the battle as an indecisive fight, in which he was deprived of victory only by the extreme weather, and it was some while before the Senate appreciated the scale of the disaster. The blow to Roman pride was probably more serious than the actual losses, for the victory persuaded those Gauls who had been wavering to embrace the Punic cause. Even so, the defeat was put down to Longus' mistakes, whilst the success of the Roman infantry in the centre seemed to confirm that the courage of their soldiers had not failed.

Hannibal's victory gave his campaign sufficient momentum to carry it through the months of virtual inactivity forced upon him by the winter weather. His soldiers now knew that they could beat their enemy in the open field, further increasing their faith in their commander. As a general Hannibal had consistently outperformed both of his Roman opponents, controlling his soldiers so tightly that a battle was only fought at a time and place of his own choice. He had been able to exploit the advantage given by his numerical superiority in cavalry, added to the flexibility derived from the mixture of light and heavy horse. At the Trebia his army had fought as a co-ordinated unit, focusing all its strength on the Roman wings. To further the anticipated success of his cavalry over the outnumbered Roman horsemen, the best of his infantry, the Libyans and Spanish, were placed on the flanks of the infantry centre, their attack given even more power by the support of the elephants. Mago's ambush had added to the confusion in the Roman ranks and probably reduced much of the forward impetus of their assault, in particular by involving the third line in combat, but the battle had already effectively been won by the success on the wings. The escape as a formed body of such a large part of the Roman infantry was regrettable, but once the Romans broke through the Gallic infantry there was little that Hannibal could do to stop them. Nevertheless the Roman eagerness to escape from the battlefield rather than renew the fight demonstrated that they had admitted defeat.

The Battle of Lake Trasimene, c. 21 June 217 BC

The Senate was shocked by the defeat, but began the new year grimly determined to prosecute the war with greater success. The other theatres were not ignored, but the main focus of Roman effort was to be against the enemy on their own soil and both consuls would go north against Hannibal. An air of normality was provided when Longus returned briefly to Rome to preside over the consular elections, which were won by Cnaeus Servilius Geminus and Caius Flaminius. We do not have a detailed breakdown of the citizens and allies levied in this year, but Geminus and Flaminius both seem to have been given the standard consular army of two legions and two *alae*, composed of a mixture of newly raised troops and the remnants of the armies defeated at Trebia. The legions may have had a stronger than usual complement and it is also possible that the armies contained a very high proportion of cavalry, perhaps as a reaction to Hannibal's superiority in this arm. Geminus' army is said to have included at least 4,000 horsemen, which was a very high proportion for a Roman army and probably consisted in the main of allies.[14]

Polybius' account suggests that little military activity occurred during the winter, and although Livy supplies a dramatic account of an action in which Longus gained an initial advantage, but which was ended by bad weather, this is most probably an invention. It may even derive from Longus' own self-serving account of Trebia. The usually sober Polybius does, however, recount the bizarre story of how Hannibal, distrusting many of his newfound Gallic allies, adopted a range of disguises, including a variety of differently coloured wigs, to conceal his true appearance. Perhaps the apparent ability of appearing in different forms enhanced his reputation as a powerful leader with the tribesmen, but this is no more than a conjecture.[15]

When the new campaigning season opened in the spring of 217, Hannibal had two real alternatives. Remaining in the Po valley would achieve nothing, and the continued consumption of their food by his soldiers might in time weaken Gallic support, whilst moving west into Liguria would not help to weaken Roman resistance and meant passing through country where foraging would be difficult. Hannibal needed to keep up the pressure on the Romans and this meant continuing his advance deeper into their territory. There he could feed his soldiers from the produce of enemy fields, provide them with plentiful booty, and any victories he won would be that much more disturbing to the Romans and perhaps do more to encourage the defection of their Italian allies. The direction he took could not ignore that most important feature of Italian geography, the Apennine Mountains, that solid barrier which cuts the Peninsula in two and which could only be crossed by an army in a few places. Therefore Hannibal could either move east to the sea and advance down the Adriatic coast into Picenum, or go south to the passes of the Apennines and then swing west into Etruria. These alternatives were as clear to the Senate as they were to Hannibal, and their solution was to place one consul in a position to oppose each threat. Geminus moved to Ariminum (modern Rimini) to cover the eastern coast, whilst Flaminius went to Arretium, where he could best cover the various passes over the Apennines.[16]

Caius Flaminius was to play the most prominent role in the forthcoming campaign and has suffered in our sources because he too presided over a Roman disaster and, unlike Sempronius Longus, was killed and so unable to justify his actions. Nor was his family a prominent one at Rome, so that there were few descendants able to have much influence on the widely accepted version of events, for Flaminius was a *novus homo*, a new man who was the first in his family to reach the consulship. Both Polybius and especially Livy depict him as an aggressive demagogue, a man of bold words but little talent who had based a career on pandering to the desires of the poorest citizens to overcome the opposition of most of the Senate. His career up to this point had certainly been controversial, but it had also been exceptionally distinguished, even by the standards of the third century, and especially so for a new man. We have already seen how as a tribune of the plebs in 232 he had passed a bill to distribute land in Cisalpine Gaul to poorer citizens, and in his first consulship in 223 had celebrated a triumph over the Insubres. He had also been the first praetorian governor of Sicily. Elected one of the two censors in 220 he had carried out several major projects, including the construction of the Circus Flaminius in Rome and the *via Flaminia* which ran from the city to Ariminum, connecting the city with the newly colonized land. He was clearly something of a maverick, a politician who achieved his ambitions by methods that were anything but traditional. His land law had been disliked by many in the Senate, and he had gained a reputation for impatience during his first consulship, refusing to be recalled on religious grounds and only celebrating his triumph by Popular vote, after the Senate had refused him this honour. The most successful politicians at Rome were the men who got what they wanted quietly and without such crises. Men like Flaminius made many enemies who only waited for them to become vulnerable to exploit this weakness. In his case they were allowed to savage his reputation after his death.[17]

Flaminius' election was no protest by a 'democratic party' against the Senate's handling of the war. As we have seen such terms have no relevance for Roman politics, and anyway Flaminius' candidature almost certainly predated the news of Rome's early defeats. That he was an experienced man, who had fought successfully against the very Gauls now joined with Hannibal, may well have been useful in his election campaign, but Flaminius must have had some support in the Senate, even if few wished to admit to this after his defeat. Certainly he must have won the votes of many of the wealthier citizens and cannot have relied simply on the poorest to have been successful in the *Comitia Centuriata*. It is important not to confuse modern concepts of 'popular support' with Roman or be taken in by the language of political insults at Rome. It is possible that Flaminius exploited a body of support outside the traditional family systems of patronage which tended to dominate the Roman assemblies, for his career as tribune and censor had given him many opportunities of winning the favour of the wealthier classes outside the Senate. The distribution of the *ager Gallicus* and his building projects all gave opportunities to award lucrative contracts and win important friends.

Flaminius proved impatient to begin operations, flouting convention by taking up office on 15 March not in Rome, but at Ariminum. Livy says that he was afraid that his rivals in the Senate would manipulate the auspices and delay him in Rome as long as possible, hoping to deprive him of his command, fears which were probably not groundless. To avoid this, he pretended to leave the city on private business and instead went to join the army.[18] Militarily this made sense, since it was important to have his army in position to cover the approaches to Etruria before Hannibal made any move and the armies last year had withdrawn to this town. It did mean that Flaminius did not properly carry out the rituals normally presided over by an incoming consul, and further alienated the Senate by ignoring the commission sent to recall him to Rome. As with Claudius at Drepana, the consul's disrespect for the gods was later held to be a major factor in his defeat.[19]

Hannibal moved as soon as the arrival of spring made it easier for his army to forage. As usual he moved quickly and in an unexpected direction. He had decided to cross the mountains into Etruria, partly because the area was fertile enough to support his soldiers, but also because it would allow him to pose a more direct threat to Rome. He crossed the Apennines probably by the Porretta, or perhaps the Colline pass, and forced his way through the marshes around the River Arno, which had flooded after the winter rains, driving his army hard to push it quickly through this difficult terrain. His most disciplined infantry, the hard-marching Africans and Spanish, led the way with the baggage train, setting a fast pace which the Celtic warriors, unused to the rigours of campaigning, found difficult to maintain. It is anyway always harder and more aggravating to march in the rear of a column. Hannibal's cavalry brought up the rear and chivvied along the Gallic stragglers. It took three days and nights to get through the marshes and the army suffered much in the process, the men finding it difficult to rest on the muddy ground so that some were only able to sleep by lying on pack saddles, or the corpses of the many baggage mules which collapsed and died during the journey. Hannibal himself suffered badly from ophthalmia, eventually losing the sight in one eye since the conditions did not allow proper treatment, and had to be carried for much of the journey by the sole surviving elephant with the army, perhaps the brave 'Syrian' mentioned by Cato.[20]

Once again Hannibal had done the unexpected, getting his army across a major obstacle in spite of the difficulties and without interference from the enemy. He was now in position to begin the next stage of his campaign. Granting his men a few days' rest when they emerged from the marshes somewhere near Faesulae, Hannibal sent out scouting parties to locate the Romans and gain as much information about the area as possible. Learning that Flaminius was at Arretium, and confirming that the rich plain of Etruria should offer plentiful food to support his army and booty to encourage his soldiers, he decided to push past the Roman army and lure them into following him south. He is said to have realized that Flaminius was a rash commander who was likely to pursue incautiously and so give opportunity for a battle in conditions favourable to the Carthaginians.

Such a move would also draw the Roman army further away from the support of whatever forces they had stationed east of the Apennines – Hannibal is unlikely to have known the precise location of Geminus' army – who would doubtless attempt to join Flaminius as soon as they had confirmed which way Hannibal was going. Other factors made such a plan both feasible and desirable. Hannibal had established no permanent base from which he intended to keep his army supplied and so had no lines of communication which the Roman army could cut if he left it in his rear. Instead he relied on gathering food and forage from the land through which he was passing, carrying just enough in his baggage train to keep men and horses fed until the next opportunity came to stop and scour the neighbourhood for supplies. Although this granted his army considerable freedom of movement, it also meant that the army could never afford to stop moving for any length of time, since they would swiftly consume all the available resources of that locality. The problem was made more acute now that he had left behind the allied tribes of Cisalpine Gaul. Therefore, to move on Arretium, and hope to draw Flaminius into battle on favourable terms before his army ran out of food and had to disengage, was highly risky. Hannibal simply could not afford to fight too many indecisive battles, or win minor victories at the cost of high casualties amongst his irreplaceable experienced soldiers. Bypassing the Roman army gave Hannibal the initiative and ensured that he would dictate the course of the campaign.[21]

Flaminius immediately responded as the Carthaginian had predicted, and indeed as any other Roman commander of this period, and certainly the consuls of 218, would have acted. As soon as he realized that the Punic army had passed him and was devastating the land of Rome's allies, he marched out of Arretium in pursuit. He is supposed to have ignored the advice of his senior officers, as well as a series of bad omens, such as when his horse threw him, and the standard bearers had difficulty pulling the standards free from the ground where their iron butts had been planted to hold them upright. It is possible that some officers advised the consul to wait until he had been reinforced by his colleague, since Flaminius' soldiers on their own were significantly outnumbered by the enemy, but this is more probably part of the tradition which placed the sole blame for the disaster on the commander. As the Roman army marched south, it passed through the area laid waste by the enemy, through villages pillaged and burned. It was immensely humiliating when an enemy could violate the fields of a state or its allies without any interference from the army of that state, and reflected badly on its military prowess. It is important to

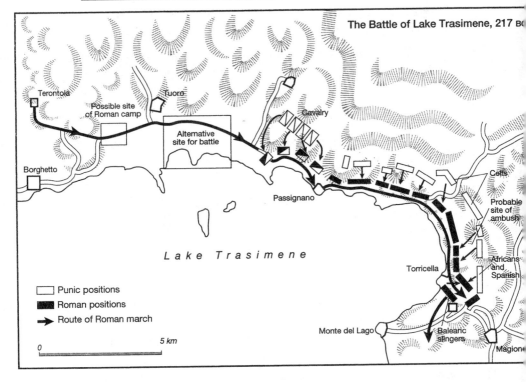

The Battle of Lake Trasimene, 217 BC

Terontola

Possible site of Roman camp

Tuoro

Cavalry

Alternative site for battle

Borghetto

Passignano

Celts

Probable site of ambush

Lake Trasimene

Torricella

Africans and Spanish

☐ Punic positions
◼ Roman positions
➤ Route of Roman march

Monte del Lago

Balearic slingers

Magione

0   5 km

remember that the Roman army was still largely recruited from a rural population of farmers and their sons, commanded by officers who were themselves landowners. They retained much of the old hoplite ethos which held the preservation of the community's land to be the highest duty of the citizen under arms. When the enemy openly ignored a Roman army and felt free to plunder the land at will, this implied that it held Roman might in contempt and issued a direct challenge to prove otherwise. Few, if any, states in the ancient world were able to resist such provocation without admitting their own weakness. The Romans were no exception, especially since they were still convinced of the superiority of their infantry despite the defeat at Trebia.

As Flaminius and his army hastened to catch up with the enemy in the first weeks of June, it may well have seemed that the Carthaginians were fleeing because they were terrified of Roman arms. According to Polybius the Roman column was swollen by volunteers anticipating an easy victory and bringing along fetters and chains they expected to use on the prisoners they would capture and sell as slaves.[22]

Hannibal continued south, deliberately provoking the Romans with the savagery of his depredations. They were now no more than a day's march behind him. Passing the city of Cortona, he came to Lake Trasimene and saw an opportunity as the main route continued through a defile with the shore on one side and a line of hills on the other. On 20 June the Carthaginian army marched past the lake and very visibly pitched a camp at the far end of the line of hills. During the night Hannibal divided his troops into several columns and led them round behind the hills, taking up positions parallel with the path. Such night marches are never easy and it was no small feat for an army composed of so many different nationalities to make their way quietly to the correct positions without confusion or discovery by the enemy, who had pitched camp near the lake shore late in the day. Most, if not all, of the troops were positioned on the reverse slopes of the high ground, concealed from the enemy's view when the sun came up. The cavalry were on the flank nearest to the Romans, ready to swing round behind the enemy column once it had completely entered the defile and cut off their retreat. The Celts formed the centre and the African and Spanish foot the left flank near the Punic camp. The javelin skirmishers and Balearic slingers were probably to the left of these troops ready to close the exit to the defile. Precisely where on the northern or eastern shores of Lake Trasimene the ambush was set is now impossible to know, since our sources are unclear and sometimes contradictory. It is also uncertain where the third-century shore-line lay in relation to the modern lake and possible that it has changed considerably.[23]

Flaminius' army was ready to move at dawn on the 21st, clearly expecting to close with his quarry today. The morning was misty, the line of hills mostly obscured, but it is possible that he could see the Punic camp at the far end of the defile. He may well have formed his army into the three columns ready to wheel into the *triplex acies* which was the normal way to approach the enemy, but our sources are vague, and much would depend on the width of the level ground between hills and lake in the third century BC. Had the army been in a single column this would have stretched for at least 5 miles and probably considerably more, making it unlikely that the whole force could have fitted into any of the likely ambush positions. Flaminius did not send out scouts, but it was rare for Roman armies at this time to take much care over reconnoitring their line of advance. It was normally assumed that in daylight any enemy numerous enough to present a threat would be clearly visible for some distance.[24]

As the Roman army marched steadily along the lakeside Hannibal's waiting soldiers maintained admirable discipline. It was only when the Roman vanguard – usually composed of Roman and allied cavalry and the *extraordinarii* followed by one of the Latin *alae* – bumped into the left of

187

the Punic line, either the skirmishers or the Libyans and Spanish, that Hannibal sent orders for the remainder of his army to attack. Soon attacks began to come in downhill from all directions. The Roman army was thrown into confusion. The soldiers could see little, since the mist still lay heavy in the defile and visibility was limited, and instead they heard enemy war cries and the sounds of fighting from many different directions simultaneously.

From the moment that the ambush was sprung Hannibal's victory was certain, for the Roman army was in a hopelessly bad position. Nevertheless there were to be three hours of heavy fighting before that victory was complete. The Romans may well have been marching in three columns, but it took time and considerable supervision to turn this formation into anything resembling a proper fighting line. At Trasimene there was little or no time, and anyway none of the officers knew where and facing in which direction to form a line. In some places there was panic as the soldiers fled from real or imagined foes looming out of the mist. Elsewhere the legionaries clustered together, often led by their centurions, sometimes by tribunes, and held their ground with that grim determination which so often characterized the Roman soldier. The fighting was especially heavy in the centre where the Gallic warriors suffered heavy losses as they gradually beat down the Roman resistance.

Polybius claims that Flaminius panicked and fell into despair, until he was killed by unnamed Gauls, but Livy, who has little else to say in favour of the consul, describes behaviour more appropriate for a Roman senator in the face of crisis. In this version, Flaminius galloped around the army, shouting out encouragement to the soldiers and trying to organize their resistance. Rallying a group of the bravest soldiers, he charged to the aid of his men wherever he saw them sorely pressed. Easily recognizable by his splendid equipment, the consul became the focus for enemy attacks, particularly from Hannibal's Gallic allies, who are supposed to have recognized him as the man who had defeated their warriors and laid waste their lands in 223. According to Silius Italicus' epic poem, Flaminius had adopted the further provocation of wearing a Gallic scalp on the crest of his helmet. This work is often fanciful and this may simply be a lurid invention, although if it is true it presents a far more savage image than we normally associate with the civilized Roman aristocracy. Finally, an Insubrian cavalryman, whom Livy names Ducarius, charged the Roman lines, killed Flaminius' personal bodyguard and then impaled the consul himself with his spear. However, a group of legionaries, *triarii* according to Livy although he may have been using the term generally, drove the Gauls back and saved the consul's corpse from being despoiled and beheaded.

The confusion may not all have been on the Roman side. Hannibal's army had started the battle spread over a wide area of hilly ground and had to cope with the same problems of visibility as the Romans, so their attacks may not have been as perfectly co-ordinated as our sources suggest. The Roman vanguard broke through the enemy opposing them, perhaps the light infantry, and pushed on up the road. At some point they had lost contact with the troops behind them, perhaps as some officer drew them off to form a line facing one of the other threats. About 6,000 men pushed on in this way and found no more enemies in front of them, but it was only as they climbed out of the defile and the mist began to thin that they were able to look back and see the scale of the disaster which had befallen the rest of the army. Organized resistance had largely collapsed with the consul's death. Men were killed as they ran, abandoning their weapons, or drowned as they tried to swim to safety across the lake. Others waded out into the water, submerging up to their necks, and later the Punic cavalrymen amused themselves by swimming their horses into the water and hacking at the bobbing heads. The vanguard could do nothing useful by turning back, so marched on to take sanctuary in a nearby village. Later in the day, Hannibal sent Maharbal with some Spanish troops supported by the javelinmen to surround the place. The vanguard surrendered on the promise that their lives be spared and, according to Livy, that they be allowed to go free with the clothes they wore, but nothing else. Hannibal did not approve the agreement made by his subordinate. The Romans were enslaved, but as usual the allies, who probably formed the bulk of this group, were well treated and allowed to return home with the assurance that he was fighting on their behalf against their Roman masters.

Fabius Pictor claimed that 15,000 Romans were killed, whilst 10,000 men were dispersed and gradually made their way back to Rome. It is unclear whether this figure included prisoners, such as the 6,000 men of the vanguard, but Polybius says that Hannibal captured around 15,000 men. He also gathered a great quantity of booty and in particular military equipment. Soon the Libyan infantry were re-equipped as Roman legionaries, each man being given mail, a bronze helmet and an oval *scutum*, although it is unclear whether they also adopted Roman *pila* or swords. Hannibal's own losses were much less, either 1,500 or 2,500 depending on the source, the vast majority Gauls, but including thirty senior officers. A loss of 3–5 per cent was not too high a price to pay for the annihilation of the enemy as an effective force, but, given the tactical advantages enjoyed by the Punic army, it testifies to the ferocious resistance put up by many of the Roman and allied soldiers. Hannibal buried his own dead, and particularly his officers, with some care and attempted to locate the body of Flaminius in order to pay the consul the same courtesy, but was unable to find it. Perhaps the Insubres had disposed of it after their own fashion, but it may simply have been lost amongst the many dead, or quickly stripped of its armour and clothing by looters thus becoming unrecognizable.[25]

Within a few days the Romans suffered another disaster. Geminus had been hurrying to join his colleague and had sent on ahead 4,000 cavalry under one Gaius Centenius. Hannibal learned of their approach before the Romans knew of Flaminius' defeat. Maharbal took another column out and launched a surprise attack on the Roman horsemen. Those who were not killed in the first onslaught retired to some high ground, but were surrounded and surrendered the next day. The loss of its cavalry effectively removed whatever threat had been posed by the other Roman army in the field.[26]

Few commanders have been able to repeat Hannibal's feat of ambushing and effectively destroying an entire army. He had dictated the course of the entire campaign, luring Flaminius on into a hopeless position. These operations highlighted not only Hannibal's superiority as a general, but the greater flexibility of his army. Not only had his troops had the skill to move into ambush positions under the cover of darkness, without getting lost or ending up in the wrong place, and then demonstrated their discipline by not attacking prematurely, but the ability of his subordinates was demonstrated by the two successful columns taken out by Maharbal. The Romans still expected battles to be open and formal, where the courage of their legions, closely controlled by their officers, would win the day, and did not take the same care as their opponent to keep the enemy under constant surveillance and always, where possible, to surprise him.

The 'Delayer'

This second disaster, following only six months after Trebia, shocked Rome. As rumours spread and the first survivors began to reach the city, the urban praetor, Marcus Pomponius, climbed onto the Speaker's platform in the Forum and announced simply that 'We have been defeated in a great battle' (*pugna magna victi sumus*). Livy's dramatic accounts of wives, mothers and fathers waiting at the city gates to search for husbands and sons amongst the fugitives are often dismissed as rhetorical, but it is important to remember that much of the population will have had family or friends in the army. This defeat had occurred not too far from Rome itself and it must have appeared that there was little to stop the enemy marching on the city. News of Centenius' defeat arrived three days after the reports of Trasimene and added to the despondency.[27]

One consular army had been destroyed, and the other, temporarily crippled by the loss of its cavalry, had withdrawn back to Ariminum to counter the increased Gallic raiding provoked by Hannibal's presence. In this crisis the Senate decided that a military dictator must be appointed to co-ordinate the defence against Hannibal, the first time this had been done since 249. This meant that the *imperium* of all other officials lapsed and for six months Rome had a single supreme magistrate. Only the powers of the tribunes of the plebs, who did not have a military role, remained unchanged during a dictatorship. Normally dictators were appointed by one of the serving consuls, but since Geminus was unable to reach the city, an election was held to fill the post, although Livy may not have been correct in claiming that this meant that the man's title would actually be *prodictator* or 'acting dictator'. The assembled centuries of the People chose Quintus Fabius Maximus as dictator, with Marcus Minucius Rufus as his *Magister Equitum* (Master of Horse) or second-in-command.[28]

Both were experienced men. Fabius Maximus – the title 'the Greatest' had been awarded to an ancestor several generations earlier – had been twice consul, in 233, when he triumphed over the Ligurians, and in 228, as well as holding the censorship in 230. He was now about 58, rather old by the standards of Roman generals, but was to prove an active commander and emerge as one of the greatest Roman heroes of the entire conflict, holding the consulship three more times in the next decade. It is, however, probable that he would never again have held senior public office had it not been for the crisis of the Hannibalic war. Nicknamed Verrucosus or 'spotty' as a result of a prominent facial wart, Fabius had been considered a dull child, lacking in initiative, and it was only during his adult career that he earned widespread respect. We know far less about Minucius, who had been consul in 221, but the two do not seem to have been close and their relations were to prove strained during the forthcoming campaign. To depict them as members of different parties is to misunderstand Roman politics and Minucius' advocacy of a more aggressive strategy was typical of the other commanders fielded by Rome so far in this conflict, and represents the instinctive reaction of most senators.[29]

The two men threw themselves into the organization of the city's defences immediately after their appointment. As yet they may not have known that Hannibal had turned aside and had no intention of marching directly on Rome. Fabius publicly emphasized Flaminius' failure to carry out the proper religious rites earlier in the year, persuading the Senate to consult the Sybilline Books and appoint one of the praetors to oversee the performance of the rituals necessary to propitiate the gods. Reassured by this explanation for the recent disasters which offered the promise that traditional Roman virtues of courage and piety would carry them through the crisis, and energized by the activity of Fabius and Minucius, all levels of society threw themselves into preparations to continue the war.[30]

Fabius was careful to emphasize the traditional dignity of his own office as he travelled to take over the army commanded by the surviving consul and add them to the newly raised troops. Geminus had been instructed to march his troops down the *via Flaminia* and the two forces met at Narnia. The dictator was escorted by twenty-four lictors, equal in number to those of both consuls whose power he in effect combined. Fabius sent a messenger ahead to inform Geminus that he was no longer entitled to symbols of office and should come into the dictator's presence as a private citizen. Taking over his soldiers, Fabius sent Geminus to Ostia to take command as proconsul of the fleet being mustered there. However, in one respect Fabius decided to abandon a traditional restriction imposed on the dictator, and was allowed by the Senate to ride a horse. This old ban was probably a legacy of the former dominance of the hoplite class of heavy infantry who wanted a commander to remain on foot, fighting, and if necessary dying, with them as part of the infantry phalanx. Hence it was the dictator's subordinate, or Master of Horse, who traditionally led the cavalry. Given the size and more sophisticated organization of the army by the late third century BC, it was essential for a general to be mobile if he was to command effectively.[31]

After Trasimene, Hannibal had moved east to recross the Apennines and invade Picenum, reaching the Adriatic coast after ten days' march. En route, his soldiers plundered and ravaged the land they passed through, brutally sacking and storming the villages and small towns they passed. Both men and horses were still not fully recovered from their long journey to reach Italy and the two rapid campaigns fought subsequently. The men showed signs of scurvy, and the horses of mange, both caused by vitamin deficiency. On reaching the coast he rested the men and allowed them to recover through eating the plentiful produce gathered from this rich area. The horses were bathed in the sour wine or *acetum*, which had been captured in great quantities, restoring the condition of their coats. Even when resting his troops, he was still forced to move his camp periodically as the army consumed the food and good forage in its immediate vicinity. Hannibal had to keep moving because of his need to feed his men and animals, but the marauding progress of his army through the heart of Roman Italy displayed to all sides the inability of the enemy to oppose him. Once on the Adriatic, he was for the first time able to send a message by sea to Carthage, reporting his successes since he left Spain. The Carthaginians were delighted at his success and promised aid to support his campaigns and his brother's operations in Spain, although little was ever to reach Hannibal.[32]

His army restored to health, Hannibal continued his advance down the coastal plain of eastern Italy, capturing amongst others, the Roman colony of Luceria. The Punic army then moved south-west towards Aecae where it once again came into contact with a Roman army. Fabius with his army of four legions and allies, at least 40,000 men, camped 6 miles away from the enemy. He had been advancing cautiously, carefully scouting ahead to give him plenty of warning of the enemy's presence, for the location of the Carthaginian army was not known with any certainty. Hannibal's immediate response was to form his army up and offer battle outside the Roman camp. No response came from the Romans, so after waiting long enough to impress his own men with the enemy's timidity, he led his army back into camp. It swiftly became clear that Fabius had no intention of risking a battle under any circumstances. This was certainly wise, since at least half his army consisted of very raw soldiers, and all were in awe of the enemy who had twice defeated Roman armies in less than a year. As Hannibal continued westwards and crossed the Apennines once again, Fabius shadowed his march, but refused to fight a major action. The hilly country of this region favoured the Romans, allowing Fabius to keep to the high ground and always occupy and camp on positions which Hannibal would never risk attacking. The dictator's plan was to weaken the enemy indirectly, depriving him of food supplies, a ploy later known to the Romans as 'kicking the enemy in the stomach'. Whenever possible the Romans attacked the Carthaginian foraging parties, not inflicting many casualties, but making it difficult for them to gather food and fodder. The local population were instructed to seek refuge in fortified strongholds, taking with them or destroying their animals and food, although it is unclear how perfectly this order was obeyed.[33]

It required great skill on Fabius' part to keep close to the enemy without giving him an opportunity to fight, but the local knowledge of the Romans and their allies were a great advantage. However, by the time Hannibal crossed into Samnium and plundered the fertile land around Beneventum, the Roman army had fallen between one and two days' march behind the enemy. The Carthaginian then decided to attack into Campania and devastate the rich *ager Falernus*, famous for its wines, feeling that the threat to this area farmed by Roman citizens must either provoke Fabius to battle or demonstrate finally Rome's weakness. It may be that he already had hopes that Capua and other cities might defect to him, as they were in fact to do a year later, having been encouraged by the promises of Campanian prisoners. In fact the cities remained loyal, as did the remainder of Rome's allies at this time, in spite of Hannibal's victories and Rome's obvious weakness shown by her inability to stop him devastating the country at will.[34]

Fabius followed the enemy, but once again refused to be provoked and the Roman army watched from the safety of the mountains whilst the Carthaginians looted and burned. It was now late in the season and Hannibal was faced with the problem of establishing a base where his army could winter and enjoy the spoils of its raiding. This meant first escaping through one of the few passes in the mountains which ring round the Falernian plain and Hannibal decided to employ the same route which he had used to enter. Fabius correctly anticipated him and managed to occupy the pass with 4,000 men whilst the remainder of his army camped on a hill in front of it. Hannibal's army halted and pitched camp on the plain beneath. The way in which he now extricated his army became a classic of ancient generalship, finding its way into nearly every historical narrative of the war and being used by later military manuals. His officer in charge of supplying the army, one Hasdrubal, was instructed to gather oxen and fasten wooden branches to their horns. The soldiers were ordered to eat a meal and get as much rest in the evening as possible. In the night, the army moved out. The torches tied to the cattle's horns were lit and the animals driven up onto the ridge, the javelinmen assisting the drovers to keep them moving in the right direction. Simultaneously the main column started to ascend the pass, the Libyans led wearing their Roman equipment, the cavalry and baggage came behind and the Gauls and Spanish brought up the rear.

The Roman troops holding the pass saw the mass of torches and left their position to attack the presumed enemy. Reaching the milling animals, they halted in confusion and were suddenly attacked by the javelinmen, with whom they fought a desultory skirmish until both sides disengaged. Fabius saw the torchlight and heard the noise of fighting, but refused to move from his camp in the darkness, despite the urgings of his officers and Minucius in particular. Given the problems of fighting at night and the relative inexperience of his soldiers, this was probably the correct decision, and it is questionable whether the Romans would have been able to locate and intercept the enemy in time to achieve anything if they had moved out. Hannibal's main column was able to travel through the pass without any interference and escape with all its booty, apart from the cattle used in his ploy. The next morning revealed the Punic javelinmen facing the Roman detachments on the ridge beside the pass. Hannibal responded more quickly than his opponent and sent a force of Spanish *caetrati* to their aid. Lightly armed and used to rugged terrain, the Spanish not only brought the javelinmen back with them, but inflicted heavy losses on the Romans.[35]

Fabius had been humiliated, allowing his enemy to escape from an apparently hopeless position. From the beginning many in Rome and with the army had resented the dictator's passive policy. Officers and soldiers who despised his caution nicknamed Fabius 'Hannibal's *paedagogus*', for following him around like the slaves who accompanied children to school, carrying their books. The Roman instinct was to wage war aggressively, escalating a conflict rather than enduring losses patiently. Fabius' operations conformed with the military wisdom of the Hellenistic Age, that a commander who could not realistically expect to win a battle should avoid one until such a time as his strength increased in relation to that of the enemy, but as yet few if any Roman aristocrats appreciated such subtleties. When the dictator had to return to Rome to supervise some religious rituals, Minucius ignored his orders and attacked. Hannibal's army was not concentrated, busy as it was in gathering enough supplies to last the winter, and the Romans won a large-scale skirmish outside Gerunium, which Hannibal had stormed and intended to use as his winter quarters. Exaggerated accounts of this action caused widespread rejoicing in Rome, with the belief that at last they had found a commander willing and able to fight. In an unprecedented move, the tribune of the plebs, Metilius, passed a law granting the *Magister Equitum* equal *imperium* to the dictator. In effect it was a return to the normality of having two senior magistrates and when Fabius returned to the army it was divided into two, Fabius and Minucius each taking the equivalent of a consular army. The result was predictable. Hannibal lured Minucius into a trap and severely mauled his army before Fabius arrived and extricated them, but Fabius refused to engage further. Voluntarily, the Master of Horse returned to being a subordinate, hailing the dictator as father, a powerful figure in Roman society with power of life and death over his children, and bidding his men refer to Fabius' soldiers as their patrons, as if they were freed slaves.[36]

The year ended with the Roman army maintaining a respectful distance from the enemy, but sporadic skirmishing occurring between patrols and foraging parties. Around December 217, the six-month term of the dictatorship expired and Fabius and Minucius returned to Rome, leaving the army under the command of Geminus, the surviving consul, and Marcus Atilius Regulus (the son of the consul of 256), who had been elected as suffect or replacement consul and had held the magistracy itself ten years earlier.

Quintus Fabius Maximus was greatly revered by his own and later generations as the man who had saved Rome by avoiding battle. He earned the nickname 'Cunctator' ('the delayer'), which was clearly a considerable improvement on 'Verrucosus'. His dictatorship gave the Romans a breathing space to recover from the defeats at Trebia and Trasimene, in which they could rebuild their strength. In our sources he is depicted as an isolated figure, who alone realized that the Romans could not defeat Hannibal in battle and refused to be swayed by persuasion or mockery from his decision not to fight.

CHAPTER 8

Cannae and the Crisis for Rome

ON 2 AUGUST 216, Hannibal won his greatest victory in the plain north of the small, hilltop town of Cannae in southern Italy. By the end of the day his outnumbered mercenaries had enveloped and massacred the greater part of the largest army Rome had ever fielded, turning this into one of the bloodiest battles ever fought, rivalling even the industrialized slaughter of the twentieth century. For the Romans Cannae became the yardstick by which other defeats were measured, never surpassed and only once or twice equalled in the next six centuries. Cannae remains one of the most famous battles ever fought, frequently alluded to in modern military writing, and Hannibal's tactics are still taught in the military academies where today's officers are trained. The UN commander in the Gulf War, General Norman Schwartzkopf, claimed to have employed principles based on study of Hannibal's campaigns and Cannae in particular in the planning and control of his own brief and devastatingly effective campaign. In the nineteenth and early twentieth centuries the disciplines of Ancient History and Archaeology were overwhelmingly dom- inated by German scholarship, and it was perhaps a reflection of this that the study of ancient warfare was taken very seriously by the Prussian and German military. Von Schlieffen, the architect of the plan for the invasion of France in AD 1914, was obsessed with Cannae, studying it in incredible detail throughout his life, and attempting in his war plan to achieve just such a total victory. Cannae became the shorthand term for a complete success for many German generals. In AD 1941, as Rommel drove the British army back towards Tobruk, he wrote in his diary that 'a new Cannae is being prepared', and a year or so later in December 1942 during the Stalingrad campaign, the commander of the 6th Panzer Division produced a boastful report of a successful day's fighting around the obscure village of Pakhlebin, calling the engagement 'the Cannae of Pakhlebin'.[1] Yet in spite of having fought 'the perfect battle' Hannibal ultimately lost the war and, having achieved no other victories as great as this, but still undefeated in battle, was forced to evacuate Italy twelve years later. How and why the Romans were able to survive this disaster is the theme of this chapter.

Cannae, August 216 BC

If we are to understand the Cannae campaign and the battle itself, we must constantly remind ourselves that at the time no one could have guessed at its outcome and that, even during the battle itself, there were several stages when things might have turned against Hannibal for all the brilliance of his tactics. Livy's account of the preliminaries to the battle is dominated by a sense of impending disaster, as once again an impulsive Roman commander recklessly led the army to defeat, ignoring the advice of his more experienced colleague. The sense of inevitable catastrophe pervading the narrative is utterly false.

The Roman Senate had resolved on mounting a major effort for the campaigning season in 216. The magistrates for the year were a distinguished group, with one of the consuls and three out of four praetors all having held the consulship before, whilst the other consul and all the praetors had held the praetorship in an earlier year. For the first time ever each consul was given a double-sized army of four legions which were expected to fight together. In 225 the consuls had also each commanded four legions, but the participation of both armies in the battle of Telamon had been coincidental. The legions themselves were each to be larger than normal, expanding to the size the Romans felt appropriate for the current crisis, so that each mustered 5,000 infantry as well as the usual complement of 300 horsemen. We do not know the size of the allied *alae* attached to each army, but can safely assume that their infantry were roughly equal in number to the Roman foot, whilst their cavalry was more numerous. Sometimes the unprecedentedly large size of this army has been doubted, especially since Livy mentions that there were a variety of traditions about the number of troops enrolled in this year. However, Polybius clearly believed that there were eight legions in the united army of the two consuls and there is no good reason to doubt him. This was not the only Roman army to be fielded in this year. In addition to the forces in Spain and Sicily, an army of two legions was sent north to face the tribes of Cisalpine Gaul which remained in open rebellion. This expedition was commanded by Lucius Postumius Albinus, who had been twice consul in 234 and 229 and was now probably nearly 60 years old.[2]

The incoming consuls given command of this, the largest army Rome had ever put into the field, were Caius Terentius Varro and Lucius Aemilius Paullus. The latter was the grandfather of Scipio Aemilianus and therefore receives a very favourable treatment from Polybius and all subsequent historians. This was his second consulship, as in 219 he had fought successfully against the Illyrians and celebrated a triumph, although he seems to have been involved in the scandal associated with the campaign which had led to the retirement from politics of his colleague, Marcus Livius Salinator. Paullus was to fall in battle, but, unlike Flaminius, he was a member of a wealthy and well-established aristocratic family, who were more than capable of defending his reputation in later years. A convenient scapegoat was found in the person of his colleague, who survived the fighting, but was a new man and vulnerable to the propaganda of such powerful families. Varro's descendants continued to gain membership of the Senate, but none had distinguished careers and the family never gained admittance to the core of senatorial families who dominated the senior magistracies till the end of the Republic.

Livy portrays Varro as a demagogue much like Flaminius. This conforms with his theme that it was the radical, popular politicians who caused most of the disasters to befall the state, when the mob ignored the wise leadership of the experienced aristocrats in the Senate. He tells us that Varro's family was undistinguished, that it was said his father was a butcher. Such an accusation is typical of the exaggerated invective that was a normal feature of Roman political debate and should not be taken seriously. Varro is supposed to have been one of the main supporters of Metilius' bill to grant Minucius equal power to Fabius Maximus the year before, but otherwise, even by Livy's account, his career had not been a radical one. As with Flaminius, he must have had considerable support from the wealthier classes in the *Comitia Centuriata* to have won election to the consulship. Livy even claims that he was the sole choice of the Assembly at the election, which strongly attests to his popularity, and that he actually presided over the vote to appoint his colleague. His success also makes it certain that he possessed considerable support amongst his fellow senators and, given that the presiding magistrate could do much to influence the outcome of an election, it is unlikely that he and his fellow consul were hostile to each other. There is no good reason to accept Livy's depiction of Aemilius Paullus as an adherent of Fabius' strategy of avoiding battle. It is not even certain that Fabius himself believed this to be the right way to proceed in the spring of 216, and that he continued this strategy in the years after Cannae does not necessarily mean that he advocated it before this disaster.[3]

Even if Fabius still advocated his policy of delay, then the plans of the

Senate for the campaigning season of 216 make it clear that he was in a minority, and that they expected a direct confrontation with Hannibal. Fabius' six-month dictatorship had given the State time to recover from the defeats at Trebia and Trasimene. His army of four legions was relatively well-trained and had won some minor successes, even if part of it had also been defeated under Minucius. To this force they added four new and less experienced legions, so that around 80,000 infantry and 6,000 cavalry would face Hannibal's 40,000 foot and 10,000 horse. A continuation of Fabius' strategy did not require such a large force and concentrating so many soldiers and mounts greatly increased the problems of supply. Morale was good both in the population as a whole and amongst the soldiers, who were eager for battle. Many senators and their sons were serving either as tribunes, in the cavalry or on the commanders' staffs. One of the tribunes was the former Master of Horse, Minucius. The allied soldiers in particular were desperate to fight and avenge the devastation Hannibal's progress had wrought on Italian fields. Polybius claims that the Senate told Paullus to seek battle and attributes a speech to him in which he explained to the soldiers the reasons for Hannibal's recent victories and assured them that the enemy would not be able to stand up to the combined might of both consular armies. In Polybius' version, Varro and Paullus did not disagree over whether or not to fight a battle, but instead over when and where to do so.[4]

At the opening of the campaigning season in 216, Hannibal was still at his winter base at Gerunium in Apulia, watched warily by the army commanded by Geminus and Regulus. Both of these men had their power extended as proconsuls for this year, but it is not clear whether Regulus remained with the army for the coming campaign. Livy claims that he gained permission to return to Roman on the grounds of age and infirmity, and certainly Polybius' statement that he was killed is untrue, since he became censor in 214. Once the crops had ripened enough to make foraging possible, Hannibal led his army south. The proconsuls followed him at a safe distance and sent repeated messages to the Senate asking for instructions, explaining that they could not close with the enemy without being forced to fight a battle. This was plausible enough, since the country the armies were marching through was open and fairly flat. Hannibal pressed on and captured the ruined stronghold of Cannae, which was still in use as a Roman supply depot.[5]

It is not certain when the new consuls arrived and the two parts of the army were joined together. Polybius implies that this was not until after Hannibal had taken Cannae, less than a week before the battle, whereas

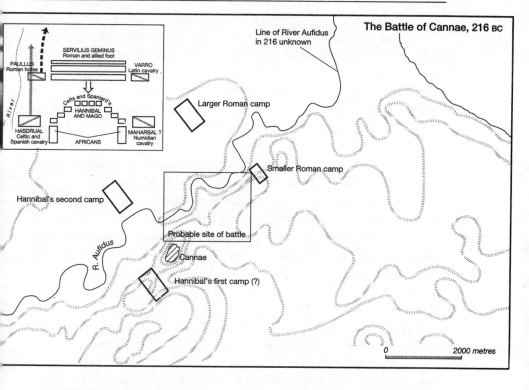

The Battle of Cannae, 216 BC

Line of River Aufidus in 216 unknown

Larger Roman camp

Smaller Roman camp

Hannibal's second camp

Probable site of battle

Cannae

Hannibal's first camp (?)

R. Aufidus

River

0   2000 metres

PAULLUS Roman horse

SERVILIUS GEMINUS Roman and allied foot

VARRO Latin cavalry

Celts and Spaniard's

HANNIBAL AND MAGO

HASDRUAL Celtic and Spanish cavalry

AFRICANS

MAHARBAL ? Numidian cavalry

Livy tells of their arrival before he had left Gerunium. Polybius' account is probably to be preferred, not only because of the implausibility of much of Livy's account of Hannibal's withdrawal, but also because the difficulties of feeding such a large army make it unlikely that the Roman force remained concentrated for such a long period. Further uncertainty exists over the precise location of the battlefield, chiefly with regard to which side of the River Aufidius it was fought on. We do not know what the course of the river was in the third century, but it is clear that this differed from its present-day line. Although some authorities have placed the battle to the north – the term is used loosely, the river actually running from south-west to north-east – on what is normally referred to as the left bank, it is an easier reading of our best sources to locate the fighting on the south, or right bank, assuming that the river's course originally lay further away from the hillock of Cannae itself. Such a positioning makes the movements of both armies more intelligible and will be followed here.[6]

The Romans advanced carefully in pursuit of Hannibal, having learned from Flaminius' failure to scout properly before Trasimene. They seem to have come along the coastal plain, perhaps to avoid having to pass any suitable ambush positions. On the day they came into sight of the enemy army,

201

they stopped and camped 6 miles away. The Romans were to the east on the flat and open plain which runs down – there is a very slight gradient – to the sea. The consuls held command of the army on alternate days, the normal practice on the rare occasions both consuls operated together, but one which Fabius had refused to adopt with Minucius in the previous year. Paullus is supposed to have advised against advancing directly on the enemy in this country which favoured Hannibal's more numerous cavalry, but the next day was Varro's turn to command and he decided to press on. As the Romans marched across the plain, the column was attacked by Hannibal's cavalry and light infantry and thrown into some disorder before the Romans formed up part of their forces to drive the enemy back. The Roman *velites* and cavalry fought with formed maniples of legionaries in close support, giving them an edge over the opposition. Skirmishing lasted till nightfall, and it is doubtful that the Romans had covered many miles by the time they made camp. The next day Paullus continued the advance and brought the army up to camp by the river bank, only a couple of miles from Hannibal's position.

Polybius claims that Paullus still did not like the ground, but felt that the armies were now too close together for the Romans to disengage safely. It may be that Polybius was simply trying to shift the blame for the defeat onto Varro, but the difficulty of withdrawing in the face of the enemy was genuine. The Romans would be vulnerable as they withdrew across the open plain and anyway such a retreat would have had a demoralizing effect on the soldiers. It should never be forgotten that the legions at this time were not composed of the highly disciplined, professional soldiers of later years, but were still a volunteer militia of citizens who looked forward to returning to civilian life as soon as the campaign was over and the threat to their State ended. At the moment the army was enthusiastic, confident in its own numbers and encouraged by the promises of its leaders and the victories in the skirmishes over the winter. If their commanders appeared to lack a belief in victory and decided to flee from the enemy who was freely devastating Roman and allied fields, then the army's spirit would begin to drop. Apart from the risk of lowering morale, there was another pressing reason for the army to seek an early battle. Feeding so many men was an immensely difficult and never-ending problem, made far worse by the loss of the supplies at Cannae. If the campaign were prolonged, then the two consuls would be forced to divide their forces in order to keep men and horses fed. Paullus divided his army and sent the smaller portion across the Aufidius into a separate camp with the express intention of protecting the foraging parties which were to be sent out on this side of the river.[7]

Hannibal faced similar problems, made far worse by his lack of any immediate source of supplies beyond what his soldiers could forage or capture. Livy claims that immediately prior to the battle the situation had got so bad that many of his mercenaries, and particularly the Spanish contingents, were contemplating desertion. Hannibal is even supposed to have considered making a run for Gaul with his senior officers and cavalry, although his desperation may simply be another attempt to emphasize the wisdom of Fabius' strategy if only it had been followed. The capture of Cannae was only a temporary solution to his army's requirements and with the Romans so close he could no longer risk spreading his army out into detachments to forage. Both sides thus needed to seek battle in the immediate future if supply problems were not to put pressure on them to retreat or disperse, both of which would put them in danger. Yet the size of the Roman army was daunting and one of Hannibal's officers, a certain Gisgo, is supposed to have commented on their superiority. The general is said to have looked solemn and then quipped that whilst there may be a lot of Romans over there, there is not one called Gisgo, prompting a burst of laughter, perhaps forced, nervous, sycophantic, or a mixture of all three, from his assembled staff.[8]

Several days followed during which the armies stared at each other and skirmished in the usual way. Though both sides were eager to fight a battle, neither wanted to provoke one until they felt ready. By this time Hannibal had moved on from the hilltop citadel of Cannae itself and crossed the river, camping on the same side as the larger Roman camp. The most likely location for his camp is the high ground on which the modern village of San Ferdinando di Púglia now lies. On the next day, 31 July, the Carthaginian army was ordered to prepare for battle, cleaning their armour and sharpening the blades of their weapons. On 1 August Hannibal's army marched out to deploy on the open plain in front of the ridge. This was Paullus' day of command, but his only move was to deploy strong covering forces in front of both of the Roman camps. Hannibal seems to have been content with giving his soldiers this demonstration of Roman timidity. Numidian light horsemen crossed the river and rode up to harass the slaves gathering water for the smaller camp. Paullus remained on the defensive and Hannibal made no further moves to force a battle.[9]

The Roman commander's reluctance to fight in the open plain is understandable given Hannibal's marked superiority in cavalry, but Polybius tells us that his soldiers resented his passive behaviour, a natural mixture of enthusiasm and nervousness making them long to get the anticipated battle over with. Varro is supposed to have been similarly roused by the sight of

Numidian cavalry riding up to the Roman camp, and when he took over command of the army on the next day, decided to give battle. However, he did not plan to do so under the same circumstances which his colleague had just refused, but across the river on the narrower plain north of Cannae itself. Livy claims that he issued the orders without even bothering to consult Paullus, but this is extremely unlikely and not claimed by Polybius. It may be that Paullus did not believe it wise to fight, but this would then make his willingness to close with the enemy in the first place rather strange, and it is distinctly probable that he agreed with Varro's decision. One scholar has even suggested the ingenious and attractive theory that the battle was actually fought on Paullus' day of command, but this is impossible to prove and it is safer to stick with our sources.[10]

Early on the morning of 2 August, Varro had the red *vexillum*, the square Roman flag carried by the consul's bodyguard, displayed outside his tent in the traditional signal for battle. It is probable that orders had been issued to the tribunes during the night, giving them time to prepare their men, for just after dawn the army began to march out of the larger camp and cross the river. Joining the troops from the smaller camp, the Romans formed a single line of battle with its right flank resting on the river. This vital position was held by the Roman cavalry who should have been 2,400 strong if all eight legions had their full complement of horsemen. The left flank, resting against the hill of Cannae itself, was held by the Latin and allied cavalry who composed the remainder of the army's 6,000 horse, and were thus probably around 3,600 strong. The *alae* were normally supposed to supply three times as many horsemen as the legions, but the lower proportion at Cannae may have been a result of the heavy losses suffered by Centenius' force the year before. However, it is equally possible that some of the legions were below strength in horsemen, in which case the allied contingent would have been larger.

The centre of the army was composed of its strongest component, the heavy infantry of the legions and *alae*. There were perhaps 55,000 heavy infantry supported by 15,000 *velites*, allowing for the contingents left out of the battle for various reasons. They were in the usual *triplex acies*, but with one major difference, for Polybius tells us that the maniples were placed closer together than usual, each one's depth 'many times' wider than its frontage. We do not know the precise dimensions of this formation and estimates have varied from a total depth for the three lines of between fifty and seventy ranks, giving a frontage for the centre of perhaps half a mile to a mile, with perhaps each maniple deploying five men abreast. There were several reasons for adopting this formation. The first was simply one of space, for the flat land between the hills and the river was narrow and would not have permitted all of the legions and *alae* to deploy in their normal, shallower formation, but given that the Romans had chosen to fight in this position they clearly did not believe this to be a major problem. The deeper, narrower formation allowed both the individual maniples and the army as a whole to move more quickly whilst the ranks kept their dressing, for the wider a formation is, the quicker it will fall into disorder as it marches across even the flattest ground. Although some of the Roman soldiers had been in service since 218, and a good number had experience from the previous year, more than half the army consisted of recent recruits whose standard of drill cannot have been high. Moreover, the entire army had had little or no time to train together, and none of the officers had experience of leading or serving in such an unprecedentedly large force. The formation adopted was simple enough to work with such material and was able to create tremendous forward pressure. Visually it was intimidating to any enemy in its path, whilst the Roman soldiers enjoyed the security of being surrounded by so many of their comrades. The deep formation would also make it harder for any of the soldiers to flee. The men in the front ranks would be unable to escape until the men behind them had given way and these were removed from the immediate risks and stress of combat. Once the Roman mass had begun its lumbering advance it would be difficult to stop. At the very least it ought to have far greater staying power than Hannibal's less numerous infantry. The price was a loss of flexibility, for the reduction in the gaps between the maniples made it virtually impossible for these to change formation or wheel to face another direction.

Varro placed himself at the head of the Latin cavalry, whilst Paullus commanded the Roman horse and the proconsul Servilius Geminus led the infantry centre. Paullus' position with the prestigious Roman cavalry has been used as evidence by those who believe that the battle was fought on his day of command, but it is actually uncertain whether there was a normal position for the supreme commander of an army. In the few battles where both consuls were present they do not appear to have placed themselves in any particular precedence, since traditionally they were not expected to fight together.[11] The entire army must have occupied a frontage of between 1 and 2 miles and it is distinctly probable that it was angled back from the river, facing roughly south-west, to allow it to fit into a plain which was no more than 1⅓ miles wide. The Roman plan was simple and based upon their experience in earlier battles. At Ticinus and Trebia the Roman cavalry had been outnumbered and outfought, allowing the enemy cavalry to outflank the entire army. Yet at Trebia the Roman infantry had broken through the enemy centre, whilst even in the disorganized fighting at Trasimene they had put up a strong resistance and the vanguard had actually smashed through the Punic line. The strengthened Roman centre should be able to repeat these successes and crush the Carthaginian centre. All that was required of the cavalry wings was for them to protect the flanks of the infantry long enough for them to win the battle in the centre. Terrain prevented the cavalry wings from being outflanked by their numerically superior enemy and the Roman tactics here were to be purely defensive, designed to hold their ground for as long as possible. It was probabiy for this reason that the two consuls held command of these critical positions, their presence intended to inspire the cavalry to stand against their more numerous foes. With his infantry beaten and scattered, Hannibal's army would be permanently defeated, even if his cavalry were eventually successful in their combat with their Roman counterparts. Varro's plan was not subtle, and nothing illustrates Polybius' earlier comment on the Romans' reliance on brute force better than their tactics at Cannae, but it might easily have worked and anything much more sophisticated would have been impossible with the army under his command. Hannibal had been brought to battle on ground of the Romans' choosing where they hoped to negate his cavalry superiority and could be sure that no ambush lay behind their lines. He no longer had the elephants which had panicked earlier Roman armies and now he would be crushed by the numbers and courage of Rome's greatest strength, her sturdy citizenry of farmer-soldiers.[12]

There was no guarantee that Hannibal would accept battle in the narrow plain. Paullus left 10,000 men to guard the larger camp which remained on the same side of the river as the enemy. It is not certain whether these were a whole unit, perhaps a legion with its *ala*, or detachments from several units. There is no good reason to believe that the entire *triarii* were given this task, since, contrary to some claims, this was not their normal role. Paullus is said to have ordered them to attack the Punic camp if Hannibal took the bait and crossed the river to fight. If this is true, then this was a bold plan, but characteristically Roman, and the capture of Hannibal's camp and baggage would make sure that the enemy had no chance of reforming his army to continue the struggle. At the very least it might compel the enemy to weaken their force by leaving a detachment to protect the camp while the rest of the army fought the main battle. In fact, the Punic commander quickly decided to accept the challenge to battle and does not seem to have made any special provision for the defence of his base.[13]

Hannibal responded quickly to the sight of the Romans crossing the river, which may suggest that his army was at least partially prepared to move out in any case. His slingers and javelinmen were sent across the river as a covering force to allow the remainder of his army to move out and deploy. The main body forded the Aufidius in two places, which suggests that they were formed into two columns. The army then wheeled into line facing the Romans, its left flank resting on the river. The 10,000 cavalry were divided between the wings, but in this case Hannibal put all of his Numidians opposite the Latin Horse and concentrated his close order cavalry, who rode with saddles and bridles, on the left. It is unclear just how many of each nationality were present, but at least 4,000 of the cavalry were Gallic and several thousand Spanish, so it is probable that the Punic left wing significantly outnumbered the Romans facing them. The Numidians may have been roughly equal in numbers to the Latins, but certainty is impossible. Hannibal had 40,000 infantry, but this total included the light infantry. He had had 8,000 of these at Trebia and it is doubtful whether his recruitment of Celts had added substantially to this total, for skirmishing was not common in Gallic warfare. This left 32,000 close order foot, of whom the majority were Celts, perhaps as many as 20,000, for he had received no more drafts of Libyans or Spanish. Possibly there were 8–10,000 Libyan infantry and around 4,000 Spanish.

Together the Spanish and Gallic infantry formed the army's centre, deployed in alternate companies. Polybius uses the word *speirai*, one of the terms he uses to mean 'maniple', and it is likely that he uses it to mean units of a few hundred men, although there was probably no standard size. This interspersion of companies from two distinct ethnic groups suggests that Gauls were now fully absorbed into Hannibal's army, so that there was no need to place them in larger, tribal contingents. The Libyans were split into two halves, each roughly the strength of a Roman legion, and placed on the wings, formed into deep columns. Although this is not clear from our source, it is probable that they were actually behind the edges of the line of Spanish and Celts, out of sight of the Romans. They may well have composed the second of Hannibal's columns, crossing the river upstream of the main force, concealed from enemy gaze. Once the army had reached its positions, Hannibal led forward the centre companies of his infantry, causing the whole line to bulge towards the enemy, the units echeloned back on either side of the new, narrow front. The general himself, with his brother Mago, was with the Gauls and Spanish, while Hasdrubal led the heavy cavalry, and Livy says that Maharbal controlled the Numidians. Hannibal had rightly guessed that the main Roman effort was to be made in the centre and had adjusted his deployment and issued orders accordingly. His plan was to use the enemy's own strength against him, but it easier to describe how this was achieved than to anticipate the action.[14]

It must have taken hours for both the armies to reach their positions and deploy into battle, the tribunes scurrying about to join the two Roman armies together and jostle the men into place. When they were ready, over 125,000 men and 16,000 horses were gathered in an area no larger than 5 or 6 square miles, whilst more soldiers and tens of thousands of slaves, servants and camp followers looked on from the three camps. The noise of their movements drowned out the constant chirruping of the cicadas which fills the air on summer days in this plain. So many feet and hoofs threw up clouds of dust which swirled in the strong gusts of the hot Volturnus wind which blows from the south-east. The dust was another irritant to men beginning to swelter in their heavy armour under the hot glare of the sun. On the Roman side the army presented a fairly uniform appearance, although we must remember that these were citizen soldiers and there is no good reason to believe that they wore tunics of the same colour or that shields were painted with unit insignia. Our sources were most struck by the diverse dress of the enemy army. On the one hand were the Libyans, dressed in Roman helmets and armour, and with oval *scuta*, then the Gauls stripped to the waist (since this is probably what Polybius means by 'naked'), and the Spanish in their white tunics with purple borders, to which we might add the unarmoured Numidians with their distinctive hairstyles and riding their small, shaggy horses. It is uncertain how accurate this picture is. The Spanish had left home two years before and one may wonder how many still wore their native garb and had not replaced it with whatever was available locally or could be made in camp. However, they probably had retained their native weapons, the Spanish carrying their short-stabbing swords, and perhaps a few of the curved blades similar to the Greek *kopis*, whilst the Gauls had their long slashing blades.

For a while the armies stared at each other, whilst their light infantry skirmished between the lines. Neither side seems to have gained much advantage in this combat and eventually the skirmishers pulled back behind the main lines of their infantry. Hannibal's light troops may then have moved to support his cavalry on the wings as they did at Trebia, for early in the fighting Paullus was hit in the face by a slingstone cast by one of the Balearic slingers. The Roman *velites* seem to have pulled back through the small intervals left in the line of *hastati*. However, the first close combat occurred when Hasdrubal led his Spanish and Gallic cavalry against the Roman horse. A vicious mêlée developed, the sources once again stressing that it was unlike most cavalry combats, consisting not of charges and pursuits, but of a standing fight. Again we hear of men dismounting to fight on foot. Eventually the ferocity of Spanish and Gallic horsemen proved too much and the Romans were killed or put to flight. It is unclear how much advantage Hasdrubal had from his numbers, for the confined space between the infantry centres and the river may have prevented him from bringing them to bear. It may simply be that the Roman cavalry had got as used to being beaten by the Punic horsemen as the latter had to winning. In hand-to-hand combat confidence was often of greater importance than numbers or equipment. The Romans fled, but many found that their escape was cut off by the river and were slaughtered by their exultant opponents. The combat had been fierce, but according to Livy had not lasted very long, although it is always difficult to know what to make of such vague allusions to time. Before it was finished the heavy infantry had met in the centre.[15]

Hannibal's men do not seem to have advanced further once he had formed his convex line pointing towards the enemy, so it was probably the Romans who marched forward, eager as they were to decide the combat before their cavalry were beaten. The cacophony of noise can only have been appalling as the Romans cheered, blew their trumpets and clashed their weapons against their shields, the Celtic and Spanish warriors answering them with their own war cries as each side tried to terrify the other into submission. As they came closer, the Roman line checked and began to hurl their *pila*, the enemy replying with showers of their own javelins. Despite their numbers the Romans did not throw many more missiles than their opponents, for the men in the rear ranks even of the maniples of *hastati* could not do so without severe risk of hitting their own front ranks. Soon the Romans, encouraged by their officers and the men behind, surged forward into contact. The combat fell into the usual pattern, with brief flurries of savage hand-to-hand fighting, after which the exhausted participants pulled back a few yards to draw breath, taunting and lobbing missiles at their enemies, until they regained the confidence and energy to renew the fight. Livy speaks of the Romans 'for a long time repeatedly pushing forward', before they began to win ground against strong opposition.[16] The Gauls were renowned for their ferocity in the early stages of battle, but supposed to weary quickly and lose heart if they did not seem to be winning. At Cannae, as at Telamon, they confounded the literary cliché of the fickle and easily tired barbarian, and put up a long and sturdy resistance. There were several reasons why they were able to do so. In numbers they were roughly equal to the Roman *hastati* and, since they occupied roughly the same frontage, their companies were formed in similar depth. The stiffening of experienced Spanish infantry may also have helped to steady the Gauls, and they were inspired by the presence of Hannibal and Mago, who rode around, close behind the fighting line, yelling encouragement to their warriors. Pride probably had a lot to do with it, for both the Gauls and Spanish were products of warrior societies which prized military glory above all else. At Cannae these men had been specially chosen as the first to meet the enemy, even being advanced ahead of the main army where all could witness their valour, in a gesture not unlike that of the Gaesatae at Telamon, running naked ahead of the whole army, challenging the enemy and daring them to come on.

Only slowly did the Romans force the Celts and Spaniards back, and at first they did so step by step, still facing forward. The bulge in Hannibal's line was flattened, and still the Romans pushed on, till in the centre they drove the enemy back further, so that now the line was concave instead of convex. More of the front lines were in contact and the fighting general, but the main effort was still in the centre where the two sides had first met and where the Romans were winning. Roman officers, including the many tribunes, the proconsul, and Paullus himself who had ridden to the centre after the defeat of his cavalry, urged the legionaries on, led them in charges, and fed in maniples from the reserve lines to support the *hastati*, desperate to keep the forward momentum going and exploit this success. Gradually the Roman infantry lost their neat formation, as the narrow gaps between the maniples vanished and the units merged into one great crowd. The intervals between the three lines had probably also been reduced by the deep formation of the individual maniples. There was always a tendency for very large mass formations to lose order and degenerate into a mob of men pushing forward, (as Napoleon's army was to discover when the declining quality of its infantry led to the use of gigantic formations at Wagram, Albuera and Waterloo). Yet the forward pressure created by the densely packed mass of Roman infantry was inexorable and, eventually, the Gauls and Spanish began to break. In the centre they at last gave way, and the Romans surged forward, victory in sight. It was probably now that the Gauls suffered a good proportion of the many casualties, as those who did not run quickly enough or were slowed by their wounds were hacked down by the elated legionaries. The Roman mass burst through the centre of the enemy army and, in the rear, the Roman commanders urged more men on to support them.

On either side of the victorious Roman infantry were the columns of the Libyan infantry. We do not know whether Hannibal had given their commanders instructions to begin to move when the enemy reached a certain point, or whether he now sent orders by courier for them to do so. Calmly, the columns turned to face inwards, and although there has been considerable debate over precisely how this manoeuvre was performed, this need not concern us, since so much depends on the details of the formation they started the battle in, concerning which we have no precise information. Then, ranks neatly dressed, they advanced to take the mass of Roman infantry from both sides. The disorganization amongst the Romans was appalling and no one was able to assemble a coherent fighting line to face these new threats. The maniples were hopelessly confused and the men turned as individuals and small groups to confront the advancing Libyans. Most of the Romans were weary from the fighting, since even those not actually in the front ranks had endured the stress of close combat, and now they faced men who were well formed and fresh. It is even possible that they did not immediately realize that these new troops were enemies, for the African soldiers were dressed in Roman equipment and in battle men often become disorientated and lose their sense of direction. All forward movement in the Roman centre ceased, the two bodies of Africans compressing the mass of soldiers like a vice. In the lull, the Gauls and Spanish who had broken began to rally and return to the fight.[17]

Varro must have watched the early stages of the battle with some satisfaction, as his infantry started to achieve the breakthrough which was to smash the enemy army. His own command was faced only by skirmishing Numidians, who never risked a charge and fled whenever the Latins advanced towards them. His men suffered a steady drain of casualties, but there was no reason for him to advance and drive the enemy back, since as long as he remained in place and protected the flank of the infantry the legions could perform their task and win the battle. It is doubtful that the consul could have seen the defeat of the Roman cavalry on the opposite wing, but even if Varro had knowledge of it, there was nothing that he could have done to prevent it. Various rumours circulated in the aftermath of the battle to explain the Roman defeat, and one of these was that a party of Numidians had pretended to surrender, only to produce swords which they had concealed on their persons and attack their captors in the rear, but Polybius does not mention this and it is most likely untrue.[18]

On the opposite flank, Hasdrubal had allowed his cavalry to pursue the fleeing Roman horse for a short distance along the river, but soon rallied them. It was always difficult to reform cavalrymen once they had begun to scatter in pursuit of a helpless enemy and it is a tribute to Hasdrubal's ability and the discipline of his men that he so quickly re-established order. The narrowness of the plain probably helped to keep the pursuers together and they were prevented from charging off too far into the distance by the smaller Roman camp, only a mile or so along its bank. The Spanish and Gallic cavalry then moved round behind the Roman army and prepared to charge into the rear of the Latin horse. Without waiting to receive them, Varro and his men fled in panic as soon as they perceived the threat. Such routs were not uncommon when a force was unexpectedly confronted by a new threat, but the ground may have added to the Latin horsemen's nervousness, for if they stayed to fight they would have been trapped between the Numidians, Hasdrubal's men, their own infantry and the steep slopes of the high ground around Cannae. Once again the commander of the Punic left wing displayed admirable control over his Celtic and Spanish warriors, halting them and leaving the pursuit of Varro's troopers entirely in the hands of the Numidians. The fact that his men had not actually made contact with the enemy probably made it easier to keep them in order. Hasdrubal wheeled them round and began a series of charges against the rear of the Roman infantry. The *triarii* may no longer have been a clearly distinct line, having been absorbed into the general mass, and anyway there were probably few senior officers in the rear of the army to organize resistance as most will have made their way forward to control the critical fighting against the Punic infantry. There was no question of a line of spearmen being able to turn around and ward off the approaching cavalry. In some places a dense group of men presented a wall of spear points to deter the oncoming horsemen, in which case they were bombarded with thrown javelins, but elsewhere the Punic horsemen were able to charge home into the panicked and disordered men.[19]

The Roman foot were now almost completely surrounded. Such was their disorder that they could make little use of their numbers, which were still greater than the enemy's. In the milling mass of men there were no formed reserves to be sent forward to reinforce a combat. Everywhere they were steadily driven back, pressing the crowd more closely together and adding to the confusion. Still the Romans fought on, although admittedly for many of them flight was impossible. This phase of the battle is passed over briefly by our sources, and often by modern commentators as well, since it is not a story of tactical brilliance, but of prolonged butchery. It must have taken hours for the Carthaginians to massacre their enemy. The pauses between the brief minutes of furious hand-to-hand combat doubtless grew longer as the Punic soldiers had to overcome their exhaustion before renewing the killing. For hours they pressed on, their shields and the chests of their horses stained red with blood, the edges of their swords blunted by so much killing. Hannibal lost 4,000 Gauls, 1,500 Spaniards and Libyans and 200 cavalry, a total of about 11.5 per cent of his entire army, still more if these figures only included the dead and need to be increased to include wounded. This was a staggeringly high loss for a victorious army in the ancient world and a testament to the long and ghastly struggle fought to destroy the surrounded Roman host.

Our sources give various figures for the Roman casualties. The normally reliable Polybius is obviously confused at this point, because his figures for their losses produce a total higher than the one he gives for the entire army at the beginning of the battle. Livy says that 45,500 Roman and allied infantry and 2,700 cavalrymen were killed and in this case his version seems more plausible. Some 3,000 foot and 1,500 horse were captured immediately, but to these we must add the roughly 17,000 men who surrendered in both the Roman camps by the next day, since only a small proportion of the fugitives who had fled to these were willing or able to fight their way to safety. The losses amongst senior officers had been especially bad. Paullus was killed, allegedly after refusing the offer of his horse from the tribune Cnaeus Lentulus, who had found the wounded consul sitting on a rock in the midst of a mob of fugitives. Geminus was dead, as were Minucius Rufus, both of the consuls' quaestors, and twenty-nine out of forty-eight military tribunes. In addition Livy says that eighty other senators, or men due to be enrolled in the body at the next census, had also fallen.[20]

These figures need to be put into perspective. On 1 July AD 1916, the British army began its offensive on the Somme, suffering an appalling 60,000 casualties on this first day. It was a disaster which still haunts the national psyche, much as Cannae was to remain a powerful image to the Romans for the remainder of their history. In the popular mind the losses to the mostly volunteer army is often equated with 60,000 dead, but in fact out of the total of 61,816, there were 8,170 killed, 35,888 wounded and 17,758 listed as missing, 10,705 of whom were later found to have been killed. The French suffered even higher losses on the first day of Nivelle's offensive the following year. In each case these casualties were spread along a front many miles in length – on the Somme the British Expeditionary Force attacked along a 16-mile front.[21] At Cannae, over 50,000 corpses lay heaped up in a few square miles of open plain. Livy's description of the appalling sights on the battlefield on the next day may owe much to his imagination, but does convey something of the horror. He speaks of 'so many thousands of Romans, infantry and cavalry mingled', bloodstained men rising from amidst the slain only to be cut down by the Punic soldiers, others unable to walk, begging to be put out of their misery, some who had scraped holes in the ground to bury their heads and smother themselves; and he tells the story of a Numidian, pulled alive from underneath the body of a Roman soldier who, in his death throes, had bitten into the man's nose and ears.[22]

Polybius commented that the battle proved that it was better to fight a battle with half as many infantry as the enemy, but with a great superiority in cavalry than to fight with roughly equal numbers of both, but it must be emphasized that it was only through Hannibal's tactical skill that the victory had been possible.[23] The Carthaginian general had exploited the diversity of his multiracial army to defeat the homogenous forces of his opponents. Thus his Numidians had kept the Latin cavalry occupied, whilst his heavier horse routed the Romans, and in the infantry centre his wild but ill-disciplined and poorly armoured tribesmen had engaged the enemy in a hard struggle, before they finally gave way and the Romans were lured forward in pursuit, exposing their flanks to the Libyan foot in reserve. It is probably a mistake to assume that the Gauls and Spanish were exposed in this way because they were expendable in comparison to his trained African phalanx. Only the Libyan infantry had the training necessary to wait quietly in reserve and then manoeuvre to trap the enemy. However, the eventual scale of the Punic victory should not conceal the many phases where the complex plan might have collapsed. The Spanish and Gallic cavalry might not have been able to defeat the Romans as quickly as they did, nor was it certain that Hasdrubal would be able to restrain them from pursuing first the Romans and then later the Latin cavalry. The warriors in the centre might not have held out for as long as they did in the face of the tremendous Roman pressure. If they had broken quickly, then the advancing legionaries may still have been in good enough order to face the massively outnumbered Libyans. Hannibal's decision to stay with his centre emphasizes the importance of this. He had had to rely on Hasdrubal's skill to keep his heavy cavalry well under control. Luck had favoured Hannibal, as it has most successful commanders.

Hannibal's Dilemma and the Aftermath of Cannae

Hannibal spent 3 August gathering booty and mopping up the survivors in the Roman camps, who capitulated without putting up much of a struggle, most of them still too stunned by the scale of the disaster. Once this was completed the Carthaginians buried their own dead, and are said also to have given a proper burial to Paullus, although the rest of the Romans were left where they fell. In the towns round about, dazed remnants of the Roman army began to gather. Varro had only seventy horsemen still with him when he took refuge in Venusia. A much larger group numbering thousands had fled to Canusium, where four tribunes, including the 19-year-old Publius Scipio and the son of Fabius Maximus, took charge. Scipio is supposed to have drawn his sword and threatened to kill some young aristocrats who were speaking of fleeing abroad, forcing them to take an oath pledging never to abandon the State. Eventually nearly 10,000 men mustered in the small town and Varro arrived to resume command. The question was, what would Hannibal do now?[24]

Livy was in no doubt about what he should have done. He describes Hannibal's officers clustering around him and congratulating him on his victory, telling him that

' ... since he had concluded so great a war, he should allow himself and his weary soldiers to rest for the remainder of the day and the following night. Maharbal, the cavalry leader, reckoned that they ought not to delay. 'No,' he said, 'so that you will appreciate what this battle has achieved, in five days' time you will feast as a victor on the Capitol! Follow on! I shall go ahead with the cavalry, so that they will only hear of our approach after we have arrived.' This idea was too great and joyful for Hannibal to grasp immediately. And so he praised Maharbal's attitude; yet he needed time to consider his counsel. Then Maharbal said, 'Truly the gods do not give everything to the same man: you know how to win a victory, Hannibal, but you do not know how to use one.' This day's delay is widely believed to have saved the City and the empire.[25]

The scene is probably imaginary, and Polybius does not even mention Maharbal in his account of the battle, although it is possible that he was the unnamed commander of the Numidians. Whether or not Hannibal should have led his army on Rome immediately after Cannae became a commonplace of Roman oratory, and generations of schoolboys learned rhetoric by composing speeches on this theme. It is unfortunate that Polybius' continuous narrative ends with Cannae, and none of the surviving fragments from his later books deal with Hannibal's movements and intentions in the immediate aftermath of the battle. Modern commentators have continued to debate the matter and some, notably Field Marshal Montgomery, agreed with Maharbal's verdict. However, most now take the opposite view and argue that an advance on Rome was both impracticable and unlikely to succeed. In the first place Cannae is nearly 250 miles from Rome and it is questionable whether even a small body of cavalry could have covered this distance in five days. It is also argued that Rome was not entirely defenceless and an apparently impressive array of forces in or near the city have been listed, utterly insufficient to fight an open battle, but strong enough to defend fortifications. This, it is argued, would have made it extremely difficult for Hannibal to take the city by direct assault, and he could not afford a long siege, when it would be difficult to feed his army and he would have had to fight off relief attempts by Rome's still numerous armies. In addition to this the belief that Hannibal's strategy was to break Rome's power by causing her allies to defect suggests that it was wiser for the Punic army to stay in the south of Italy, where many communities were disaffected and would soon join him.[26]

It is probably correct that Hannibal would have been unable to capture Rome if its defenders had put up any sort of resistance. The crucial but unanswerable question is whether the Romans would indeed have fought, or felt forced to sue for peace with the invader who had arrived outside their walls in the wake of his massive triumph. Any other contemporary state would certainly have done so, as Carthage did with Regulus in 255 and would do again with Scipio in 204 and 202. Hannibal now posed a greater threat to the Roman Republic than any other foreign power would ever do throughout its entire history. That on other occasions the Romans endured great defeats without ever losing their belief in ultimate victory does not prove that they would have done so in 216. Nor does their solid defence against Hannibal's actual appearance outside the city in 211, since Rome's fortunes had been greatly revived by this time. Certainly, if any state could have coped with such pressure, then it was Rome, but it is impossible to know that they would have done so.

Hannibal did not attempt to march on the city in 216. Instead his army remained for some time near Cannae, resting and recovering from the exertions and their own heavy losses. Hannibal himself had been very active during the battle and was almost certainly physically and mentally exhausted in the days afterwards. His main concern was to organize the ransoming of the 8,000 or so Roman citizens taken prisoner. A price was agreed and ten representatives chosen from amongst the captives to go to Rome and arrange matters with the Senate. The delegation took oaths to return to the Punic camp regardless of the outcome. With them went one of Hannibal's officers, a certain Carthalo.[27]

Exchanges of prisoners had been occurring since the beginning of the war and this regular communication between the opposing armies is too often forgotten. Quickly they had revived the conventions of the First War, when the side which had more prisoners to return was paid per head for them and when more than one Roman consul seems to have undergone a period of captivity. Lucius Cincius Alimentus seems to have been captured in the early stages and ransomed, going on to hold the praetorship in 210. According to Livy he cited conversations with Hannibal as the source for some of his statements in his subsequent history of the war. When discontent was at its highest with Fabius Maximus' cautious strategy in 217, his opponents in the Senate denied him money to pay for the ransom of prisoners after he had agreed the details of the exchange with Hannibal. The dictator sent his son back to Rome to sell one of his rural estates, and used this money to redeem the captives. This incident seems to imply that ransoms were normally provided by the State, but it is possible that the old obligation for a man's clients to aid his family in providing the necessary money was still sometimes employed.[28]

In August 216 the situation was different. The Romans had few, if any, Punic prisoners to exchange, whilst Hannibal had thousands of captives, many of high rank. An important feature of all peace treaties ending conflicts between the great states and kingdoms of the third century BC dealt with the terms by which each side's prisoners would be returned. The amount paid to redeem captives was as much a gauge of victory and defeat as the forfeiture of territory or the payment of an indemnity. The addition of Carthalo to the delegation of prisoners suggests that Hannibal expected to begin peace negotiations with the Roman Senate, for by the standards of the day he had very clearly won the war. In the last two years he had incited rebellion on Rome's northern frontier, and won three major battles. He was free to roam at will through the territory of the city and her allies, laying them waste and destroying whatever forces had been sent against him, including now the largest army Rome had ever fielded. In the two years of war, the Romans and their allies had suffered at least 100,000 casualties, over 10 per cent of the population eligible for military service. Casualties amongst Rome's political élite had been especially severe. In the first two years of this war at least one third of the Roman Senate had been killed in battle, and many of those left had lost family members. The catastrophes at sea in the First Punic War had never in this way struck at the heart of Rome's élite. Hannibal repeatedly stressed that he was not fighting to destroy Rome, but for 'honour and power', desiring to remove the limitations imposed on Carthage after the First War and reassert her dominance in the western Mediterranean. He had by this time proved his military superiority and made it clear that if the Romans refused to accept defeat and seek terms, he could continue to inflict real damage on their population and their property. The Romans were beaten and ought to have the sense to realize it.[29]

The Senate refused even to see Carthalo and sent messengers ordering him not to enter the city. Both the Punic emissary and his master were shocked by this outright rejection. Similarly Pyrrhus had been equally surprised when after defeating the Romans in battle he had naturally attempted to begin negotiations to conclude a peace, only to have the Senate declare that they would never treat with an enemy still on Roman or allied soil. In 216 the Romans reinforced this refusal to concede defeat by a public demonstration of their continued determination. A vote was narrowly carried in the Senate that the State would not pay the ransoms for the prisoners taken at Cannae, nor would it permit private citizens to redeem family or friends. Tradition held that some of the ten delegates from the captives tried to remain in Rome, having attempted to circumvent their oath by returning to the Punic camp on some pretext before resuming their journey, but that the Senate had them sent back to Hannibal. In an alternative version of the story they were allowed to remain, but publicly humiliated and ostracized by the rest of the population. Hannibal had some of the 8,000 captives executed and sold the rest into slavery. Soon afterwards the survivors of Cannae were formed into two legions which were sent to Sicily and not allowed discharge or to return to Italy until the end of the war. Some were in fact still serving twenty years later.[30]

The determination of the Roman people under the leadership of the Senate to continue the war in spite of the catastrophe at Cannae was a source of immense pride to later generations of Romans. The Roman aristocracy justified its right to rule by the obligation of its members to lead in war. In the first two years of the war they had paid the price of this duty, suffering disproportionately high losses. Thus Livy's dramatic portrayal of a city stunned by the scale of the disaster probably is not far from the reality. As after Trasimene, news of another disaster soon arrived to add to the despair. Postumius, the praetor sent to Cisalpine Gaul to restrain the Gallic tribes whose aggressive raiding had gone unchecked since Hannibal's arrival, had been ambushed and the bulk of his two legions and allies massacred. The praetor had been beheaded, his skull cleaned and gilded to be used as a vessel in tribal rituals. Yet still the Romans refused to compromise and come to terms with Hannibal. That a few men panicked and despaired should not surprise us; what is truly remarkable is that the majority remained so determined to fight on. Roman victory was still over a decade away and there were other disasters still to come before this was achieved, but with hindsight this was the most serious crisis the Romans faced during the war and the nearest they came to defeat. Whether or not the immediate advance of Hannibal's army on the city after Cannae would have been just enough to tip the balance and shatter Rome's will to resist must remain one of the great unanswered questions of history.[31]

Rome's refusal to negotiate can only have surprised and perhaps discouraged Hannibal, but on balance his situation in late August 216 seemed very good. His army had fully established itself in Italy and displayed its superiority over the best that Rome had sent against it. Soon most of southern Italy would defect to him, and the Gallic tribes of the Po valley remained in open revolt. There was no reason to think that continued pressure on Rome would not eventually force her to acknowledge defeat.

Within a short time the Romans started to recover from the shock and take practical measures to rebuild their strength. A levy was carried out to form new legions, enrolling many 17-year-olds and even younger soldiers. It may have been around this time that the minimum property qualification for military service was lowered to include poorer citizens. Soon there were at least four legions at Rome, although Livy suggests that these were slightly under strength in cavalry, an indication of the severe losses suffered by the equestrian order. An appeal was made to the slave households of citizens, promising freedom and the franchise on discharge for those willing to fight Hannibal; in response 8,000 volunteers (*volones*) came forward and made up two legions, their owners receiving compensation from the State. Another 6,000 men were provided from criminals awaiting punishment and debtors, all of whom were promised amnesty if they were willing to fight. Equipment was in short supply, so the Romans went to the temples of the city and stripped them of the many trophies of foreign armour and weapons from past triumphs, giving the newly raised troops a motley appearance. The released criminals were issued with Gallic weapons and armour captured by Flaminius in 223.[32]

When Varro was recalled to the city he received a rapturous reception, Senate and People praising him for 'not having despaired of the Republic'. Whether or not he caused the defeat at Cannae and whatever the circum-. stances of his flight during the battle, in its aftermath he had behaved as a Roman commander should, regrouping his soldiers to renew the struggle, and refusing to admit defeat or negotiate with the enemy. Varro assisted in the organization of Rome's renewed war effort, and continued to hold commands for the remainder of the war, although he never again led an army in a major battle. The surviving praetors were also heavily involved in the raising and equipping of the new legions and the contingents of allies to support them, but overall command was once again invested in a military dictator. This was Marcus Junius Pera, who had been consul in 230 and censor in 225, with the able Tiberius Sempronius Gracchus as his

Master of Horse. Near the end of the campaigning season of 216, Pera was able to lead a field army of 25,000 men out of the city.[33]

As after Trasimene, the Romans paid great attention to their religious duties. Mourning was officially limited to thirty days by the Senate, but even so they allowed the annual festival to the goddess Ceres to lapse, since this could only be performed by married women who were not in mourning. Two Vestal Virgins were accused of breaking their vows of chastity and in the tense atmosphere were condemned to the traditional punishment of being buried alive, although one girl managed to commit suicide before the sentence was imposed. One of their lovers was scourged so severely that he died as a result. The Sibylline Books were consulted to discover how this offence to the goddess could be propitiated and as a result the Romans made one of their rare recourses to human sacrifice, burying alive a Greek and Gallic man and woman in the Forum Boarium. Fabius Pictor, the later historian, was sent to the famous oracle of Apollo at Delphi in Greece to seek guidance on how the Romans could best restore the favour of the gods and whether as a People they would survive the recent disasters. Polybius found the Romans' obsessive adherence to obscure religious rites at times of crisis rather odd, and certainly un-Greek, but we should never doubt its importance to the Romans themselves.[34]

By the end of the campaigning season of 216 the war in Italy had irrevocably changed. Throughout southern Italy many states defected to Hannibal, including parts of Apulia, nearly all of Samnium and Bruttium, and, most disturbing of all, Campania. The Carthaginian army now had bases from which it could draw supplies and was no longer forced to keep moving simply to feed itself. It also had allies to protect from Roman retribution, a pressing need if other communities were to be persuaded to rebel against Rome. Like the land operations in Sicily during the First War, the Italian campaigns now became dominated by fortified towns and strongholds. The Romans strove to protect their remaining outposts in enemy-held territory whilst steadily attacking their rebellious allies, as Hannibal attempted to overcome these last bastions of Roman authority in the south and defend his new allies. Pitched battles were less common in these years, and invariably fought to protect or threaten a city or town, not with the primary object of destroying the enemy's field army. Skirmishes, blockades and sudden raids were the most common activities for both sides. Much of the campaigning took place in the rugged country of central Italy, near the Apennines, terrain which made it exceptionally difficult to force a battle on an unwilling opponent. The Romans' massive resources of manpower came into play in these years more than ever before, as they fielded unprecedentedly large numbers of legions. Yet unlike 216, these were not massed into one great army, but dispersed into several forces, each not much bigger than a conventional consular army, which operated simultaneously in several theatres. The odds were against Hannibal in this type of warfare, despite his continuing ability to outwit and surprise his opponents. Ultimately he could not match the enemy's numbers and one by one the armies formed by his Italian allies were cornered and defeated, although the Romans were never able to inflict more than minor reverses on Hannibal himself and his mercenaries. In 211, in an effort to lure the Romans away from his beleaguered allies in Capua, Hannibal once again surprised the enemy and made a rapid march to Rome, camping outside the walls of the city. In contrast to 216 the city was well defended, with more troops hurrying to its aid. Later tradition claimed that an auction was held to sell the piece of land on which Hannibal's army had actually camped and that the plot went for the normal market price. Hannibal's response was to hold his own auction and sell off the major banks based around the Roman Forum. Having achieved nothing, for the blockade of Capua had not been interrupted, Hannibal was forced to march away as his food was beginning to run short and sizeable Roman forces were approaching. Whatever threat he had posed to Rome itself was at last laid to rest, but the war was far from over.[35]

CHAPTER 9

The War in Italy 216–203 BC

H ANNIBAL'S FIRST THREE campaigns in Italy have been described in some detail. They are well documented and included three of the largest and most important battles of the entire war. They also provide a good picture of the way in which armies moved and fought during this period. Polybius' continuous narrative of the war ends with Cannae, and only a few fragments exist for the remainder of the thirteen years Hannibal spent in Italy. Livy provides a detailed account of these years, but his reliability is often suspect. Many of the battles he describes seem to be inflated accounts of small skirmishes, perhaps exaggerated by the propaganda of senatorial families who wished to add to the reputations of their ancestors, and little reliance can be placed on Livy's descriptions of these. During these years the rival armies marched and counter-marched across much of southern Italy, frequently passing again over the same areas, both sides struggling to control the important cities and towns, such as Capua, Tarentum, Nola and Beneventum. A simple chronological account of these years would be long, wearisome and confusing to those unfamiliar with the landscape of third-century Italy. Instead, this chapter will attempt to explain why the campaigns developed in this way.

City states in the Graeco-Roman world were inherently unstable, hence the widespread admiration for the 'Mixed Constitutions' of Rome and Carthage which appeared to preserve them from political upheaval. In most communities there seemed always to be individuals or a faction which wished to dominate the state, or a group on the fringes of the established political class who were willing to raise a charismatic leader to the dictatorship if he promised to favour them. Livy presents a picture of fierce factionalism in most of the cities of southern Italy, claiming that in the majority of cases it was the poorer classes which favoured rebellion against Rome and the wealthier citizens who hoped to preserve the alliance, although he does mention a few exceptions to this rule. Livy had little sympathy for politicians who relied on the masses for their support, blaming many of the ills which befell the Republic on such demagogues, and it may be that his association of popular politics with Rome's enemies was a deliberate attempt to condemn them. However, it is not unreasonable to suppose that the leaders wishing to supplant the existing élite were both the most likely to appeal for popular support, and also to favour revolution and so a new alliance with Carthage.[1]

The attitude to the Carthaginians of even those allies who did change sides seems to have been ambivalent at best, for they were alien in language and culture both to Italian and Greek. Rarely did all the communities of one region rebel simultaneously. Many Campanian cities remained loyal even after the defection of Capua and this was true in each area that rebelled, so that even some Samnites remained loyal. In some cases communities were held in check by Roman garrisons, but elsewhere the existing élites were content with Roman rule and themselves suppressed any elements favouring a change. The strength of the Roman network of alliances was demonstrated at this time of crisis, the Latin communities proving especially staunch. Although eventually much of southern Italy defected to, or was captured by, Hannibal, the bulk of Rome's allies remained loyal. In part this may have been due to fear. For much of the war the Romans maintained a strong army in Etruria, and the Senate responded very quickly to reports of discontent and potential rebellion at Arretium. In Sicily during the First War the cities had felt little affinity to either side and had tended to switch allegiances and join whoever they believed to be the stronger. Despite the appearance of invincibility gained by Hannibal after Cannae, this did not happen to anywhere near the same extent in Italy.[2]

Those communities which did join Hannibal had no sense of common identity or purpose. In 215 one of Hannibal's officers, Hanno, led an army primarily composed of Bruttians against Rhegium, Locri and other Greek cities in the south-west of Italy. The Bruttians were amazed when Locri surrendered and was granted allied status by the Carthaginians, for they had eagerly anticipated plundering the city as enemies. They promptly proceeded to besiege Croton without Punic aid to ensure that they alone enjoyed the prizes of this victory. The Roman system had always placed Rome at the centre of a network of otherwise unconnected communities. When allegiance to Rome was removed, then there was no common bond between the Italian communities, since none favoured the prospect of shifting their allegiance to Capua or any other big city. Each tended to look to its own interests and expected Hannibal to provide them with full protection from Roman reprisals. On several occasions the Campanians and Samnites complained that Hannibal was not doing enough to defend them against attacks and expected him to rush to their aid with his main army.[3]

Capua was the most important city to defect to Hannibal in the aftermath of Cannae. Its population held Roman citizenship, but without the right to vote or stand for office in Rome, and the aristocrats of the city had close connections with many senatorial families, marriage alliances being relatively common. Hannibal guaranteed that Capua should be self-governing and retain its own laws, which would be enforced by its own magistrates. No Carthaginian officer or magistrate was to have jurisdiction over the city, and neither could they compel Campanian citizens to serve in the army or perform any other duty against their will. Arrangements were also made to provide the city with 300 Roman prisoners who could be exchanged for a similarly sized detachment of Campanian horse serving with the Romans in Sicily. In fact these cavalrymen chose, or felt compelled, to remain loyal and were later rewarded by the Romans. It was clear that the city did not envisage a close, subordinate relationship with Carthage. Perhaps the leaders at Capua hoped that after the Punic victory in the war, their city would replace Rome as the dominant power in Italy. It is difficult to know to what extent the Capuans were motivated by discontent with their relationship with Rome or despair over their ally's prospects after the string of defeats culminating in Cannae. Livy claims that a deputation had been sent to Varro after the battle and that his sense of despair persuaded them that Rome's defeat was inevitable, but this may simply be another piece of propaganda intended to blacken the consul's name. Romans in Capua were arrested and imprisoned in a bath house, where they were suffocated by the extreme heat of the furnace. It is unclear whether or not this act was deliberate and, if so, who ordered it, but it is clear that feelings against Rome ran high after Capua had rebelled.[4]

Most of the cities which defected to Hannibal did so only on the approach of his army. When a city did not act in this way, Hannibal immediately resorted to force or the threat of force in an attempt to overawe them with his might and prompt their surrender. Twice in late 216 the Punic army swept down on Naples, hoping to force it into submission. Some Neapolitan cavalry were heavily defeated in a skirmish outside the walls, but the magistrates and senate held the population loyal to Rome and no faction willing to seize power or betray the city to the enemy appeared. Hannibal withdrew as soon as this became clear and moved off to try his luck elsewhere, starving Nuceria into submission and making the first of his unsuccessful threats to Nola. Only very small communities were ever subjected to direct assault, for an attack on a well-fortified city had little prospect of success and risked heavy casualties and the diminution of his reputation for invincibility. As in the First War in Sicily, the principal ways of taking a city were by stealth or blockade. Stealth relied on gaining knowledge of a weakness in the defences or an offer of betrayal from inside and was therefore only viable in some places. Blockade required the army to stay in one place for months or even years and the willingness of Hannibal to employ his main army in this way was usually a sign of the importance of the place under siege.[5]

After the fall of Capua, Hannibal began the siege of Casilinum late in 216 and reinforced the blockading force with much of his army early in the next spring. The city lay on the River Volturnus, commanding the routes north out of the Campanian plain along the *via Appia* and the *via Latina*. It was heroically defended by a garrison of allied soldiers, a cohort of about 500 Latins from Praeneste commanded by Marcus Anicius and another of 460 Perusians with a few mixed stragglers from Roman field armies. Short of food the defenders foraged for roots and grass outside the walls, planting turnips when Hannibal ordered the ground ploughed up. A Roman army under the *Magister Equitum* Gracchus hovered in the area but was unwilling to close with the Carthaginian army. To aid the defenders, at night the Romans floated large jars full of grain down the river. For several nights the plan succeeded until Hannibal's men noticed the pots caught in the reeds near the river bank and established a firmer guard, sealing off this means of supply. Eventually the garrison ran out of food and surrendered after Hannibal had promised to ransom them at the rate of seven tenths of a pound of gold per man. This was duly paid – presumably by their communities although our sources are not explicit – and the men released. Livy tells us that Anicius later erected a statue of himself at Praeneste to fulfil a vow made during the siege. About half of the garrison had perished before the capitulation. The Praenestians were offered Roman citizenship by the Senate and interestingly refused the honour, a sign of the strong loyalty of many Latins and Italians to their own communities. Hannibal left Casilinum to the Campanians, bolstering their new garrison with 700 of his own men, for the Romans would need to regain control of this place if they were to threaten Capua itself.[6]

After 216 Hannibal was faced with the permanent problem of protecting his new allies and their territory. Defections to him did not greatly increase the number of soldiers at his disposal. At various times predominantly Italian forces were formed, sometimes bolstered by detachments of mercenaries from the main army and commanded by a Carthaginian officer. The army defeated at the River Calor in 214 consisted of 17,000 Bruttian and Lucanian foot supported by 1,200 Numidian and Moorish light horse under the leadership of Hanno. This army had earlier enjoyed some success in persuading the Greek cities of the south-west to submit. In 212 it was again heavily defeated near Beneventum, when the Romans surprised Hanno whilst the bulk of his men were out foraging. At this action, a cohort from Praeneste once more played a distinguished role, being the first to break into the Punic camp. Most of Hannibal's Italian allies were unwilling to commit large numbers of their troops to campaigning outside their own territory, another sign of the lack of common cause between these communities as well as the fear of Roman reprisals. It was rare for there to be more than one sizeable force available to operate in support of Hannibal's main army and, as Hanno's defeats showed, their performance was poor. The Romans fought with great determination against their former allies and were certainly not in awe of them, as they still were of Hannibal and his army. Few Italians had ever exercised high command, since such posts were the preserves of Roman citizens, and Carthaginian officers could only gradually create a bond with Italian soldiers and develop some sort of command structure to control these new armies. As at the River Calor, most of these predominantly Italian armies were weak in cavalry, denying them one of the greatest advantages Hannibal himself had always enjoyed over the Romans. This meant that the only force which could consistently face and defeat Roman armies in battle was Hannibal's own main army. Some Italians were incorporated into this and performed well, but its heart remained the Libyan, Numidian, Spanish and Gallic contingents. Its numbers were steadily diminished by casualties, disease, and the need to detach groups to bolster allied resistance. Only once, in 214, did Hannibal receive a significant reinforcement when Bomilcar and a Punic fleet managed to land troops, elephants and supplies at Locri.[7]

The Roman situation was utterly different. We have already seen how quickly they had mustered new legions in the months after Cannae, making use of slaves and criminals. There is some suggestion that during these years the minimum property qualification for service in the legions was significantly reduced, adding to the already large pool of citizen manpower which was to prove Rome's great advantage in these years. Record numbers of legions were enrolled for the remaining years of the conflict. Livy is our main source for the number of legions fielded in each year, although there are some problems and apparent contradictions in these passages, for instance the inconsistency with which he includes the armies in Spain in his figures, so that certain scholars have modified his total. There were at least twelve and probably fourteen legions in service in the spring of 215 and eighteen in 214. The number continued to rise until there were twenty-five legions at the peak of Roman mobilization in 212–211, representing a theoretical strength of at least 100,000 infantry and 7,500 cavalry, supported as always by a similar number of allied soldiers. The bulk of these troops were invariably deployed in Italy. However, they were not concentrated into one or two great armies intended to confront and defeat Hannibal in open battle. In the decade after Cannae there were between four and seven consular-sized, two-legion armies operating in the Italian Peninsula, supported by several single-legion forces as well as smaller garrisons and detachments. The increase in the number of active field armies made it relatively easy for the Romans to threaten defecting Italian states.[8]

There was also far more continuity in the Roman command. Fabius Maximus held his third consulship in 215 with Tiberius Sempronius Gracchus, the dictator Pera's *Magister Equitum*, as his colleague. In 214 he was again consul, this time with Marcus Claudius Marcellus, who had held the office in 222. The next year Fabius' son, also called Quintus Fabius Maximus, was elected consul in what was seen as a gesture of favour for his father, and Gracchus won his second term of office. Marcellus held the consulship again in 210 and 208, and the elder Fabius once more in 209. In 212 and 209 Quintus Fulvius Flaccus held his third and fourth consulships, over twenty years after he had first held the post in 237. All of these men also held pro-magisterial commands during the years between their office, so that Marcellus served without a break from 216 until his death in 208. The electorate's preference for experienced men to hold the senior posts indicated a realization that the current crisis required able commanders, but was also a result of the appalling casualties suffered by the major senatorial families in the first years of the war. The Senate's ranks had been replenished by men with distinguished records, but these were invariably too young or too poor to stand for the highest magistracy with any chance of success. Marcellus, Fabius and Fulvius Flaccus were all in their late fifties or sixties, members of the generation which had grown up and fought during the First Punic War. Serving with the same legions for several years in succession greatly increased the bond between commander and soldiers. The legions of *volones*, the slaves recruited after Cannae, showed particular affection for Gracchus, dispersing and having to be reformed after he was ambushed and killed in 212.[9]

Several of the elections in these years were controversial. In 215, Gracchus and Lucius Postumius were originally elected consuls, and the

Assembly voted for Marcellus to replace the latter when he was ambushed and killed in Gaul. However, on the day that Marcellus formally assumed the office, the college of augurs reported hearing thunder and his election was declared invalid on religious grounds. Another election was held and Fabius Maximus chosen. It is difficult to know what lay behind this incident, although manipulation of the State religion for political ends was not unknown at Rome. Those who understand Roman politics purely in terms of factions have had trouble reconciling Fabius' apparent desire to prevent Marcellus holding office, with his willingness to have him as a colleague the next year. Fabius himself presided over the election for 214 and is supposed to have asked the leading centuries of the *Comitia* to reconsider, when they had initially chosen two former praetors whom he considered to be unsuitable for the current situation. Livy tells us that the Senate informally stated that it was improper to have Marcellus and Gracchus as colleagues, since both were plebeians and it was traditional to reserve at least one of the consulships for a patrician. If this was in fact behind the whole business, then it would indicate the same sort of emphasis on scrupulous normality in spite of the current crisis which also characterized the regulation of the State religion at this time. The continuation of the normally fierce competition for office throughout the Hannibalic war is another indication of the strength of the Roman political system. Roman senators battled furiously to gain magistracies and senior commands against the State's most dangerous enemy. None ever dreamed of joining that enemy and seeking his aid to gain power in a defeated Rome.[10]

Although the Roman armies fielded in these years did not mass together, they often operated in mutual support. Campania was the main focus of Roman attention until 211. In 215 Fabius and Gracchus both went there, whilst Marcellus based himself with another two legions at Nola. Gracchus relieved Cumae on his own, but afterwards both consuls acted together against the outposts protecting the approaches to Capua. In 214 Marcellus brought his army into the area to cover Fabius whilst he besieged and eventually captured Casilinum. Later, near the end of Fabius' year of office, a nobleman from the city of Arpi in northern Apulia came to him and offered to betray the city to the Romans in return for a reward. This man, one Dasius Altinus, informed them of a weakness in the city's defences. Fabius approached as if to conduct a regular siege, but then employed a picked body of 600 men in a night attack. The weather favoured the Romans as a thunderstorm reduced visibility and forced most of the sentries to seek shelter. Setting ladders against the weak spot in the wall, the Roman force climbed into the city and moved silently to seize the gates and admit the remainder of the army into the city just before dawn. For a while the population and the Punic garrison tried to resist in the streets, but the Arpini surrendered and turned on their erstwhile allies. The Carthaginians in turn capitulated and were allowed to rejoin Hannibal's main army, but nearly 1,000 Spanish deserted to the Romans who rewarded them with double rations, perhaps an indication of one of their grievances with Carthaginian service conditions. This was the second serious desertion suffered by Hannibal's army, for 272 mixed Spanish and Numidian cavalrymen had defected to Marcellus' camp outside Nola the previous year. Such losses in the years when Hannibal's strength and fortune appeared at its greatest are striking, but this was not entirely a one-way process, for some Roman and Italian deserters proved willing to fight with the enemy. On the whole Hannibal's soldiers of all nationalities proved remarkably loyal.[11]

Like so many of the other strongholds to fall during the Punic Wars, Arpi was captured by treachery and stealth. Hannibal had some successes elsewhere during these years, usually by the same means, but his repeated attempts to capture Nola, which lies on the edge of the Campanian plain, failed. The Romans were ruthless in their attacks on allies who had rebelled, but their commanders paid careful attention to winning back the loyalty of the disaffected Italian noblemen before they committed themselves to the enemy. At Nola Marcellus rewarded and lavished praise on the bravery of Lucius Bantius who had been captured at Cannae and released as part of Hannibal's plan to win over the Italians. Fabius also took care to foster the loyalty of his allied soldiers, for instance rewarding a Marsian soldier, who was believed to be planning to desert, and publicly stating that the man's achievements had been unfairly overlooked in the past.[12]

The Fall of Tarentum

Hannibal was especially eager to capture a port. The Roman refusal to concede defeat after Cannae and the continued loyalty of most of her allies had made it clear that the war would not be won quickly. In the struggle to control the walled towns and cities of southern Italy, Hannibal was at an increasing disadvantage as the Romans mobilized more and more soldiers. His main army remained undefeated in any serious engagement and he repeatedly led it against the strongholds loyal to Rome, hoping to force their defection or discover a means of capturing them. The Roman armies kept to the higher ground on the fringes of the Apennines as far as possible and avoided the plains where the superiority of the Carthaginian cavalry was unchallenged. Roman commanders offered battle only from strong defensive positions, which the Carthaginian was rarely willing to attack. In the hilly country around places such as Beneventum and Nola it was hard to fight a decisive battle. Rarely were the open plains wide enough to deploy large armies and there was always higher ground for a beaten side to retire to and recover. Even a general of Hannibal's genius could not force a reluctant enemy to fight pitched battles in this country. His army needed to remain concentrated if it was to threaten the Romans. Wherever it appeared, the Romans' movements had to become cautious, but the army could only be in one place at a time and the Roman forces elsewhere inevitably became very aggressive. Unprotected, his allies were attacked and their fields raided. Hannibal's rapid and unexpected marches during these years displayed all his familiar genius and the continued efficiency of his army, but even this could not entirely overcome the enemy's vastly superior numbers.

Late in 216 Hannibal had sent his brother Mago to report to the Carthaginian Senate. There, perhaps in the same hall where Fabius Buteo had let slip war from the fold of his toga, Mago ordered his attendants to pour onto the floor heaps of the gold rings taken from the bodies of slain Roman senators and equestrians as evidence of the slaughter Hannibal had wrought on the state's enemies. He ended with an appeal for immediate reinforcement and supplies of grain to feed the army. Livy claims that Hanno, the old opponent of the Barcid family, mocked the catalogue of Hannibal's achievements, complaining that the general was asking for aid as if he was losing rather than winning the war. In spite of this criticism, the majority voted to send support to the army in Italy as well as reinforcing the position in Spain. The problem was how to get reinforcements and supplies to Italy. Without a port, and some degree of control over the waters off Sicily, no sizeable reinforcement could reach Hannibal without following the land route he had taken himself.[13]

Hannibal had failed at Cumae and Naples. In 214 five noblemen from the great maritime city of Tarentum came to the Punic camp. All had been captured at Trasimene or Cannae and released. They claimed that they had the support of most of their city and that it would immediately defect if the Carthaginian army approached in force. Hannibal was currently on the west coast outside Cumae and made another attempt at Naples, before marching once more on Nola. From there he set out at night, reaching Tarentum whilst the Roman armies were all occupied elsewhere. The Roman garrison were on their guard and had recently been reinforced by the fleet from Brundisium. No rising occurred in the city and none of the noblemen appeared to fulfil their promises, so after a few days Hannibal withdrew.[14]

In 212 hostages from Tarentum and Thurii attempted to escape from Rome and were arrested and executed, enraging opinion in these and many other Greek cities. Another conspiracy was formed at Tarentum by a group of young aristocrats led by Philemenus and Nico (Nikon in Greek). Hannibal had placed his winter camp three days' march from the city and before the spring he was approached by the conspirators, who were ostensibly on a hunting expedition. Hannibal accepted their offer and sent them back, driving cattle from his baggage train which they claimed to have found grazing and captured. In the next weeks the ruse was repeated on several occasions as the noblemen negotiated the conditions of their betrayal. Tarentum was granted much the same terms as Capua, being guaranteed freedom to be ruled by its own laws and magistrates, that the city would not pay tribute to Carthage nor accept a Punic garrison against its will. Only the property of Roman citizens living in the city was to be seized by Hannibal and these, as well as the Roman garrison, would be taken prisoner by the Carthaginians who could then ransom or sell them as they wished.[15]

The detailed accounts of the capture of Tarentum provide a good example of the type of operations which occurred when other cities were betrayed and are worth recounting in detail. Philemenus took to hunting at night, allegedly to avoid Punic patrols, and regularly returned with prizes which he liberally shared with the sentries and commander at the side gate he used. So familiar did the guards become with this routine that they happily opened the gate whenever they recognized his whistle. Hannibal picked 10,000 mixed horse and foot for their speed and agility to form his attack column, issued four days' rations, and led them out in the middle of the night. Interestingly they included three bands of Gauls, a total of 2,000 men, which shows how effectively these warriors had been absorbed into the army, when compared with the criticisms of the Gauls' lack of speed and stamina in marching during the 217 campaign. The column was screened by 80 Numidian horsemen, who had orders to capture or kill anyone they met but otherwise give the impression that they were no more than a normal foraging party. Hannibal's force marched them to within 14 or 15 miles of the city, keeping the men tightly under control and not permitting any straggling. He rested them for the remainder of the day in a gorge where they were hidden from view, holding a briefing for his officers in which he stressed that they must keep their men tightly under control and obey his orders to the letter.

The commander of Tarentum's Roman garrison, one Marcus or Caius Livius, was attending a feast when he received a report of the marauding

Numidian cavalry. He saw no serious threat in their actions and merely ordered a cavalry patrol to be sent out the next day. The conspirators had deliberately chosen this day in the belief that Livius would be distracted and some of them kept him drinking after the celebration and escorted him home in no state to command. That night Hannibal was guided towards the city by Philemenus and made the prearranged signal by lighting a bonfire. When the conspirators answered with a fire-signal of their own, Hannibal extinguished the beacon and divided his force into three. The 2,000 cavalry were to remain outside, ready as a reserve to cover their retreat or exploit their success. Philemenus led 1,000 Libyans towards the gate he habitually used for his hunting expeditions, whilst Hannibal led the remainder cautiously up the main road towards the Temenid Gate. The conspirators surprised the guards there and massacred them, killing the majority in their sleep, and admitted the Carthaginians when they arrived. In the meantime Philemenus and three others approached the other gate carrying a boar as if returning from the hunt. Hearing Philemenus' whistle, the sentry admitted them through the postern door next to the main gate. As the man leaned over to view their prize, Philemenus killed him with a hunting spear. Thirty Libyans had followed close behind the four men and swiftly entered, dealing with the guards and opening the main gate for the rest of the force. Pushing into the city, the whole body joined Hannibal, who had by this time reached the Forum. From there he dispatched the three bands of Gauls guided by some of the conspirators to take control of all the routes into the marketplace. All Romans encountered were killed, most without managing much resistance. Further confusion was added when the conspirators brought out some Roman military trumpets and began to sound contradictory orders. Livius escaped in a rowing skiff to the citadel which lay on a narrow promontory and was the only part of the town to remain in Roman hands. The Tarentines, faced with an enemy already controlling their streets, were assembled and soon accepted the terms presented to them by the conspirators.

Hannibal took immediate steps to reduce the citadel, which commanded the entrance to Tarentum's harbour. A wall and ditch were constructed cutting the promontory off from the main city, and a Roman sally to hinder the work was heavily defeated. However, the Roman garrison remained confident and was able to draw supplies and reinforcements from the sea. The entire garrison of Metapontum was shipped into the citadel, although their withdrawal prompted the defection of that city. A direct assault failed and Hannibal left the blockade largely in the hands of the Tarentines. He once again demonstrated his ingenuity by showing the citizens how to drag their galleys from the harbour and down one of the main streets to float them again in the open sea, allowing them to close the blockade by sea.[16]

Rome Resurgent

The capture of Tarentum was a heavy blow to Rome and a great, if incomplete, victory for Hannibal. Yet in the same year the Romans advanced to begin a full-scale siege of the other major city to join him, Capua. As early as 215 Fabius Maximus had mounted a series of heavy raids to ravage Campanian territory. Grain can most easily be burned for only a short period before harvest and the Romans took care to mount their attacks each year at this time. With cities such as Arpi and Casilinum back under their control both consuls were able to move against Capua itself in 212 and begin its blockade. In answer to the Capuans' appeal, Hannibal sent only 2,000 cavalry and several officers to their aid, but made vague promises of more substantial assistance. The Campanian cavalry were very good and had always been highly thought of by the Romans. Reinforced by the detachment from Hannibal's main army they won several small actions. However, the Romans' morale was restored when one of their own horsemen accepted the challenge to single combat issued by a Campanian with whom he was linked by ties of hospitality. This is the second such duel between Roman and Campanian described by Livy, in both of which he patriotically avers that the Roman proved successful.[17]

Soon afterwards Hannibal did march his army to the relief of Capua. Three days after his arrival he offered battle in front of the Roman camps. Livy's account of the action is confused, although not necessarily impossible, since he claims that battle was ended when both sides saw a distant column approaching and, assuming them to be enemies, broke off the action. Whatever the actual details of the fighting, it seems to have been indecisive, but at the very least discouraged the Roman consuls. Their two armies decided to part company and march in opposite directions to lure Hannibal away from Capua, knowing that he could only pursue one of them, so that the other could return. Livy tells the strange story of a former senior centurion named Marcus Centenius, who had requested a command from the Senate, claiming that his intimate knowledge of the area would allow him to raid it with great effect. With 8,000 men under his command he ran into Hannibal who had just given up his pursuit of one of the retreating consular armies. Centenius died heroically, but his men were massacred in the brief action or the ensuing pursuit so that barely 1,000 escaped.[18]

In the meantime both consular armies had returned to Capua to renew the blockade. Supplies were massed in a depot at Casilinum and strong-holds established to control the River Volturnus so that bulky material such as grain could be carried in safety along it to feed the armies. Great care was taken to organize an effective system of supply, for large numbers of Roman troops would have to remain in one position if the blockade were to be successful. The two consular armies were joined by another com-manded by a praetor, Claudius Nero, and the six legions set to work building a wall and ditch to encircle the city and another facing outwards. A last plea for assistance was sent to Hannibal by the city before the line of circumvallation was closed, but the Carthaginian was interested in other projects, hoping to capture Brundisium by treachery. The Romans offered free pardon to any Campanians who surrendered to them before the lines had been closed. None responded, although 112 equestrians had deserted to the Romans the year before.[19]

In 211 the siege of Capua remained the main priority of the Senate in Italy and both the consuls and Nero had their commands extended as pro-magistrates. The Campanian horse continued to enjoy frequent successes, until a Roman centurion, one Quintus Naevius, came up with the idea of forming a picked body of *velites* who would ride behind the Roman horse-men. In action they dismounted and fought in close support of the cavalry, acting as a solid bulwark in the shelter of which the horsemen could rally and reform to charge again. The new tactic gave the advantage to the Romans in all subsequent encounters. This incident has sometimes been depicted as a major reform of the cavalry and light infantry of the legions, but in fact it was simply a local expedient to deal with a particular situation. It reflected the growing experience of the Roman armies, rather than any fundamental change in their composition.[20]

Capua would inevitably fall if the blockade were not broken, so Hanni-bal decided that he must act. Leaving the heavier part of his baggage train with the Bruttians he hastened to Campania. The Roman armies were now in the open country around Capua where his more numerous and effective cavalry could normally be expected to have given Hannibal the advantage, but the Romans refused to leave their fortifications and fight a pitched battle. The proconsul Appius Claudius was not to be drawn out when Hannibal sent skirmishers up to the pickets outside the Roman camp in the way that he had lured other Roman commanders into unfavourable battles. Desperately Hannibal launched a direct assault on the Roman camps, whilst the Capuans sallied out to attack the defences from the other side. At one point a unit of Spanish infantry led by three elephants broke through the fortifications and threatened Fulvius Flaccus' camp, only to be repulsed as the Romans counter-attacked inspired by the heroic example set by several officers including Naevius. Hannibal's attack failed and his army quickly began to run short of food. They had carried only a small supply with them and the Romans had picked the land around clean of anything that could be foraged. It was then that Hannibal decided to march on Rome in the effort to lure the legions away from Capua described in the last chapter. When this failed, he abandoned Capua to its fate and returned via Samnium and Apulia to Bruttium in the south-east.[21]

Even the Carthaginian officers left in the city felt betrayed and abandoned by their commander, but the angry letters they dispatched to him were all intercepted by the Romans, who cut off the hands of the couriers (who had pretended to desert) and returned the men to the city. Capua's population was now facing starvation. A few of the more anti-Roman senators committed suicide, but the remainder surrendered the city, opening the gates to admit the Romans. Soon afterwards the outlying communities of Atella and Calatia also capitulated. Fifty-three Capuan senators who were held principally responsible for the rebellion against Rome were arrested. They were subsequently executed by the proconsul Fulvius, seemingly on his own authority and against the wishes of his colleague, although there were apparently several traditions concerning this incident. Later the Roman Senate decided to dissolve Capua as a city state with institutions, magistrates and laws of its own. In future it was to be governed by an official appointed by Rome.[22]

In 209 Hannibal's other great prize, the city of Tarentum, was recaptured by Rome. Once again the city was betrayed to an attacker. This was the last campaign fought by Fabius Maximus. During these years the Roman garrison had managed to cling onto the citadel of the city and much hard fighting had occurred as attempts were made to run supplies through the Tarentine blockade. In the spring two of the seven two-legion armies operating in Italy in that year were sent to keep Hannibal's army occupied, whilst Fabius led his own men against Tarentum. A further diversion was provided by a group of Bruttian deserters and an irregular force from Sicily based at Rhegium who were sent to raid widely, a task they carried out with considerable enthusiasm. Tarentum had surrendered on the condition that it could not be forced to accept a Punic garrison, but it is clear that it had willingly accepted one at some point. Under the overall command of Carthalo, this garrison included a band of Bruttians whose commander happened to be in love with the sister of a Tarentine man in Fabius' army. With the approval of the consul, the Tarentine pretended to desert and used the connection to befriend the Bruttian officer. (In another, even more romantic version of the story, this officer was actually in love with Fabius' former mistress.) The officer was persuaded to defect and bring his men with him. When Fabius launched an assault on the city he sent a group with ladders to the stretch of wall guarded by this unit. The Bruttians helped the Romans into the city and despite some fighting in the streets, the issue was never in doubt. Nico and some of the other conspirators died fighting, Philemenus disappeared and was presumed killed. Carthalo trusted to ties of guest friendship with Fabius, but was overtaken by a group of soldiers and cut down before he could reach the consul. The Roman soldiers ran amok, killing Tarentines and Carthaginians indiscriminately, and even some of the Bruttians were deliberately or accidentally slaughtered. An immense amount of booty and 30,000 slaves were taken. By the time that Hannibal had heard of the threat to the city and marched to its relief, it was all over.

The brief campaign had demonstrated once again that Hannibal could not deal with all the Roman threats simultaneously. He had fought some confused and indecisive actions against the proconsul Marcellus outside Canusium not far from Cannae when Fabius had begun his drive on Tarentum. Hoping to inflict at least a minor reverse on the victorious Romans, the Carthaginian sent a false message to the consul's camp alleging that some noblemen were willing to betray Metapontum. Fabius is supposed to have taken the bait, but cancelled the expedition because of unfavourable omens, or perhaps just his instinctive caution.[24]

Despite its losses – 500 of his best Numidian cavalry were killed or captured when Salapia was betrayed to the Romans in 210 – Hannibal's army still remained a formidable force. It is difficult to avoid the suspicion that Livy's accounts of the many minor Roman victories, or battles ended by nightfall or weather before a decision could be reached, conceal tactical defeats, but even he records a number of outright Punic victories. In 212 the praetor Cnaeus Fulvius Flaccus was defeated with the loss of 16,000 men outside Herdonea, when Hannibal repeated his trick from Trebia of concealing men behind the enemy line. In 210 the proconsul Cnaeus Fulvius Centumalus was defeated near the same city, losing 7,000 or 13,000 men depending on the source. Although the coincidence of the Roman commanders' names and the location has sometimes led to suggestions that Livy has mistakenly described the same battle twice, there is no good reason to accept this and some evidence to corroborate his version. In the second battle, the Romans are supposed to have deployed not just in the usual *triplex acies* but with entire legions in reserve, a practice which Livy claims was followed in other battles in these years. If these accounts are accurate, the tactic may simply be a reflection of the lack of reasonably open ground in the hilly country in which the armies chiefly operated during these years, so that there was rarely space to deploy all the units of an army side by side. It is also worth remembering that when the Roman army deployed from column of march it did so by wheeling its three parallel columns to the right to form the *triplex acies*. If the enemy was encountered unexpectedly, it may well have been easier and quicker to wheel each *ala* and legion separately into line where it stood, so that at least the lead units could present an organized fighting line to any enemy threat. Many of the actions appear to have been unanticipated encounter battles without the days of cautious manoeuvring and observation of the enemy which had preceded battles like Trebia and Cannae.[25]

The survivors of the disasters at Herdonea were sent to replenish the ranks of the Cannae veterans fighting in Sicily and obliged to serve under the same conditions as these. The praetor Fulvius was prosecuted for his incompetence and exiled, only narrowly escaping the death penalty. Serious though these defeats were, a far greater psychological shock came in 208 when both of the consuls, Marcellus again and Titus Quinctius Crispinus, were ambushed by Hannibal whilst carrying out a reconnaissance. Marcellus was killed in the initial attack, along with a tribune and two prefects, and his colleague mortally wounded. Hannibal treated Marcellus' corpse with respect, but also tried to take advantage by using the consul's signet ring in an attempt to recapture the town of Salapia. A letter was sent bearing Marcellus' seal and instructing the local authorities to receive him and a body of troops. A column was formed headed by a group of Roman deserters still dressed in their old uniforms. However, Crispinus had realized the danger and sent messages warning all the towns in the area to be on their guard. The garrison of Salapia let the leaders of the approaching column pass through the gate and then dropped the portcullis behind them. Six hundred men, mostly the deserters, were massacred in the confined space.[26]

By this time the area still controlled by Hannibal had been reduced to the extreme south of the country. In spite of his continued successes, the pressure of Roman numbers and the constant aggression of the annually appointed Roman commanders gradually reduced his allies. More and more individuals and whole communities returned to their original allegiance to Rome, encouraged by the good treatment which such defectors received in comparison to the punishment of states recaptured by force. In 209 the Hirpini and Lucanians surrendered and were reprimanded, but not punished for their earlier defection. The Bruttians were offered the same treatment if they too returned to Rome, and some of their noblemen welcomed this. The drift was not entirely in one direction. As the Salapian incident showed, there was still a tiny minority of Roman soldiers willing to fight for the enemy, as there were Libyans, Spanish, and Numidians willing to desert and serve against their former comrades. Yet overwhelmingly the trend in defections was now in favour of Rome.[27]

The mobilization of so many soldiers and the maintenance of a war fought on a huge scale and on many fronts simultaneously had placed Rome under tremendous strain. Not all citizens had patriotically devoted themselves to serve the interests of the state. In 213 a scandal occurred when it was revealed that the contractors paid by the state to supply the armies in Spain had been falsifying their returns and scuttling empty ships to claim massive compensation for losses to storms. In 209 the censors made an example of those equestrians from the highest centuries who had been 17 or older in 218, but who had failed to serve in the army for a single campaign during the war, by downgrading them to a lower class. (These were exceptions to the general rule, for an overwhelming majority of Roman citizens proved remarkably willing to submit to long years of legionary service and sacrifice themselves to defend their state.) A more disturbing incident had also occurred in 209 when twelve out of the thirty Latin colonies which formed the heart of Rome's network of allies declared that they could no longer contribute soldiers or funds to the war effort. This seems to have been a result of exhaustion more than disloyalty and the remaining colonies stressed their loyalty and the willingness to fulfil their obligations. Rome was winning the war of endurance, but that does not mean that the city and her allies were not feeling the strain of maintaining the struggle for so long.[28]

The Battle of Metaurus, 22 June 207 BC

Only one draft of reinforcements ever reached Hannibal by sea, when Bomilcar landed at Locri in 215. A combination of Hannibal's lack of a major port, the Carthaginians' failure to drive the Romans from Sicily and win naval dominance of the sea routes around the island, and apathy amongst the leadership at Carthage, prevented a repeat of this convoy. It seems clear that from the beginning Hannibal hoped to be reinforced by an army from Spain following the overland route he had taken himself. Hasdrubal Barca is said to have been planning such an expedition in 216 when it was rendered impractical by Roman successes in Spain. The need to restore Punic fortunes in Spain also led to the redirection of the troops raised in Europe by Mago Barca which had originally been intended to go to Italy. Hasdrubal tried again in 208 and successfully led an army out of Spain despite being defeated in a rearguard action at Baecula. He seems to have followed a similar route to his brother but does not appear to have had to fight the local tribes as often, with the result that his smaller army suffered fewer casualties. Perhaps it helped that he was spending gold lavishly to hire mercenaries from amongst the Gallic tribes. Massilia sent messages to warn the Romans of his progress. Roman ambassadors were sent and through links of guest friendship between Massiliotes and some Gallic chieftains discovered that Hasdrubal expected to cross the Alps into Italy early in the spring of 207.[29]

The news caused panic at Rome. For a decade they had waged war against an enemy army on their own lands. Vast numbers of soldiers had been enrolled and kept permanently in service. Casualties had been huge and the financial cost to the state enormous, whilst wide swathes of the Italian countryside had been foraged over and devastated by the rival armies. After all the effort Hannibal remained undefeated and although he had been hemmed into a corner of southern Italy he was still capable of outwitting their commanders. The declaration of the twelve colonies in 209 might suggest that the State was nearing the end of its resources. Now another of Hamilcar Barca's sons was set to invade Italy with fire and sword. What if the two brothers were to join forces? Were there to be new 'Trebia's and 'Cannae's, and if so, could Rome survive?

One of the new consuls, Marcus Livius Salinator, who had only a few years before returned to political life following a self-imposed retirement after the scandals of his first consulship in 219, was sent north with an army. He was supported by one of the praetors, Lucius Porcius Licinus, who had two understrength legions based near Ariminum, whilst Varro led a similarly sized force on the other side of the Apennines in Etruria. Just like his brother in 217, Hasdrubal would be forced to choose which side of these mountains to advance down, so once again the Senate deployed armies to guard against both options. The Carthaginians descended from the Alps earlier than the Romans had expected, although Licinus heard of his advance and sent a message warning Rome and urging the consuls to join their armies as soon as possible. Once in the Po valley, Hasdrubal marched on Placentia and began to besiege the colony. Perhaps he wanted to rest his men after their march, or as Livy suggests wanted the prestige of an early victory, which might certainly encourage the Gallic tribes to muster to him. However, the town's defenders proved more resilient than he had anticipated and he abandoned the blockade. Six riders, two Numidians and four Gauls, were sent with sealed letters to find Hannibal. As usual in the campaigning season, Hannibal's army was constantly on the move and it was near Tarentum that some of the messengers were arrested by a Roman patrol. After interrogation their letters were discovered and sent to the Senate, who read in them that Hasdrubal hoped to meet his brother in Umbria. Livy provides no detail as to precisely where in this large area the rendezvous was supposed to occur. Clearly it was somewhere on the east coast, perhaps near the southern edge of the *ager Gallicus*. Hannibal remained in the south as his brother began to push down the east coast of Italy.[30]

This was not like 218. The Romans were in a far higher state of mobilization, their leaders and armies more experienced and effective. Their response to the news of the Carthaginians' intentions was rapid. Somewhere, perhaps near Sena Gallica, Hasdrubal was confronted by the combined armies of Salinator and the praetor Licinus, who had retreated ahead of the enemy, delaying their march as much as possible. The other consul, Caius Claudius Nero, had a somewhat ambiguous reputation for boldness verging on rashness. At the beginning of the year he had been sent to lead the armies containing Hannibal in the south and was near Canusium when he received the intercepted message. Nero decided to take the pick of his army, some 6,000 foot and 1,000 cavalry, and lead them north to join his colleague. Instructions were sent out to the communities along his planned route ordering them to prepare food and supplies for his soldiers who were to march unburdened. The towns were also to make ready carts and mules to give lifts to the weary men in the column. Then, spreading a rumour that he intended a surprise attack on a nearby city, Nero marched out of camp at night and after a short distance swung north towards Picenum. As they marched crowds cheered them on their way, furnishing the requested supplies. The reaction in Rome to the report of the consul's move was less certain, as many feared that the remainder of the army he had left in Apulia might be vulnerable to Hannibal's attack. Livy does not say how long this forced march of around 250 miles took Nero's men, although he does claim that the return journey was completed even more quickly, in only six days. Clearly it was fast enough to surprise Hasdrubal, and the Romans took care to conceal this reinforcement. Messengers were sent ahead to Salinator and it was arranged for the column to march in under cover of darkness and that the men were then to be led as quietly as possible by the individual soldiers in the camp to the tents they would share. Although Hasdrubal's camp was a mere 500 paces – half a Roman mile – away, the deception worked.[31]

The next morning Nero persuaded his colleague and the praetor to risk a battle immediately, preferring the benefit of surprise over allowing his footsore soldiers to rest. Hasdrubal had already formed his army in battle order outside his camp as the Romans marched out to deploy. However, he is said to have noticed amongst the Roman line men with old shields he had not seen before, and cavalry with lean horses, as well as having a general impression of an increase in Roman numbers. Worried, Hasdrubal refused battle and the Romans, as was usual, did not force an engagement with an enemy who refused to advance far from his camp. Patrols were sent out to observe the separate camps pitched by Licinus and Salinator. Livy tells us that they reported two trumpet fanfares in the consul's camp and only one in the praetor's camp, which Hasdrubal correctly understood as meaning that a second consul must also be present. The size of Hasdrubal's army is unclear, but it seems probable that the addition of the equivalent of a strong legion to the Roman armies facing him convinced him that a battle was unwise. In the night he retreated towards the River Metaurus. Livy claims that his guides, presumably local men, deserted and that the Punic column went astray in the darkness, but night marches have always been difficult and it is possible that the mistake was accidental. Later in the night Hasdrubal reached the river bank and ordered his units to follow it, hoping to strike the proper road by the light of dawn and so discover a crossing place.

The Romans began the pursuit as soon as they realized that the enemy had retreated. Nero led with the combined cavalry of the three armies, followed by Licinus with the *velites* and Salinator, under whose auspices the battle was fought, with the main army. They caught up with Hasdrubal when the latter had decided that his men needed rest and so had begun to construct a camp on a hill overlooking the river. As the various elements of the Roman armies arrived and began to form a battle line, the Carthaginian ordered his men to stop work on the camp and deploy. Both sides must have been tired after their march, but the Roman commanders were eager for battle and did not intend to delay. The precise location of the battle of Metaurus is unknown and the suggestions have varied widely. The terrain seems to have been fairly uneven and the open space limited, and this, combined with the haste with which each side formed up, made the battle less regular than Hannibal's early campaigns and more like the fighting in southern Italy. Nero commanded the Roman right wing, apparently with his own infantry and cavalry; Licinus held the centre and Salinator the left. It is unclear whether all the cavalry were divided between the extreme left and right wings as was the usual practice, although Livy seems to imply that the bulk of the Roman cavalry were with Salinator on the left which may mean that Nero had the allied horse. Hasdrubal stationed his ten elephants (fifteen according to Appian[32]) ahead of his centre, and placed his best troops, the Spanish, on the right and the Gauls on the left. According to Livy his centre behind the elephants was composed of Ligurians, but Polybius does not mention their presence at all in his account, although he may simply have lumped them in with the Spanish. Neither Livy nor Polybius make any specific mention of Carthaginian cavalry. The Gauls were on high ground in a very formidable position, certainly impossible to take by a frontal attack and perhaps difficult even to reach. The Punic centre and left were deployed unusually deep, probably a reflection of the confined space and the haste with which they had formed up. The Romans are unlikely to have had many more than 40,000 men and Hasdrubal significantly fewer, but these numbers must remain conjectural.

The battle began when Hasdrubal launched his main assault against Salinator and the Roman left, who advanced to meet him. Livy claims that the elephants disordered the *hastati* and created a temporary advantage, but then panicked and spread confusion on both sides. The fighting was fierce and no clear advantage was achieved by either side as both Salinator and Hasdrubal were closely involved in the fighting, directing and encouraging their men by personal example. On the right, the Romans could make no headway against the position held by the Gauls and were unable to find a way of outflanking it. Nero then made a remarkably bold and imaginative decision on his own initiative. Taking many of the men from his wing, he led them in a march behind the Roman battle line and around the enemy's extreme right flank. They then attacked the Spanish in the flank, turning the tide decisively in the Romans' favour. The Punic right and centre collapsed into rout under this unexpected onslaught. Hasdrubal, realizing that the day was lost, died fighting heroically or, according to another tradition, committed suicide. The Romans rolled up the entire army, driving the Gauls from their hilltop and storming the Punic camp. More Gauls are said to have been discovered there, most lying in a drunken stupor in their tents. It is possible that Hasdrubal's recently recruited Gallic allies had as poor march discipline as the tribesmen Hannibal had had to drive along in 217. For troops unused to campaigning, the long and confusing night march would have proved very fatiguing.

Polybius tells us that 10,000 of Hasdrubal's men fell in the battle for the loss of 2,000 Romans, far more plausible figures than the huge totals given by Livy. Six elephants were killed and the other four rounded up in the aftermath. It was a great Roman victory and the entire campaign demonstrated the higher efficiency and greater flexibility of Roman armies compared to the beginning of the war. The Romans had responded quickly to news of the enemy's intentions, arranging to intercept Hasdrubal with two armies, which were then reinforced by a strong detachment from a third. Nero's march was a triumph not just for discipline and determination, but for the logistical organization which allowed him to arrange in a matter of days for supplies to be prepared in advance along his route. His decision to march from one wing to outflank the enemy on the opposite end of the battlefield displayed a degree of tactical flexibility unimaginable in the legions of 218. The same level of skill was also to be shown by Scipio Africanus' armies in Spain and Africa.[33]

The relief at Rome was overwhelming when news of this victory was received, and three days' public thanksgiving was declared by the Senate. Even more so, according to Livy, when it was learned that Nero had rejoined his own army in Apulia before Hannibal had been able to take advantage of his absence. The last great crisis of the war in Italy had been averted. Livius Salinator was awarded a triumph for his victory, and Nero, who had been his subordinate, the lesser honour of an ovation. However, Livy claims that when Nero rode on horseback behind Salinator's chariot the cheers were louder for him, the crowd believing that he had been the real architect of the victory. By archaic tradition Roman soldiers who marched in a triumph sang ribald verses at their commander's expense. Nero received the slightly dubious honour of being the target of more of these jibes than his senior colleague.[34]

Evacuation

In 205 Hannibal's remaining brother, Mago, landed near Genoa with 2,000 cavalry and 12,000 infantry, some recruited during the past winter from the Balearic Islands. Subsequently he was sent a draft of seven elephants, 800 horse and 6,000 foot along with funds to recruit from amongst the enthusiastic and warlike Ligurian tribesmen. Mago's campaign never really gathered momentum and he does not appear to have made a concerted effort to join his elder brother. Perhaps the objective was simply to keep the war going on another front. In 203 he was brought to battle in the territory of the Insubres by the praetor Publius Quinctilius Varus and the proconsul Marcus Cornelius Cethegus with an army of four legions. According to Livy's problematic account, the Romans once again deployed the legions in more than one line. Mago was hit by a javelin in the thigh and his withdrawal from the field is supposed to have triggered the collapse of his army. Soon afterwards he was ordered to return with his army to Carthage to defend it against the Roman invaders, but died of his wound en route. His expedition had not caused the same level of panic as Hasdrubal's invasion in 207. By this stage of the war, the Romans were beginning to reduce their war effort, demobilizing some of their legions and encouraging citizens to return to their farms.[35]

In 203 the same order came to Hannibal himself, instructing him to evacuate Italy and return to the defence of his homeland. He embarked his army at Croton and sailed back to Africa, allegedly after massacring all the Italian soldiers who refused to come with him, although this is most probably a piece of Roman propaganda. He spent sixteen campaigning seasons in Italy and, if he had in the end found himself forced into an ever decreasing corner of the Peninsula, he had not been defeated in a single important battle. For many years his soldiers had been vastly outnumbered by their enemies, but even the more experienced, better drilled and more flexible Roman armies, which had defeated his brothers with such dismissive ease, lacked the confidence to face up to and beat Hannibal and his veterans. Hannibal had failed to win the war in Italy, but neither had he truly lost it. In the meantime the Romans had proved successful on every other front, establishing peace with Macedonia and winning outright victories in Spain and Sicily, so that they were in position to mount an invasion of Africa. It is to these campaigns that we must now turn.[36]

CHAPTER 10

Spain, Macedonia and Sicily

NEARLY ALL THE FIGHTING in the First Punic War had occurred in and around Sicily, apart from Regulus' invasion of Africa and sporadic raiding of the Italian and African coastlines. The Second War between Rome and Carthage spread over a much wider area. Hannibal with the best of the Punic armies invaded Italy from his base in Spain, and there too the greatest number of Roman soldiers took the field, but the Carthaginians were later also to attempt the re-conquest of Sardinia and Sicily. From the very beginning, the Romans threatened the Punic province in Spain, and they were to end the war by mounting a second invasion of North Africa. Some of this widening of the conflict had been anticipated by both sides. In 218 the Roman Senate had expected the year's consuls to fight in Africa and Spain, and Hannibal had made provisions for the defence of both areas. In other cases the war spread unexpectedly. Philip V of Macedon, long nervous of growing Roman influence in Illyria, chose to ally himself with Hannibal, impressed by the latter's victories in 218–216. The king's intervention was purely opportunistic and more bitterly resented by the Romans as a result. For a decade a Roman fleet and army operated in Greece and Illyria to prevent a feared Macedonian expedition to Italy. The naval skirmishing around Sicily only escalated into a major war when political turmoil in Syracuse finally led to an alliance with Carthage.

There was some interconnection between the different theatres during the war. Spain was the base from which Hannibal had launched his invasion of Italy and one reason for the Romans' persistence in maintaining the long struggle there was fear of a repeat of this expedition. In fact, Hasdrubal Barca made an unsuccessful attempt to move on Italy in 215 and actually succeeded in 208–207. Had the Carthaginians re-established themselves in Sicily, its ports would have allowed them to support Hannibal's

245

army in Italy far more closely. In reality Hannibal and the Punic and allied commanders in Sicily gave each other little direct aid. A more direct impact on the Italian campaign resulted when both Hannibal and Mago were recalled to counter Scipio's successes in Africa. The slow pace of communications made it difficult to co-ordinate the operations in different theatres. Hannibal and Hasdrubal singularly failed to unite and support each other when the latter finally arrived in Italy in 207. The main role of central authority was in the allocation of men and resources to the different regions, along perhaps with dictating the priorities of the commanders there. The Roman Senate annually reviewed the state's war effort, how many troops should be in service, where they were to operate, how they were to be supplied, and who was to command them. Even when Hannibal was marauding through Italy, shattering one army after another, the Senate was still able to take thought for operations elsewhere. The Carthaginian war effort lacked such clear direction, imposed at a fundamental level on the Roman state by its tradition of annual magistracies. In 218 Hannibal appears to have disposed the military effort in both Africa and Spain, but once in Italy, he had only limited contact with either area. The authorities in Carthage were less intimately linked with military organization than their Roman counterparts. They did provide resources for and urge actions upon commanders in Spain and Sicily, but their directives were occasional and many decisions were reactions to Roman moves rather than the product of concerted objectives of their own.

Spain 218–211 BC

The Spanish Peninsula was occupied by three major peoples. In the west, in an area roughly equivalent to modern-day Portugal, were the Lusitanians. In southern and central Spain were the people who gave the region its name, the Iberians, whilst the land to the north was the territory of the Celtiberians, a mixture of migrating Gallic tribes and the indigenous population which had merged to create a distinct culture. All three peoples were tribal, but these tribes were far less coherent than their Gallic counterparts and the focus of loyalty for most tribesmen was the town or city. Invariably fortified and usually set on a hilltop, most of these communities were small, little more than villages. A few on the southern coast, like Saguntum, had grown much larger, possessed a literate culture and were by this period hard to distinguish in prosperity from the Greek and Punic colonies in the region. Various kings and chieftains appear in the narrative of the operations in Spain, but their power does not appear to have been fixed, depending instead on personal charisma and particularly on a reputation as warriors and leaders of warriors. Strong leaders, who had proved themselves in war, might control many settlements in both their own and other tribes' territories, the area loyal to them changing in size as their prestige, and that of rival leaders, fluctuated.

Warfare, particularly raiding, was endemic throughout the Spanish Peninsula. Like the tribes of Gaul, the peoples of Spain habitually raided their neighbours, and it was a dispute of this sort which had provided the ostensible reason for Hannibal's attack on Saguntum. Tribes or towns perceived to be weak were mercilessly raided, every successful attack encouraging similar enterprises. A leader could only expect to command the loyalty of allied communities for as long as he was able to protect them from depredations. A reputation for military might, achieved primarily by aggressive campaigns against others combined with swift reprisals to avenge any attack, deterred raiding, but this was hard to maintain and even a small defeat encouraged more raids. Both Rome and Carthage relied overwhelmingly on Spanish soldiers, who formed the most numerous element in almost every army in the Peninsula. Some of these troops were mercenaries, but the bulk were allies, whose loyalty was based above all else on a belief that whichever side they had joined was the stronger, at least locally. Defections followed rapidly when either Rome or Carthage came to be seen as weak. The old Carthaginian province covered only a small area, with its heartland around New Carthage and Gades. Elsewhere, although rapid campaigns had overrun other tribes, the Punic position had not yet been consolidated.[1]

In 218, having failed to intercept Hannibal on the Rhone, the consul Publius Scipio had sent his brother Cnaeus with the bulk of his army on to his province of Spain, before returning himself to confront the enemy in Cisalpine Gaul. Cnaeus had two legions and a strong allied contingent, an impressive army of perhaps 20,000–25,000 men. Sailing along the coast, he landed at the Greek colony of Emporion, a city with which Rome already had some sort of relationship, either directly or through her ally Massilia. Other communities in the area proved ready to ally with Rome. Hannibal had swept through the area north of the Ebro in a few months, leaving Hanno with 10,000 foot and 1,000 horse to control it. Soon after disembarking his army, Cnaeus advanced against this force and easily defeated it at a place called Cissa, probably somewhere near Tarraco (modern Tarragona). Hanno was captured along with the heavy baggage which Hannibal had left under his protection before setting out for Italy. Also captured was a chieftain of the Ilergetes, a man named Indibilis (Andobales in Polybius) who appears to have been one of those strong leaders able to dominate communities from other tribes as well as his own. The Romans spread out and soon most of the tribes and cities north of the Ebro were defeated or voluntarily defected. Hasdrubal Barca, left in overall charge of Spain by his brother, hastily put together an expeditionary force when he heard of Scipio's arrival and, according to Polybius at least, of Hanno's defeat. With 8,000 foot and 1,000 horse he crossed the Ebro and attacked elements of the Roman fleet which had scattered around the coastal areas to raid the local communities. Dispersed and careless, several groups of Roman marauders were caught by the Carthaginians and cut to pieces. The survivors fled and several officers were punished by Cnaeus for their unnecessary defeat. Hasdrubal withdrew after this minor success, having neither the troops nor, probably, the supplies, to risk a longer campaign or an encounter with the main Roman force.[2]

The Romans had established themselves in Spain, gaining allies amongst not just the Greek cities on the coast, but the native tribes of the interior. Cnaeus detached some troops as garrisons to defend both the captured cities and his new allies, before returning to winter with the bulk of his army at Tarraco. Distributions of booty, especially the prizes from Hannibal's baggage train, added to the soldiers' good spirits. In the spring of 217 Hasdrubal mustered larger forces to mount an offensive against the Roman enclave. Crews were found for a few more of the ships left to him by Hannibal, so that forty galleys, the majority 'fives', sailed from New Carthage under the command of Hamilcar. These cruised along the coast, keeping pace with Hasdrubal's army on land, under whose protection the ships could beach and the crews rest each night. We do not know the size of the Punic army, but we must assume that it was substantial since Cnaeus decided that it was unwise to follow his first instinct and face it in battle. Instead the Romans loaded thirty-five ships with marines picked from the legions. At least some of this squadron was provided by Massilia, a maritime city whose sailors had a high reputation. Moving south along the coast, Cnaeus paused about 10 miles from the enemy and sent two small Massiliote ships forward to scout. When these reported that the Punic fleet was beached near the mouth of the Ebro, Cnaeus decided to launch an immediate attack in the hope of catching the enemy unprepared. However, Carthaginian scouts along the coast had already spotted the enemy fleet and warned Hasdrubal, who rapidly ordered Hamilcar to embark and put to sea. The rival squadrons engaged willingly, but the fighting did not last long and ended in a clear Roman victory, perhaps due mainly to the actions of the Massiliotes. Polybius argued that the presence of the Punic army did less to encourage their sailors than to offer them an easy prospect of flight to safety. Perhaps more importantly, at least a quarter of the Punic crews were recently raised, and even the existing ships' companies may not have been especially well-trained. Marauding expeditions rather than naval fighting were a far more common activity for the Punic fleet in Spain. Two Carthaginian ships were lost, four more lost their oars and marines, whilst the rest fled to the sanctuary of the army, beaching themselves in panic. Twenty-five enemy vessels were captured by the Romans, who had arrogantly rowed inshore and towed away many of the beached ships. The Roman fleet may have mounted a few raids along the Punic-held coastline later in this year, but the details are obscure. More Iberian communities sought alliance with Rome after this display of strength. Livy's narrative of this period is not supported by any of the extant passages of Polybius, but he claims that tribesmen from the Ilergetes raided communities friendly to Rome and were in turn attacked by Cnaeus, whilst the Romans managed to persuade some Celtiberians to ravage Carthaginian territory.[3]

Encouraged by Cnaeus' successes, and in particular his naval victory, the Senate decided to send reinforcements to Spain under the command of his brother, Publius, now recovered from the wound suffered at Ticinus. In late 217 Publius arrived with twenty or thirty warships and a draft of 8,000 men along with food and supplies. The brothers, both given proconsular *imperium*, were ordered to take the offensive and under all circumstances to prevent troops, supplies or money being sent from Spain to support Hannibal. With their combined forces, Cnaeus and Publius pushed across the Ebro and advanced towards Saguntum, where the treachery of a Spanish leader brought them an unexpected reward. This man, Abilyx, outwitted the local Punic commander into freeing a group of hostages, mostly the sons of aristocrats taken from the tribes by Hannibal, and handed them over to the Romans. Abilyx's action was prompted by his belief that the Romans were now stronger and more likely to prevail than the Carthaginians, to whom he had been conspicuously loyal in the past. Returning these to their home communities, the Romans were able to persuade more of the tribes to join them, Abilyx pleading their cause with great enthusiasm.[4]

Hasdrubal was in the meantime occupied with suppressing the rebellion of a tribe that Livy calls the Tartesii, incited in part by men, presumably tribesmen, who had deserted from the Punic fleet. In 216 he received from Carthage a small reinforcement of soldiers and orders to mount an expedition to join his brother in Italy. Hasdrubal replied that he lacked the resources to undertake this and still protect the Punic province in Spain and only after receiving more troops under Himilco did he begin serious preparations for a move to Italy. As Hasdrubal began to move out, either in late 216 or more probably at the very beginning of the campaigning season in 215, the Romans concentrated their forces and confronted him near the town of Ibera, just to the south of the Ebro. For several days the rival armies camped about 5 miles apart, but neither side felt ready to offer battle. Then, apparently on the same day, both armies deployed in battle order and advanced to contact. The Romans deployed in the usual *triplex acies* with cavalry on the wings. Hasdrubal placed his Spanish allied foot in the centre of his line, flanked by Libyan and mercenary infantry on the left and Carthaginians on the right. It is distinctly possible that this last contingent consisted of troops from the Punic colonies in Spain rather than Carthage itself. The cavalry were divided between the wings, the right being held by a contingent of Numidians. The cavalry, or perhaps the flanks of the infantry line were strengthened by a force of elephants, perhaps the twenty-one left by Hannibal in 218. Numbers were roughly equal on the two sides, but our sources supply no figures for either army. Hasdrubal's deployment has frequently been compared to his brother's formation at Cannae, and the assumption made that he wanted the Romans to push back his centre and so make it easier to envelop them. This is certainly an error. The tactics of Cannae were peculiar to the local situation. Perhaps there is some similarity to Trebia, when Hannibal put his best infantry on the flanks to support the anticipated success of his cavalry wings. Livy tells us that Hasdrubal's centre of Spanish troops was solid, not deliberately thinned as Hannibal's was at Cannae. Even so, these warriors gave way quickly, which probably explains the mistaken comparison with Hannibal's victory in 216, although his centre held out for some time. Livy claimed that the Spanish were unenthusiastic about marching away from their homeland and gives this as the reason for their flight, which occurred after only a brief exchange of missiles before the two sides had closed to hand-to-hand contact. The Roman legions then did what the manipular system was designed to do, the reserve lines exploiting the breakthrough and wheeling to right and left to roll up the flanks of the enemy line. The Libyans and Punic troops put up a much harder fight against the flanks of the Roman line, but without reserves of his own there was nothing that Hasdrubal could do to plug the gaping hole in his centre. There was apparently little serious fighting between the cavalry and the Carthaginian horse fled after seeing the destruction of their own infantry. Cnaeus and Publius completed their victory by storming the enemy camp and plundering it. The threat of a second invasion of Italy was ended for the foreseeable future and this triumph persuaded even more tribes to abandon Carthage and side with the Romans.[5]

Livy's narrative for the next few years of the war in Spain presents many problems. The defeat at Ibera prompted the Carthaginians to send more troops to Spain, notably the forces under Mago Barca originally intended to go to Italy. In the years after Cannae there was far less prospect of reinforcement for Cnaeus and Publius Scipio, who on at least one occasion complained to the Senate of their lack of resources, a problem exacerbated by the corruption of some of the companies contracted to supply the legions in Spain (already mentioned in the last chapter). However, although numbers had started to favour the Carthaginians, the Romans were not their only enemy. Controlling a much larger area of the Peninsula required the dispersion of their forces to protect their allies from attacks and suppress rebellions by tribes bribed by the Romans or encouraged by their successes. Three main armies were formed, but each commander tended to concentrate on the problems of the area under his immediate control. This, perhaps coupled with personal disagreements, frequently prevented the effective co-ordination of and mutual support between the Punic forces. Their problems were not solely confined to Spain. Appian claims that Hasdrubal and a large force had at some point to return to Africa to suppress a rising by the Numidian King Syphax. Livy also tells us that Cnaeus and Publius negotiated with this monarch, as Scipio Africanus was later to do, and even sent him centurions to train his army in Roman drill and discipline. More often they devoted their efforts to raising rebellion amongst the Carthaginians' Spanish allies. The years after 215 were ones of steady progress in Spain for the Romans, although their sphere of influence was still predominantly in the north. Raids were sent further into Punic-held territory, minor encounters won and towns captured.[6]

In 211, or, according to Livy but less probably, 212, the Roman commanders in Spain decided to launch a major offensive. Two of the Punic armies led by Mago Barca and Hasdrubal Gisgo had for once united and were a mere five days' march away, whilst Hasdrubal Barca was slightly closer to the Romans near a town called Amtorgis. The Romans had added 20,000 Celtiberian allies or mercenaries to their army and felt themselves strong enough to confront both enemies simultaneously. Together the brothers advanced as far as Amtorgis, but then Publius led out two thirds of the old army, the legions and Italian allies, to face Mago and Hasdrubal, whilst Cnaeus with the remaining third and the Celtiberians confronted Hasdrubal Barca. The latter made use of the usual days of waiting before a battle to hold secret negotiations with the Celtiberian chieftains, who were bribed to return home. The tribesmen considered this breach of faith entirely honourable, since they were not actually being asked to fight against their allies. To the dismay of Scipio and his soldiers, the Celtiberians simply marched away. This was not the only occasion when these warriors, who had a great reputation for ferocity when they did choose to fight, behaved in such a manner. Now greatly outnumbered by Hasdrubal, Cnaeus had little choice but to retire in haste.[7]

By this time Publius Scipio had already suffered disaster. As the Romans drew near to the adjacent camps of Mago and Gisgo, their column was severely harassed by Numidian light horsemen, inspired by the leadership of a young prince named Masinissa, who was later to play a major role in events. The Roman outposts and foragers suffered severely and the repeated attacks made the soldiers nervous. Scipio discovered that the Carthaginians were soon to be joined by the chieftain Indibilis and 7,500 tribesmen from the Suessetani and decided to intercept the approaching force and destroy it. Leaving a small garrison in camp, he led his troops out in a night march, a typically bold action. The resultant encounter was confused, neither side managing to form a proper battle line. Things rapidly started to go wrong for the Romans. Masinissa and his Numidians found them and attacked suddenly from one flank. Later the main Punic army arrived and the pressure became overwhelming. Publius Scipio, riding round the front lines as a Roman general should to inspire and organize the men, was killed by a thrown javelin. As the news of his death spread, the Roman army dissolved into rout, to be massacred as they fled by the eagerly pursuing Numidians and Punic light infantry.

The two Carthaginian generals hurried to join Hasdrubal Barca and reached him before Cnaeus had any news of his brother's defeat and death. However, the arrival of enemy reinforcements, wherever they had come from, made it clear that he must continue his retreat. Leaving camp at night he was able to steal a march on the enemy, but by the end of the following day the Numidian cavalry had caught up with him. Harried by the agile horsemen, the Roman column made less and less progress, continually having to deploy to drive the enemy back. Near nightfall Scipio led his weary men onto a hill where they formed a ring around the baggage and his own outnumbered cavalry. By this time the vanguard of the main Punic armies was in sight. The ground was too rocky for the legionaries to dig the usual ditch and rampart around the camp, so the Romans laid out a line of pack saddles and piled their baggage onto it to form a crude barrier. For a while this delayed the enemy, but soon the vastly outnumbered Romans were overwhelmed. A few survivors escaped in the night and managed to reach Publius' camp and the small garrison he had left behind. Cnaeus was killed during either the fighting or the subsequent pursuit. In just under a month the Carthaginians had smashed the Roman armies in Spain. Many of Rome's allies abandoned them after this display of their weakness. An equestrian, Lucius Marcius, who was serving as either a tribune or a senior centurion, rallied the survivors of the brothers' army and managed to hold onto some territory north of the Ebro, although Livy's account of his successes may well be exaggerated. The Punic armies dispersed to reassume control over the remainder of the Peninsula.[8]

The defeat of Cnaeus and Publius Scipio was sudden and all the more unexpected because of their previous record of success. For years, the Romans had been able to take comfort from the campaigns in Spain when elsewhere everything seemed to be going disastrously wrong. All this had been achieved at relatively little cost in funds or manpower to the Roman state. More importantly a disproportionate amount of enemy resources had been drawn to Spain and another invasion of Italy prevented. The Scipios had proved themselves able enough commanders, though Cnaeus may well have been more gifted than his younger brother, and typically aggressive in the Roman manner. Throughout the years of war they had continually raided into enemy territory and sought to gain as many allies as possible from the indigenous tribes. However, Hasdrubal's manipulation of the Celtiberians may point to his superior knowledge of the customs of these wild warriors. Whether or not the Romans could have defeated the three Punic armies if their allies had remained loyal is impossible to know. Even with these warriors, the Carthaginians may well have had a significant numerical advantage although, given the limitations of intelligence gathering in this period, it is questionable that the Roman generals knew this.[9]

The First Macedonian War 215–205 BC

The war in Greece grew directly from the main conflict between Rome and Carthage, but differed from every other theatre of operations in several important respects. It was overwhelmingly a struggle of Greek against Greek. The Romans committed fewer troops to the area than any of the other main theatres, rarely sending more than a single legion supported by naval squadrons, whilst the only direct Carthaginian involvement consisted of a late and largely ineffectual appearance by a Punic fleet. The Romans were never Macedonia's sole or even main opponent, but simply another participant in the ongoing struggle for control of Greece. In the only pitched battle of this extended conflict, at Mantineia in 207, not a single Carthaginian or Roman soldier was present. Most of the fighting consisted of raids and sieges, with armies rarely mustering more than 4,000–5,000 men.

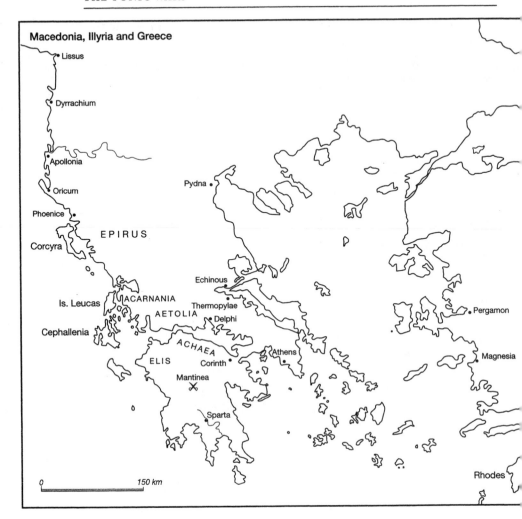

Macedonia, Illyria and Greece

In the late third century Macedonia was not much larger than it had been before the conquests of Philip II and Alexander. Its influence and control over neighbouring Thrace, Illyria and Greece varied according to the strength of each Macedonian king and the current level of unity of the communities in that region. The instability of the Thracian and Illyrian tribes made it difficult to establish lasting control over, or even peace with, these peoples. In Greece, two powerful Leagues had developed, out-stripping the power of the surviving independent city states, such as Sparta and Athens, and the lesser regional leagues. Much of the Peloponnese was dominated by the Achaean League, whilst the Aetolian League occupied central Greece. The Leagues, city states and Macedonia itself competed for domination, allying with each other to oppose mutual enemies. Each state

254

understandably pursued its own interests, so that such alliances often proved unstable. The Achaean League had more to fear from their neighbours the Aetolians than from the Macedonians, so were natural allies of the latter. Lacking the strength to overrun Greece by force, the Macedonians based their control of the area on a network of alliances. Warfare was common between the main players and their allies, but no side ever gained enough of an advantage to destroy its rivals. New territory and cities were acquired through military action, but the conflicts were invariably ended by treaties, which usually provided no more than a period of rest before a renewal of the conflict along the same, or similar, lines as alliances altered.

In 217 Philip V, the 21-year-old King of Macedonia, achieved an acceptable peace settlement in his long struggle with the Aetolian League. The Macedonians had long been nervous about the growth of Roman influence on their western border along the Illyrian coast. Following their successful operations against the pirates of the region in 229 and 219, the Romans had taken into their alliance and under their protection a number of cities in the area, including Apollonia and Lissus in the area of modern Albania, although these had not been formed into a province or provided with a permanent garrison. Hearing of Rome's difficulties in Italy, and the disaster at Trasimene in particular, Philip is said to have decided on a direct attack to overrun Rome's Illyrian allies, encouraged by Demetrius of Pharos, one of the Romans' chief opponents who had fled to the royal court. Employing local shipwrights, 100 biremes of the type used by the Illyrian pirates and known as *lemboi* were constructed. In the summer of 216, the new fleet put to sea and spent some time in training, before Philip sailed with them to the islands of Cephalania and Leucas. There he awaited information of the location of the Roman fleet and, learning that this was concentrated around Sicily, began to move up the western coast of Greece. Off Apollonia, a fresh report of approaching Roman warships caused panic and led Philip to decide on the immediate abandonment of the project. In fact, it was later discovered that only ten Roman ships were *en route* to support their Illyrian allies. These operations once again highlight the problems of gathering strategic intelligence in this period, a factor overlooked far too often by many modern commentators.[10]

Hannibal's continued successes in Italy, culminating in his massive victory at Cannae, encouraged Philip in his belief of Rome's current vulnerability. In 215 a delegation headed by an orator, Xenophanes of Athens, was sent to negotiate an alliance with Hannibal. The envoys seem to have had considerable difficulties in reaching their destination, and on the return trip were captured along with several Carthaginian officers by a

Roman squadron. Xenophanes attempted to bluff his way out of the encounter, claiming that they were in fact a delegation sent by Philip to Rome, but the accents and dress of the Punic officers gave the game away. The group were arrested and a copy of the treaty as well as a letter from Hannibal to the king discovered. Later another embassy went from Macedonia to Hannibal in Italy, confirmed the alliance and returned safely. The treaty pledged mutual protection between Philip V, Macedonia and its allies in Greece and Hannibal, Carthage and its current and future allies in Italy, Gaul, Liguria, and North Africa. Each was to deal fairly and honestly with the other and be the enemy of the other's enemies. In particular, they were to be allies in the war with Rome until victory was achieved, and Hannibal should not make peace with Rome without ensuring that the Romans would not continue fighting Philip and would leave the king in possession of certain named cities along the Illyrian coast and restore territory to Demetrius of Pharos. If in future Rome made war on either Macedonia or Carthage, the other should come to its aid.[11]

The treaty is somewhat vague over precisely what sort of co-operation was envisaged between Hannibal and Philip during the war and, since nothing came of this, our sources' beliefs remain conjectural. Philip's main preoccupation was clearly with driving the Romans from Illyria. The treaty anticipated Rome emerging from the war with sufficient strength to attack either of the allies at some uncertain date in the future, a point we have already discussed in the context of Hannibal's war aims. The alliance with Philip and the assurance that he would attack Roman interests on yet another front offered a means of putting still more pressure on the embattled Roman Republic. What is clear is that Philip V saw this as a limited war to gain specific objectives. It was not to be a war to the death with Rome, ended only by the utter defeat of one or the other side. Cynically, the king took advantage of Rome's apparent vulnerability to further his own local ambitions.

Livy certainly believed that the Romans feared raiding or a direct Macedonian invasion of Italy. In the autumn of 215 a praetor, Marcus Valerius Laevinus, was sent to Brundisium to protect the coast, his province including the war with Macedon. Rome's Illyrian allies lay almost directly opposite Brundisium, separated by the narrowest part of the Adriatic. Laevinus had under his command two legions recently withdrawn from Sicily. By the next year, this was reduced to a single legion, but this was supported by the sizeable fleet which had been mustered, and Laevinus remained in command as a propraetor. He received reports sent by the city of Oricum that a Macedonian fleet consisting of 120 *lemboi* had launched a surprise attack on Apollonia and, having been checked there, had moved against Oricum and stormed it in a night assault. Laevinus embarked the majority of his legion and sailed to relieve the city, the small Macedonian garrison being rapidly defeated, and sent a detachment to the relief of Apollonia. These troops entered the allied city at night and then proceeded to sally out and surprise the poorly guarded camp of the Macedonian besiegers. Even if Livy's account may exaggerate the scale of the Roman success, Philip's offensive against the allied communities had been repulsed.[12]

Laevinus remained with his forces at Oricum for the next year, his command again being extended by the Senate. Philip V made no more aggressive moves against the Roman enclave and Laevinus' posture was entirely defensive so that no serious fighting occurred. In 211 the Romans concluded a treaty with the Macedonians' recent enemy, the Aetolian League, the terms of which are partially preserved on an inscription from Acarnania. The Aetolians agreed to begin operations against Philip V which were to be supported at sea by a fleet of at least twenty-five Roman quinqueremes. Detailed provision was made for the division of the spoils of success. All territory, cities and fortifications captured by the allies as far north as Cocyra, and in particular the region of Acarnania on the west coast, were to belong to the League. However, from these, the Romans were allowed to take movable booty. Both sides pledged not to conclude an independent treaty with Philip which would leave him free to attack the other. Provision was also made for other communities and leaders hostile to Philip and friendly to the Aetolians to join the alliance with Rome under precisely the same terms, and specific mention was made of Sparta, Elis, the kingdom of Pergamum, and certain Illyrian chieftains.[13]

The terms of the treaty were far more characteristically Greek than Roman and reveal far less determined objectives than was usual in Roman war-making. Clearly, in the same way that the alliance between Hannibal and Philip V had not envisaged the destruction of Rome, it was expected that Macedonia would survive the war with enough strength to represent a potential threat to either the Romans or the Aetolians on their own. The primary aim of the Aetolians was to extend their territory, adding other communities to the League. They were very much the dominant partner in the alliance, who would provide the bulk of the troops. The expectation that other powers in Greece and Asia Minor might wish to join the struggle against Philip V emphasized how much the Aetolians viewed this as the continuation of earlier conflicts. The clauses dealing with the distribution of plunder reflect its traditional importance in Roman campaigns. The prospect of loot seems to have been an important additional incentive for

Roman legionaries, in addition to their fierce patriotism. The Senate also expected the defeated enemy to provide at least some of the funds to pay for the cost of the campaign waged against them, so that capitulating states were frequently obliged to supply considerable stocks of food, clothing or material for the Roman army. The need to fund his operations may have been a particular concern for Laevinus, who must have realized that his province was not the Senate's highest priority when it came to the allocation of resources.[14]

It had taken several years from the opening of hostilities between Rome and Macedon before the Aetolians were willing to ally with Rome, and it was not actually till 209 that the treaty was formally ratified by Rome, although co-operation between Laevinus and the League began immediately. Macedonia was its natural enemy, but the League had needed to be convinced of the value to them of an alliance with Rome. Similarly it was only after the Romans and Aetolians had won some victories that other likely opponents of Philip V and his allies felt that this was an opportune moment to enter the war. Elis joined the alliance in 210, Sparta soon afterwards, and King Attalus of Pergamum at the end of the same year. The Achaean League, threatened by both Sparta and the Aetolians, rallied to Philip's cause.[15]

The Aetolian and Roman campaign began with a series of raids against Philip and his allies, the Roman squadron making sudden descents on coastal communities. An early attack on Acarnania failed. Most of the successes, especially the capture of cities, were due to the speed and surprise of an attack, or as elsewhere the result of treachery by some of the defenders. Philip V was faced by many threats simultaneously, as chieftains in Illyria raided his lands and the Aetolians, Romans, and their growing number of allies attacked his adherents in Greece. The young king responded with tremendous energy, rapidly marching his soldiers to face one threat after another. Like the other Hellenistic kingdoms, Macedonia possessed a relatively large army of professional soldiers. Early in the second century, Philip was able to field a force of over 20,000 of these, its core being the well-trained infantry of the pike phalanx. We have far less detail about the army during this period, but it is highly unlikely that so many men were ever concentrated in one place. Cavalry, a far lower proportion of the total force than they had been under Alexander the Great, figure prominently in the brief accounts of these campaigns. On at least some occasions Philip V commanded in the same manner as his illustrious predecessor, charging spear in hand at the head of his cavalry, narrowly escaping death or capture on several occasions. The professionalism of the Macedonian army was reflected in a greater effectiveness in siegecraft, shown for instance in the capture of Echinous in 210.[16]

Philip V displayed great skill in these campaigns, winning a number of large skirmishes, but he could not be everywhere at once and the Aetolians and Romans continued to enjoy some limited successes. When Laevinus returned to Rome to hold the consulship in 210 he even recommended the demobilization of the legion he had left in Greece, and the Roman military presence in the area was certainly reduced under his successor, Publius Sulpicius Galba. In spite of this confidence, the balance of power steadily shifted in favour of Philip V. Livy claims that ambassadors from several powers including Ptolemaic Egypt, Athens and the wealthy island of Rhodes came to the king in 209 and attempted to persuade him to negotiate a peace with the Aetolians. They were concerned that he might soon achieve a complete military victory that would give him an overwhelmingly powerful position in Greece for the foreseeable future. A thirty-day truce, another common feature of wars between Greek states, was agreed, but no permanent settlement concluded and the war recommenced at the end of this period. Philip V continued to make every effort to protect his allies, either in person or by sending detachments of soldiers to their aid. In 207 Philip led a large and determined raid into the territory of the Aetolian League. In the Peloponnese, the newly trained and reorganized army of the Achaean League under the leadership of the gifted soldier and politician Philopoemen shattered the Spartan army at Mantineia, a battleground which had already witnessed several of the largest battles in Greek military history. These twin blows sapped the will of the Aetolian League to continue the struggle. Like any other Hellenistic state, they expected wars to be concluded by a negotiated settlement and in 206 the Aetolians agreed on peace terms with Philip.[17]

The capitulation and withdrawal from the war of Rome's main ally did not mean the end of the fighting. Roman forces in the area were increased, the command given to a proconsul rather than a propraetor. This man, Publius Sempronius Tuditanus, brought 11,000 soldiers and thirty-five quinqueremes with him in 205. Some aggressive moves were made by both sides, Philip repeating his earlier attack against Apollonia, but the Romans refused the king's challenge to fight a pitched battle. The operations at this stage were confined to the western coastal area of modern Albania where the conflict had first originated, since without major allies in Greece it was impractical for the Romans to operate there. Ambassadors from Epirus approached both sides and successfully negotiated a peace treaty, the Peace of Phoinike. Under the terms of this Philip V gave up some of the towns he had captured, notably those allied to Rome, but retained many of his other conquests. Unlike other Roman treaties to end a conflict this was negotiated between equals. Macedonia was recognized as a fully independent power, in no way absorbed into Rome's dominion of subordinate allies.[18]

The outcome of the First Macedonian War was unlike that of any other conflict fought by the Romans in the third century BC. Dissatisfaction with the failure to defeat Philip V, combined with the strong legacy of hatred and mistrust resulting from his unprovoked attack on Rome during its worst crisis, ensured that a new war with Macedonia followed almost immediately after the eventual defeat of Carthage. In the context of the Second Punic War, the fighting with Macedonia had allowed the Romans at minimal cost to prevent Hannibal from gaining any tangible benefit from his alliance with Philip. It had essentially been a Greek conflict, fought mostly by the Hellenistic states according to their own military conventions and concluded in the normal manner of Hellenistic warfare.

Sicily 215–210 BC

Sicily was divided into two, the west and north being governed directly by Rome and the remainder under the control of Hiero's Syracuse. In 218 Sempronius Longus had been sent there to prepare the planned invasion of North Africa and had been involved in some naval fighting as the Carthaginian fleet began to raid the island, before he was recalled to face Hannibal in Cisalpine Gaul. In subsequent years the Senate maintained a garrison, usually of at least two legions, and strong naval forces in Sicily. In late 216 the two legions formed from the survivors of Cannae replaced the existing garrison of the island, their ranks later replenished by the troops defeated in the two battles at Herdonea. In 215 a Carthaginian attempt to reclaim Sardinia failed due to a mixture of bad luck, when storms delayed the fleet, and the rapid response of the Roman Senate, who sent an army to the island under the command of one of its original conquerors, Titus Manlius Torquatus. Manlius had first been consul in 235 and was another of the experienced men, like Marcellus and Fabius Maximus, who were given commands despite their advanced years during the crisis of the Hannibalic War. The Punic fleet returning from Sardinia was harried by Roman squadrons operating from Sicily.[19]

Another reminder of the past was Rome's old ally, Hiero, who was in his seventies at the beginning of the Second Punic War, but proved just as loyal as he had in the First War, sending a strong force of mercenary light infantry, including Cretan archers, and supplies of grain to support the

Roman war effort in 217 or 216. Either in late 216 or early 215, the old man died and with him perished the political stability which had endured for over fifty years during his tyranny. His son having died some years before, Hiero was succeeded by his 15-year-old grandson, Hieronymus, guided by a council of advisers. Almost immediately the fierce factionalism which so often bedevilled the internal politics of Greek cities gripped Syracuse. Hieronymus was young, lacked the experience, achievements and ability of his grandfather and failed to control events. His advisers competed to control the youth, whilst other groups plotted to end the monarchy and restore some sort of Republic. It is tempting but mistaken to characterize these groups primarily on the basis of their attitude towards Rome and Carthage, since it is unlikely that this was the dominant factor in these disputes. More often a group simply sided with the opposing group to rival factions. In 215 Hieronymus began negotiating first with Hannibal and then with the authorities in Carthage itself, his demands increasing so that eventually he demanded the rule of all Sicily once the combined might of Syracuse and Carthage had driven the Romans from the island. However, no formal break with Rome actually occurred and, after a thirteen-month reign, Hieronymus was murdered by a faction at Leontini, one of the cities controlled by Syracuse. His uncle Adranodoros became one of the elected magistrates which replaced the monarchy, but he too, along with most of the rest of Hiero's descendants, was murdered by another group bidding for power.[20]

Active at the time were two brothers, Hippocrates and Epicydes, descended from a Syracusan exile who had settled in Carthage. They had been sent as part of Hannibal's delegation to Hieronymus, having served with his army in Spain and Italy. In 214 the brothers were elected to two of the senior magistracies left vacant by the massacre of the royal family, but their power was challenged by other leaders more disposed to maintain the treaty with Rome. Hippocrates was sent to garrison Leontini with 4,000 troops, a mixture of mercenaries and deserters from the Roman army in the west of Sicily who were fiercely opposed to Rome and threatened the stability of the state. Later joined by his brother, Hippocrates declared the city independent and began raiding the Roman province. The recently arrived Roman commander, Marcellus, currently holding his second consulship, was informed by Syracuse that they no longer controlled Leontini, so advanced and stormed the city in his first assault. Most of the garrison was captured. The Roman deserters suffered the traditional punishment of citizens who had turned against the State, being first flogged and then beheaded. Hippocrates and Epicydes escaped from the disaster and met up

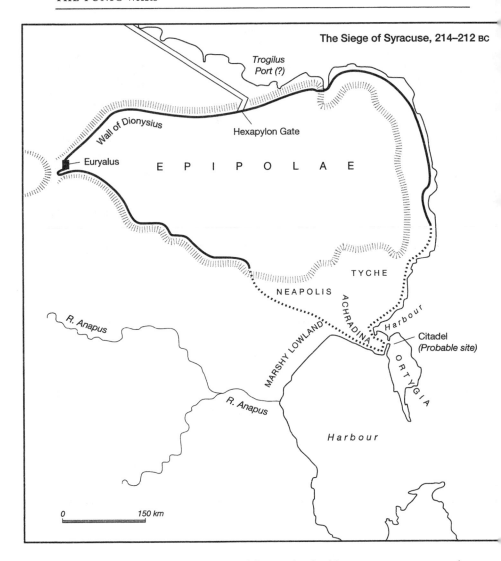

The Siege of Syracuse, 214–212 BC

with a body of 8,000 Syracusan soldiers, who had been sent to support the Roman attack on Leontini on the condition that the rebellious city should be returned to their rule. Aided by rumours of widespread massacre of Leontini's entire population, the brothers were able to win over these troops and led them back to Syracuse where, after a brief fight, they killed their rivals and gained unchallenged control of the city. War with Rome was now inevitable.[21]

Probably in early spring 213 the Romans launched a full-scale assault on Syracuse. Marcellus as proconsul was in overall charge, supported by the propraetor Appius Claudius Pulcher. Marcellus had four pairs of galleys specially prepared, removing the starboard oars from one and the port from the other, before lashing the two together. On their bows were mounted solid scaling ladders which could be lowered against a wall by pulleys attached to the mast, earning the devices the nickname *sambuca* after their similarity to the musical instrument. With these the Romans were able to attack the city walls from the sea, whilst another assault was mounted from the landward side. This was to be one of the very few attempts to take a well-fortified major city by direct attack during the course of the three wars. The result was an utter failure. The walls of Syracuse had been strengthened over the years by various tyrants, and the city had a tradition of producing some of the most advanced siege engines in the world. Many of those used to repulse the Romans had been designed by Archimedes, the renowned geometrician. A relative of Hiero, the ageing philosopher played a major role in organizing the deployment of his artillery and other machines. As the Romans approached the city walls they were bombarded with missiles fired with great power, catapults of different sizes firing at each range. Archimedes had also designed other machines, which lowered hooks to lift the Roman ships out of the water and then drop them, shaking the crewmen out and dashing the ship to pieces. Much later sources even claimed that he invented some sort of mirror device to concentrate the rays of the sun and direct them onto an enemy ship, setting it on fire. However, Plutarch tells us that Archimedes did not bother to write down the details of his designs, considering the practical uses of his studies far less important than theory itself, so it is hard to know how accurate the descriptions of his engines are, but Polybius writing less than a century later certainly believed in the devices called 'claws' which smashed the *sambucae* and others which lifted ships out of the water. Plutarch tells the highly plausible story that the Roman besiegers became so nervous of Archimedes' contraptions that the sudden appearance of any beam or pole on the city walls was liable to cause a panic. Eventually, after suffering heavy casualties, Marcellus abandoned any hope of direct assault and resolved to blockade the city into submission. There is no doubt that the genius of Archimedes had contributed significantly to the successful defence of Syracuse, but it is worth remembering that direct assaults on strong fortifications were so rare precisely because they seldom succeeded and risked heavy casualties.[22]

Appius Claudius kept two thirds of the Roman army to invest the city, whilst Marcellus led the remainder to attack the other communities which had followed Syracuse into rebellion. The situation changed dramatically when a strong Carthaginian army of 25,000 foot, 3,000 horse and twelve elephants under the command of Himilco landed at Heraclea Minoa on the south coast. He soon moved east to occupy Agrigentum, which may well have welcomed the invader. Other cities followed its example and declared for the invader. Marcellus failed to reach Agrigentum in time to prevent its loss, but chanced upon a Syracusan army led by Hippocrates which was moving to join their new allies. In a surprise attack on the enemy camp, Marcellus killed or captured the bulk of the enemy's 8,000–10,000 foot, so that only Hippocrates and his 500 cavalry escaped to join Himilco. The Roman column then returned to Syracuse, followed soon afterwards by the Carthaginian army.

The ability of Hippocrates to break out from the Roman blockade of Syracuse emphasizes just how insecure the blockade was at this stage. This was confirmed soon afterwards when a Punic fleet of fifty-five galleys led by Bomilcar was able to sail into Syracuse's harbour. However, around this time Marcellus was reinforced by another legion, giving the Romans a total of three or four legions as well as allied contingents. Himilco did not stay long outside Syracuse. He may now have been outnumbered, but there is no record of either side challenging the other to battle. The Carthaginian army moved off in an attempt to persuade more of Rome's Sicilian allies to rebel and so draw their forces away from Syracuse. Several communities responded, especially after the Roman garrison commander at Enna massacred a population he suspected of disloyalty. The Romans had a pragmatic attitude to such atrocities, believing them acceptable if likely to be effective, but in this case it turned other communities against them. Despite this, and the loss of a major supply depot at Murgantia, the Romans continued their blockade up to and throughout the winter, whilst Himilco withdrew to winter quarters at Agrigentum.[23]

Syracuse was a large city by ancient standards, divided into several sections each protected by its own line of defences. Direct assault had failed to make any impression on the defences and a faction within the city plotting to betray it to the Romans was discovered and suppressed. However, early in 212 Marcellus resolved upon attempting a surprise attack. A series of negotiations concerning the ransom of prisoners had taken place outside the city wall near a tower called Galeagra. One of the Roman negotiators calculated the height of the fortifications by counting the number of courses of stone, which in this area happened to be of even size. With this information the Romans were able to work out the height needed for ladders to scale the wall. The opportunity came when it was reported that the Syracusans were celebrating a festival dedicated to the goddess Artemis, for which Epicydes had distributed large amounts of wine, in part to compensate the citizens for the scarcity of bread. On the third night of the feast a Roman storming party crept up to the wall near the Galeagra tower. Their information proved correct and the ladders were high enough. The sentries were keeping a poor watch and most had gathered in the towers, where they were surprised and quickly overpowered. The storming party then made their way to the Hexapylon Gate and seized it, admitting the bulk of Marcellus' force at dawn. Epicydes made some attempt to repel the incursion, but did not realize the scale of the Roman attack until too late. Within hours, the Romans controlled the entire area of the city on the high ground known as the Epipolai. Shortly afterwards another stronghold of the defences, the fort of Euralus, was surrendered by its commander. In spite of these successes, the area known as Achradina, the harbours and the peninsula citadel of Ortygia remained firmly in Syracusan hands, so Marcellus settled down to continue the blockade.[24]

Too late to prevent these Roman successes Himilco and Hippocrates arrived to threaten the besieging army. After some ineffectual skirmishing, disaster struck the Punic army when virulent disease broke out in their camp. It was early autumn and the Carthaginians were camped in low-lying marshy ground, and according to Livy the soldiers were unused to the climate. The tighter organization of the Roman camps may have provided at least a basic level of sanitation and was perhaps another reason why the Roman army suffered less than their opponents. Both Hippocrates and Himilco died along with the bulk of the Carthaginian soldiers and the remainder were left in no state to fight. The Punic fleet had continued to run past the Roman blockade and take some supplies of food into the city. Late in 212 Bomilcar returned with a massive convoy of 700 merchantmen protected by 150 warships. It is unlikely that the Roman fleet gathered by Marcellus to intercept the convoy was as large as this, although we cannot be certain of its numbers. It is possible that the Roman ships were more heavily provided with marines drawn from the besieging army than their Punic counterparts. The rival fleets waited on either side of Cape Pachynus down the coast on the southernmost tip of Sicily, whilst a storm which would have made fighting difficult blew itself out. Then, when the weather changed and Marcellus led his fleet towards the enemy, Bomilcar decided to avoid battle and, after sending the transports back to Africa, sailed instead to Tarentum, captured earlier in the year by Hannibal. The reason for Bomilcar's action will never be known, but he has often been accused of losing his nerve.[25]

The last hope of relief for Syracuse had gone. Epicydes escaped from the city and fled to Agrigentum. The Sicilian troops and the Syracusan population both favoured surrender to Rome, but they were opposed by the mercenaries and in particular the Roman deserters who feared the brutal punishment they would receive on capture. Ortygia was betrayed to the Romans by a Spanish officer called Moericus, who opened a gate to admit a party of Roman soldiers carried across the harbour in a merchant ship towed by a quadrireme. Soon afterwards Achradina surrendered and the Romans plundered the city. Marcellus had given orders for his men to take Archimedes alive, but the old man was killed by a legionary, according to the commonest tradition when he refused to be interrupted until he had solved the mathematical problem he had been sketching in the dust.[26]

Some cities had returned to Rome after the fall of Syracuse had demonstrated the difficulty of resistance. Resistance to Rome now centred around Agrigentum where Himilco's successor, Hanno, was supported by Epicydes. Still presumably weak in numbers the Carthaginians concentrated on raiding the territory of Rome's allies. Some reinforcement had come from Hannibal's army in Italy, including an officer called Muttines, a Liby-Phoenician rather than a pure-blooded Carthaginian. Put in charge of a force of Numidians he displayed great skill in ravaging the territory of states loyal to Rome, whilst protecting the lands of the cities which had joined Carthage. His successes encouraged the Carthaginians to advance from Agrigentum as far as the River Himera, where Muttines won several skirmishes with the outposts of Marcellus' army. He was then recalled to deal with the mutiny of 300 Numidians at Heraclea Minoa, and in his absence Hanno and Epicydes gave battle only to be utterly defeated. Livy claims that the Numidians still with the army had agreed with Marcellus not to take part in the fighting. Punic casualties in killed and captured numbered in thousands, and eight elephants were taken to be displayed in Rome. Late in 211 Marcellus returned to Rome to win the consulship for the next year. As the war in Sicily was still unfinished, he was not allowed to celebrate a full triumph and had to make do with an ovation. The booty from Sicily, including artworks stripped from temples and monuments, was more lavish than that ever displayed before by a Roman commander, and some later moralistic writers condemned Marcellus for encouraging a love of luxury in the hitherto austere Romans.[27]

The war was not quite over. More Punic reinforcements arrived from Africa, totalling 8,000 infantry and 3,000 Numidian light cavalry. Muttines continued to lead these light horsemen with great skill, moving rapidly, burning crops and farms. With Rome unable to defend them, more cities defected to the enemy. The Roman troops on the island felt neglected and ignored by their government, especially the Cannae legions, topped up with survivors of Herdonea, who were still barred from returning home in spite of their successes. In 210 Marcellus' consular colleague and the man who had directed the early years of the war with Macedonia, Marcus Valerius Laevinus, arrived to take command in Sicily. The province had originally been allocated to Marcellus, but this was changed after complaints against him from Rome's allies on the island. Mustering a strong army Laevinus mounted an offensive directly against the main Punic stronghold at Agrigentum. Rivalry amongst the Carthaginian commanders played into the Romans' hands and gave them a rapid and spectacular victory. Hanno had become jealous of Muttines' success and growing reputation, despising him for his origins, and had finally dismissed him and given the command of the Numidians to his own son. Muttines, whose men remained loyal to him, was outraged at Hanno's slight and began negotiations with Laevinus. When the Roman army arrived outside Agrigentum, Muttines' men seized one of the gateways and opened it to admit the enemy. Hanno and Epicydes escaped by sea, but the bulk of the garrison were captured by the Romans. Once again a major city had fallen to treachery. Livy mentions that in the aftermath of this success, forty towns and cities voluntarily surrendered, twenty were betrayed to the Romans and only six taken by direct assault. This illustrates not only the extent of the rebellion against Rome even at this late stage, but also the difficulty of storming well-fortified cities. Laevinus punished the leaders of defeated states and rewarded those who had returned to alliance with Rome before being compelled to do so. Muttines was rewarded with Roman citizenship and continued to serve as a commander of Roman auxiliary troops. The Iberian Moericus and his men who had betrayed Syracuse's citadel to Marcellus were likewise rewarded with citizenship and land taken from defeated rebels.[28]

The war in Sicily had ended in an outright Roman victory, the first achieved in the Second Punic War, encouraging the Romans after the major setbacks in Spain and the continued presence of Hannibal in Italy. A Carthaginian victory in Sicily might well have altered the course of the entire conflict. Since the conquest of the island its fertile lands had become an increasingly important source of grain for the growing population of Rome. Sicilian grain had played a major role in allowing the Romans to field so many legions during the war with Hannibal. Laevinus took great care to encourage the revival of agriculture before he left Sicily at the end of 210. The importance of Sicily as a naval base was noted in the discussion of the First War. One of the reasons for the unimpressive performance of the Punic navy in the Second Punic War was its lack of bases on the

Mediterranean islands. If the Carthaginians had managed to establish themselves firmly in at least part of Sicily then they might have been able to supply Hannibal with enough men and supplies to make a difference in Italy, assuming that there was the political will in Carthage to do this.[29]

Considerable resources were committed to the war effort in Sicily, with the dispatch of Himilco's army and its significant reinforcement in spite of the loss of Syracuse, whilst the Punic fleet operated in considerable strength around the island and did much to prolong the resistance of that beleaguered city. In spite of this they failed to inflict a major defeat on the Romans either on land or sea. The Romans seem never to have maintained more than four legions in Sicily, which may have given them a numerical advantage, although by no means an overwhelming one. The need to garrison allied and captured cities reduced the number of troops which both sides, and particularly the Romans who controlled most of the island, could concentrate in one place. The Carthaginian command lacked aggression in comparison to Marcellus, Laevinus and the other Roman generals in Sicily, who consistently and in classically Roman fashion adopted the offensive. Their behaviour was often lethargic, with the exception of Muttines, whose successes made him unpopular. It is by no means clear whether Himilco was capable of breaking the blockade of Carthage, even before his army was devastated by plague, whilst Bomilcar's refusal to risk battle was timid in the extreme. The desertion of such a senior officer as Muttines was unimaginable in the Roman high command.

Ultimately much depended on the choice of the communities in Sicily and, whilst many did rebel against Rome and join Carthage, the majority did not. Whether through fear of reprisals or loyalty to their ally, most communities did not risk rebellion and the Carthaginians never won enough local victories to persuade most states that it was in their interest to abandon Rome. Syracuse took over a year to break with Rome, allowing the Romans some time to recover from their losses in 216 and ensuring that there were legions available to go to the island. There, as in most other cities, the aristocracy were fiercely divided in their attitudes towards the rival powers. Throughout the war it was the Romans who benefited most from the willingness of elements within the rebellious cities to betray the defenders.

CHAPTER 11

The Rise of Scipio, 210–205 BC

Spain 211–205 BC

AFTER THE DISASTER IN 211 the remnants of the Roman armies had managed to cling onto a small enclave north of the Ebro. Lucius Marcius, elected leader by the soldiers and styling himself 'propraetor', drove back the few Carthaginian thrusts directed against the area, but the three Punic armies rapidly dispersed. It was difficult to feed too many troops when they were concentrated and apart from that each commander was eager to return to his own region of the province and restore order there. The Scipios defeated, the Romans were no longer the main enemy for the Carthaginians in Spain. Marcius wrote to the Senate reporting his activities and requesting supplies of food and clothing, but his adoption of a magisterial title caused considerable offence. Late in the year Caius Claudius Nero, the man who would later engineer the victory at Metaurus, was dispatched to take over the command. He brought with him reinforcements of, according to Livy, 12,000 infantry, half-Roman and half-Latin, and 300 Roman and 800 Latin cavalry; although Appian claims that there were only 10,000 foot and 1,000 horse. Probably in the next spring, Nero led an expedition across the Ebro and inflicted a minor defeat on Hasdrubal Barca.[1]

At the end of 210, Nero returned to Rome and was replaced in the Spanish command by Publius Cornelius Scipio, the eldest son of the consul of 218. During the next five years he showed himself to be the most gifted Roman commander of the war, utterly reversing the situation in Spain, so that at the end of his command the Carthaginians had been completely expelled from the province. Scipio's success should not blind us to the utterly unprecedented nature of his appointment, being given proconsular *imperium* in spite of the fact that he was a private citizen. Other men had received similar grants of power since early in the war, but invariably they had held high magistracies at some point earlier in their careers. Scipio had been *curule aedile* in 213, but even during the height of the war with Hannibal this post was still essentially a civil office. In his mid twenties, he was far too young to have held the praetorship or consulship, although as a result of his father and uncle's premature deaths, he was head of one of the most distinguished and influential patrician families in Rome. Like most of his generation, the young Scipio had extensive military experience, having reached adulthood at the very beginning of the war. In 218 he had served with his father and perhaps saved his life at Ticinus. He had certainly been present at Trebia and may even have been at Trasimene. As a tribune of the Second Legion he had escaped the disaster at Cannae and played a prominent part in rallying stragglers from the battle and turning them back into some sort of organized force. Our sources are silent, but it seems probable that he saw active service in at least some of the campaigns in Italy during the next few years.

Livy claims that the Senate decided to hold an election in the *Comitia Centuriata* to choose a proconsul to send to Spain, but that no one seemed to want the post until the young Scipio appeared and was unanimously elected. This is very strange, because pro-magistrates were not elected officials, but appointed by the Senate. It also seems highly unlikely that in the closed world of senatorial politics that Scipio's intentions were not widely known before the event. Perhaps the formal vote was intended to legitimize a decision already made and confirm the legality of Scipio's power, but this does not explain why he was chosen. Attempts to understand the incident in terms of factional politics once again fail to convince and rely on far too many unjustified assumptions about the 'policies' of different families. The Romans were somewhat short of experienced commanders after the heavy casualties of the early years of the war, but there must have been men available who had held senior magistracies. Livy may be right to say that the Spanish command was not an attractive one. Even before their disastrous last campaign the Scipios had complained of lack of supplies. The new commander would continue to face an enemy greatly superior in numbers which would make it extremely difficult to achieve anything significant. There were far better opportunities for distinction in the operations in Italy, which could more easily be translated into future electoral success in Rome. Another factor certainly favoured the choice of Scipio, although it is impossible to know whether or not the Senate were aware of it. The loyalty of the Spanish tribes and chieftains tended to focus around individual leaders rather than states, as the Barcid family had shown. Scipio's name might well prove more useful in regaining lost allies who had once followed his father or uncle than prestige won elsewhere by an experienced, but unknown Roman senator. We can never know precisely how and why Scipio was chosen to go to Spain, but his appointment illustrates the flexibility of the Roman political system at this period just as much as the willingness to give multiple consulships to experienced commanders.[2]

Scipio Africanus was one of the most charismatic figures produced by the Romans during the Punic Wars. In many respects he conformed to the ideal of the youthful military genius which has done much to shape Western ideas of heroism since Alexander the Great. He was that familiar mixture of the man of action and the sensitive, intelligent lover of culture, particularly that of the Greek world. His operations were imaginative, bold and aided by good fortune, so that it is sometimes easy to overlook the careful preparation and planning which underlay the sense of youthful impatience. Polybius' adherence to Scipio Aemilianus ensured that all his ancestors received favourable treatment, but the author's admiration for Africanus seems to have been genuine. He was at great pains to emphasize Scipio's skill as a commander, that the risks he took were the result of sober calculation and not unthinking rashness. A rational Greek with a somewhat cynical view of religion as a useful tool for controlling the masses, Polybius argued that Africanus did not believe the stories of divine assistance which he used to inspire his men. This may be so, but other sources present Scipio as a man who believed that he possessed a special relationship with the gods. This was not unique amongst Roman commanders; both Sulla and Caesar later claimed to be especially lucky because of their personal favour with particular gods and found that their soldiers responded to such claims.[3]

New Carthage, 209 BC

Scipio took with him to Spain a further reinforcement of 10,000 infantry and probably some cavalry, increasing the Roman army in the province to 28,000 foot and 3,000 horse. This total was barely equal to any one of the three armies maintained by the Carthaginians. Landing at Emporion late in the campaigning season of 210, Scipio concentrated his forces at Tarraco and spent the winter there, negotiating with Spanish leaders. Even before his arrival, Scipio had been contemplating a bold strategy for his first full year's campaigning and the winter months gave the opportunity for the gathering of intelligence and detailed planning, as he later explained in a letter to Philip V which Polybius was to consult. The three Punic armies were widely dispersed, Hasdrubal Barca fighting the Carpetani roughly in the area of modern Toledo, his brother Mago near the Pillars of Hercules

(Straits of Gibralter), and Hasdrubal Gisgo amongst the Lusitanians. It might be possible for the Roman army to march and confront one of these forces before the others could intervene. However, even if Scipio were able to move into contact there was no guarantee that he would be able to force the enemy into a decisive and successful battle. The longer the campaign continued without result, the greater chance of the arrival of overwhelming enemy forces and the risk that he would suffer at best a humiliating retreat and at worst a disaster similar to 211. Secretly, Scipio decided that he would instead move against one of the most important strongholds of the Barcid province, the city of New Carthage. The dispersion of the enemy armies made it feasible for the Romans to advance this far without meeting serious opposition, but there was no certainty that they would then be able to take the city, for direct assaults were rarely successful and there would certainly not be sufficient time to blockade the city into submission before relief arrived. Intelligence reports indicated that the garrison was relatively small, whilst fisherman from Tarraco who plied their trade along the coast provided the valuable information that the lagoon apparently preventing access to one side of the city's walls was in fact readily

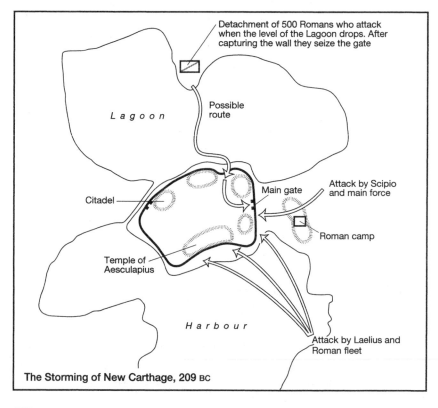

Detachment of 500 Romans who attack when the level of the Lagoon drops. After capturing the wall they seize the gate

Lagoon

Possible route

Attack by Scipio and main force

Main gate

Citadel

Roman camp

Temple of Aesculapius

Roman camp

Harbour

Attack by Laelius and Roman fleet

The Storming of New Carthage, 209 BC

fordable in several places. Scipio's preparations were careful and thorough, but this, and his eventual success, should not conceal the great boldness and high risks of this operation.[4]

Keeping their destination secret, Scipio led 25,000 foot and 2,500 horse into the field next spring, whilst his friend Gaius Laelius took the fleet along the coast to New Carthage. Polybius tells us that Scipio reached the city after a seven-day march, but does not tell us where he started from and this seems a very short time to move from Tarraco or anywhere else north of the Ebro. Whatever the details of this operation, it is clear that the Romans arrived rapidly and unexpectedly outside the city. Scipio pitched camp, but made no attempt to surround the city with a wall of circumvallation. Assembling his troops, he made a speech explaining his reasons for wanting to capture the city and promising rich rewards for men who distinguished themselves, in particular the first man to get over the wall. Finally he claimed that the entire plan had been given to him in a dream by Neptune. Like all speeches supposedly given to massed armies, it is probable that this was delivered to smaller sections in turn.[5]

The garrison commander, another Mago, had 1,000 mercenaries supported by 2,000 armed townsfolk to meet the next day's assault. The eager but untrained citizens were stationed behind the main gate, ready to sally out, whilst the mercenaries were split into two, half holding the citadel and the remainder the hillock on the eastern, seaward side of the town, where there was also a temple to Aesculapius. The next morning's attack was met by an immediate counter-attack as the armed citizens charged out of the gate and engaged the Roman attacking columns. The defenders of ancient cities often displayed a willingness to fight outside their walls even when greatly outnumbered by the attacking army. Such sallies were a sign of confidence and served the practical purpose of delaying the start of any siegeworks by the attacker, who was forced to fight to gain control of the approaches to the defences. In this case the narrow isthmus connecting the city and mainland in the east prevented the Romans from overwhelming the citizens, despite the delay before all 2,000 had deployed into a fighting line, caused by the column having to leave the city by a single narrow gate. The two sides clashed about a quarter of a mile from the gate, nearer to the Roman camp than to the city walls. Polybius tells us that Scipio, anticipating just such a sortie and planning to inflict serious losses on the defenders, had deliberately kept his men back so that they could fight with every advantage. Despite their lack of training, the citizens fought well and the combat was long and hard, but as the Romans fed in more and more reserves to reinforce the maniples in the fighting line the pressure finally became too much. The Carthaginians broke and fled back to the city, many being cut down as they ran or injured as the mob tried to force its way back through the narrow gateway.[6]

The Romans followed up eagerly, assault parties racing forward to set ladders against the high city walls. Simultaneously Laelius led the fleet against the southern, seaward side of the city. Scipio himself directed the fighting from high ground near the walls, sheltered from missiles by three soldiers carrying large shields, a measure of prudence which Polybius admired. The Romans attacked with great determination, but made no headway as the barrage of missiles swept men from ladders. As the day drew on and the attacks continued to fail, Scipio had his trumpeters sound the recall. At this stage Mago may well have been satisfied with events. Although his sally had been repulsed, it had delayed the Roman assault and may have reduced its momentum. Neither the Roman army or fleet had made any impression on his walls and the best part of his garrison was still intact. There seemed every reason to believe that he would be able to hold out until relieved by one of the Punic field armies. Polybius claimed that none of the armies was further than ten days' march away.[7]

It came as some shock to the defenders when the Romans decided to renew their unsuccessful attacks. Usually several days' rest were given to troops before they attacked again after a failed assault. Once again the storming parties rushed against the walls, this time carrying even more ladders than in the earlier advance, more having been issued as the troops rested. Much of their ammunition exhausted, the garrison found it harder to hold back the Roman escalade and only narrowly succeeded in doing so. In the meantime, Scipio had positioned a specially picked unit of 500 men on the northern side of New Carthage, at the edge of the wide lagoon. He had deliberately waited until later in the day when the fishermen of Tarraco had told him that the tide lowered the depth of the water still further. Without difficulty, the Romans waded through the shallows of the lagoon, following the guides Scipio had brought. Mago had stripped the northern walls of defenders to hold back the onslaught against the isthmus and the 500 men were unopposed as they set their ladders up and ascended. To the east, the rest of the army were inspired by the visible evidence of Neptune's favour and renewed their efforts. Holding their long shields over their heads in the famous *testudo* formation, soldiers approached the gate and began to hack at its timbers with axes. The 500 men made their way along the wall, their body shields and short swords ideally suited to disposing of any defenders who tried to stop them. Reaching the gate they secured it and let in the attacking party, whilst elsewhere the defenders began to give way and allowed many of the escalading troops to climb onto the walls.[8]

Getting into a city did not ensure its fall. It took time for the attackers to get many men into the city through narrow entrances or still using assault ladders and there was always a danger that the defenders would rally and, using their better knowledge of the city's layout, counter-attack and drive them out. As more and more troops entered the city, Scipio kept 1,000 men tightly in hand and led them to secure the citadel, where Mago surrendered after a brief resistance. The remainder were let loose into the streets with orders to kill anyone they met. Polybius tells us that he had witnessed the aftermath of the Roman sack of a city – probably when he accompanied Scipio Aemilianus on campaign in Africa or Spain – and had seen the dismembered bodies of men and even animals lying in the streets. There is some later archaeological evidence to support this picture of wide-spread atrocities. He believed that the practice was intended to inspire terror, both to overawe the population and prevent further resistance, but also to deter other cities from opposing a Roman army. The Roman sack of a city was brutal even by ancient standards, which assumed general mas-sacre of men and rape of women. However, it is important to remember that the Roman soldiers who behaved with such brutality had undergone two major assaults against the city, during which they had suffered griev-ous casualties whilst making no headway or being able to injure the enemy. The skeletal evidence from towns sacked by the Romans suggests more wild frenzy than calm murder. In addition, the citizens of New Carthage were not peaceful neutrals, but active participants in the defence. This does not condone the Romans' behaviour, but it in part explains it.[9]

It may well be that Polybius exaggerates the tight control Scipio exer-cised over his men, who did not begin to plunder until a given signal, but the Republican army had a tightly controlled system for the central distri-bution of booty. The system may have had its roots in the old predatory warfare of archaic Italy, but had been reinforced as the army grew more organized and required men to remain to guard the camp or stay under arms when others were free to plunder. All legionaries were more likely to perform their duties if they knew that they would receive a fair share of the profits of victory. The collection of plunder into a central spot and its care-ful distribution under the supervision of the tribunes emphasized the communal spirit of the Roman army as representative of the entire State under arms. This distribution was carried out the day after the capture of the city. Later Scipio also took care to reward those who had distinguished themselves. The *corona civica*, the crown given to the first man over the wall and the additional prizes Scipio had promised for this deed were fiercely contested by a centurion of the Fourth Legion, Quintus Trebellius, and a marine, Sextus Digitius, who had presumably attacked under Laelius from the seaward side of the city. After a detailed investigation and fierce rivalry between soldiers and sailors, Scipio gave the crown to both.[10]

There has been much debate over the precise nature of the information Scipio had about the level of the lagoon, whether the drop was caused by tide or wind, and whether it was a daily or occasional phenomenon. It is unlikely that these issues will ever fully be resolved. The Roman commander had used the knowledge that the lagoon was fordable with great care. Had the party attacking from this direction found the wall held in any strength at all, it is unlikely that they would have been able to force an entry by escalade. The initial Roman attack concentrated on the southern and eastern approaches, focusing enemy attention on these areas. The renewal of this assault with increased force confirmed Mago's belief that these were the sole points in danger and drew in his reserves. Scipio was willing to accept the high casualties inevitable in these direct frontal assaults to draw the enemy's attention away from the wall running along the side of the lagoon. Had Mago possessed a larger garrison this plan would have had far less chance of success, but Scipio had fairly accurate knowledge of the enemy forces and was willing to gamble on stretching the garrison so thinly that his unexpected attack had a good chance of succeeding.[11]

New Carthage contained considerable stores of material and war engines, as well as housing a rich Punic treasury, carefully catalogued by the quaestor Flaminius, son of the consul killed at Trasimene. Prisoners included Mago and several distinguished Carthaginians. Of the 10,000 men captured, the citizens were released, the non-citizen artisans of the type found in many mercantile cities were made public slaves but promised release at the end of the war, and from the remainder,who were mostly slaves, suitable men were selected to serve as rowers in the Roman fleet. Perhaps the most important prize was the more than 300 hostages taken from the noble families of the Spanish tribes to ensure their good behaviour. Scipio treated the hostages with great courtesy, rewarding them and sending them back to their families as a way of opening negotiations with the tribes. Several stories grew up concerning Scipio's chivalrous treatment of the noble women numbered amongst the hostages, similar in many respects to Alexander's treatment of captive women from the Persian royal family. Many, including the sister-in-law of the prominent chief Indibilis of the Ilergetes, were taken under his personal protection. When the soldiers brought an especially beautiful young woman to offer to their commander, Scipio thanked them, but took care to hand the girl back to her father. In

Livy's version the girl was betrothed to a young nobleman and Scipio is supposed to have reassured the man that the girl's honour was intact. This is typical of the romantic embellishments which grew up around the charismatic figure of Africanus. The good treatment given to the hostages served a practical purpose, furthering the Roman cause with the tribes, but that does not mean that we need believe that Scipio was acting against his true nature.[12]

The Battle of Baecula, 208 BC

Soon after the fall of the city Laelius sailed in a quinquereme to carry the news to Rome, Scipio anticipating that this great success should coax more support from the Senate. He remained at New Carthage for some time, subjecting his army to a rigorous training programme, before retiring to winter at Tarraco. The situation in Spain was beginning to change. The loss of New Carthage was a major blow to Carthaginian prestige as well as depriving them of resources and a vital base. Since the Punic victories in 211 their treatment of the Spanish tribes had become harsher, since there was less need to keep them content and prevent defections to Rome. Many leaders responded to the Roman diplomacy, including Indibilis of the Ilergetes who had remained staunchly loyal to the Carthaginians up until this point, in spite of his capture in 218. Scipio seems to have planned to confront one of the main Punic armies in the next campaigning season, drawing men off from the fleet to bolster the strength of his field army. Carthaginian objectives are harder to reconstruct. Hasdrubal Barca was clearly already planning the expedition to Italy which he would in fact lead later in the year. He resolved to seek a decisive encounter with Scipio, although it is hard to credit Polybius' statement that he only definitely planned to move on Italy if he lost the battle.[13]

When Scipio led his army out of Tarraco in the spring of 208 he found Hasdrubal near Baecula, almost certainly the modern town of Bailén, in an area famous for its silver mines. It was in the same rugged country that Napoleon's army suffered one of its first serious defeats when General Dupont was forced to surrender to a Spanish army in 1808. As soon as he received reports of the Romans' approach, Hasdrubal camped on high ground, his rear protected by a river, and his flanks by rocky hillocks. In front, at the top of the slope, he positioned a strong guard of formed troops to protect the camp. In was a very strong position, one which no general would relish attacking, which makes it a strange choice if Hasdrubal actually wanted to fight a battle. Perhaps he was hoping to keep the Romans occupied until Mago or Hasdrubal Gisgo could arrive to overwhelm them with numbers, or possibly that the fear of this would make the Romans fight in such unfavourable circumstances. For two days Scipio observed the enemy from the valley below, before deciding that he must attack in case the other Punic commanders were approaching.[14]

Scipio sent some *velites* supported by formed infantry in battle order straight up the slope to engage the Punic covering force. Attacking with great enthusiasm, the Romans slowly drove the enemy back. Livy even claims that the army's slaves, the *calones*, joined in the advance, picking up stones from the ground and lobbing them at the enemy. As they approached the more level summit, the willingness of the *velites* and the formed maniples to close to hand-to-hand combat proved too much for the Punic light troops, persuading Hasdrubal to order out the remainder of his army and begin forming them in a line near the top of the ridge. Scipio had already divided the remainder of his army into two halves, leading one himself and putting Laelius in charge of the other. It was now that the months of training began to prove their value as the two Roman columns marched to outflank the enemy. Scipio led his section of the army to the left, climbing the high ground and reaching the summit where they deployed into a fighting line threatening the enemy flank. Laelius troops performed the same manoeuvre on the right. The Romans had gained the high ground before Hasdrubal had fully formed his army up and there was no time to alter his orders and place some of the troops to face either flank. As the Romans attacked, the Punic army rapidly gave way, Hasdrubal ordering the unengaged troops to withdraw.

Livy claims that 8,000 Carthaginians fell in the pursuit, although Polybius gives figures of 10,000 foot and 2,000 horse for the prisoners. Both he and Polybius state that Hasdrubal began to withdraw very early in, or even before, the fighting, sending away his slow-moving elephants and his treasury. Rallying as many fugitives as possible, he then led them north towards the valley of the Tagus and began his long march to Italy. His actions must raise the question of whether or not he had really wished to fight in the first place. Even if he had, the reverse at Baecula does not seem to have been a serious enough defeat to upset his plans, unlike Ibera in 215. Scipio did not attempt to block Hasdrubal's escape and it seems unlikely that his small army could have done this. Even after Hasdrubal had left the Peninsula Scipio was still outnumbered by the Punic forces there. The victory at Baecula certainly encouraged more Spanish leaders to join the Romans, some of them saluting Scipio as king, a title so alien to the Roman system that he was at pains to stop its use.[15]

It may be that the scale of Scipio's success at Baecula has been exaggerated by sources favourable to his family. Even so, the battle demonstrated once more his boldness and imaginative tactics. The manipulation to his advantage of the formal manoeuvring before a battle and the ability to wrong-foot the enemy commander were to be a feature of several of his later battles. This was made possible by the tactical flexibility of the legions under his command, the product of long and careful training.

The Battle of Ilipa, 206 BC

After two aggressive campaigns, Scipio appears to have been far less active in 207. A Roman column seems to have had a success when it surprised Hanno, the Punic officer sent to replace Hasdrubal Barca, whilst he was recruiting soldiers amongst the Celtiberians. The Carthaginians were still as concerned with maintaining their control over the Spanish tribes as they were with defeating the Romans. When Hasdrubal Gisgo made a demonstration of force in Baetica, in the far south of Spain around Gades, Scipio concentrated his forces and advanced towards him. Hasdrubal dispersed his men to garrison the region's cities and refused to be drawn into a pitched battle. As in the earlier campaigns when Scipio had lunged deep into Punic-held territory, he could not afford to stay there for any length of time, as supply would become a problem and the enemy's numbers would steadily increase and eventually overwhelm him. He sent his brother Lucius, serving as his *legatus*, to capture the city of Orongis to ensure that the Romans achieved a token victory, before they withdrew north and returned to winter quarters in and around Tarraco.[16]

The next year the Carthaginians decided on a major effort and massed a large army with which to overwhelm the bold young Roman commander. Polybius tells us that Hasdrubal Gisgo led out 70,000 infantry and 4,000 cavalry, supported by thirty-two elephants, although Livy says that there were only 50,000 foot and 4,500 horse. He camped near a town called Ilipa, placing his camp on readily defensible high ground with an open plain in front of it. This was probably in the region of modern Seville, near Alcalá del Rio. It was a clear message to the Romans that this time Hasdrubal was ready and willing to fight. When Scipio had called in the various detachments of his army, they mustered around 45,000 foot and 3,000 horse. Only just over half of these were Romans or Italians, the two legions and two *alae* composing the standard consular-sized army which he seems to have had since 210. The remainder were allied troops, many recently raised from Rome's new allies amongst the Spanish tribes, similar to the warriors whose desertion had precipitated the disaster suffered by his father and uncle. Even with these additional men, Scipio had at best rough

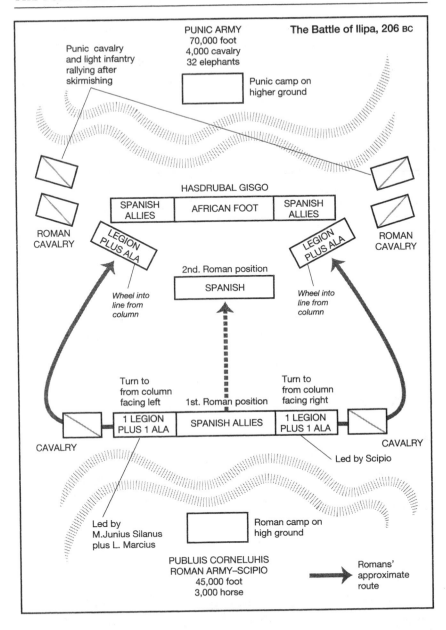

Punic cavalry
and light infantry
rallying after
skirmishing

PUNIC ARMY
70,000 foot
4,000 cavalry
32 elephants

The Battle of Ilipa, 206 BC

Punic camp on
higher ground

HASDRUBAL GISGO

| SPANISH ALLIES | AFRICAN FOOT | SPANISH ALLIES |

ROMAN CAVALRY

LEGION PLUS ALA

LEGION PLUS ALA

ROMAN CAVALRY

2nd. Roman position

SPANISH

Wheel into
line from
column

Wheel into
line from
column

Turn to
from column
facing left

Turn to
from column
facing right

1st. Roman position

| 1 LEGION PLUS 1 ALA | SPANISH ALLIES | 1 LEGION PLUS 1 ALA |

CAVALRY

CAVALRY

Led by Scipio

Led by
M.Junius Silanus
plus L. Marcius

Roman camp on
high ground

**PUBLUIS CORNELUHIS
ROMAN ARMY–SCIPIO**
45,000 foot
3,000 horse

Romans'
approximate
route

parity with the enemy and may even have been significantly outnumbered.
Nevertheless, eager to fight the decisive action which had eluded him the
year before, he advanced to confront Hasdrubal.[17]

As the Roman army pitched camp on a line of low hills facing the enemy,
Mago led the Punic cavalry in a sudden attack, hoping to catch them
unprepared. The skirmish gave another indication of the careful prepara-

tion that underlay the overt boldness of Scipio's operations. In addition to the usual outpost placed to cover the construction of a camp, a unit of cavalry had been concealed behind one of the hills. As the Punic horsemen, led by Masinissa's Numidians, swept down on the outposts and the main column still marching up to the camp site, the Roman horse charged unexpectedly against their flank, spreading disorder. The momentum of the Punic charge was lost, and there was time for the outposts to be reinforced by units specifically kept in battle order and also by some men drawn off from the construction. The Carthaginian cavalry were slowly pushed back, until their retreat turned into panicked flight and they were pursued with some loss back to their own lines.[18]

This success raised the morale of the Roman army. For the next few days the rival armies deployed to offer battle in the plain between their camps, but neither advanced far enough to force the other to fight, contenting themselves instead with sporadic skirmishing between the cavalry and light troops. Success in these small fights and single combats were believed to give a good indication of the relative courage and prowess of each side. Neither side marched out to form up too early in the day, an indication of their lack of desire for an immediate fight. Each day the Carthaginians moved first, and it was only in apparent response that Scipio gave the order for his own columns to march out of the camp gates and form up. Hasdrubal placed his best foot, the Libyans, in the centre, stationed his Spanish warriors on their flanks and had the cavalry and elephants on the wings. Scipio's formation was equally conventional, with the Roman legions in the centre, the *alae* to their flanks and the Spanish foot to their right and left, with the horse on the wings. Neither side possessed a great superiority in cavalry and as was normal in Spain these formed a lower proportion of the total army than was common elsewhere, especially in Hannibal's army. This battle, like most others in Spain, would be decided primarily by the close order infantry.

Scipio decided once again to wrong-foot his opponent. Orders were issued for his soldiers to have fed themselves and be ready in battle order by dawn the next day. Summoning his tribunes to his *consilium* he issued new orders, altering the army's battle order. It was probably then that he also explained the complex manoeuvre planned for the next day. At, or a little before, first light the Roman cavalry and *velites* were sent out with orders to push up as close to the enemy camp as possible. Behind them the remainder of the army marched out in columns and wheeled into a battle line with the Spanish in the centre and the Romans and Italians on the flanks. The Punic outposts were rapidly driven in and Hasdrubal responded by ordering first his own horse and light troops and then the entire army to march out and deploy. The Carthaginian soldiers did so before they had a chance to eat breakfast and in the same order as on previous days. It was only after pushing back the Roman light troops and forming his own line on the level ground beneath his camp that Hasdrubal realized that Scipio had altered his deployment, and by then it was too late to change the orders for his own troops. Half a mile, or a little more, apart the two lines stared at each other for a long time – perhaps hours – as their respective light troops continued to skirmish, periodically retiring through the intervals between the formed troops to rally, before returning to their long-range combat.

Scipio then recalled his *velites* and ordered them to the wings of his army, before beginning a general advance. The Spanish troops in the centre had been ordered to move slowly and it is unclear who commanded them. The wings were composed of the cavalry as well as the legions and Latin *alae*, and Scipio himself led the right wing. The left was commanded by Marcus Junius Silanus and Lucius Marcius, the equestrian who had salvaged the situation in 211 and had been treated with great honour by Scipio. Having initially deployed his men in the usual *triplex acies* facing the enemy, Scipio ordered them to turn to the right so that they now formed three columns parallel to the enemy line. The left wing turned to the left to mirror this formation change. The Roman commanders then wheeled the heads of their columns towards the enemy and advanced in column directly towards them. A narrow-fronted column will always move faster than a line, for it encounters fewer obstacles and there is less need for its officers to halt and reform the ranks at regular intervals, so they further outstripped the Spanish allies. Nearer the enemy, the Roman wings wheeled again to 90 degrees and marched out to form the *triplex acies* facing the enemy again. The Roman troops were now close to the edges of Hasdrubal's Spanish infantry, so much so that the *velites* and cavalry were able to outflank the enemy position. Scipio's manoeuvre was a variation on the normal Roman method of deploying an army, but it had never before been performed so close to and under the gaze of a formed enemy. Only the exceptionally high discipline and training of his army made this possible.

The Carthaginian army had watched, mesmerized, as the Roman columns had arrogantly come straight at them. Hasdrubal did nothing. It was one thing for the Romans to carry out a carefully planned and prepared manoeuvre, but far harder for him on the spur of the moment to issue new orders, sending some of his line forward to face them. If his Libyan foot had been sent forward to outflank the Roman wings, they would in turn have exposed their own flanks to the Spaniards forming the Roman centre. Attempting to shift his units to face a different direction risked splitting the army up, confusing his battle line without achieving anything positive. In any case the Roman manoeuvre will not have taken much time, perhaps as little as an hour, reducing the Punic response time.

The Roman wings attacked with great enthusiasm, the *velites* bombarding the elephants with missiles, causing many to stampede. The legions and *alae* charged into the Spanish foot, who met them with considerable determination. In the centre, the pick of the Punic army remained unengaged for some time, inactive observers of the fighting, until the Romans' Spanish allies eventually came into contact. On the wings the Romans gradually started to make headway. Polybius mentions that hunger weakened the resilience of the Spanish warriors as the fight continued through the heat of the day, whilst we may suspect that the Roman multiple line system allowed them to inject renewed impetus into their fighting line. Hasdrubal rode around the line urging his men on, and probably the Roman officers did the same on the other side. At first the Spanish and then the whole Punic army went back step by step, still facing the enemy. Then the pressure grew too much and, as the Romans surged forward, they broke and fled. For a while they seemed to rally at the base of the hill beneath their camp, but as the Romans came on to renew the fight, the rout started again. Our sources tell us that the Romans were only prevented from storming the enemy camp by a sudden deluge of rain which ended the fighting.[19]

Our sources do not give casualty figures for Ilipa. The details of the manoeuvre performed by the Roman army has, like so many other aspects of the war, been endlessly debated by scholars. All agree that it demonstrated a far higher standard of corporate discipline than Roman armies had possessed in the early years of the war. Sometimes attempts have been made to compare the battle to Cannae, measuring Scipio's tactical skill against Hannibal's mastery. This is a mistake, since they were very different battles fought in very different circumstances. What the Roman general had shown was his ability to manipulate to his own advantage the rituals of a formal battle, with its days of delay, skirmishing and displays of confidence. He had dictated how and when the battle would be fought, surprising and wrong-footing his opponent. In this sense he had displayed the same sort of superiority over Hasdrubal that Hannibal had shown over the Roman commanders in 218–216.[20]

After a miserable night spent in the pouring rain, Hasdrubal found on the next day that his Spanish contingents were already abandoning him.

Giving up any thought of continuing the fight, he ordered a retreat. It was always difficult to disengage from close contact with the enemy and the Romans, elated by their success, pursued with great enthusiasm. Hasdrubal and Masinissa managed to make their way to the coast and took ship for North Africa, whilst Mago fled to Gades. Abandoned by its leaders, the Punic army in Spain dissolved, whilst the Spanish tribes flocked to pledge their allegiance to Scipio. The Romans divided to mount a series of punitive expeditions against those chieftains who did not submit readily enough. Some of this fighting was very bitter, the population of one town allegedly murdering their families and committing mass suicide rather than surrender. A conspiracy by some deserters from Gades to betray the city to the Romans was discovered by Mago and suppressed, but it was an indication of the collapse of Carthaginian power in the Peninsula.[21]

Around this time, Scipio fell seriously ill and a rumour of his death spread rapidly throughout the tribes. Indibilis, the powerful chieftain of the Ilergetes, saw this as an opportunity for rebellion and rallied many Iberian and Celtiberian warriors to his call, leading them in raids against Rome's allies. Perhaps this was a sign of the fear that now that the Romans were supreme in Spain they might become as repressive as the Carthaginians. More probably it was just a reminder that the loyalty of the Spanish tribes focused upon individual leaders rather than foreign states. Simultaneously, a force of 8,000 Roman soldiers garrisoning the town of Sucro mutinied, complaining that they were owed much back pay and wanted either to return to campaigning with its prospects of booty or to be sent home and discharged. Some of the soldiers in Spain had been there for over a decade, most for half that time, so that the desire for discharge now that the war seemed won may be understandable. Others in fact would later choose to stay in Spain, settling in the new colony of Italica. However, most military mutinies throughout history have occurred when troops were inactive, and have frequently had very complex causes. The ringleaders of the mutiny were executed, whilst the remainder were paid, brought back under tight discipline and forced to renew their oath by a commander now recovered from his sickness. Scipio then led the bulk of the army against Indibilis, defeating him in a battle in which once again his troops displayed their skill at manoeuvre and their commander his ability to dictate how the battle would be fought. Perhaps as a result of years of fighting with or against the Carthaginians, or because it was part of native military culture, the Spaniards seemed to expect battles to occur in the same formal way as Rome, Carthage and the Hellenistic world. However, these fiercely individualistic warriors were hard for any chief to control and the movements of their army clumsy in the extreme. The revolt was crushed, but Indibilis escaped, only to be killed when he rebelled again after Scipio had finally left the province.[22]

Mago's hopes may briefly have revived when he saw the Romans experiencing problems. Soon he was ordered off to prepare his Italian expedition, but not before he had alienated the population of Gades. The city surrendered soon after his departure and several hundred years of Carthaginian presence in Spain ended. Scipio returned to Italy to deliver his report, being greeted by the assembled Senate outside Rome although, because he had never held a magistracy, he was denied a triumph. His fame was such that he easily secured election to the consulship of 205, despite the fact that he was well below the normal minimum age. Scipio's achievement was undoubtedly spectacular. Marcius and Nero had helped to prevent the utter expulsion of the Romans from Spain, but when Scipio had arrived in 210 the balance of power was absolutely in favour of Carthage. In just four campaigns the young, untried commander had utterly reversed the situation and ejected the enemy from the Peninsula. He had achieved this success with very modest resources, far less than those at the disposal of his opponents. Conditions had changed in Rome's favour, particularly the widespread resentment amongst the tribes against the increasingly harsh Punic rule, but the main factor in his success was Scipio's own ability. He combined the traditional aggression of Roman commanders with careful preparation, planning and training. This was a combination which, when a means was established of permanently keeping Roman armies at a high level of skill and efficiency, would later make Rome militarily dominant for the best part of five centuries.

Rebellions began to break out in Spain soon after Scipio left, confirming the personal nature of the loyalty amongst the chieftains and tribes, but his eyes were already further afield. Even whilst still in Spain he had begun to anticipate a campaign to strike at the Punic heartland in Africa. He made several attempts to form alliances with Numidian princes, sending men to negotiate with Masinissa in an attempt to lure him over to join Rome. He resumed the contact his father and uncle had had with King Syphax, even sailing across the Straits of Gibralter to visit him in his kingdom. This resulted in the bizarre incident when both Scipio and Hasdrubal Gisgo with their respective officers sat down as guests at the royal table only a few months after Ilipa. Ultimately the negotiations with Syphax failed, but in Masinissa Scipio made an important ally who would do much to affect the outcome of the Roman invasion of Africa. It is to this that we must now turn.[23]

CHAPTER 12

Africa

SCIPIO MADE IT VERY clear that as consul he wanted to be sent with an invasion force into Africa, proclaiming that if permitted to do so he would win the war. The idea was not entirely new, since Sempronius Longus had been sent to prepare such an expedition in 218 before he was recalled, but the Romans' confident mood in that first year of war had long since been shattered by Hannibal. Eventually the Senate decided that the consular provinces for 205 should be southern Italy and Sicily and it became almost certain that Scipio would get his way. Publius Licinius Crassus, the other consul, was also *pontifex maximus*, Rome's senior priest, and so for religious reasons needed to remain in Italy itself, ensuring that he would go to Bruttium to face Hannibal, and Scipio to Sicily. The war there had been over for five years and the island was ideally placed to act as a base for an invasion of the Carthaginian heartland. Yet from the beginning there was intense opposition in the Senate, both to the idea of sending an army to Africa and to granting Scipio the command. Rumours circulated then and later that the young consul was willing to use radical methods to get his way, planning to persuade a tribune to pass a law in the Popular Assembly giving him Africa as his province if the senators denied him. Technically legal, such a move would have been utterly unprecedented, threatening the stability of a political system which relied so much upon convention and was in fact to begin breaking down in this way less than a century later.[1]

Most prominent of Scipio's opponents was Fabius Maximus, now too old to serve in the field himself and nearing the end of his long life. Our sources depict Fabius as still obsessed with avoiding all military risks and perhaps a little jealous of Rome's new hero, but the arguments attributed to him were reasonable enough. Hannibal was still in Bruttium, undefeated in a serious battle after more than a dozen campaigns on Italian soil. The

Romans may already have been aware that Mago Barca was planning to join him, perhaps reviving the fears which had flourished back in 208 when Hasdrubal was poised to cross the Alps. The threat to Italy itself was still very real. Fabius was old enough to remember how Regulus' defeat in 255 had revived the flagging Carthaginian war effort, prolonging for over a decade a war which had seemed to be nearly won, and pushing Rome almost to the limit of her endurance. Landing an army on the other side of the Mediterranean and then supplying it were difficult tasks in themselves, without having to face an enemy fighting on their home ground and so inevitably superior in numbers. Fabius may well have felt that Scipio's Spanish campaigns had not prepared him for such an enterprise.

In the end a compromise favouring Scipio was reached. He was given Sicily as his province with permission to cross to Africa if he believed it to be in Rome's interest. Our sources claim that his opponents still tried to restrict his action by preventing him from levying a new army, although this tradition has sometimes been doubted. The garrison of Sicily was still substantial enough to provide an invasion force and in addition such was Scipio's popularity that volunteers flocked to join him: 7,000 men came forward, including a cohort of 600 from the city of Camerinum, whilst other communities provided food and equipment. Etruria proved especially enthusiastic, perhaps to prove their loyalty which had been suspected by the Romans earlier in the war. The size of the army eventually taken to Africa is unknown. Livy mentions three different totals given by unnamed sources, ranging from 10,000 infantry and 2,200 cavalry, through 16,000 infantry and 1,600 cavalry, to a maximum of 35,000 of both arms. The heart of the army was the two Cannae legions, now numbered Fifth and Sixth. Scipio had removed the old and unfit from the ranks of these units and replaced them with his volunteers, to produce two exceptionally strong units of 6,200 foot and 300 horse. There is no record of legions as large as this in the third century BC and Livy's figure has as a result sometimes been doubted, but this is to deny the essential flexibility of the Roman military system. It was normal to increase the size of legions when faced by an especially dangerous enemy and Scipio's army was about to undertake a difficult operation, so there is no good reason to reject this figure. It is probable that the legions were supported by the usual two *alae*, giving Scipio a standard consular army. Assuming that the allies were roughly equal in size to the citizen troops, then this would have brought the army's total number of combat soldiers up to somewhere around 25,000–30,000 men, to which we must add servants and camp followers. It is doubtful that more than one in ten of the soldiers were cavalrymen and the ratio may have been even lower, given the difficulty of transporting horses by sea. If this estimate is near the mark, and it must remain conjectural, then this was one of the largest armies to be transported by sea to a hostile shore throughout the entire course of the wars.[2]

Scipio went to Sicily in 205, but did not actually launch the invasion until the following year. A squadron of thirty warships from the Sicilian garrison was put together and sent on a plundering expedition against the North African coast. In charge was Gaius Laelius, once again serving as Scipio's senior *legatus*. The raid caused an invasion scare in Carthage, before it was realized that it was only on a small scale. It also allowed Laelius to make contact with Masinissa, who was busy fighting a civil war to control his late father's kingdom, and complained about the delay in the Roman invasion. It was not only contemporaries who expected the invasion to occur in 205, for some historians have also wondered why Scipio delayed. This is to misunderstand the scale of the planned invasion and the preparations it required, which could not have been completed in a few months. A large fleet, particularly of transport ships, had to be assembled and crews provided. One difficulty was encountered when the galleys Scipio had brought with him to the island proved to have been constructed from improperly prepared wood and needed to be beached for extensive maintenance. The perennial problem of supply posed particular problems for an army that planned to operate so far from its bases. It would have been difficult to feed such a large army through foraging, especially in the winter months, and the requirement to do this would have placed serious limitations on Scipio's freedom of action in Africa. Instead, for the two years that the African campaign would last, the bulk of the food consumed by the Roman army was brought across by sea from Sicily or Italy. The troops themselves had also to be prepared for a new type of campaign. The Cannae legions had served continuously under arms longer than any other units of the Roman army, but for the last decade they had fought in Sicily where pitched battles were exceptionally rare and most of the fighting consisted of raids and sieges. In addition a good number of the men in their ranks, perhaps as many as 50 per cent, were recent replacements from Scipio's volunteers. An extensive training programme was needed to absorb the new recruits and raise the standard of drill and discipline to the same level that had allowed the legions in Spain to undertake the complex battlefield manoeuvres of Baecula and Ilipa. Scipio spent about a year preparing for the invasion, a fairly typical period for a major expedition in the ancient world. It was once again an indication of the thorough planning and preparation which formed the basis for his bold operations.

According to Livy the general knew that landing an army in Africa was not difficult. The problem was in keeping it there and defeating the strong defences arrayed against it. Scipio's attitude made military sense, but did assume that his command would be extended for at least another year and probably much longer. He appears to have been confident that his friends and supporters in the Senate were numerous and influential enough to ensure that this happened, or perhaps that the entire state realized that he was the best man for the job. During the months in Sicily a scandal occurred which challenged this assurance.[3]

Late in the campaigning season of 205, a group of Locrian prisoners offered to betray the city's citadel to the Romans. Scipio leaped at the chance to deny Hannibal one of the few cities still loyal to him and gave orders for 3,000 men commanded by the tribunes Marcus Sergius and Publius Matienus to march from Rhegium to Locri. One of his *legati*, Quintus Pleminius (who is attributed propraetorian rank by Livy, perhaps anachronistically), was detailed to assist in the operation and seems to have assumed overall command. Although not every aspect of the plan went smoothly, the Romans were eventually successful and the Punic garrison retired from the city to rejoin Hannibal. The Carthaginian occupation of the city had been particularly repressive, but Pleminius and his garrison rapidly proved themselves to be worse. Houses and temples, including a famous shrine to Persephone, were plundered, citizens assaulted and their wives and daughters violated. The war in south-west Italy had long consisted of brutal plundering raids by both sides and the troops in the area had degenerated into little more than bandits. The garrison divided as the tribunes' soldiers and those of Pleminius formed two rival bands. A squabble over booty escalated into open fighting which was won by the tribunes' men. As punishment Pleminius ordered the tribunes flogged, an extremely harsh punishment for men of their rank. He was in turn attacked by their angry soldiers, battered around the head and left unconscious. Hearing of the disturbances, Scipio sailed to the city where he supported his *legatus*. The tribunes were arrested and put in chains to be sent to Rome for judgement. The consul then returned to Sicily, leaving Pleminius in charge of the city. Angry at what he considered to be the lenient treatment of the tribunes, the *legatus* had them tortured and then executed, repeating the procedure with any of the city's leaders who dared to oppose him.[4]

Eventually the Locrians managed, early in 204, to send ten ambassadors to Rome where they reported on their mistreatment. The news caused an uproar and provided valuable ammunition for those senators opposed to Scipio, although fortunately for him this occurred after the provinces for the year had been allocated and his command extended as proconsul. The Locrian emissaries reported that complaint had been made to Scipio in Sicily, but that he was so preoccupied with the final preparations for the invasion and so well disposed to Pleminius that they had received no response. Fabius Maximus was again prominent in his condemnation of Scipio, accusing him of failing to impose proper discipline on his soldiers, who had also mutinied in Spain. Other rumours circulated about the young general's behaviour, claiming that he and his staff wandered about dressed in Greek fashion and lived the leisured lifestyle of Hellenistic aristocrats in the gymnasia of Syracuse, whilst the army and navy fell into neglect. Marcus Porcius Cato, Scipio's quaestor, was one of the equestrians with a good military record who had been enrolled in the Senate to replace the casualties of the early years of the war. Later he would establish a reputation as a stern personification of traditional Roman virtues which were increasingly under threat from the corrupting influence of Greek culture. During these months Cato provided a rich source of stories discrediting his commander. In spite of this, Fabius failed to have Scipio removed from his command. There was, however, a general consensus supporting Fabius' harsh treatment of Pleminius, who was arrested and brought to Rome for trial on capital charges, although Livy records several traditions concerning his precise fate. Faced with a serious problem, the Senate fell back on a very Roman way of dealing with it, sending a Commission of ten to Sicily to judge Scipio's responsibility for the recent crimes. The board was treated to several days of rigorous manoeuvres in which the army and fleet demonstrated the fruits of their months of training. Fully satisfied with this and the other visible signs of the preparations for the coming invasion, the commissioners confirmed the proconsul in his command and returned to Rome. It is impossible to know how impartial a group these men were, but there is no good evidence to portray the majority as close adherents of Scipio and his family. His only fault had been placing too much trust in his own subordinate and not properly investigating the problems at Locri during his brief visit.[5]

Invasion, 204–203 BC

Early in the campaigning season of 204, the Roman invasion fleet left Sicily, its departure accompanied by much ceremony. The traditional sacrifice was performed, Scipio personally flinging the innards of the slaughtered animal into the sea. Altogether, there were about 400 transports escorted by only forty warships. In addition to the men and animals there was fresh water and food for forty-five days, the food ration for fifteen days pre-cooked –

the grain probably baked into bread or hard tack – and ready for issue. The fleet sailed in close convoy, lights being hung from their sterns to allow them to keep station at night, each galley carrying one, the transports two and the flagship three. The warships were divided into two squadrons, those sailing to the left of the transports commanded by Laelius and Cato and those on the right under Scipio and his brother Lucius. Their small number suggests that the Romans did not anticipate strong opposition from the Punic navy, whose performance in the war up to this date had been dismal. Alternatively, Scipio may have had insufficient trained rowers to crew more galleys and been forced to gamble on not encountering an enemy fleet. If so, the gamble paid off, for the Romans sighted the African coast without difficulty on the second day out from Sicily.[6]

Livy claims that the Romans had originally planned to land far to the east of Carthage, near one of numerous trading communities known as Emporia, but that after sighting Cape Bon, his pilots steered to the west and made landfall on the third day at the promontory 'of the Beautiful one' (or god), modern-day Cap Farina or Ras Sidi Ali el Mekki. It is difficult to know what to make of his account, especially since we lack Polybius' narrative at this point, but it seems certain that the Romans did in fact land at Cap Farina not far from the city of Utica. Their arrival prompted a widespread flight by the local villagers who fled with their cattle into the cities, and particularly to Carthage itself. Scipio showed the same skill in deploying outposts to screen his army as he had before Ilipa, for 500 Carthaginian cavalry on a reconnaissance were easily defeated. Both the overall commander, one Hanno, and the cavalry's own leader were killed. Despite the exodus of much of the population, the Romans gathered considerable booty and 8,000 captives to send back to Sicily in the transport ships.[7]

Soon afterwards Masinissa arrived to join the Romans. His people, the Maesulii, had had a succession of leaders during the civil wars which followed the death of Masinissa's father, Gala. Numidian tribal politics were highly complex, since the throne was not hereditary and disputes were frequently settled by violence. The various protagonists all sought aid from external powers, including other Numidian kings, such as Syphax, the Carthaginians and eventually the Romans. Masinissa's main opponent, one Mazaetullus, had married the widow of another king. She was the granddaughter of Hamilcar Barca, offspring of the daughter he had married to Navaras, emphasizing the often close ties between the Punic aristocracy and the Numidian royal families. Masinissa had defeated this man, but then Syphax intervened, fearing that a strong king of the Maesulii might begin to threaten the power of his own people, the Masaesulii. Although he had dabbled with the idea of an alliance with Rome, Syphax had finally been persuaded to stay loyal to Carthage by Hasdrubal Gisgo, who had given him his daughter Sophonisba in marriage. By all accounts a remarkable woman, she gained great influence over the king and used it for the good of her father and her homeland. Syphax won a victory in which Masinissa was wounded and most of his army dispersed so that by the time he joined Scipio he may have had as few as 200 men still with him, although Livy also mentions that other sources gave him 2,000.[8]

The Carthaginians sent another cavalry force to probe the Roman positions. It was led by another Hanno, described variously as the son of Hamilcar and the son of Hasdrubal Gisgo. With around 4,000 men, mostly recently raised Numidians but including a contingent of Carthaginian citizens, Hanno moved to the city of Salaeca, around 15 miles from the Roman camp. Scipio is supposed to have commented scornfully on a cavalry commander who kept his men in a city during the summer months when they ought to be active. He ordered Masinissa to attack and then lure the enemy into a rash pursuit to a position where the Roman cavalry would be concealed in ambush. It was the same type of tactic which Numidian cavalry had used in the past against Roman armies and proved just as effective. Hanno fell and 1,000 of his men were killed or captured in the initial fight, 2,000 of the rest in the 30 mile pursuit. The coincidence of names between the two commanders of the Punic cavalry defeated in different skirmishes has led to the suggestion that there was in fact only one action, which our sources have confused, but even Livy was aware of this possibility and believed that there were two distinct encounters. After this success the Romans continued to ravage the surrounding land, sending their plunder and prisoners back to Sicily in the convoys of ships which regularly brought them supplies.[9]

At this point Scipio began the siege of Utica itself, hoping to capture the city and its port to use as a base. The Roman army established itself on a site which was still known as *castra Cornelia*, or the camp of Cornelius (Scipio), in Julius Caesar's day over a century and a half later. As was usual when there was no opportunity to seize the city by stealth or treachery, the siege proved slow going, continuing throughout the winter of 204–203. Observing the Roman army from a distance were the two armies of Hasdrubal Gisgo and Syphax, which had finally moved against the invaders late in the previous summer. Polybius and Livy both claim that Hasdrubal had 30,000 foot and 3,000 horse, and Syphax 50,000 and 10,000 respectively, but this seems unlikely since it would have been very difficult to feed such a large concentration of troops throughout the winter. Even so, it is probable that the Romans were significantly outnumbered and perhaps especially so in cavalry, since Numidian armies traditionally included a high proportion of these. The two armies built separate camps, a little more than a mile apart and around 7–8 miles from the Romans. Knowing that they would be there for some time, the Punic soldiers had built fairly solid timber huts, but the Numidians, perhaps following a native style or merely because there was not enough timber left by their allies, had employed reeds. Syphax's camp was far less organized than Hasdrubal's, many of the men even sleeping outside the rampart.[10]

During the winter, Scipio tried once again to win Syphax over, hoping that he had by now tired of Sophonisba. The king replied by offering to mediate between Rome and Carthage, suggesting a peace by which the former would leave Africa and Hannibal evacuate Italy. Scipio included centurions disguised as slaves in his delegations to the enemy camps, who assessed in detail the layout and the readily combustible nature of the construction. At the beginning of spring 203, Scipio openly prepared to continue the siege of Utica and made public pronouncements to the soldiers that they were soon to attempt a direct assault. Yet he also suggested to Syphax that he was ready to accept the proposed terms, until at the last minute he reported that his *consilium*, or council of officers, was opposed to the treaty, so that they needed more time for discussion. In the meantime he prepared a night attack on the two enemy camps. The tightening of the blockade around Utica was intended more to prevent its garrison sallying out and threatening the Romans from the rear than to further the capture of the city. On the day chosen for the assault, Scipio summoned his tribunes at noon and briefed them in detail on the proposed attack. The trumpet fanfare sounded each night in the Roman camp, to mark the end of the day's duties and the beginning of the night watch, was on this night to be the signal for the legions to march out of camp. Information provided by scouts sent to reconnoitre the ground and from Masinissa's local knowledge had been carefully analysed to establish the best route for the attacking columns.

Half of the main force, supported by Masinissa's Numidians, went under Laelius to attack Syphax's camp, whilst Scipio led the remainder against Hasdrubal. Laelius was to attack first, but before doing so Masinissa carefully stationed men to cover all the routes in and out of the Numidian camp. The Romans then attacked, setting light to the rudely constructed huts, which began to burn furiously. Unaware of any enemy threat and assuming that the blaze was accidental, many of the Numidians were cut down as they fled. The confusion spread to the Punic camp, some of the mercenaries rushing out to help their allies fight the fire. Just as suddenly, Scipio sent his men into the attack, putting to the torch the Carthaginians' timber camp. Again men were killed as they fled, or perished in the flames which spread rapidly through the closely packed timber huts. Surprise was complete and the attacks devastatingly successful. By the end of the next day's pursuit, both armies were demoralized and dispersed, Polybius claiming that Hasdrubal had only 500 cavalry and 2,000 infantry still with him. The attempt to relieve the pressure on Utica and hem the Roman army into the narrow peninsula around it had failed utterly.[11]

Polybius praised the conduct of this night attack as one of Scipio's greatest achievements. A night attack was always difficult, especially a relatively complex one requiring several columns to co-ordinate their movements. The skill with which the Romans undertook this operation provides another indication of Scipio's careful preparation and the high standard of training of his army. Care had been taken to deceive the enemy concerning Roman intentions at Utica, but ultimately the deception plan rested upon convincing Syphax and Hasdrubal that Scipio sincerely wanted peace. Although Polybius believed that Scipio's message to the Numidian king claiming that his officers opposed the treaty made it clear that negotiations were incomplete, and that therefore the two sides remained at war, this was legally questionable by the standards of the day.[12]

After the victory Scipio divided his forces between the siege of Utica and plundering expeditions in which he threatened the recently defeated enemy. Loot was so plentiful in the Roman camp that the merchants who habitually followed the army were able to buy at abnormally low levels. The army had also gathered herds of cattle and some food, but huge amounts of grain were still being brought by sea from Sicily and also Sardinia. Large granaries were built in *castra Cornelia* to preserve the stockpiles of food. In addition Livy mentions supplies of clothing, for instance one batch of 1,200 tunics and 1,200 togas, although perhaps by the latter he meant military cloaks.[13]

The Battle of the Great Plains, 203 BC

News of the disaster caused a fresh outbreak of panic in Carthage, some calling for the return of Hannibal and his army, whilst others even suggested seeking peace with Rome. However, at this stage the majority of the Punic senate summoned by the suffetes were still in favour of continuing the struggle, so they ordered messages to be sent to Syphax, urging him to rejoin Hasdrubal. The king was at the city of Abba, where he had begun reforming his army. He remained loyal to Carthage, urged on by his wife, but also encouraged by the arrival with Hasdrubal of a contingent of recently raised Celtiberian warriors. There were in fact 4,000 of these tribesmen, but rumours encouraged by the Carthaginians inflated the number to 10,000 and spoke in extravagant terms of their ferocity and prowess. The Carthaginians' continued ability to raise mercenaries in Spain, despite their expulsion from the country gives an interesting indication of the minimal control the Romans exercised over the greater part of the Spanish Peninsula. Syphax went to join Hasdrubal after thirty days and their combined forces, something like 30,000 men, encamped in a strong position on the area known as the Great Plains, probably the modern Souk el Kremis.[14]

As soon as Scipio received reports of this new concentration of forces, he decided to march and confront them. Leaving his fleet and part of the army to continue the siege of Utica, he led out the remainder, reaching the edge of the Great Plains on the fifth day. It is uncertain how large the Roman force was, but likely that it was smaller than the enemy army. The Romans left behind their heavier baggage, clearly planning on a swift campaign. Scipio camped just under 4 miles from the enemy position and rested his army. On the next day, the Romans marched out into the plain and deployed into battle order a little less than a mile away from the Punic army. There was the usual skirmishing between the cavalry and light infantry, but neither side chose to force a general action on that day or the next two. On the fourth day, the rival commanders seem to have mutually decided to fight a battle and advanced their lines so far forward that a clash became inevitable. Hasdrubal formed his centre from his most reliable troops, the Celtiberians. Next to them on the right were the infantry salvaged from his old army, flanked by his cavalry, and on the left Syphax's Numidians. The Roman deployment was similar with the legions in the centre, presumably flanked by the *alae*, the Roman and Italian cavalry on the right flank and Masinissa's Numidians on the left.

The battle was decided very quickly as Masinissa's Numidians and the Italian horse swept away their counterparts in the first charge. Most of the Punic and Numidian infantry seems also to have collapsed into rout, probably pushed by the *alae* if these were in fact present, leaving the Celtiberians isolated. The fleeing troops all preserved the memory of recent defeat when these same Romans had stormed their camps, and their morale had evidently not yet recovered. Abandoned, the Celtiberian warriors continued to fight hard against the Roman legions, Livy claiming that their unfamiliarity with Africa deterred them from joining the flight. In numbers they at the very least roughly equalled the *hastati* of the two legions who probably formed the centre of Scipio's line. The Romans had deployed in the usual *triplex acies*, but rather than feed the rear lines into the combat, the legions performed another of the manoeuvres which were becoming the trademark of Scipio's armies. The *principes* and *triarii* turned into column and marched out from behind the *hastati*, wheeling to attack the Celtiberians in both flanks. It is unclear whether one entire line went to the right and the other to the left, or the separate legions divided so that half of the *principes* and *triarii* moved against each flank. Enveloped, the Spanish warriors were destroyed as an effective unit, very few escaping, but their sacrifice allowed much of the rest of the army to get away.[15]

After this victory Scipio summoned his *consilium* to discuss their next move. Roman magistrates serving in any capacity were expected to seek the advice of experienced men, but, whilst considering other viewpoints, a general was expected to make the actual decisions himself. The gathering of senior officers was then a convenient way of explaining a plan to the subordinates who would carry it out. Scipio decided to divide his army, keeping the main force himself to ravage the surrounding area, whilst Laelius took the remainder and went with Masinissa to restore the prince to power within his own tribe. Once again Scipio's men gathered rich plunder from the wealthy plains and began to find that some of the Libyan communities, weary of the heavy taxes imposed on them to support the Punic war effort, were willing to surrender to Rome. Encouraged, the general decided to make a demonstration against Carthage itself.[16]

Despite the dismay caused by another defeat, the Carthaginian Senate remained resolute, giving orders to prepare the city itself for a siege. In the last months considerable effort had been directed towards equipping and crewing a fleet, originally with the intention of threatening the Roman supply lines with Sicily. It was decided to send the fleet to Utica, which was now surrounded by a comparatively weak Roman force. At the very least this might raise the siege, but plans were also made to attack the Roman fleet which was, correctly, believed to be unprepared for naval combat. In addition, the momentous decision to recall Hannibal and his army was taken, a party of Punic senators being dispatched by sea to carry the message to the general.[17]

Scipio moved against Tunis, which was abandoned by its garrison. He was now about 15 miles from Carthage itself, able to see the city and its harbour. As the Romans watched they saw the Punic fleet putting to sea and immediately realized the threat to their own naval squadrons at Utica. Scipio gave the order to abandon the new camp and hastened back to *castra Cornelia*, the general perhaps riding on ahead, for he reached his base before the enemy ships. Realizing that there was no time to prepare the Roman squadrons for battle, since many had been adapted to carry siege engines, he had the ships lashed closely together, the transports three or four deep around a central line of galleys. On board were stationed 1,000 picked men, equipped with a great quantity of missiles. The Punic fleet had not hastened to reach Utica, and did not attack until the next day. This may simply have been a tactical error on the part of their commander, brought on by over-confidence, or perhaps reflected a desire to give the crews some sea training before they engaged. When they did attack, the Punic ships were able to make little headway against the solid barrier of Roman ships, especially since the transports were significantly higher than the low-slung galleys. However, the Carthaginians managed to cut sixty transports free and towed them in triumph back to Carthage.[18]

It took around fifteen days for Laelius and Masinissa to reach the kingdom of the Maesulii. Syphax had raised another army to face them, mostly from his own tribe. In a confused battle his more numerous cavalry initially gained an advantage, but as Laelius' legionaries came up to support Masinissa's horsemen the tide began to turn. The close formations of the Roman infantry gave stability to the line, and provided solid points behind which their own horsemen could rally and reform before charging again. Steadily the Roman line pushed forward until finally Syphax's army broke. The king himself attempted to rally his men by personal example, but when his horse fell beneath him he was captured and taken to Laelius. On Masinissa's suggestion, Laelius then moved on Syphax's capital Cirta, taking it by surprise and easily capturing it. Sophonisba surrendered herself with great dignity to Masinissa, begging him not to hand her over to the Romans. Without informing Laelius, Masinissa impulsively decided to take her as his own wife. The creation of such a link between their closest ally in Africa and the Carthaginian nobility was obviously most unwelcome to the Romans, who believed the Numidians to be a fickle race in their loyalties, but Laelius agreed to allow Scipio to decide what should be done. After mopping up the few garrisons still loyal to Syphax, the victorious leaders returned to join Scipio. The captured Syphax bemoaned his fate, blaming his misfortune on Hasdrubal's daughter who had led him against his inclinations to war with Rome. Subtly, he claimed that he was glad that his enemy Masinissa would now fall under her spell and suffer the consequences. This added to the Roman commander's suspicion of the young Numidian's action, perhaps especially because of his own refusal of similar temptations at New Carthage. Scipio declared that both Syphax and

Sophonisba were captives not of Masinissa but of Rome, and could not be disposed of without his permission. The emotional Numidian sent a gift of poison to his new bride who, the product of a culture which told many tales of aristocratic suicide, took it without hesitation. So ended one of the most romantic and tragic episodes of the war. The next day Scipio confirmed Masinissa as king of his tribe in a public ceremony, lavishing him with praise and honours.[19]

Peace Negotiations and the Return of Hannibal, Autumn 203 – Spring 202 BC

The Punic army in North Africa had been dispersed, Syphax, their most important ally, utterly defeated, and the minor success won by their fleet too late to pose a serious threat to the invader. The Roman expeditionary force remained at large, its numbers set to grow with the addition of more Numidians rallying to Masinissa. By the end of the campaigning season in 203 the voices in the Punic Senate calling for a continuation of the struggle were drowned out by those advocating peace. The thirty most senior members, the *gerousia*, were sent to Scipio's camp to begin negotiations to end the war. The delegation blamed Hannibal and his supporters for starting the war. Like all treaties which proved short-lived, it is difficult to know how much reliance can be placed on the terms listed in our sources. Livy says that Scipio demanded that the Carthaginians should release all captives, deserters and runaway slaves, withdraw their armies from Italy and Cisalpine Gaul, permanently sever their last ties with Spain, renounce their claim to the islands in the Mediterranean, and hand over all but twenty ships from their navy. In addition they were to supply large quantities of grain, 500,000 *modii* (*c.* 3,390 metric tonnes) of wheat for the men and 300,000 *modii* (*c.* 2,034 tonnes) of barley for the animals, to feed the Roman army in Africa. There were several different amounts given for the financial indemnity to be imposed.[20]

The Carthaginians accepted the terms, although Livy claims that they were simply playing for time, hoping that the return of Hannibal's army could restore the military situation. An embassy was dispatched to Rome to confirm the treaty, which needed approval from the Senate and ratification in the *Comitia Centuriata*. Rome had already received a report of the recent campaigns delivered by Laelius, resulting in the declaration of four days of public thanksgiving. There is now a conflict in our sources, for Polybius later tells us that the treaty was approved by Rome, whereas Livy describes the talks breaking down as the Carthaginian delegation attempted to alter the terms agreed with Scipio and return to a version of the Catulus treaty. He claims that the Senate decided to expel the ambassadors from Italy and voted to give Scipio, as the man on the spot, authority to advise whether or not future peace proposals should be accepted.[21]

The armistice continued throughout the winter months, in spite of the arrival in Africa of Hannibal and his forces. Scipio's army was still dependent on supplies brought by sea from Sicily and Sardinia, especially during the winter. During the armistice, probably at the beginning of spring 203, a convoy of 200 transports and thirty warships was brought by the propraetor Cnaeus Octavius from Sicily, but was struck by a sudden change in the weather. The oared warships were able to row against the wind and reach their intended landfall, but the sail-powered merchantmen were swept eastwards along the coast and scattered, many ending up in the wide bay overlooked by Carthage itself. Encouraged by popular demonstrations, the Punic Senate were unable to resist the temptation to profit from this opportunity. Hasdrubal was sent out with fifty warships to round up the Roman transports, most of which were abandoned by their crews. The prizes were then towed back to Carthage and their cargoes added to the city's grain reserves, which may well have been running short for a population swollen by the influx of refugees from the rural areas.[22]

Scipio sent a delegation of three ambassadors on board a quinquereme to Carthage to demand the return of the ships and their supplies, complaining that their seizure had violated the armistice and, if Polybius is right, the Peace Treaty agreed in Rome. The mood in Carthage had changed once again, encouraged by the return of Hannibal and his veteran soldiers. All classes were now overwhelmingly in favour of renewing the war, hoping for a victory which would allow them to gain far more favourable terms. The Roman delegation was mobbed and only escaped injury through the protection of the city's magistrates. The Roman galley was given an escort of two triremes to take it to within sight of its own fleet. As the quinquereme passed the Carthaginian fleet observing the Romans near Utica, three Punic triremes (or quadriremes in Livy's version) put out to intercept it. Skilful handling by the Roman captain and crew avoided the enemy rams, and the superior height and numerous marines of the 'five' deterred attempts at boarding, but the ship was deluged with missiles and suffered many casualties.[23]

Campaigning began again with renewed energy almost immediately. Scipio became more ruthless to demonstrate his determination to the end the war decisively. Cities which surrendered voluntarily were no longer offered terms, but their populations enslaved as if they had been taken by storm. The Roman general had been pleased by the Senate's acceptance of the peace terms he had framed, despite the swift collapse of the Treaty. It showed that he was still popular with the majority of senators. Particular glory was reserved for the Roman commander who completed a major war and there was always a danger that rivals would seek to replace a general in the closing stages of a conflict and steal much of the credit. In 203 the Senate had extended Scipio's command until the war had been won, but there was no guarantee that this decision might not be reversed. Now that Hannibal had left Italy, Africa offered by far the greatest chance of distinction. One of the consuls of 203, Cnaeus Servilius Caepio, is supposed to have travelled to Sicily late in the year, with a view to crossing to Africa. He seems to have been recalled by the dictator appointed to hold the elections for the following year. Both of the successful candidates for the consulship of 202 hoped to be given Africa as their province. Scipio still had enough supporters in the Senate, notably Quintus Caecilius Metellus, to refer the matter to the People, who voted overwhelmingly to continue Scipio's *imperium*. Nevertheless, one of the consuls was sent to Africa in command of a fleet of fifty quinqueremes. This was Tiberius Claudius Nero, cousin of the victor at Metaurus, who was ordered to support by sea the operations of Scipio's army. For the moment, Africanus' popularity with the people and allies within the Senate had defeated the attempts to replace him. The scene was now set for a direct clash between Scipio and Hannibal, without doubt the ablest commanders produced by each side in the Second Punic War.[24]

The Battle of Zama, 202 BC

The brutality of the Roman campaign against the African towns prompted the authorities in Carthage to bombard their commander with orders to join battle. Hannibal refused to be hurried and remained in his camp near Hadrumentum. He knew that his army was weak in cavalry and managed to persuade a relative of Syphax's named Tychaeus to join him with 2,000 Numidian light horse. Scipio was equally concerned that Masinissa should now justify his support by bringing a strong force of auxiliaries to assist the Roman army, and sent repeated messages to him. Finally Hannibal decided to break the stalemate and advanced his army to Zama, five days' march west of Carthage. Pausing there, he sent spies and scouts out to locate the enemy and assess their strength. Three spies were captured by the Romans, and on Scipio's orders they were given guided tours of his camp and told to report everything to Hannibal. It was the sort of stratagem which demonstrated a general's confidence, but it is also possible that the inten-

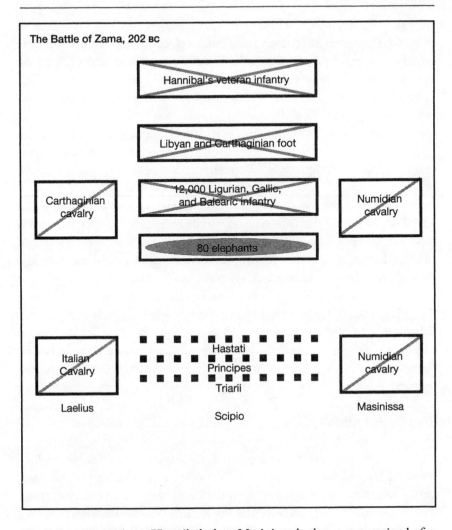

The Battle of Zama, 202 BC

Hannibal's veteran infantry

Libyan and Carthaginian foot

Carthaginian cavalry

12,000 Ligurian, Gallic, and Balearic infantry

Numidian cavalry

80 elephants

Italian Cavalry

Hastati
Principes
Triarii

Numidian cavalry

Laelius

Scipio

Masinissa

tion was to convince Hannibal that Masinissa had not yet arrived, for Polybius claims that the king rode into the Roman camp on the next day. He brought with him a reinforcement of 4,000 cavalry and 6,000 infantry, the latter perhaps including some of Laelius' command. Livy repeats these figures, but believed that the king had arrived before the capture of Hannibal's spies and that their report discouraged the latter. Both authors report that the Carthaginian was eager to meet his young adversary and that the two commanders met for a parley, but it is questionable whether the speeches attributed to them preserve anything of their actual conversation.[25]

The Roman army was encamped on a hill outside a town called Maga-ron by Polybius and Naragarra by Livy. As usual it has proved impossible to locate the battlefield with any certainty, although it was clearly some-where to the west of Zama. The Roman position was good with close access to a plentiful water supply. Hannibal advanced and camped on another hill just under 4 miles away. It was a stronger position but lacked a good water supply. On the next day the commanders met for their parley and it was on the second day that the armies marched out to fight. Such a swift confrontation, without the usual days of skirmishing, indicates the eagerness of both commanders for battle. The willingness to fight imme-diately created an impression of confidence in the outcome which could have an adverse affect on the opposing side's morale.[26]

We do not know the size of the opposing armies, but it is probable that the Romans had fewer infantry and significantly more cavalry than their opponents. Appian gives figures of 50,000 men for Hannibal's army and 23,000 foot and 1,500 horse plus Masinissa's Numidians for the Romans, but his account of the battle is generally unconvincing and needs to be treated with caution. Scipio massed the Roman and Italian cavalry on the left wing, putting Laelius, who was now serving as his quaestor, in charge. Masinissa's 4,000 Numidian light cavalry formed the right. In the centre were the legions and *alae* in the usual *triplex acies* with one slight variation. Instead of stationing the maniples of *principes* to cover the intervals between the maniples of *hastati*, they were drawn up directly behind them, with the *triarii* in turn behind them. This created a series of wide lanes running right through the Roman formation. Groups of *velites* were sta-tioned in these gaps, probably in skirmish order, although it is possible that initially they were formed up to conceal the nature of the Roman deploy-ment. These men were given specific orders to deal with the elephant attack which it was clear would open the battle. More than eighty of these beasts formed a line in front of the Punic army. Hannibal divided his cav-alry between the two wings, the Numidians facing Masinissa and the Carthaginians and other nationalities opposite Laelius. The infantry in the centre were split into three lines, mirroring the Roman formation. The first line was composed of Ligurians, Gauls, Balearic slingers and some Numid-ians. This appears to have been the remains of Mago's army brought back from Italy. The second line consisted of troops raised for the defence of Africa, Libyans and a strong contingent of Punic citizens, making a rare appearance as a formed unit during the wars. One tradition claimed that there was also a strong force of Macedonians in this line, but since it would be most unusual for Polybius not to mention the involvement of Hellenic troops this is normally rejected. The last line, held back a couple of hun-dred yards behind the second, consisted of his own veterans, a mixture of many races nearly all now equipped with Roman armour and shields. The narratives of the battle suggest that they were roughly equal in number to the entire Roman heavy infantry, so perhaps there were between 15,000–20,000 of them.[27]

The two sides' deployments were very similar and showed just how much the two military systems had learned from each other during the long years of war. This was the first time that Hannibal had copied the Roman practice of keeping the majority of his infantry in reserve. He had always known that the strength of the enemy lay in the close order foot of the legions. Now that he no longer enjoyed the superiority in cavalry which had marked his earlier battles, Hannibal realized that he stood little chance of enveloping the Roman centre as he had done at Trebia and Cannae. The only alternative was to punch straight through the middle of their line. The Roman system of multiple lines gave their determined legionaries great staying power in combat, allowing fresh troops to be fed into the fighting line as the battle drew on and the enemy wearied. The strong force of elephants would first charge straight into the Roman front line, causing casualties and hopefully spreading disorder, as a similar attack had done to Regulus' army in 255. Hannibal's infantry lines could then advance to exploit this confusion, the reserve lines continually renewing the army's forward impetus as fresh troops were fed in. Ideally all three Roman lines would have been committed to the fight before Hannibal's own veterans, who significantly outnumbered the *triarii*, moved forward to complete the victory. It was not an especially subtle plan, but it was certainly the most practical in the circumstances. Scipio was too able a commander to be outwitted into fighting in unfavourable circumstances in the way that Hannibal had defeated his opponents earlier in the war. More importantly his own army was not as good as the one he had taken to Italy in 218, whilst Scipio's was one of the best trained forces ever produced by the Roman militia system. Hannibal's veterans, experienced and confident both in themselves and in their officers, composed less than half of his total force. His first and second lines were each formed from the remnants of two different armies, as unfamiliar with Hannibal as they were with each other. There had simply not been the time over the winter months to convert these disparate elements into a single army with a clear and homogenous command structure. Therefore Hannibal's deployment had the added advantage of effectively allowing the three different armies composing his force to operate independently. It is notable that whilst Hannibal made a speech to his own men, he ordered two distinct sets of officers to speak to the first and second lines. It was far easier for Scipio to ride along the ranks of his own army, encouraging the men, for, except for many of Masinissa's warriors, his soldiers had served under him for the past three years and army and commander were well known to each other.[28]

It took several hours for the two armies to march out and deploy, during which time there was only some sporadic skirmishing between the Numidian horsemen serving on both sides. Eventually when both were ready and the commanders had finished making speeches each side raised a cheer and sounded its trumpets in the customary gesture intended to demonstrate confidence and intimidate the enemy. The sudden burst of noise startled the elephants and seems to have caused them to attack prematurely. The far larger than usual number of war elephants suggests that the vast majority had recently been rounded up and were probably poorly trained. On the left a number of the animals panicked and stampeded back through the ranks of their own cavalry. Masinissa spotted the opportunity and led his men forward in an immediate attack on Hannibal's Numidian allies, routing them almost immediately. The remainder of the elephants surged forward against the Roman infantry. It must have been a truly intimidating sight as so many of the huge animals bore down on the waiting Romans. The *velites* skirmished forward, throwing showers of javelins at the oncoming beasts. Wounded, or their crews killed, the elephants became even more inclined to panic. Some *velites* fell and others fled back to shelter behind the formed maniples of *hastati*, but few of the elephants charged into the heavy infantry. Instead most of them stampeded through the lanes deliberately left in the Roman formation. Later they were disposed of at leisure in the rear of the army. Some on the right swerved towards the Roman cavalry, but changed direction again when they were greeted with a volley of javelins. Now completely out of control, they burst back through the Carthaginian cavalry. Laelius then copied Masinissa's example and charged forward against the disordered enemy horse, putting them to flight.

The elephant attack had failed and Hannibal had lost both of his cavalry wings in the opening stages of the battle. However, both Laelius' and Masinissa's horsemen had chased the enemy off the battlefield, driving them hard to prevent any attempts to rally. This meant that the Roman cavalry would be unable to intervene in the main action for some considerable time. It has occasionally been suggested that Hannibal deliberately ordered his cavalry to flee to draw the numerically superior enemy horse away from the action, but this is certainly incorrect. The Punic cavalry would have been more useful to their commander if they had remained and kept Scipio's cavalry busy for as long as possible. Our sources were convinced that it was not so much the numerical superiority of the Romans and Numidians, but the confusion caused by the stampeding elephants which produced the rapid flight of Hannibal's cavalry.[29]

The first two lines of Punic infantry had probably begun to advance as soon as the elephants attacked. The third line remained stationary under Hannibal's direct orders. The Roman foot went forward to meet them once the elephants had been repulsed or passed through their lines. As usual both sides advanced noisily, the men cheering and trumpets blaring. Polybius mentions again the Roman custom of banging their weapons against their shields, the *principes* and *triarii* in reserve urging on the *hastati*, and contrasts this with the discordant yelling of the many races in the enemy ranks. This was a theme as old as Homer's *Iliad*, which in fact Polybius quotes in this passage, repeated often in narratives of the Greek victories over the Persians. Yet the whole point of shouting during the advance was to frighten the opposition and to encourage yourself, and many sources testify to the importance of noise and appearance in deciding the outcome of encounters. The Romans may in fact have gained some advantage over the enemy in this way, although if so, it was not an overwhelming one for the first Punic line put up a very good fight. Polybius' text is slightly corrupted at this point, but he appears to have said that the two sides did not spend much time throwing missiles at each other, but rapidly charged into contact, a sign of their enthusiasm.[30]

Mago's old army attacked with great enthusiasm, inflicting significant losses on the *hastati*. After each lull in the fighting they renewed the combat, but gradually their charges slackened, whilst the Romans kept steadily pushing forward. Livy claims that the legionaries used the bosses of their shields to punch at the enemy, unbalancing them. Standard practice in the later, professional army, this was harder to do with the heavy shields of this period, which seem to have weighed over 20 lb (about 10 kg). The *principes* kept up close behind the front line, but do not yet seem to have joined the fighting. The Ligurians, Gauls and others in the Punic first line received little aid from their supports, the second line of Libyans and Carthaginians hanging back. The failure of the two lines to co-operate properly is probably another indication of the lack of unity in the disparate elements of Hannibal's army. Our sources even claim that fighting broke out between the two lines as men from the first attempted to retreat through the second. It is possible that Hannibal had issued instructions to the reserve lines not to let fugitives through their ranks, as he had with his veterans. Some sort of fighting line was established, merging elements of the first and second lines. For a while the advance of the *hastati* ground to

305

a halt. Polybius implies that at least some of the maniples of *principes* were then fed into the fighting and that the injection of these fresh troops into the combat renewed the forward impetus of the Roman infantry, putting the enemy to flight. The *hastati*, their order gone after two hard combats, surged forward in pursuit, hacking down at the enemy as they ran. This was always the time when most casualties occurred and it was particularly difficult for men wounded in the legs to escape.[31]

Hannibal's veterans refused to break their ranks and presented a levelled row of spear points at their comrades fleeing towards them. Officers bellowed at the men to go around the flanks of the third line and rally behind it. At least some of the units may have recovered and formed up to reinforce the last reserve of the Punic army. Hannibal's veterans were intact and apparently unperturbed by the rout of the other mercenaries and citizen troops. However, it is possible that the flight of the forward lines made it impossible for Hannibal to send the third line forward in a counter-attack against the Romans, who were now in some disorder. The *hastati* were for the moment out of control, chasing the men who had inflicted considerable losses on them earlier in the day, whilst even the *principes* had fought a short combat and lost some of their order. An attack might have been able to profit from the confusion in the Roman lines. However, between the Romans and the veterans the ground was strewn with corpses and slick with blood, difficult ground for a formation to move across whilst retaining its order. Hannibal may have preferred to remain where he was, the ranks of his men in perfect order, and allow the Romans to come to him, hoping that in their current state their advance would be improperly co-ordinated and lack power.[32]

Scipio's army then gave another proof of its high level of discipline, not by carrying out a complex manoeuvre, but by the even more difficult task of reforming in the middle of a battle. Trumpets sounded to recall the *hastati* from their pursuit. In the time taken for these men to come back and form up once more, the wounded were taken to the rear and other troops given some time to rest. Scipio, and probably his officers of all ranks, busied themselves reforming the line. The *hastati* reformed in the centre, whilst the *principes* and *triarii* were brought up on either flank. For once the Roman legions reverted to the tactics of the old hoplite phalanx, forming a single dense line matching the enemy's. When ready the Romans resumed their advance, and Hannibal's men came on to meet them. It proved a hard struggle, for the two sides were roughly equal in number and similarly equipped. Some of the soldiers on both sides were veterans with over ten years' service. The Romans were probably more tired, but were confident from their recent defeat of the first and second lines. A prolonged slogging match ensued. In the end it was decided by the return of Laelius' and Masinissa's rallied cavalrymen who returned to the battlefield and took Hannibal's veterans in the rear, making them suffer as they had once made the legions suffer at Trebia and Cannae. It was the final irony of the war that the Cannae legions won Rome's greatest success.

The Carthaginian losses were heavy, 20,000 killed and as many captured according to Polybius. The Romans lost 1,500 men, around 5 per cent of their total if their army numbered 30,000 (and it is unlikely to have been any larger). This was a substantial loss for a victorious army, testimony to the hard fighting, and there is no need to prefer the higher figure of 2,500 given in some later sources. The outcome of the battle was not inevitable, despite the great advantage the Romans possessed in Masinissa's cavalry. Hannibal's basic plan was sound and might easily have succeeded. Had Scipio not arranged his formation to let the elephants pass through between the maniples, then their charge might have inflicted as much damage as a similar onslaught had on Regulus' legions in 255. Hannibal's use of three lines of infantry, with the best troops in the last line, did much to weary the Roman foot, exhausting the *hastati* and taking the edge off the *principes*. It was only Scipio's ability as a commander and the discipline and high morale of his men that allowed them to reform and then hold their own in the final engagement. It is impossible to know which phalanx would eventually have prevailed if the Roman cavalry had not returned to take the enemy in the rear. Hannibal's tactics were not intended to surround and annihilate the enemy to the same degree as his earlier victories. He did not need such a complete victory. Now the Romans were the invader with the small, outnumbered army far from their home bases, just as Hannibal had been in the early years in Italy. If Scipio had suffered a clear defeat then it would most probably have meant the end of the African expedition, even if much of his army had escaped.[33]

The End

After the battle Hannibal and his staff fled back to his main base at Hadrumentum. The Romans rounded up their prisoners and looted the Punic camp. Scipio received the encouraging news of a fresh convoy of supplies arriving near *castra Cornelia*. Laelius was sent once again to carry the news of victory to Rome. The defeat of their last army left Carthage with no choice but once again to seek peace. Scipio led his fleet in a demonstration of force right up to Carthage itself to place further pressure on it to submit. In military terms the Romans could pose little direct threat to such a well-fortified city. Even with his entire army the siege of Carthage would have been a massive undertaking of uncertain outcome. Scipio swiftly rejected the idea, even though it is claimed by Livy that several of his officers advocated the plan. Therefore despite his initial rebuff of a Punic peace embassy, the Roman commander was eager to settle. In particular he may have been once more concerned about keeping his command and retaining the glory which his victory had won. In fact one of the consuls of 201 did try to replace Scipio in the African command at this late hour, but after intervention by some of the tribunes of the plebs and further senatorial debate, he in fact replaced Nero in the naval command.[34]

The terms of the Treaty dictated by Scipio were harsh. All Roman prisoners and deserters were to be handed over without ransom. All war elephants were confiscated and the fleet was reduced to a mere ten triremes. Carthage kept most of its territory in Africa, but all its overseas possessions were lost. Even in Africa they were forced to acknowledge Masinissa in a substantially enlarged kingdom. An indemnity of 10,000 silver talents was to be paid in annual instalments over a fifty-year period, a constant reminder of their defeat. Another indication of their new status was the stipulation that they should not make war outside Africa and only there with Rome's permission. Although Carthage continued to be ruled internally by its own laws it was now clearly subordinate to Rome in all external affairs. Finally the Carthaginians were to provide food and supplies for Scipio's army for a three-month period and provide their pay until the treaty had been confirmed. As a reminder of what the Romans considered to be their recent treachery they were also to make reparations for loss of Roman property when the truce was broken and the convoy attacked. Hostages were selected from the noble families of the city to act as surety during the negotiations so that there would be no repeat of this incident.[35]

The message of the Treaty was clear, and perhaps reinforced if as Appian claims the Carthaginians were now to be styled 'Friends and Allies' of the Roman People, the same formula used for Rome's subordinate allies in Italy. For that was what they now clearly were, subordinate allies of a greater state to which they paid annual tribute and to whose authority they submitted in important matters of foreign policy. The overseas empire and the once proud fleet which had protected it were abolished. It is unsurprising that some of the Punic leaders wanted to refuse such a harsh peace. Hannibal, always a realist, physically dragged one senator down from the speaker's position when he embarked on a speech in this vein. He excused his behaviour by saying that after a thirty-six-year absence from Carthage he had forgotten the etiquette of its politics, but then urged the leaders forcibly not to reject a peace which in their position could have been far worse. In the end the Punic Senate accepted and delegations were sent to Rome to confirm the terms.[36]

It was early spring 201 before the Senate finally confirmed their earlier decision to accept whatever peace terms Scipio proposed. Immediately on the return of the envoys along with representatives of the Roman priest-hood, the fetials, to oversee the important rituals involved, the provisions started to be put into operation. A great number of Punic warships, 500 according to some of Livy's sources, were rowed out of the city's great harbour and then burned. A grim fate awaited the deserters who had fought for the Carthaginians, the Romans being crucified and the Latins beheaded. Scipio returned to Rome to celebrate a spectacular triumph.[37]

CHAPTER 13

Rome, the Beginnings of Empire

The Reckoning

ROM THE BEGINNING the Second Punic War was a far more serious struggle than the First, which began in Sicily and remained primarily a struggle for control of the island. Regulus' invasion pushed the Carthaginians close to capitulation, but resulted in defeat and was never repeated by the Romans. The conflict became one of endurance, decided eventually when the last Punic fleet was destroyed at the Aegates Islands. The resultant Peace Treaty left Carthage strong in Africa and still capable of expansion in Spain, but came to seem more harsh after the Roman seizure of Sardinia.

The Second Punic War was a much simpler struggle for dominance in which territory was only ever of secondary importance. The Carthaginian attempt to retake Sardinia was feeble, and the moves against Sicily did not begin until several years into the war. In each case the initiative came from leaders on these islands and not from Carthage. Land was taken from the enemy and allies persuaded to defect as a means of exerting pressure, not as an end in itself. The treaties guaranteeing the independence from Carthage of states like Capua and Tarentum make it clear that a permanent Punic province in southern Italy was not anticipated. The war was fought to force the other side to submit and accept a treaty greatly favouring the victor. In 218 both sides planned to strike at the enemy's heartland, the Romans in Africa and Spain, and Hannibal in Italy. Despite setbacks, distractions and disagreement amongst the rival leaderships, these aims remained until the end, Hasdrubal and Mago renewing the invasion of Italy, and Scipio ending the war in Africa. The war extended into other theatres as each side seized opportunities to mount additional attacks on the enemy and so apply more pressure, but these were always subordinate to the main effort.

The greater intensity of the Second Punic War is illustrated by the balance between the three main types of fighting, battles, sieges and raids. Massed battles were far more common, although naval encounters were few and small-scale, none rivalling the great fleet actions of the First War. There were about twelve pitched battles from 218 to 202, which is three times the number fought between 265 and 241; and perhaps two dozen other sizeable actions. The brief accounts of many encounters make it difficult to be certain of their scale, nature and sometimes even their outcome, forcing these figures to be a little rough. Just over half of the major battles were fought in Italy, the remainder in Spain and Africa. As in the First War, the terrain in Sicily did not favour formal pitched battles and this was also true of much of Spain, Illyria and Greece, but in addition to the concentration of massed clashes to certain regions, they also tended to occur in brief, highly intense periods of campaigning. Hannibal fought three major battles and several sizeable actions between 218 and 216 and far fewer in later years. Scipio Africanus fought a battle in Spain in 208, tried unsuccessfully to force one in 207, and completed his victory with a final encounter in 206. In Africa he repeated this pattern, fighting major actions in both 203 and 202. Battles were most likely to occur when one commander acted exceptionally aggressively, usually by penetrating deep into enemy territory, for instance in the initial invasions of Italy and Africa, or Scipio's deep forays into the Punic province in Spain. The Roman response in particular was to meet such threats in open battle and it was only after successive defeats that commanders like Fabius Maximus injected a degree of caution into Roman operations in Italy. Such a high degree of mutual consent was required to produce a massed battle that even such able commanders as Hannibal and Scipio were frequently incapable of forcing an unwilling enemy to fight. This makes Scipio's decision to attack such a formidable position as Hasdrubal's at Baecula as remarkable as its success.[1]

The Romans lost several smaller actions, but were only defeated in a pitched battle by Hannibal in Italy. The defeats of Publius and Cnaeus Scipio in 212 occurred in a series of scrambling fights produced by a markedly unfavourable strategic situation. Elsewhere Roman armies displayed a marked superiority in open battle against all the other Punic armies and commanders. There is no doubt that Hannibal's army in Italy was the best ever fielded by Carthage, due to a combination of his charismatic leadership and the long years of campaigning in Spain. Another advantage came from its exceptionally high cavalry to infantry ratio, which reached between 1:3 and 1:4 at its peak, more than double the average for both sides. Hannibal's continued successes over the Romans gave his army an advantage in morale which it never really lost to the very end of the Italian campaign. Other Punic armies had a similar mix of nationalities and troop types, but performed very poorly on the battlefield. Most other commanders were far less able leaders and tacticians than Hannibal, and did not have the opportunity to turn the disparate contingents under their command into a cohesive unit through a combination of long training and successful operations under familiar officers. Frequently a single element is presented in our sources as the only truly reliable and efficient part of an army, for instance the Libyans at Ilipa or the Celtiberians at the Great Plains. Even Hannibal failed to weld together the three armies in Africa for the Cannae campaign in the short time he had available.

The Roman militia system produced armies which were far more homogenous in terms of language, command structure, drill and organization. This made it far easier to integrate legions from different commands into the same force. Prolonged service steadily increased the effectiveness of a Roman army, but the process occurred far more readily than with a Punic force of mixed nationalities. The legions in the Second Punic War served for far longer than any Roman troops before this date, so that by the latter stages of the war many were as well-trained and confident as any professional soldiers. The tactical flexibility shown by the Romans at Metaurus, Ilipa and Zama was the tangible evidence of this. Both men and their officers were now capable of feats unimaginable in 218. Such armies were far superior to most Punic forces and could defeat significantly more numerous enemies, as Scipio was to demonstrate. As the war progressed, the disdain which the Romans had shown for all Carthaginian armies and commanders apart from Hannibal began to be based more and more on reality.

Despite the large number of battles and sizeable actions fought in the Second Punic War, they were still rare events in the experience of most soldiers, who far more often took part in raids or sieges. Raiding was not primarily intended to provide food for an army, although it could be combined with this activity. Its main objective was to inflict as much damage as possible on the enemy-held countryside, killing or capturing the population, destroying farms and villages, burning crops and stealing livestock. All of these activities took time and effort, whilst some, for instance the destruction of crops, could only be done for a brief season of the year in the weeks immediately before harvest. Damage tended to be confined to a small area and had little long-term effect, although it was doubtless appalling for those immediately affected. Yet if raids continued over a long period they could have serious consequences for a region. Losses amongst the rural workforce to capture, death or conscription, and prolonged damage to fields, crops and livestock reduced productivity and created a shortage of food which in turn weakened the population and encouraged disease, resulting in further declines in production. Some areas, especially Bruttium and the other parts of southern Italy where Hannibal and his army were confined for years, were repeatedly raided by both sides and must have suffered greatly. One of the major controversies of the Second Punic War, which we shall discuss in a later chapter, is its impact on the population and rural economy of Italy.[2]

The most immediate consequence of raiding was damage to the enemy's prestige for failing to defend his territory. The sight of burning farms left in the wake of Hannibal's march in 217 incited Flaminius to pursue him incautiously, eager to avenge this humiliating display of Roman weakness. Later in the same year Fabius Maximus became very unpopular because he refused to act and prevent such depredations. A state which proved unable to defend its allies against enemy depredations lost face and was likely also to lose its allies. This was especially true in areas such as Sicily and Spain where the communities showed understandably little strong commitment to either side. Hannibal's failure to protect many of his Italian allies from raiding was a major factor encouraging their inexorable drift back to Rome.

Walled cities were safe from raiding, and only the smallest were ever likely to fall to direct assault. For most of the peoples involved in the conflict, towns and cities provided their political centres, controlling wide areas of the surrounding land. Raiding could intimidate the population of a region, but only the occupation of their important strongholds allowed their permanent control. The Roman victory in Sicily came from the capture of the two main enemy strongholds at Syracuse and Agrigentum. Neither side was capable of ending the entire war by capturing the enemy's capital, which were too large and too well protected, although on several occasions both Rome and Carthage believed themselves to be under direct threat. The capture of fortified positions has always been extremely difficult, one of the main reasons for the prominence of sieges in the propaganda of 'Great Kings' from the Pharaohs onwards. Only when the professional Roman army combined engineering skill with a willingness to accept the casualties inevitable in an assault did the balance shift away from the defender. As we have seen, direct attacks on a large city were only successful when they combined surprise with treachery from inside or special knowledge of a weakness in the defences. Blockades took much longer and required a large force to remain in one place for months or years, increasing the problems of supply. The Romans' superiority in numbers and ability to feed their armies allowed them to mount the long and ultimately successful sieges at Capua and Syracuse.[3]

The devastation of the countryside, the capture of towns and open battles were the three main ways of eroding the enemy's will to fight on. The balance between the three varied from theatre to theatre, but everywhere a major defeat in battle had the greatest impact. The war was finally ended by the Roman victory at Zama, as the First War had been ended by the Aegates Islands. Other battles provided more complete tactical victories, but failed to have such a decisive affect. This is especially true of the series of overwhelming battlefield victories which Hannibal won in Italy and which forced the Romans to admit that they could not face him in the open field. He devastated the lands he passed through and persuaded many of Rome's allies in the south to defect. In spite of all this the Romans refused to seek peace, as any other contemporary state would have done, so Hannibal continued to apply pressure on them by the same methods, although his successes were never again to be quite so spectacular. Still the Romans refused to give in. By the time that Capua and Tarentum, the most important of the defecting states, had been recaptured by the Romans, Rome had also regained the larger part of the areas which had defected and Hannibal's power in Italy was in decline. No Latin city ever joined him. Attempts to reinforce him with new armies failed and it became clear that he could not win. In the meantime the Romans had regained Sicily, expelled the Carthaginians from Spain, and established themselves in Africa.

It is difficult to see what more Hannibal could have done to attain victory. We can never know how close the Romans came to conceding defeat. Perhaps a march on Rome after Cannae would have broken the Romans' nerve, but we cannot be sure of this and such a move would have been a great gamble. One major problem for the Carthaginians was that they had one superb commander with an excellent army, whilst elsewhere they had poor commanders with average armies or average commanders with poor armies. From the beginning the Romans were able to produce in considerable quantity armies which were average in their quality and the skill of their commanders, giving them an advantage over all but Hannibal. As the war progressed and Roman leaders and soldiers gained experience, their superiority over the other Punic armies became even more marked. Had the Romans not found the troops to fight and win the campaigns on the fronts outside Italy, then the outcome of the war would surely have been very different. It is to the immense credit of the Roman Senate that it continued to commit men and resources to distant theatres when disaster appeared to threaten in Italy.[4]

There was a fundamental difference in the behaviour of Rome and Carthage when under threat. When a Roman army appeared outside their walls in 255, 203 and 202, the Carthaginian leadership responded by seeking peace. Livy believed that they were insincere in 203, and both then and in 255 they renewed the war after failing to win terms which they considered appropriate to their still considerable strength. In neither 216, 212 nor any of the other low points of the war did the Roman Senate or any Roman commander seriously consider conceding defeat and negotiating with the enemy. Despite their appalling losses, the string of humiliating defeats, the defections of some Italian allies and the continuing malevolent presence of Hannibal's army in Italy, the Romans simply refused to come to terms with the Carthaginians, as they had earlier refused to treat with Pyrrhus. They were then able to beat the enemy on every other front and force the undefeated Hannibal to evacuate Italy and return to protect Carthage. The Carthaginians expected a war to end in a negotiated peace. The Romans expected a war to end in total victory or their own annihilation, something which no contemporary state had the resources to achieve. This attitude prevented the Romans from losing the war and ultimately allowed them to win it.

Rome's huge pool of military manpower was probably the most important factor in allowing her to adopt such a rigid attitude. Her losses were appalling, far heavier than those of the First War, and this time fell especially heavily on the wealthier classes, the senators, equestrians and the yeoman farmers who served in the heavy infantry of the legions. Perhaps 25 per cent of the men qualified for military service were lost through casualties and defections in the first few years of the war, but in spite of this the number of legions in service increased. Some extraordinary measures were taken to replenish the pool of recruits, so that younger and older men than usual were enrolled, the minimum property qualification for service reduced, and legions of convicts and slaves formed. On the whole this expansion was made possible by the willingness of ordinary citizens to submit to years of harsh military discipline and extremely dangerous campaigning. It is vital to remember that all classes at Rome and amongst most of the allies felt very strong bonds of loyalty to each other and the State. There were some exceptions, most notably the refusal of the twelve Latin colonies to supply more men in 209, but they were extremely rare. It should also be noted that the colonies merely stated that their resources had been exhausted. They did not recommend a settlement with the enemy or make any move to defect. Similarly some men tried to avoid military service, others sought to profit at the expense of the troops they were supposed to be supplying, whilst a very few deserted and fought with the enemy, but the overwhelming majority did not and were led by fierce patriotism to sacrifice themselves for the State.

The Carthaginians suffered much lower casualties, both in number and in proportion of the total citizen body. Punic citizens only took the field in significant numbers in Africa, and their losses at the Great Plains and Zama were not high. Money never seems to have been lacking to hire more mercenaries, although time to recruit them and mould them into an effective army often was. Carthage was simply not geared to warfare to the same degree as Rome, where war-making was an integral part of the political system. Every year the Roman Senate decided on the allocation of commands and military resources and it was simply a continuation of normal procedure to do this throughout the Hannibalic war. It is questionable whether or not the Romans made war more frequently than other contemporary peoples, but they certainly did so with greater efficiency and wholeheartedness. Polybius was surely right to highlight Rome's political organization, social structure and military institutions as the keys to their victory over Carthage. During the Hannibalic War all of these had to be modified to cope with the crisis, so that multiple magistracies and pro-magistracies became common, the ranks of the Senate replenished *en masse* and slaves recruited into the army, whilst the legions were trained to an unprecedented level of efficiency. Each of these institutions had proved flexible enough to adapt without changing their essential nature. In the next half century they would give Rome mastery of the Mediterranean world.

World Empire, 201–150 BC

The war with Carthage ended in 201, but it left a legacy of continuing conflict which was to occupy Rome for several decades. Hannibal had launched his invasion from Spain, and in order to prevent anyone else following his example two provinces were created and a Roman military presence permanently maintained in the Spanish Peninsula. This involved the Romans in near constant warfare, in part prompted by the resentment of Spanish communities at the presence of a new occupying force, but also as they became involved in traditional patterns of warfare. Roman rule was only secure so long as they were able to protect their allies from raiding. After over two decades of intensive campaigning, Tiberius Sempronius Gracchus, son of the consul killed in 212, managed to create a lasting settlement through a judicious mixture of force and diplomacy. This produced a period of relative tranquillity for nearly a generation.[5]

Hannibal's invasion was just another episode in the ongoing struggle between Rome and the tribes of Cisalpine Gaul. His victories and those won by the Gauls themselves inspired a new generation to resist Roman incursions in the Po valley. One Carthaginian officer, a certain Hamilcar who had probably arrived with Mago, remained with the tribes and continued to lead them in battle after 201. Complaints were sent to the Punic authorities, who denied that the man was acting under orders, but the problem was only solved when Hamilcar was killed. In the first decade of the second century more consuls and more legions went to Cisapline Gaul than any other area, and the Senate exercised close control over the campaigns there, which was after all not far from Rome's heartland. This effort brought about the final defeat of the Gallic tribes in the Po valley, some of which were virtually destroyed as political entities and others absorbed. The suppression of the Ligurians took longer, their loose political structure, independent nature and rugged homeland prolonging their resistance and making it necessary to defeat each village in turn. A sizeable part of the population was transplanted and given land in southern Italy left vacant after the Hannibalic War, where they proved successful and peaceful farmers.[6]

In 200 the consul Publius Sulpicius Galba presented a motion to the *Comitia Centuriata* for the declaration of war against Macedonia. The pretext was an appeal from Athens for aid against Philip V. Nearly all of the voting centuries voted against the proposal, one of the very few occasions when the Roman People seemed reluctant to go to war. The prolonged effort against Carthage had left all classes weary and hesitant about embarking on a major overseas war. The *Comitia Centuriata* was not a forum for debate and could simply vote for or against a proposal. Before Galba summoned the Assembly to vote again, he addressed the centuries at an informal meeting (or *contio*). Livy gives the consul two main arguments in favour of the war. Philip V had shown himself to be Rome's enemy by his unprovoked attack during the crisis of the Second Punic War. If the Romans did not attack him now and fight the war in Greece, then at some time in the future the Macedonians might use their sizeable fleet to land an army in Italy. Athens must be protected from Philip, since the failure to defend another ally, Saguntum, from Hannibal had encouraged him in his plans to attack Italy. When the *Comitia* voted a second time, the motion was passed easily and war declared on Macedonia. There may have been other reasons for the decision. Philip V and the Seleucid King Antiochus III had secretly decided to benefit from the accession to the Egyptian throne of a minor, Ptolemy V, by carving up his territory. This

317

threatened to upset the balance in power between the three great king-doms, but it is difficult to know to what extent the Romans were aware of this. In the end, Philip V was a clear enemy and the settlement at the end of the First Macedonian War had been most unsatisfactory by Roman standards. As a result, the renewal of war was almost inevitable.[7]

The Second Macedonian War led on directly to conflict with the Aeto-lian League, Rome's former allies, and in turn to the Syrian War with the Seleucids. All of these enemies had been utterly defeated by 189 BC, the conflicts being swifter and far more quickly decisive than the First Mace-donian War. Defeat in a single pitched battle was enough to persuade the Hellenistic kingdoms to concede defeat. The Roman armies which achieved these victories were not especially large, nearly all being the stan-dard consular-sized force of two legions and two *alae* with the addition of local allies, just like the army which had won at Zama. At one point two such armies were operating, one in Greece and the other in Asia, but there proved no need to draw heavily upon Rome's reserves of manpower in these campaigns. Hellenistic armies were far more homogenous than the mixed mercenary and allied forces of Carthage. Their soldiers were mainly professionals, highly trained and disciplined, but relatively few in number and hard to replace.

The principal strength of every army was the phalanx, eight or more ranks deep of men armed with 21-foot (6.4 m) *sarissae* or pikes. These were held in both hands and weighted near the butt, so that two thirds of the weapon reached in front of the soldier. When the army was properly formed the spear points of the first five ranks of a phalanx projected in front of the formation, whilst the men in the rear held their pikes up at an angle, the dense mass of shafts providing some protection from missiles. The Hel-lenistic phalanx was very difficult for other infantry to defeat in a frontal attack and tended to win combats because of its immense staying power. The close-packed, very deep formation and the physical presence of the long *sarissae* made it very difficult for the men to flee. The phalanx was also a very intimidating sight as it bore down on the enemy, one Roman com-mander describing it as the most frightening thing he had ever seen in his life. Philip II and Alexander had used the pike phalanx to pin the enemy army and exert steady pressure, creating opportunities for devastating cav-alry charges to be delivered at a weak point in their line. By the later period the role of cavalry had diminished, largely because none of the Successor Kingdoms were ever able to field as high a proportion of good cavalry as their predecessors in the fourth century. Instead the phalanx delivered the main attack, a task for which it had never really been intended.[8]

The Romans first met a modern Hellenistic army in the war with Pyrrhus and Tarentum in 280–275. Defeated in two hard-fought and bloody battles, the legions had finally prevailed in a third and final encounter. The second-century encounters proved to be less close. The Roman soldiers who fought in the eastern Mediterranean in the early second century rapidly showed themselves to be markedly superior to their professional opponents. These legionaries were the men who had grown into manhood during the long struggle with Hannibal. The vast majority of them had many years of military experience, far more than was normal for most Roman armies. The army sent to Greece in 200 even included a sizeable contingent from the Cannae legions, the unfortunate men still waiting for their discharge. The officers of all ranks in these armies were on average both younger and more experienced than was usual. Many former praetors and consuls served as *legati* or even military tribunes. Titus Quinctius Flamininus, the man who brought the Second Macedonian War to a successful conclusion, won the consulship in 198 at the age of 30, and without having held the praetorship. His success was the last example of the constitutional flexibility which had allowed the rise of Scipio Africanus. Soon the career pattern was to become far more rigid. The combination of experienced soldiers and leaders led to exceptionally efficient armies, as well-trained and tactically flexible as those of the last years of the Punic War.[9]

This was amply demonstrated in the major battles of these conflicts. At Cynoscephalae in 197, Flamininus' and Philip V's marching columns unexpectedly bumped into each other as they approached a pass from opposite directions. In the usual way, the rival armies deployed into a battle line by wheeling their columns to the right. In each case the right wing of the army and thus the head of the column was able to form up more quickly and charge, routing the unprepared enemy left wing. Philip's army was composed of a single line, according to normal Hellenistic practice, and had no reserves. The Romans were in the usual *triplex acies* and an unnamed tribune with the right wing of the army peeled off twenty maniples and led them round to outflank the successful Macedonian right. Philip was unable to respond and his men were massacred. In 190 Lucius Cornelius Scipio, younger brother of Africanus, faced Antiochus III at Magnesia. The king, leading after the manner of Alexander the Great, personally led a cavalry attack which seems to have broken through one of the legions. Without reserves, and with their commander too closely involved to see what was going on in the rest of the battlefield, the Seleucids were unable to exploit this success. Antiochus' cavalry were first stopped by the pickets left outside the Roman camp, which they had rashly attacked, and

319

then beaten as reserves were brought up by one of the Roman subordinate commanders. In the meantime, the gap in the Roman line had been filled by reserves and everywhere else the enemy was in rout. At Pydna in 168 bickering between the outposts of the Roman and Macedonian armies escalated into a full-scale battle as more and more troops were fed into the fight. This confusion, and the long distance traversed in formation, speeded the usual process by which the phalanx broke up into its constituent units. After the Romans had put together enough of a fighting line to stop the Macedonian advance, individual centurions took the initiative and started to lead men into the gaps between the different sections of the phalanx. Pikemen were defenceless against flank attacks and, as the Macedonians began to panic, the whole formation collapsed into rout.[10]

Pydna decided the Third Macedonian War (172–167), and was really the last gasp of the Second Punic War generation. Even by this time there were beginning to be concerns that recruits for the army no longer possessed the martial virtues of their predecessors. In an effort to restore traditional practices, Lucius Aemilius Paullus was elected consul for the second time in 168. The son of the man who fell at Cannae, he was now over 60, far older than most field commanders since Fabius Maximus and Marcellus. Paullus took with him many experienced officers, carefully trained the army in Greece and brought the campaign to a successful conclusion. The causes of the war help to illustrate the Roman attitude to defeated enemies. After Cynoscephalae Philip had accepted peace terms similar to those given to Carthage. He was no longer allowed to wage war outside Macedon without Rome's permission and had to pay an indemnity of 1,000 talents over a ten-year period. The king acknowledged the independence of communities in Greece and Asia Minor, withdrawing from those subject to him in both areas. In addition the Macedonian fleet was reduced to a token force, removing Roman fears of an attack on Italy, and all Roman prisoners and deserters were returned without ransom. In fact, during the years Flamininus spent in Greece organizing the settlement, he discovered a number of slaves who had been captured by Hannibal, probably in the Cannae campaign, and sold to traders when the Senate refused to permit their ransom. Scrupulously, Flamininus purchased the freedom of these men and returned them to Italy.[11]

The Treaty ending the Second Macedonian War made it clear that the kingdom was now subordinate to Rome, even if it remained free to regulate its internal affairs. Rome now directed its foreign policy, arbitrated in disputes between Philip and the Greek cities and expected him to behave as a loyal ally. The army that had beaten the Macedonians was fed, at least in part, on grain from recently defeated Carthage. When Lucius Scipio took his army into Asia against the Seleucids, Philip V used a mixture of diplomacy and force to secure their route through passes controlled by predatory Thracian tribes. When the Roman army returned by the same route under the command of Manlius Vulso, he failed to request assistance from Macedon and as a result suffered badly in a series of ambushes. Antiochus III was obliged to accept similar peace terms to those agreed by Philip V after Magnesia. He agreed to withdraw from Asia Minor, was forbidden from making war in Asia or Greece, and was only to fight defensively if attacked by another state in this area. An indemnity of 15,000 talents was to be paid to Rome, more than had been demanded from Carthage, but not an impossible sum for the wealthy Seleucids. In addition, Antiochus gave up almost all of his warships and war elephants.[12]

Although Philip V studiously obeyed the terms of his treaty with Rome, both he and his son Perseus made every effort to strengthen their power within Macedonia. The army was increased and carefully trained, more control gained over the Thracian and Illyrian tribes on their borders, and connections renewed with cities in Greece. This was not the behaviour the Romans expected from a subordinate ally, although entirely legitimate by Greek standards. It is extremely doubtful that Macedonia posed a threat to Rome in the way that Livy claims, or that Perseus had any plans for an invasion of Italy, but clear that the Romans viewed these developments with extreme suspicion. Military strength and an increasingly independent foreign policy were not to be tolerated in former enemies. After the defeat of Perseus, the kingdom was abolished, although the Romans were still very reluctant to add another province to their existing four. Instead Macedonia was divided into four self-governing regions or *Merides*, each with its own laws and magistrates. Elements of this settlement were to last for several centuries.[13]

Roman Politics, 201–150 BC

Roman politics was changing in the early part of the second century. The Senate was filled mainly with the equestrians enrolled *en masse* during the war and the new generation of the established families whose senior members had been lost in the war, who had now reached maturity. The heavy casualties inflicted by Hannibal had drastically thinned the ranks of the older, experienced senators and particularly the ex-consuls. The Punic Wars had also produced an increase in the number of permanent provinces, reflected in a corresponding rise in the number of praetors elected each year. There had only been one of these magistrates in 265, but this was increased to two during the First War, to four in the early 220s and finally to six in the decade after 201. Before 265 the praetorship had carried purely judicial responsibility in Rome itself and many consuls never held the post. Flamininus was the last man to do so in 198. In the early second century many praetors went out to command overseas provinces, commanded armies and won victories, perhaps even securing a triumph. They returned to Rome with glory and wealth, both of which added to their chances of future electoral success. There were still only two consuls elected in each year, and the simple arithmetic meant that only one in three praetors could hope to secure the highest magistracy. This greatly increased the already fierce competition in the consular elections. The dominance of the old, established families was weakened. Their wealth, extensive network of clients and family reputation still brought them much electoral success, but it was now far less likely that it would permit them to hold the consulship more than once. More families could now challenge for the higher offices, although it must always be remembered that the majority of senators were still unlikely to reach the praetorship. Provincial commands were actively sought by most magistrates, so that far less use was made of promagistrates than during the war. Most provincial governors served for a single year and needed to take immediate advantage of the opportunities for profit. In this climate of tighter competition, there was increased regulation of the political career. Minimum ages were set and enforced for each office – 30 for the quaestors, 36 for aediles, 39 for praetors and 42 for consuls – and a ten-year interval imposed before the same magistracy could be held again by an individual. For half a century this system worked.

Roman war-making in the early decades of the second century was highly profitable. A great part of the wealth derived from booty and the sale of war captives into slavery remained in the hands of the commanders who led the Roman armies in these campaigns. Warfare in the Hellenistic east proved especially lucrative. During the Second Punic War Marcellus' ovation after the capture of Syracuse and Scipio's African triumph had included unprecedentedly lavish displays of plunder. In the next decades the triumphs of Flamininus over Philip V, Lucius Scipio over Antiochus, Cnaeus Manlius Vulso over the Galatian tribes of Asia Minor, and Aemilius Paullus over Perseus were each said to have been the most spectacular and richest processions ever seen in Rome. Those senators able to gain military commands were becoming more and more wealthy, especially the few who secured the leadership of major wars in the east, and the gap between rich and poor in the Senate was widening. This wealth allowed families to increase their prestige by lavish spending on public entertainments, like the gladiatorial fights which were becoming increasingly popular. It is also in this period that construction of monumental buildings in Rome began to gather pace, as successful commanders constructed basilicas, temples and aqueducts from their spoils. In this way senators commemorated their achievements and helped their own and their families' chances of future electoral success.[14]

Political careers were increasingly expensive as men were forced to spend extravagantly to keep pace with their rivals. Electoral success was costly and put many men in debt, making it all the more pressing for them to profit from the senior magistracies. Manlius Vulso was accused and nearly condemned for provoking a war with the Galatians which had not been approved by the Senate and was not in Rome's interests. Only the number of his friends and political allies at Rome narrowly prevented his condemnation. A rich man could use his wealth to win many such allies, making loans to aid those struggling to keep pace with the costs of political life, but this required ability which not everyone possessed. Most of the commanders who won spectacular victories came under fierce attack from rivals in the Senate. Manlius Vulso and Aemilius Paullus both had to struggle to win the right to celebrate their triumphs. Flamininus' brother Lucius was expelled from the Senate by the censors in 184, charged with improper behaviour, including executing a captive at a feast to please a male prostitute. The most successful attacks of all were directed against Publius and Lucius Scipio.[15]

Africanus was only in his mid thirties in 201, still too young to have held the consulship according to tradition and the soon-to-be-enacted legislation. It is difficult to see how his career after the war could ever have equalled his achievements in Spain and Africa. Elected consul for the second time in 194, he campaigned competently against the Ligurians and Cisalpine Gauls, but achieved nothing spectacular. A public announcement that he would serve as his brother's *legatus* secured Lucius the Asian command, particularly as it was known that Hannibal had fled to Antiochus' court. In fact the old adversaries did not encounter each other again in battle, nor was Africanus present at Magnesia, as a result of illness – perhaps a diplomatic one allowing his brother to gain full credit for the victory. By the standards of most senators, even the generation who reached maturity between 218 and 201, Scipio had spent little of his adult life in Rome. His first consulship had been dogged with controversy, with the rumours of his willingness to use questionable means to secure the African command and the Pleminius scandal. Although a brilliant soldier and an inspirational commander, Africanus was a poor politician who had difficulty achieving his objectives in the Senate quietly and without confrontation. In the next century Pompey the Great, another successful soldier who was inexperienced in the day-to-day politics of Rome, failed to make best use of his riches and prestige when he at last returned to Rome. Scipio Africanus was the most distinguished ex-consul of his day, named first on the senatorial role as *princeps senatus* for at least a decade, his own wealth and achievements adding to those of his family, but he was also politically vulnerable. In the Roman system there were always ambitious men waiting to attack any prominent senator who appeared vulnerable.[16]

Within a few years of their return from Asia, both brothers were prosecuted in the courts, and although surviving accounts of the trials are contradictory, the main charges involved the misappropriation of funds during the Syrian War. Both men refused to answer the accusations and relied upon their past achievements and reputation to prove that they were true servants of the State. Africanus publicly tore up his brother's account books for the war to demonstrate his contempt for the charges. When his own trial was reconvened on the anniversary of Zama, he declared that he intended to go up to the temples of the Capitoline triad and give thanks for his victory. The mass of the court, apart from the prosecutors and their slaves, and all of the many onlookers thronging the Forum promptly followed him, abandoning proceedings for the day. Despite this display of the charisma which had once inspired his soldiers, and his continued popularity with the People, the prosecution was renewed and few senators actively supported the brothers. Africanus, depressed by the ingratitude of the State he had served so well, went into voluntary exile in his villa at Liternum, where he died soon afterwards in 187, or 184 according to a less probable tradition. Lucius pleaded ill-health and withdrew from politics.[17]

Cato, the same man who as quaestor in 205 had attacked Scipio's behaviour in Sicily, was associated with the attacks on the brothers and many of the other prominent figures over the next decades. He was a *novus homo*, one of the many equestrians whose proven courage prompted their enrolment into the Senate during the war. He was not the only new man to reach the consulship in these years, but this and his censorship helped to forge the great influence which he came to wield. Throughout his career, Cato presented himself as the defender of traditional Roman morals and virtues against the corrupting influence of foreign, and especially Greek culture. As consul in 195, he spoke unsuccessfully against the repeal of a law passed in 215 during the height of the war which had restricted the amount Roman women were allowed to spend on clothes and jewellery. As censor in 184 he rigorously purged the ranks of the Senate and Equestrian

Order of men he considered to be unfit, notably Lucius Flamininus. During his long life he took part in forty-four prosecutions, far more than most senior senators who were much more likely to defend their friends in court than prosecute their enemies. Always he criticized the public philhellenism of men like Titus Flamininus, and the growing popularity amongst the Roman élite of Greek education, philosophy and religion.

Cato is one of the most unappealing figures from Roman history. In his manual on farm management, *de Agricultura*, he recommended selling slaves who had become too old to work, although he did not explain where he would find a purchaser. It is easy from the modern perspective to condemn him as a mere reactionary, his hostility to Greek learning just another reason to dislike such an apparently puritanical figure. This is to misunderstand the nature of Roman politics in this period. A 'new man' needed to compete with the established families, whose names were familiar to the electorate from the achievements of past generations. To be successful, he needed to make his own name as famous and instantly recognizable as theirs, and the best way was to emphasize a single attribute at every opportunity. Cato chose to portray himself as a simple Roman from a patriotic, but relatively poor family, who despite his political success continued to live a frugal lifestyle in contrast with the decadence of those around him. In his *Origines*, the first prose history of Rome written in Latin, he did not mention Roman generals by name, refusing to celebrate past victories solely through the role of aristocratic commanders rather than the whole State. To add to the snub, he did give the name of the bravest elephant in Hannibal's army, one Surus (the Syrian). Yet Cato was not so implacably opposed to foreign influences as his public statements may suggest. *De Agricultura* was influenced by the extensive Punic literature on this subject. Although affecting to despise Greek culture and literature, he seems to have had a fair knowledge of it, making a joking reference to Homer in a conversation with Polybius. Cato's contributions to Latin literature reflected a desire to rival its achievements, rather than an utter rejection of Greek learning.[18]

In the last century Rome's growing involvement abroad had brought her far more directly into contact with Hellenistic culture. Some senators embraced the ideas and lifestyle, each striving to show himself more philhellenic than his peers. Others, like Cato, competed in the opposite way by public rejection of Greek influences. Traditionally the Romans had been willing to introduce foreign religions into their city, absorbing them into the State religion. In 205 the discovery and interpretation of a Sybilline oracle led to the Senate deciding to introduce the cult of the Idaean

Mother. After negotiations with the kingdom of Pergamum, the black stone representing the goddess was brought by sea to Ostia. There it was greeted by a crowd of distinguished matrons, headed by Publius Cornelius Scipio Nasica, Africanus' first cousin, who had been chosen as the best man in Rome. The women carried the stone by hand, passing it one to the other until it was formally installed in the Temple of Victory on the Palatine. In 186 another eastern cult, the rites of the wine god Bacchus, was brutally suppressed throughout Italy by order of the Senate. In this case an imported religion was perceived as a threat to the State, because its practices were considered immoral and perhaps also because it was not regulated by senatorial priests.[19]

Rome was now more firmly part of the wider Mediterranean world, governing as provinces the major islands and Spain, whilst in the east it acted as arbiter in disputes between its allies. In time, the deep love of Hellenistic culture would take root in the Roman aristocracy, without changing its essential nature. Great quantities of booty and slaves flooded into Italy as a result of the successful wars. The wealthy invested in huge rural estates or 'latifundia' worked by servile labour. Later concern developed that this trend towards large estates had supplanted the small peasant farmers who had always provided the backbone of the legions, but in the early decades of the century Rome was in a confident mood. The great test of the Hannibalic invasion had been overcome and now they were reaping the rewards of their might. When abroad the behaviour of Roman magistrates and ambassadors became increasingly arrogant.[20]

Carthaginian Revival, 201–150 BC

Carthage went through a brief period of political turmoil in the years after 201. As usual, the lack of sources from an insider's perspective makes it very difficult to know precisely what was going on, but there does seem to have been widespread Popular dissatisfaction with the rule of the old oligarchy. Hannibal seems to have continued in command of whatever remained of the Punic army for several years, one late source claiming that he set his soldiers to farming. In 196 he was elected suffete and began a series of confrontations with another magistrate, called a 'quaestor' by Livy, and the Council of 104, accusing many of stealing from the State. He declared that the debt to Rome could easily be paid if corruption amongst the State's officials was eliminated. Hannibal strengthened the power of the Popular Assembly at the expense of the oligarchy, but was bitterly opposed by his political enemies. Some of these went to Rome and accused him of intriguing with Antiochus III against Rome. Despite opposition from Scipio Africanus, the Senate decided to intervene and in 195 sent a Commission of three to charge Hannibal publicly in Carthage. His year of office as suffete had now expired and, aware of the strength of his enemies, Hannibal fled from the city and went into exile in the east, going first to Tyre, the old Mother city, and eventually to the court of Antiochus. His house was demolished and his remaining possessions confiscated.[21]

Perhaps Hannibal's overhaul of the public finances had the desired result for Carthage rapidly began to recover from the strain of the war with Rome. After ten years, the State was able to offer Rome the remainder of the fifty-year war debt, although the Romans declined, preferring to maintain this annual reminder of Carthage's defeat. Although some land had been lost to Masinissa's Numidia, the Carthaginians still controlled the bulk of their highly fertile territory and it was not long before agricultural production was booming. As mentioned earlier, much of the grain which fed the Roman armies in the east came from Carthage. Trade seems to have revived and Punic merchants were once more a familiar figure in the markets of the Mediterranean, including Rome. It is uncertain whether or not Rome's Carthaginian community had left during the wars, but we do hear of the arrest of suspected spies by the Romans in both the First and Second War, although these appear to have been slaves. The archaeological record suggests a high level of prosperity reflected in the widespread construction of substantial new houses within Carthage and a rich material culture. The great circular harbour of the Punic navy visible today was either constructed or heavily restored during the years between the Second and Third Punic Wars and its scale is another reflection of the city's wealth. Economically the Carthaginians do not seem to have suffered in the long run as a result of their defeats.[22]

Hannibal did not live to hear of this new prosperity, not even from afar. He had commanded a fleet for Antiochus during the war with Rome and is depicted by Roman sources as constantly urging the king to invade Italy. This he maintained was the only way to beat the Romans. When Antiochus made peace with Rome, one of the terms was that he should hand over Hannibal and certain other named individuals. Before this could occur, Hannibal had once again escaped and this time ended up in the court of Prusias of Bithynia in 183. Under pressure from a Roman delegation, who saw the king's offer of sanctuary as suspicious, Prusias had the country house where the old general was staying surrounded by his soldiers. Unable to escape, Hannibal took poison and ended his own life.[23]

Both Hannibal and Scipio had ended their lives in disappointment. One tradition claimed that the two men had met once more at Ephesus, when

Scipio was part of a Roman embassy to Antiochus III. The Roman is supposed to have asked Hannibal whom he thought were the greatest generals in history. In reply he listed Alexander the Great, Pyrrhus and himself in that order. When Scipio asked what he would have said if he had won at Zama, the Carthaginian said that in that case he would have placed himself first, carefully flattering them both. The story may well be apocryphal, but the debate over the relative merits of these two commanders and comparison with the other 'Great Captains' of history continues to this day. Whilst this may provide an entertaining diversion, it is ultimately a sterile pursuit. Better simply to say that both men were exceptionally gifted commanders by the standards of their time and cultures, that they served their States to the best of their ability, and won remarkable victories against the odds, even if one was eventually defeated.[24]

PART THREE

THE THIRD PUNIC WAR
149–146 BC

CHAPTER 14

'Delenda Carthago'

T
HE FINAL CONFRONTATION between Rome and Carthage lasted only four years and ended in the latter's total destruction. The war was fought entirely in Africa, as the Roman invaders struggled to capture the enemy capital, and its outcome was never really in doubt, unless the Romans decided to abandon the expedition. Responsibility for the earlier conflicts is not always easy to assign, but there is no doubt that the Third Punic War was deliberately provoked by the Romans, who had made a conscious decision to destroy their old enemy. Roman negotiators shamelessly exploited the Carthaginians' willingness to grant concessions in their desire to avoid war with Rome, steadily increasing their demands to force a conflict on a weakened enemy. It was a far worse display than any of the recorded examples of the proverbial 'Punic treachery'. By the standards of modern strategy the war was unnecessary, since Carthage does not seem to have posed a real threat to Rome. To understand why the Romans embarked upon such a deliberately ruthless policy, we must look again at the Roman attitude to war and the peculiar conditions of the middle of the second century BC.[1]

The Carthaginians had proved consistently loyal allies of Rome since 201. They had supplied Roman armies with grain and in 191 sent half of their tiny navy to join the fleet operating against Antiochus III. Aided by Hannibal's reform of the State's finances, the annual indemnity had been paid regularly until its completion in 151. In the series of boundary disputes with Masinissa's Numidia, Carthage had submitted to Roman arbitration, even though this had always openly or tacitly favoured the king. Whether or not there had been any truth in the accusation, it was Carthaginian noblemen who reported Hannibal's supposed dealings with Antiochus and prompted his flight in 195. They also arrested and tried his agent, Ariston of Tyre, sent in 193 to encourage the city to support the

Seleucids against Rome, although Ariston was able to escape before the trial was concluded. A deputation was sent to Rome to report this incident and assure the Senate of Carthage's continuing loyalty. We are told that three main factions dominated Carthaginian politics in this half century, a group favouring Rome headed by Hanno the Great, another favouring Masinissa led by Hannibal the Starling, and the last relying on the poorer citizens for support led by Hamilcar the Samnite and Carthalo. Hamilcar's nickname was perhaps derived from a father or grandfather who had served with Hannibal in Italy, and we also hear of one Mago the Bruttian in this period, whose name suggests a similar connection, but it is not entirely clear that the democratic party should be as closely associated with the Barcids as some scholars have claimed. None of these groups appears to have been openly hostile to Rome. It is unclear whether or not the renewed prosperity of the city resulted in some rearmament, since although our literary sources claim that this was not so, the excavations in the naval harbour suggest otherwise. What is certain is that in the middle of the century the Carthaginians were in no position to launch a serious offensive against Rome, even if they had wanted to. Even so, it is clear that the Romans were increasingly afraid of their ally at this very period.[2]

The completion of the fifty-year war debt in 151 removed the annual reminder of Carthage's defeat and the city's current subordinate status. Treaties stipulating a fixed period of peace between two states were a common feature of Greek settlements ending a conflict, but very rare with the Romans, who expected a more permanent outcome to their wars. In 265 Carthage had turned herself from a long-standing and distant ally into an enemy, a permanent change in the Romans' perception of her. Rome was never content with alliances which implied any level of equality with a former foe. War was swiftly renewed with Macedonia in 200, and again when Perseus appeared to be growing both strong and independent. A loyal ally was expected to submit to Roman interference, especially in external affairs, whenever this was in Rome's interest. Between 241 and 218 the Romans had seized Sardinia and intervened in Spain, forcing concessions from Punic leaders without placing any restrictions on themselves, and this attitude continued after 201. After 151 Carthage ceased to pay an annual debt to Rome. The city was prosperous and its power in North Africa still considerable even if some territory had been lost to Numidia. The traditions of Punic warfare did not expect a defeated state, especially one which had not been conquered and absorbed, to remain forever subject to the victor. Only the Romans thought in this way. No longer were the Carthaginians unambiguously dependent allies of Rome. That a former enemy, and one who had pushed Rome to the brink of utter defeat, was once again strong and independent immediately turned her back into a threat. This was the root of the Romans' rising fear of Carthage.

The mood was personified by Cato. By the middle of the century the 'new man' who had fought at Tarentum, Metaurus and in Africa was amongst the most influential and respected members of the Senate, one of the few of his generation still actively participating in State affairs. Probably in 153, he took part in one of the embassies sent to arbitrate in a dispute between Carthage and Masinissa. By this time he was in his late seventies, but still a vigorous and forceful orator. The Roman delegation was deeply impressed by the growing wealth and population of their old enemy. On his return to Rome Cato started to end every speech he delivered in the Senate with the same phrase, 'Carthage must be destroyed'. On one occasion he is said to have dropped some figs from the fold of his toga. These, he informed an audience impressed by their size, had been grown in a country a mere three days away by sea. Cato exaggerated the speed with which a Punic fleet might descend on Rome, although one could reach southern Italy in just a few days, and some scholars have rather pointlessly speculated as to whether he had simply bought the figs in Rome or even grown them on his own estate. This was a symbolic gesture and a powerful one which our sources considered worth repeating and is still remembered to this day. Another prominent senator, Scipio Nasica, matched Cato by ending his own speeches with the view that Carthage should be preserved. It is claimed that he believed the presence of a strong rival would preserve the Romans' virtue intact, an argument which became a continual lament in the next century when Rome was plunged into a series of civil wars. At the time few Romans seem to have agreed with him. Plutarch claimed that it was primarily Cato's influence which convinced Rome to destroy Carthage, and in some modern accounts the persistent malevolence of the old man is equally prominent. As in many other aspects of his career, Cato seems to have expressed the mood of the majority of the population.[3]

There was a growing sense of insecurity in Rome during the 150s BC. The wars in the early decades of the century had been won with great ease by Roman armies composed of highly experienced officers and men. Gradually the generation of the Hannibalic war grew too old for military service and their knowledge and skill was lost. The impermanence of Rome's militia legions ensured that as each army was demobilized, the process of training new troops had to begin afresh. Experienced soldiers were replaced by younger men who were less aware that Rome's military success was based upon thorough training, careful logistical preparation and skilled leadership and believed instead that success was their due simply because they were Roman. The second quarter of the century saw fewer troops under arms and relatively little campaigning. In 155 Lusitanian tribesmen mounted a series of heavy raids on the Roman province of Further Spain, attacks which grew larger in scale with each success. In 154 a Roman praetor was killed and his army heavily defeated. In 153 the Celtiberians inflicted several defeats on a consular army led by Quintus Fulvius Nobilior. Reports of hard and dangerous fighting in Spain produced a minor crisis in Rome when very few men came forward to serve in an army being raised to send against the Celtiberians under the command of Lucius Licinius Lucullus in 151. Only the example set by Publius Cornelius Scipio Aemilianus, grandson by adoption of Africanus, who publicly volunteered to serve as a tribune, persuaded enough men to come forth. In fact the war had already been concluded before Lucullus arrived but, eager for glory and riches, the praetor set his army on a friendly tribe, who surrendered only to be treacherously massacred. A similar atrocity occurred in the next year, when the praetor of Further Spain, Publius Sulpicius Galba, already defeated once by the Lusitanians, offered to make peace with the tribesmen. Promising to settle them on good farmland, Galba divided the Lusitanians up into three groups, disarmed them and then ordered his legionaries to slaughter the defenceless warriors. One of the few to escape from this massacre was a man named Viriathus, who was to prove himself a charismatic leader and bitter opponent of Rome. For over a decade the Romans were faced with fierce fighting against both the Lusitanians and Celtiberians. Eventually one of his subordinates was bribed to murder Viriathus in 140, but it took seven more years and massive resources before the main Celtiberian stronghold at Numantia was captured. Galba was prosecuted on his return to Rome for his breach of *fides*, Rome's cherished faithfulness, Cato joining the attack upon him. Galba was unexpectedly acquitted after bringing his weeping children into court and having them beg for their father. He was later to become one of the most famous orators in Rome.[4]

The defeats suffered in Spain highlighted the inexperience of most Roman armies. The annual replacement of provincial governors and the rarity of pro-magistracies encouraged commanders to seek glory before they were replaced, and denied them the time necessary to turn their soldiers into an effective army. This had mattered far less in the early part of the century when the quality of Rome's manpower had been higher. Even then the pressure to achieve success in a single year of office had encouraged Flamininus to begin peace negotiations with Philip V in 198, only to break off the talks and press for a military victory once his command was extended for another year. Successive defeats lowered the morale and made further reverses even more likely. The failure to protect allies amongst the Spanish communities encouraged these to defect and created more enemies to fight. At one point large parts of Further Spain had submitted to Viriathus. Losses in Spain were far enough away not to pose a direct threat to Italy, but they were a major blow to Roman prestige. The difficulties in raising officers and men for Spain in 151 were especially shocking, since even the crisis of the Hannibalic invasion had not caused such reluctance to serve amongst Roman citizens.[5]

Appian says that the Roman Senate secretly decided to seek a pretext for war with Carthage soon after Cato's return from Africa. This may or may not be correct, but their actions make it clear that this was certainly their attitude by 150–149 and it is probable that the payment of the last instalment of Carthage's indemnity in 151 contributed to the decision. All the Romans now needed was an excuse for war. Their Numidian allies were soon to provide it.

Masinissa's Kingdom, 201–150 BC

Cato provided one link between the Second and Third Punic Wars in the same way that Hiero's, Fabius Maximus' and Marcellus' careers had spanned the First and Second Wars. Masinissa was another connection with the past. In 150 he was 88 years old, but still fit enough to ride without a saddle after the manner of his people and to lead his men into battle. When he died two years later, the king left behind a 4-year-old son, one of ten legitimate and illegitimate boys he had sired during his long life. Brought up for much of his early life in Carthage, the Numidian had an extensive knowledge of Punic culture and did much to introduce many aspects of this, from literacy to religion, into the kingdom which he had struggled to create from the independent tribes of his people. Towns were encouraged, although it is unclear to what extent these were populated by an imported population rather than Numidians persuaded to abandon their nomadic way of life. Masinissa gave each of his sons a landed estate to be farmed with the most modern Punic methods, realizing that the promotion of agriculture would both strengthen the kingdom and give power to those who controlled the new sources of production. Despite his admiration for Punic culture and his distinguished service with their armies in Spain, Masinissa displayed a bitter hostility to his former ally throughout his reign.[6]

The Treaty of 201 had included the somewhat vague provision that

Carthage should restore to Masinissa all territory which had belonged to him or his ancestors. Appian claims that the limit of Punic land was marked by the 'Phoenician trenches', although the precise location of these has proved impossible to establish with much precision. The vagueness of the Treaty encouraged Masinissa to seize more and more slices of Carthaginian territory, claiming that it had once belonged to his people. Eventually his claims extended to allowing the Punic settlers only the area of the Byrsa, the original hill settlement of Carthage which according to myth Elishat had received from the local ruler. Roman delegations sent to resolve the disputes between their two allies repeatedly found in favour of the king, who was able to gain more areas of fertile land and eventually the important coastal ports in the area known as Emporia.[7]

Eventually, the politicians eager to appease and accommodate Masinissa were expelled from the city around 152–151 and the Popular party gained a temporary dominance. The exiled leaders fled to the king, who sent his sons Gulussa and Micipsa to demand their restitution. Gulussa had in the past acted as the king's representative in Rome, but on this occasion the brothers were not even admitted into Carthage. As they returned, Gulussa's party was mobbed by Hamilcar the Samnite and a group of supporters, who killed several of his attendants. In 150 the Numidians once again began to attack Punic territory, ravaging the land and besieging a city called Oroscopa, the location of which is unknown. For the first time since 201, Carthage decided to fight a war without seeking Roman arbitration or approval, and formed an army of 25,000 foot and 400 horse under the command of Hasdrubal. The cavalry are described as being raised in the City so were presumably citizens. They were few in number, but received a strong reinforcement when a dispute between Masinissa's sons and two Numidian chieftains, Asasis and Suba, led to their desertion with 6,000 light horse. Hasdrubal gained the advantage in some minor skirmishing and followed the Numidian army as it deliberately withdrew, luring the enemy into more rugged terrain, where food and water were in short supply.

Finally Masinissa decided to offer battle and a day-long fight resulted in which neither side gained a decisive advantage. The battle was watched from a distance by Scipio Aemilianus, who was in Africa using his family's link with Masinissa to persuade the old king to furnish elephants for Lucullus' army in Spain. Hasdrubal withdrew to his hilltop camp and negotiations began with Scipio acting an intermediary. The talks broke down when the Carthaginians refused to return Asasis and Suba for punishment. Masinissa's army built a wall and ditch surrounding the enemy-occupied high ground, a skill which they had probably learned through service with the Roman army. Cut off from supplies and unwilling to admit defeat and attempt a breakout, Hasdrubal's army soon consumed the supplies of food carried in its train. Immobile, the Carthaginians slaughtered and ate their pack and draught animals, then the more valuable cavalry mounts. Firewood to cook the meat which was now forming so much of their diet was soon exhausted, so the soldiers chopped up their shields and burned those. Hasdrubal seems to have expected the Numidians to run out of supplies and disperse, but the army Masinissa had created during his reign was clearly a far more organized and efficient force than anything fielded by the tribes in the past. Eventually Hasdrubal surrendered, promising that Carthage would pay a fifty-year war debt and receive back the exiled aristocrats who had fled to Masinissa. As the Carthaginian army marched out in surrender, they were attacked by a group of Numidian horsemen led by Gulussa and many cut down. Whether the attack was premeditated or not, and if so whether Masinissa was involved, is impossible to say, for it has proved similarly difficult to allocate responsibility in similar, more recent massacres. Hasdrubal and many of his officers escaped.[8]

The Roman Response
The ability of Carthage to create an army and fight a war, albeit unsuccessfully, confirmed Roman fears and suspicions. The Treaty of 201 had expressly forbidden the declaration of war in Africa without Roman approval. This was probably enough to justify strong protests, but the Roman Senate, now more experienced in diplomacy after fifty years of close involvement with the Hellenistic world, looked for a stronger pretext for open war. In the meantime, preparations for a major expedition to invade Africa were begun, without declaration of its purpose. Characteristically, the Carthaginians attempted to blame their commander in the field and deny their own responsibility for the recent war. Hasdrubal, Carthalo (the leader of the Popular Party) and several other officers were condemned to death. Hasdrubal's troops must still have been loyal to their commander, for he appears soon afterwards at the head of 30,000 men. Ambassadors were dispatched to Rome to complain of Masinissa's provocation, and to condemn the Punic officers who had rashly gone to war. The Roman response was to point out that if the Carthaginian authorities had truly opposed war then they would have condemned their commanders before they had fought. The delegation was told cryptically that they must 'satisfy the Roman People'. A second embassy failed to discover precisely what the Romans meant by this.[9]

At this point Utica defected to the Romans, its harbours providing them with an ideal base for an attack on Carthage. In 149 the Senate and *Comitia Centuriata* both approved the declaration of war. Both consuls were to go to Africa, Manius Manilius in command of the army and Lucius Marcius Censorinus in command of the fleet. As in 218 and 205–204, the Romans concentrated at Lilybaeum in Sicily before embarking for Africa. In the meantime, Carthage sent another embassy to Rome, where the Senate demanded that 300 hostages selected from the children of the main noble families should be handed over at Lilybaeum within thirty days. This was done, despite the fact that the Senate had only promised the Carthagians their territory and freedom to be governed by their own laws. The wording carefully avoided mention of the city of Carthage itself, a move similar to Scipio's technical justification of breaking the truce in 203. The hostages were conveyed to Rome in a great 'sixteen', a ship probably confiscated from the Macedonian fleet at the end of the Third Macedonian War.[10]

In spite of the Carthaginians' acceptance of their demands, the consuls still sailed across to land at Utica. Still uncertain of the Romans' intentions, another delegation was formed at Carthage and sent to the consuls, who received them in great state, seated on a tribunal flanked by their senior officers and with the army paraded behind them. It was a daunting display of Rome's might, intended to persuade the ambassadors that any resistance to the consuls' demands was hopeless. Censorinus, elected first by the *Comitia*, probably older and a better orator, spoke in answer to their appeal, demanding that the city hand over all of its stocks of arms and armour. Once again, despite their nervousness at the Roman proposal, the Carthaginians submitted. They are said to have delivered 200,000 panoplies of armour, 2,000 torsion engines, and huge numbers of javelins, arrows and catapult ammunition. As usual the reliability of these numbers is questionable and it is obvious that Roman sources would be inclined to exaggerate the military preparedness of the city they were about to destroy, but it is clear that very large stocks of weaponry were surrendered to the Roman representatives.

The arrival in the Roman camp of the convoy containing this equipment was the preliminary to another, even harsher command. Censorinus informed the ambassadors that the Carthaginians must abandon their city, the entire population moving to a new settlement which they could place anywhere they chose, providing that it was at least 10 miles from the sea. Carthage itself would then be razed to the ground, although the shrines and cemeteries associated with it would not be touched and the

Carthaginians would be allowed to visit them in future. It was an appalling blow, for the city was the physical, spiritual and emotional centre of the State. Severing the link of any new community with the sea, which had for so long been the source of Punic wealth, made it doubly so. Censorinus is supposed to have employed Platonic arguments to support the view that the sea had an unhealthy influence of the political and social life of a city. At the end of this, the ambassadors were roughly ejected by the consuls' lictors, but promised to present these terms to their own government. They even suggested that the Roman fleet demonstrate in the bay outside the city to remind the citizens of the alternative to acceptance of the Roman demands.[11]

Rumours had spread rapidly in Carthage and a nervous crowd surrounded the ambassadors when they entered the city and waited outside as they reported to the Council of 104. The Roman demand was immediately rejected. Men who had argued for the conciliation of Rome were lynched, as were any Italian traders unfortunate enough to be in the city. The 104 voted for war with Rome and began preparations to find the means with which to fight. Slaves were freed and conscripted into the army, whilst Hasdrubal was pardoned and messages sent pleading with him to aid his ungrateful fellow citizens. Another Hasdrubal, son of one of Masinissa's daughters, indicating again the close links between Carthaginian and Numidian nobility, was given command inside Carthage itself. For once, the whole Punic citizen body threw itself wholeheartedly into the war effort. Weapons were hastily produced, women sacrificing their long hair to twine into the ropes needed for torsion catapults.[12]

The Third Punic War had begun. In many ways the Romans were surprised that the Carthaginians finally decided to fight, after meekly submitting to each outrageous demand made of them. The Romans' behaviour had been cynical in the extreme, concealing their intention to destroy the city until after they had extracted as many concessions as possible. Carthage now appeared to be at their mercy, unprepared and unarmed. Yet the war was to last until 146 and prove far harder than the consuls expected.

CHAPTER 15

The Third Punic War

C ARTHAGE WAS A LARGE and well-fortified city, surrounded by over 20 miles of circuit walls. Difficult to approach and with its own harbours, the city was very hard to surround and blockade. An especially strong triple line of defence, based principally on a wall 30 feet (*c.* 9 m) wide and *c.* 50–66 feet (15–20 m) high, but fronted by a 60 feet (20 m) wide ditch and a timber palisade, ran across the 2–3 mile wide isthmus approaching the city from the landward side. This was constructed as a casemate wall with two storeys of rooms containing on the ground floor accommodation for 300 elephants and above stabling for 4,000 horses and barracks for 20,000 foot and 4,000 cavalry. In 149 the defenders lacked the animals and a well-organized army, but numerous volunteers from the population ensured that the defences were adequately manned.

The Romans had assembled a large expeditionary force to attack this formidable position. Appian claims that there were 80,000 infantry and 4,000 cavalry supported by fifty quinqueremes and 100 lighter galleys. If these figures are correct, then this was the largest Roman army to take the field since Cannae, but most scholars have assumed that Appian was exaggerating, or perhaps counting servants and camp followers as well as soldiers. A common suggestion is that there were in fact four legions, so that the army may have mustered between 40,000 and 50,000 men including allies. This would still make it a significantly larger force than even the highest estimates for Africanus' army in 204. In marked contrast to the reluctance of citizens to serve in Spain in 151, there had been a burst of enthusiasm for this war, with no shortage of recruits and many volunteers coming forward to swell the ranks of the legions. The prospect of a swift, relatively easy campaign and plentiful booty doubtless encouraged many men to come forward, but there was probably also a far greater romantic appeal to fighting Rome's greatest adversary than risking life and limb fighting against some uncouthly named Celtiberian tribe. The army in 149 was large, enthusiastic and confident, but it was not well-trained. Scipio had spent over a year in Sicily preparing his forces for the forthcoming campaign, even though most of his troops were old soldiers with many years' experience. The consuls in 149 spent only a few months in creating from scratch an army whose officers and men were on average far less experienced. It was typical of the poor preparation of Roman campaigns in this period. As the army waited at Utica for the fighting to begin it began to run short of supplies, for the consuls had expected to obtain most of their requirements locally, but found their foraging restricted by the presence of Hasdrubal's 30,000 strong army. Unlike Scipio, they do not appear to have stockpiled large reserves of grain in Sicily and arranged a system of convoys to convey this to Africa. The legions which pitched their camp on the same site as *castra Cornelia* in 149 made a poor comparison with its first occupants.[2]

The consuls moved quickly on Carthage as soon as it was clear that the Roman ultimatum had been rejected. Even at this late stage, they seem to have expected the city to capitulate and that little more than a display of strength was needed. Manilius led the army against the wall protecting the isthmus. Censorinus brought the fleet to attack a weaker stretch of wall near a narrow spit of land edging the Lake of Tunis to the south of the city. Some men landed and set ladders by hand against the wall, whilst other ladders were mounted directly on the prows of the Roman warships. Both attacks were greeted by a hail of missiles from the defenders. Surprised by this stiff resistance, the assaulting parties gave way. A second attempt was equally unsuccessful and as the confidence of the defenders grew, the Romans constructed camps outside the walls. Hasdrubal brought his army to the other side of the lake and harassed the Roman lines. A party sent by Censorinus to gather wood was ambushed by Himilco Phameas and some Punic cavalry: 500 men were killed. A third attempt to assault the city from both sides also failed. Manilius had managed to cross the outer ditch and breach the stockade, but failed to make any impression on the main wall across the isthmus.[3]

Since the attempts at escalade had achieved no success, Censorinus constructed two battering rams, filling in a portion of the lake to create a broad and solid enough road to bring these up to the wall. Each was supposedly crewed by 6,000 men, probably both to move them and to swing the rams. One crew was provided by legionaries commanded by tribunes and the other by sailors under their own officers, and rivalry between the two services spurred on both parties to be first to create a breach. Two

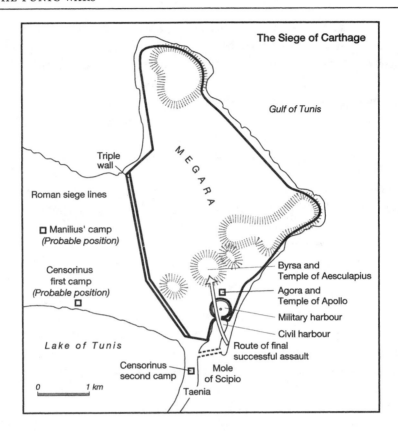

The Siege of Carthage

Gulf of Tunis

M E G A R A

Triple wall

Roman siege lines

□ Manilius' camp
(Probable position)

Censorinus
first camp
(Probable position)
□

Lake of Tunis

Byrsa and
Temple of Aesculapius

Agora and
Temple of Apollo

Military harbour

Civil harbour

Route of final
successful assault

Censorinus
second camp

Mole
of Scipio

Taenia

0   1 km

breaches were made, but the Carthaginians managed to drive the Romans back late in the day and did their best to repair the damage during the night. Under cover of darkness, a raiding party went out and managed to set fire to both of the Roman engines. Although they were not destroyed the damage was sufficient to make both rams inoperable. Daylight revealed that in spite of their best efforts, the defenders had failed to fill the gaps in their wall and at least one of the breaches was still practical. Aware of the danger, Carthaginian soldiers had formed up behind the gap in the wall, whilst a crowd armed only with missiles thronged the roofs of the nearby houses. The Romans rapidly formed an assault party and launched a furious attack through the breach. The onslaught was badly organized and after initial success bogged down. One of the military tribunes, the same Scipio Aemilianus who had served with Lucullus and begged elephants from Masinissa, had kept his men under tight control. Instead of following the main body into the city, he had stationed them to defend the wall around the breach. When Carthaginian pressure grew too much and the assaulting parties were chased back out of the city, Scipio's men

342

prevented them from being cut off and covered their retreat.[4]

Scipio was the only senior officer to win distinction in the early phases of the Third Punic War. The youngest of four sons of Aemilius Paullus, he had first seen service as a teenager at Pydna. Missing at the end of the battle, he was just about to be added to the list of casualties when he returned with a few friends, all of them heavily bloodstained from an enthusiastic pursuit of the enemy. Whilst the older brothers remained to continue the family name, the two younger boys were adopted into famous families who lacked a male heir. The third brother became Quintus Fabius Maximus Aemilianus, whilst the youngest was adopted by Publius Scipio the son of Africanus, whose ill-health had denied him a significant political career. Both of the elder brothers died before their father. The Roman aristocracy took adoption very seriously and men like Scipio Aemilianus were considered to combine the reputation of both families and were expected to live up to the standards of behaviour of both real and adopted parents. In 151 Scipio had helped to encourage volunteering for the Celtiberian war by coming forward as a military tribune. In Spain he won renown by killing an enemy champion in single combat, a deed reminiscent of the young Marcellus in the First Punic War. It was perhaps his service in Spain which taught Scipio the importance of maintaining a reserve and cautious pursuit, for the tribes of the Peninsula were quick to punish careless attackers. It was a lesson which few of the other Roman officers seem to have learned.[5]

Censorinus' camp by the lakeside was placed in an unhealthy spot. By late July disease started to spread in the camp, forcing the consul to withdraw to a position near the sea. Whenever the wind was right, the defenders sent fireships down towards the Roman fleet, causing serious losses. They also prepared a sally against Manilius' camp on the isthmus, some men being detailed to carry fascines and beams to fill or bridge the ditch surrounding it. Delivered at night, the sudden attack caused panic amongst the surprised Romans. Once again Scipio Aemilianus restored the situation, leading a body of horse out of the rear gate of the camp and bringing them round to attack the Carthaginians in the flank, driving them back in confusion. The consul subsequently strengthened the defences of his camp to prevent a repeat of this near disaster. Another fort was built near the shore to cover the landing of Roman supply ships.[6]

The Romans had failed to make any impression on the city's defences. With winter approaching and his colleague returned to Rome to hold the next year's elections, Manilius drew off a column of 10,000 infantry and 2,000 cavalry and led them in an expedition to ravage the rural areas loyal

343

to Carthage. In part this was another means of putting the enemy under pressure, but the main purpose was to gather food for men and horses and wood for cooking and building, laying in supplies for the winter which would now be spent in the siege lines around Carthage. Once again the Romans displayed their inexperience as the tribunes leading foraging parties carelessly allowed their men to disperse. Himilco Phameas, probably leading some of the Numidian and Moorish cavalry who had deserted from Masinissa in 150, ambushed and raided the Roman foragers, inflicting heavy losses. Scipio Aemilianus avoided such attacks by ensuring that his troops did not disperse too widely and that there were always groups of horse and foot kept formed and ready to cover the unarmed parties of foragers. Malicious rumours circulated in the Roman camp, claiming that Himilco was deliberately avoiding Scipio because of a bond of hospitality between one of his ancestors and Africanus. This may well suggest that Phameas was of mixed Punic and Numidian or Libyan blood. When Manilius brought his column back to the main camp, the Numidians mounted another night-time raid from within the city. This time the target was the smaller fort guarding the landing site for the transport ships. On this occasion Scipio led out the ten *turmae*, about 300 men and perhaps the cavalry element of his own legion, but this time did not directly attack the sallying force. Instead the Roman horsemen carried lighted torches and moved and manoeuvred near the Carthaginians, trying to create the impression of far larger forces massing to attack. The ploy worked and the nervous raiders withdrew.[7]

Although Himilco Phameas and his horsemen ranged widely, Hasdrubal had drawn his main army back into the area around Nepheris, in the area of the modern Djebel Zaghouan, just under 20 miles south-east of Tunis. The Carthaginians were camped beyond a small river at the end of a valley, a strong position which was difficult for the Romans to approach in anything other than a narrow column. Manilius decided to mount a direct attack on the enemy, an aggressive move typical of Roman generalship. Equally characteristically for this period the attack was badly planned, the Romans advancing directly from the march, without waiting to fortify their own camp and rest. Plunging through the river, Manilius' men made some headway and after a tough fight managed to push the Carthaginians back up onto the higher ground. It was a strong position and the weary Romans stood little chance of success in an uphill assault. Hasdrubal bided his time, knowing that the Romans could not stay where they were and would have to pull back. Disengaging from close contact with the enemy has always been a dangerous and demanding task. It was especially so for Manilius, because the fordable section of the river was relatively narrow. As the Romans fell into some confusion, Hasdrubal attacked, slaughtering the legionaries who quickly fell into panic. Scipio, who had spoken against the attack and was once again in command of 300 cavalry, rallied some more Roman horsemen and led them in a series of controlled charges. His men went forward far enough to push the enemy back, but did not pursue too far, rallying instead to prevent their formation breaking up and the horses from growing tired. The check on the Carthaginian advance gave enough time for the bulk of the fugitives to escape across the stream. There was only just time for the tribune to pull his own men back before they were overwhelmed, and as it was they galloped back across the ford under a hail of missiles. Four Roman units, maniples or possibly cohorts, were cut off during the retreat and left surrounded on a hillock. Demonstrating that he could be very bold when the occasion demanded, Scipio led some of his cavalry in a successful rescue operation. He also managed to negotiate with Hasdrubal and arrange the burial of several fellow tribunes killed in the rout.

The expedition had been a disaster. It was made even more humiliating when the retiring Roman column was attacked both by Himilco Phameas and by the defenders of Carthage on its return to camp. Scipio Aemilianus' achievements had been the only bright spot in the otherwise dismal performance of the Roman forces, a fact noted by the Senatorial commission sent out to report on operations. When reports of his deeds reached Rome, Cato once again quoted Homer when he praised Scipio as uniquely capable amongst the army in Africa. The ageing senator was to die during the next months, not living to witness the final destruction of Carthage. Another link with the past, the 90-year-old Masinissa also passed away in the first months of 148. Scipio, as the descendant of his patron Africanus, was chosen by the old king to settle his affairs and divided the rule of the kingdom between Masinissa's three legitimate sons. The Numidians had not as yet contributed any significant aid to the Roman army, but Scipio was able to persuade Gulussa, who had been placed in charge of Masinissa's troops, to join Manilius with a force of light cavalry. Very early in the spring the Roman general decided to attempt another attack on Nepheris before a new consul arrived to replace him. This time the expedition was better prepared, the legions carrying food for fifteen days. A camp was laid out before crossing the river and a ditch and wall constructed closing off the valley. Even so the operation resulted in a second failure, although it did provide an opportunity for the defection of Himilco Phameas and 2,200 of his cavalrymen, an act of treachery arranged by Scipio. This was another instance of the defection of a relatively senior Punic officer for which there is no parallel amongst the Romans. Manilius remained facing the enemy for seventeen days, so that by the time he was forced to retire his soldiers were dangerously short of food. Their plight was only eased when Scipio returned after leading Phameas' and Gulussa's men off on a foraging expedition. Universally praised by the army, the tribune then returned to Rome to present Phameas, who was rewarded by the Senate with a fine horse, splendid equipment, a tent and a considerable sum of silver. The deserter pledged himself to serve with the Romans until the end of the conflict.[8]

Only one of the consuls for 148 went out to Africa. This was Lucius Calpurnius Piso Caesoninus, who brought with him Lucius Mancinus to command the fleet, either as his *legatus* or as a propraetor in his own right. Maintaining a loose blockade around Carthage itself, the Romans decided to subdue the smaller cities of the region. Results were unimpressive, with a combined sea and land attack on Aspis unsuccessful and a prolonged siege of Hippagreta achieving nothing. The Carthaginian mood was ebullient, sending a delegation to Macedonia to form an alliance with Andriscus, a pretender to the throne of Perseus. This man had formed an army of Thracian tribesmen and invaded the four Macedonian *Merides*, defeating first the local militia and then a Roman army, killing the praetor in command. This was the worst defeat the Romans had ever suffered at the hands of the Macedonians and another sign of the decline in the efficiency of the legions. The Carthaginians received further consolation for the defection of Phameas when one of Gulussa's chieftains deserted to them with 800 men. Hasdrubal, the commander of the field army, who had once been condemned to death, was so restored to favour that he was able to assume command within the city, supplanting the other Hasdrubal who was accused of plotting treachery with his relative Gulussa and lynched.[9]

Scipio Returns, 147–146 BC

In 148 Scipio Aemilianus as a patrician planned to stand for the office of *curule aedile* for the following year. Stirred by tales of his recent exploits and the association with his illustrious grandfather, the centuries in the *Comitia Centuriata* selected his name first in the consular elections. Still only 36 or 37, he was several years below the legal age for the highest magistracy, but when the presiding consul pointed this out the voting centuries remained adamant that Scipio was their choice. When one of the tribunes of the plebs supported their demands and threatened to declare the whole election invalid, the Senate decided to fudge the issue. The law stipulating minimum ages for the important magistracies, the *lex Villia annalis*, was annulled for a single year and then immediately re-enacted. Scipio's consular colleague, Caius Livius Drusus, himself a member of a very wealthy and influential, although plebeian, family, wanted the African command and suggested that the two men draw lots in the usual way. Again a tribune intervened, declaring that the matter should be decided by Popular vote in the *Concilium Plebis*, who overwhelmingly chose Scipio. By the same law he was allowed to raise sufficient new recruits to replenish the ranks of the army already in Africa, and, like Africanus before him, take as many volunteers as came forward.[10]

This is the essence of Appian's account of Scipio's premature rise to the consulship and the African command. As with other cases where the normal electoral procedure was not followed and extraordinary appointments were made, it is impossible now to know what really happened and how much had been decided behind the scenes before the public meetings. We cannot know to what extent Scipio himself had actively sought the more senior post, although it seems distinctly probable that he did so. Nor is it clear to what extent other senators opposed the suspension of the law in his favour. It is probably a mistake to see this as the triumph of a politician relying entirely on the People for support, for it is likely that many senators were well disposed to Scipio, and others may simply have thought him the best man for the job. His military record stood out at a time when military defeats and disasters were depressingly common. The emotional appeal of sending not just a Scipio but the grandson of Africanus to defeat the new threat from a prosperous and so far successful Carthage was massive amongst all classes of Romans, who possessed such a strong sense of family characteristics. It must also be remembered that the appointment was far less radical than the decision to invest Africanus with proconsular *imperium* and send him to Spain in 210. Scipio Aemilianus was no more than five years below the minimum age for the consulship and had so far had a conventional and highly distinguished career. The strength of his support, at least as far the African command was concerned, is seen in the ease with which his *imperium* was extended to allow him to complete the war in 146.[11]

In early 147 the blockade of Carthage was being maintained by Mancinus and the fleet. Observing an apparently weak spot in the walls where the natural defences were so strong that fortification seemed unnecessary, the Romans beached their ships and attempted an escalade, provoking the defenders to sally out from a nearby gate. In the ensuing combat the Romans managed to put the Carthaginians to flight and pursued them

347

back through the open gateway. Elated by this unanticipated success, Mancinus led in as many men as he could find, some of them poorly armed ships' crews. In total there were only 500 fully equipped soldiers and around 3,000 others. A small corner of Carthage was now in Roman hands, but their hold on it was precarious for they had little food and no immediate supports to draw upon, since the main army was operating some distance away. Mancinus sent out messengers to Piso with the army and also to nearby Utica, asking for reinforcement and supplies of food. By chance Scipio had sailed into Utica that evening and received the message. Riders were at once dispatched to find Piso and preparations made to sail to Carthage in the early hours of the morning. Sacrificing the element of surprise in favour of making the enemy nervous, Scipio released some Punic prisoners and allowed them to hasten back to their city with news of his arrival. The next day the Carthaginians attacked Mancinus in great numbers, steadily pushing the Romans back. They were only checked when Scipio sailed into view, legionaries thronging the decks of his warships to suggest the arrival of a huge army merely instead of the draft of replacements that had come from Sicily. The sight stalled the Punic onslaught for long enough to evacuate Mancinus' men, who were carried away by the Roman ships.[12]

Scipio concentrated the army outside Carthage, observed by Hasdrubal with 6,000 foot and 1,000 horse as well as some of the defenders of the city camped just over half a mile away (5 stades). The discipline of the Roman army in Africa had never been especially high, but months of reverses had made things worse. Avoiding direct confrontation, the soldiers had most often served on plundering expeditions. In the same way that the legionaries involved in the constant raiding in southern Italy during the Second Punic War had degenerated into little more than bandits, service of this kind had further lowered the efficiency of the legions. Scipio made a speech declaring his intention to restore tight discipline and then expelled from the camp many of the volunteers and camp followers who had come not to fight but to loot. There was not time to train the soldiers properly. Instead he decided to mount an attack on the Megara, one of the largest of the suburbs surrounding the old citadel (or Byrsa). Two Roman assaulting parties moved forward during the night against two widely separated sections of wall. Observed by the enemy during the last stage of the approach, the attackers were repulsed by a hail of missiles, despite some initial confusion amongst the defenders. Appian tells us that the Romans then found an deserted tower adjacent to the wall, climbed it and, after throwing planks across to bridge the gap, fought their way onto the rampart. In this way the soldiers gained control of a gate and admitted Scipio with 4,000 men. The defenders panicked and fled back to the Byrsa as did the troops in the camp outside the walls, but the Romans moved forward slowly and with great care, uncertain in the dark of the routes through the Megara, much of which was given over to gardens and orchards rather than housing. Eventually Scipio decided that he was in no position to hold the ground permanently and so withdrew back to his own camp. The break-through had so frightened the defenders that Hasdrubal ordered Roman prisoners to be led onto the walls and then, in full view of the besiegers, tortured to death, believing that the gesture would demonstrate to the Carthaginians that there was now no hope of surrender. When members of the Council of 104, whose relations with the general had long been strained, protested, Hasdrubal had them arrested and executed.[13]

The Romans now decided on establishing a much tighter blockade around the city. Scipio ordered the abandoned enemy camp to be burned then moved his own position further forward onto the isthmus. There the Romans spent twenty days constructing a series of fortifications despite the best efforts of the enemy to slow the progress. An enormous rectangle of ditches was dug, backed by a rampart 12 feet high (c. 4 m) with towers at intervals, including one in the middle of the wall facing the city which was built especially high to provide an observation post. The whole complex dominated the isthmus and made access to the city from the landward side impossible. The overland route into the city had been cut off, but supplies of food were still able to get through by sea. It was very difficult for ancient oared warships to impose a tight blockade, especially in the conditions off the coast of Carthage, and a few ships kept getting through. Hasdrubal is supposed to have kept nearly all of these supplies for the 30,000 active defenders of the city, and he and his officers lived in riotous luxury whilst the civilian population began to starve. In an effort to deny the enemy this last source of supply, Scipio ordered the construction of a mole running across the channel approaching the narrow entrance to Carthage's great harbours.[14]

Ancient sieges tended to consist of move and counter-move as the attacker and defender employed their engineering skill and massive labour to gain an advantage or negate a project begun by the other side. The whole population of Carthage now threw itself into a concerted effort to keep the sea route open. Once they realized that the Roman plan was likely to succeed and that the mole was not being swept away by the sea, the Carthaginians decided to cut a new channel connecting the military harbour with the sea. The work was done at night and great secrecy maintained, with great numbers of women and children coming forward to add to the labour force. At the same time a fleet of fifty triremes supported by lighter ships was built from scratch. The Romans knew nothing of either project until at dawn one morning the new channel was cut through to the sea and the last fleet of the Carthaginian Empire sailed out.

Appian expresses surprise that the Punic ships did not immediately fall upon the Roman fleet, which, he points out, had been neglected in recent months as most of the crews were drawn off to add to the labourers working on the siegeworks. However, it is probable that the next three days were spent training the Punic crews up to at least a basic level of efficiency for it had been many years since Carthage had possessed great numbers of skilled oarsmen. When the two fleets did finally give battle, the result was a very close engagement fought close to the shore. The smaller Punic ships proved fast and manoeuvrable, stealing in to break the oars or rudders of the larger Roman warships and then escaping. No decisive result had been achieved by the end of the day, when the Carthaginians began to withdraw, the triremes covering the lighter ships. Perhaps the new channel had not been properly finished in the haste of its construction, or maybe some of the crews and captains panicked, but some of the small ships collided with each other and soon created a solid obstacle, completely blocking the route back into the harbour. Unable to retreat by that route, the Punic triremes pulled back and moored against a stretch of quayside directly under the city walls. The area seems to have been formerly used for unloading merchant vessels which could not be accommodated in the great harbour. The galleys drew up with their bow rams facing outwards. Additional protection was provided by a rampart which had been built on the quay earlier in the siege in case the Romans had tried to land at the spot. Enthusiastically the Roman ships rushed into the attack, but suffered as much as if not more than the enemy, since after each ram the galleys were vulnerable as they carefully rowed backwards to withdraw. It was only when five allied ships from the city of Sidatae (Side) in Asia Minor dropped their stern anchors before charging forward to ram and then warped themselves back that the Roman started to gain an advantage. Copying the tactic of these experienced sailors, the larger Roman ships inflicted heavy damage. Only as darkness fell were the few surviving Punic ships able to make their way back into the harbour, the blockage in the new entrance having presumably been cleared.[15]

Carthage was now cut off from the outside world and any source of supply. In time, the city would starve and be forced to capitulate, but Scipio was determined not to wait for this and continued to press his assault as closely as possible. From the newly constructed mole the Romans attacked the rampart defending the stretch of quay recently used by the Punic ships. Breaches were made with rams and the wall bombarded by artillery to prevent its repair. At night some Carthaginians swam naked across the harbour, carrying with them dry torches and the means to light them. In a furious attack these extremly brave men managed to set fire to many of the Roman siege engines, despite suffering very heavy casualties. The Roman soldiers displayed their old nervousness and ill-discipline and panicked at the noise and confusion. Scipio rode with his cavalry body-guard outside the camp and galloped about trying to stop the rout. Where the fleeing soldiers refused to stop, the general and his men cut them down, a rare but not unknown gesture by a Roman commander.[16]

Free from the barrage of missiles, the Carthaginians were able to continue repairing the damaged wall in daylight, filling the breaches and adding wooden towers to provide dominating missile platforms. The Romans returned to the attack, constructing new engines and assault ramps. Several of the new towers were set on fire and the defenders finally forced to abandon the wall. The Romans had gained control of the quay and Scipio gave orders to construct a brick wall facing and of equal height to the main city wall. When completed it was occupied by 4,000 men who were able to hurl javelins and shoot missiles at the defenders on the rampart only a short distance away. Such a massive project took considerable time and was only finished at the beginning of autumn 147. During the following months, whilst his men continued to press the siege of Carthage, Scipio decided to destroy the Punic field army which was again wintering at Nepheris. In a well co-ordinated and planned attack the Romans stormed the enemy camp, Scipio feeding reserves into the main assault against the breach until the enemy was fully occupied and then attacking with another party on the far side of the camp. Gulussa's men pursued the beaten enemy relentlessly, while the Romans moved on to take the city of Nepheris itself. The last force which might have threatened the Romans' hold on Carthage was gone. Most of the communities in the area bowed to the inevitable and surrendered to Rome.[17]

The main assault on the city was renewed in the spring of 146, using the area of the captured quay as its base. Hasdrubal guessed that the attack would come first against the rectangular merchant harbour and set light to the warehouses surrounding it. However, a party led by Caius Laelius, the son of Africanus' friend and an equally loyal companion of Scipio Aemilianus, managed during the night to slip unobserved into the inner, naval harbour and seize it. Punic resistance was, for the moment, rather feeble, due to a combination of the increasingly small rations and the hopelessness of their position. Before the end of the night the Romans had pushed forward into the Agora, or marketplace, adjacent to the civil harbour. The next morning Scipio led in 4,000 men to support Laelius but, in a display confirming the continued ill-discipline of the African army, the legionaries stopped to strip the gold from the lavishly decorated Temple of Apollo. Nothing Scipio or their officers did could persuade the men to return to duty until this had been picked clean. This incident ran directly against the ideal of Roman discipline in which all booty was gathered and centrally distributed to the army on an equal basis. Fortunately for the Romans, the Carthaginians were unable to take advantage of this delay.

Three wide streets led up from the captured Agora to the Byrsa, flanked on each side by tall buildings, six storeys high according to Appian. Excavations in this area have revealed such large apartment buildings, many with central courtyards, built on a regular grid pattern of roads in the Hellenistic manner. Even the main roads were unpaved and no more than about 21 feet across (7 m), the side streets averaging only 16 feet (5 m). Along these roads, sloping up towards the old citadel at a gradient of around 1 in 7, the Romans attacked, led by the men who had plundered Apollo's Temple, but who had not yet been involved in any serious fighting. A deluge of missiles from roofs and windows stopped the attack almost immediately. Unable to advance up the open streets, the legionaries managed to fight their way into some of the buildings on either side, taking them floor by floor. Then parties of men climbed onto the roofs and, laying down planks across the gaps, crossed to attack the adjacent buildings. As they fought their way from building to building, the quantity of missiles being thrown into the open streets slackened and assaulting parties there were able to move forward again. Like street fighting in any era, this was a vicious business and casualties were high. The Romans fed reserves into the fighting and kept the momentum of the advance going until they had reached the Byrsa. Scipio needed to improve the access for his assault parties and engines to the inner citadel, so he ordered the rows of houses running along the three streets to be burned. As the buildings collapsed, Roman working parties set about levelling the rubble to create solid, wider paths, their commander taking little rest as he constantly urged the men on. There was no time for delicacy and Appian gives a lurid description of how corpses and the injured from the buildings were heaped with the spoil and built into the Roman assault road. Finds of human bones amongst the ruins of this area suggest that his description, which probably goes back to Polybius' eyewitness account, is not exaggerated. The project took six days, by which time the Romans were ready to move against the walls of the Byrsa.[18]

On the next day a delegation carrying olive branches, the Hellenistic equivalent of a flag of truce, appeared from the citadel offering to surrender if the Roman general promised to spare their lives. The last defenders, packed into the small area of the Byrsa, with little food or water, were clearly aware of the futility of future resistance and so made none of the usual requests to be permitted to carry with them a number of garments or some of their possessions. Fifty thousand men, women and children are supposed to have marched out into captivity and a life of slavery. Only the Roman and Italian deserters, 900 in number, had been refused pardon and remained with Hasdrubal and his family. This last group had barricaded themselves into the high and inaccessible Temple of Aesculapius, but despaired of further resistance. Hasdrubal, portrayed as a poltroon by Polybius, publicly announced that he would never give in and intended to perish with his city, before abandoning his family and soldiers and surrendering. The deserters committed suicide, setting the Temple on fire and perishing in the flames. Hasdrubal's wife is said to have dressed in all the finery still left to her and appeared in plain view hurling abuse at her faithless husband. She then killed her children, throwing their bodies into the fire, and then herself stepped into the flames and died. The story may be no more than a dramatic literary invention and we can never know whether or not it actually occurred, but such a ghastly scene is a fitting end to the last day of the Carthaginian Empire.[19]

The siege was over and Scipio allowed his men several days to plunder freely, only the gold, silver and votive offerings in the temples being kept aside. Some of this was distributed to the army in the usual fashion, although the men who had plundered Apollo's Temple without orders were excluded from the division. Messengers were sent to Sicily, announcing that spoils taken from them in the past and dedicated in Carthage's temples could now be reclaimed. Unclaimed votive offerings were then auctioned off and captured weaponry and ships burned. When the news of the victory, carried in a ship containing a sample of the plunder, reached Rome it produced a spontaneous night of public rejoicing, followed by more organized celebrations and sacrifices the next day.[20]

Carthage was destroyed, fulfilling Cato's ardent wish and the Roman demand which had finally forced the unwilling Carthaginians to fight in 149. Soon a senatorial commission of ten would arrive to supervise Scipio's systematic destruction of the city. Large areas had been destroyed by fire, leaving a layer of burnt material still covering much of the site today.

Remaining buildings were demolished, although the destruction was not as total as has sometimes been assumed. Archaeologists have discovered walls still standing several yards high underneath the later Roman city. The oft repeated story of the ground being ploughed up and the earth sown with salt to prevent future cultivation is a much later invention. Yet even though the ruins of the city remained, the existence of Carthage the living state and political entity had ceased for ever. The Roman city which would one day be built on the same site shared little or nothing apart from its name and location with its Punic predecessor. As Scipio Aemilianus gazed upon the wreck of the once proud city he is supposed to have wept and quoted from a passage of the *Iliad* referring to the fall of Priam's Troy. He explained to a puzzled Polybius that he was wondering whether his own home would one day suffer a similar fate.[21]

Scipio returned to Rome and celebrated a spectacular triumph, the procession carrying the spoils being described after the pattern of recent decades as more lavish than anything ever seen before. Like his grandfather, Scipio Aemilianus took the name Africanus, but unlike him he proved more successful in the political life at Rome, perhaps as a result of his more conventional career. His circle of friends, notably Gaius Laelius, were later considered to represent the best of the Roman aristocracy, combining a traditional sense of duty with awareness of Greek culture, so that Cicero would later frame his discussion of the Roman Republic as an invented debate between these men. In 134 Scipio was again elected to the consulship amidst widespread popular enthusiasm and sent to Spain where he finally ended the Celtiberian War by capturing Numantia in the following year. So low had the confidence of the Roman soldiers in Spain dropped after repeated defeats that Scipio refused to fight a battle against the massively outnumbered Numantines and instead blockaded and starved them into submission. In 129 Scipio died, in slightly mysterious circumstances with rumours of murder circulating at the time and later, never having experienced the disappointment of his grandsire.[22]

It is as pointless to compare the generalship of Aemilianus to that of Africanus as it is to attempt to prove that any famous commander was better than another, however entertaining such a pursuit might seem. Both men won the victories that concluded a war and success was the principal criterion which the Romans themselves used to judge their commanders. The campaigns of 149–146 were very different to either of the earlier wars between Rome and Carthage, lacking the formal, pitched battles which had been especially characteristic of the Second Punic War. Although the size of the Roman expeditionary force in 149 cannot be established with any certainty, it is clear that far fewer soldiers were fielded by each side in the Third War. In most respects the armies and the majority of their commanders were far less efficient than their predecessors. The decline in the effectiveness of the legions at this period has already been noted and it must also be remembered that the Carthaginians had few experienced mercenaries or officers to call upon in 149, their only military expedition of recent years having ended in disaster. Africanus had been granted the time to train his armies to the highest peak of efficiency in Spain and in Sicily prior to the African expedition, but Aemilianus never enjoyed this luxury. To the very end of the siege, the Roman troops were prone to sudden panics and bouts of indiscipline such as the uncontrolled looting of Apollo's Temple.[23]

The fighting in the Third Punic War was confined within a small area of North Africa, reflecting the diminished territory of Carthage and its lack of any real offensive capacity. There was considerable raiding of the surrounding area, some attacks on other cities and the three Roman drives on the position at Nepheris, but these were all essentially subordinate to the main effort, the siege of Carthage. The siege illustrated once again the extreme difficulty of capturing a large and well-fortified city. Repeated attempts at direct assault failed, and even when the storming parties managed to break into the city it was rarely possible for them to hold onto the ground they had gained. Feeding in strong supports to reinforce an initial success was necessary if the attackers were not to be overwhelmed, but required a level of planning, organization and leadership which the Romans simply did not possess until near the end of the siege. The final, successful assault was mounted from the secure base provided by massive siegeworks constructed with great labour over several months. It was also delivered against defenders who were by that time very weak from starvation. The final collapse in the defenders morale came very suddenly, as it frequently did in other sieges of the ancient world, for instance at Jerusalem in AD 70. The Carthaginians' defence of their city was active and skilful. The sallies to burn the Roman rams and engines, the carefully concealed excavation of a new channel from the naval harbour to the sea and the building of a fleet all displayed a degree of flair and determination rarely shown by the Carthaginians in the earlier conflicts. This is especially notable given that the bulk of the city's defenders were Punic citizens, who had performed poorly in 255 and at Zama. When the very existence of their city was under threat, the Carthaginians fought long and hard before famine forced their capitulation. The main difference between the two sides throughout the wars was that the Romans had always fought as if this were the case.[24]

In the same year that Scipio Aemilianus presided over the destruction of Carthage, another Roman army laid waste to Corinth, one of the oldest and largest of the Greek city states. An anti-Roman faction in Corinth had won control of the city and persuaded the rest of the Achaean League to declare against Rome, only to suffer rapid defeat at the hands of the Romans who had already dealt with Andriscus. The devastation of Corinth was to serve as a warning of the futility of opposing Rome. There was also a marked change in the Roman attitude to Macedonia after the end of the Fourth Macedonian War. Victory over Philip V in the Second War had reduced the kingdom to a subordinate ally of Rome with little freedom in external affairs, and the renewal of war with Perseus had resulted in the abolition of the monarchy and State and their replacement by four self-governing regions. In 149 the governments of these *Merides* had failed to cope with Andriscus, so that in the following year a permanent Roman province of Macedonia was finally created. The Roman response and peace settlement had become progressively harsher after each fresh confrontation with Macedonia. The same progression is clearly visible in the Romans' treatment of Carthage. In the end Rome's relentless pursuit of total victory destroyed her rival both physically and as a political entity, creating the new province of Africa to administer the region.[25]

CHAPTER 16

The Legacy

'He who conquers is not the victor unless the loser considers himself beaten'

CARTHAGE DID NOT survive the struggle with Rome. Aspects of its culture persisted in the region, influencing the language, religion and architecture of the Numidian kingdoms which briefly flourished until they too came into conflict with Rome. Some cities were still styling their senior magistrates as 'suffetes' centuries later, when the region had long since become a Roman province. Religious and linguistic survivals continued in the area till at least the end of the Roman Empire in the West. Such continuity is fairly typical of the Roman presence in most provinces of the Empire. The Romans had not fought to destroy Punic culture; nor indeed had the wars ever been a struggle between conflicting ideologies, political systems, religions or cultures, but rather a simple contest for domination between rival states. Rome had waged war to subdue and finally to destroy another city state whose interests conflicted with its own and which was perceived to be a threat. This enemy, Carthage the political entity, source of its population's identity and their focus of loyalty, was utterly destroyed in 146.

The Punic Wars marked a crucial period in Rome's history, as she changed from a purely Italian power in 265 to the dominant force in the Mediterranean by 146, a process which Polybius' *History* was intended to explain. By this time six permanent overseas provinces had been created: Sicily, Sardinia and Corsica ruled as one, Nearer and Further Spain, Africa and Macedonia. All but the last named of these were acquired as a direct result of the conflict with Carthage. Two more provinces, Asia and Transalpine Gaul, were established by the end of the century. Even where the Romans did not rule directly, as in Greece itself and much of the East, Roman influence was far greater than that of any other state. Carthage proved to be Rome's last serious rival, for the Hellenistic kingdoms lacked its great resources and were rapidly overrun.

Roman imperialism was not a creation of the Punic Wars, but the process was certainly accelerated by the conflict with Carthage, as Roman armies were drawn further and further afield. The First and Second Punic Wars accustomed the Romans to massive long-term commitment of men and resources to overseas campaigns. Although after 201 the Republic greatly reduced the number of men under arms, this was never to fall back to the level normal before 265. The change was marked by the eventual rise in the number of praetors from one to six, as well as the extension of their role to include military command as a matter of course. Prior to 265 the Senate had on an annual basis decided where to send the two consuls and how many troops were to be raised and placed under their command. In the second century the process was essentially the same, but carried out on a much wider scale. Now the Senate needed to appoint governors for a growing number of provinces, deciding whether to send out one of the newly elected magistrates or extend the *imperium* of the current governor. In addition it had to judge whether or not the governor needed an army or naval forces, and if so of what size. The number of foreign embassies seeking an audience with the Senate increased dramatically as Roman influence spread, smaller states realizing that friendship with the new power could bring them great advantage. The Roman system adapted to deal with this situation without changing its fundamental nature. The number of magistrates, although not the consulship, was increased to cope, but otherwise political life continued to be much the same. For a while at least, it seemed to work well.

Their vast reserves of military manpower had allowed the Romans to persevere in spite of the colossal losses they suffered in the First and Second Punic Wars. In the ten years after Cannae there were regularly more than twenty legions in service, supported by as many, if not more, allied soldiers. Such a high level of mobilization could not have been maintained on a permanent basis, and was anyway unnecessary in the conditions of the second century. It is unlikely that there were ever more than thirteen legions in service in the twenty years after 201 and the average for each year was less than ten, and dropped further as the century progressed. Rarely, if ever, were there more than two legions and two *alae* operating in a single province at any time, although this did occasionally occur in Cisalpine Gaul. However, those legions raised did tend to remain in service for much longer than had ever been the case before the Hannibalic War. No other ancient state was ever able to combine such an extensive mobilization of its citizens with the level of military efficiency achieved by the legions. [2]

The Roman military system in this period was unique, but it is easy in focusing on the vastness of the pool of citizens and allies available for military service to ignore the economic strength underlying Rome's successful war-making. Roman armies needed to be paid, equipped, clothed and fed, tasks all made more difficult as they campaigned further and further away. Traditionally legionaries were recruited from those possessing enough property to equip themselves, but the great expansion in legionary numbers during the Second Punic War makes it very likely that more and more men were being equipped by the State. In the crisis after Cannae the trophies had been taken from Rome's temples to provide weapons, shields and armour for the penal legions, but this was a short-term measure. In the longer term the State either purchased or arranged the manufacture of the equipment and clothing needed by the armies, although the burden was sometimes spread by requiring Rome's allies to provide such things. An even greater burden had been imposed on the State's finances by the massive shipbuilding programme undertaken during the First Punic War. If the figures provided by our sources are at all accurate, then the Romans constructed nearly 1,000 warships between 260 and 241, the majority of them the large quinqueremes. This was an effort requiring immense resources and a considerable labour force, the cost of which was almost entirely paid for by the State. The scale of this expenditure was emphasized when the final fleet had to be, at least in part, paid for by loans from private citizens, the Treasury no longer being able to cope. [3]

Rome had long ago accepted its responsibility to issue rations of food to both citizen and allied soldiers. Soldiers were provided with grain, cavalrymen receiving more to provide for their mounts, and probably small amounts of meat and wine. The rise in the number of legions vastly increased the amount of grain which had to be found and then transported to each army. The Senate drew upon supplies from as far afield as Egypt as the demand increased and some productive areas of Italy were denied to them by Hannibal. In 265 the Romans had no experience of feeding an army campaigning outside Italy and the supply lines of the legions in Sicily proved precarious at best. Publius and Cnaeus Scipio complained of similar problems and lack of resources in the early years in Spain, and later there was the scandal involving companies contracted to supply the legions there, but by the end of the Second Punic War a highly effective system of supply had evolved to support Roman armies in the field. For the invasion of Africa, Scipio Africanus massed huge reserves at depots in Sicily, drawing grain from Italy and Sardinia as well as the island itself, and organizing a system of convoys to transport it across to the bridgehead established near Utica. Preparations began over a year before the actual invasion and continued till the very end of the war, although in the final months the burden was somewhat relieved when the Carthaginians agreed to feed the Roman troops in the months before the Peace Treaty was confirmed. The Romans' ability to project their military force throughout the Mediterranean in subsequent decades was made possible by the logistical arrangements developed during the Punic Wars.[4]

The economies of ancient States such as Rome have proved very hard for modern scholars to study, although there is general agreement that these must have been very different from those of modern industrialized nations. There is very little hard evidence for the workings of the Roman economy at any period, so that economic historians have tended to resort to the use of theoretical models, which are inevitably far too simplistic and often downright impractical. We can say with certainty that the Roman war effort in the First and Second Punic Wars imposed a massive strain on the Republic's finances, which on several occasions it was only narrowly able to bear. Around 213 the Roman coinage was debased, lowering the content of precious metal in each coin, but this proved a disastrous failure and in the next two years an entirely new currency was created based around the silver *denarius*. These changes can only have been prompted by the huge expenditure on Rome's war effort. It is extremely difficult to say what long-term effects this was to have on the Roman economy and in turn what impact it had on society as a whole. Some sections of society, notably the contractors supplying the army, may well have profited from the conflicts and the conquests of the following century. Rome emerged victorious from the struggle with Carthage not simply because she possessed great resources of men and wealth, but because of her willingness to expend these in great quantities, persevering in a conflict which must at times have seemed hopeless. These resources had steadily increased as the Romans absorbed the Italian Peninsula into their network of allies, so that former enemies came to contribute to future Roman wars. The Roman Republic's war-making assets were huge, but it took the pressure of the struggle with Carthage for the Romans to realize their potential. [5]

Between 265 and 146 the Romans established themselves as the supreme power in the Mediterranean, greatly increasing the territory which they ruled directly, and spreading their influence even more widely. In the subsequent 120 years the Republic was thrown into turmoil as its politics became increasingly violent and rivalry between prominent senators was commonly decided by civil wars. Stability only returned when Augustus,

Julius Caesar's adopted son, defeated his last rival in 31 BC and replaced the rule of the Senate and annually elected magistrates with a form of monarchy known as the Principate. In an apparent paradox, this period of internal chaos witnessed the most intensive period of Imperial expansion, which ended only with the death of Augustus in AD 14, by which time the Empire had reached substantially the size which, with few additions, it would maintain for the next four centuries. It would be inappropriate here to consider the reasons for the collapse of the Roman Republic, but it is worth pausing to ask whether some of the trends causing this decline were apparent in 146 and whether the struggle with Carthage had contributed to them.

Political violence began in 133 when the tribune of the plebs, Tiberius Sempronius Gracchus, and many of his followers were lynched by a mob of senators. Grandson of the man who had led the slave legions so successfully in the years after Cannae, son of the man who had brought a generation of peace to Spain earlier in the century, Tiberius fought with some distinction at the storming of Carthage in 147–146 and subsequently in Spain. In Africa he had served under the command of Scipio Aemilianus, his cousin as Tiberius' mother was Cornelia, the daughter of Scipio Africanus. In 121 his younger brother Caius, who had also tried to use the office of tribune for an ambitious series of reforms, was in turn killed in a spate of even more open fighting. Both of the Gracchi had been concerned with the decline of the rural poor and the implication this had for the recruitment of Rome's militia armies. Caius had also introduced a highly controversial bill establishing a new colony on the site of Carthage, although this was abandoned following his death.

Rome's vast reserves of military manpower had made possible her success in the First and Second Punic Wars, yet in the decades after 146 the Romans certainly believed that the class of small farmers on which the legions most relied was in decline. The poor performance of Roman armies evident from the 150s continued until the end of the century, nearly every conflict opening with embarrassing defeats and scandals. Some of the defeats were on a very large scale, notably the disaster inflicted by migrating German tribes at Arausio in 105, where the casualties are claimed by a late source to have rivalled those of Cannae. Concern over legionary recruitment was made especially relevant in the context of such military failures. This eventually led to the creation of a professional army in the last years of the century. Recruits were no longer required to possess a minimum level of property and as a result tended to come from the poorest classes for whom the army's steady, if low, pay offered an attractive living. The greater permanence of the new legions allowed them to retain the experience which had invariably been lost when the old militia armies were demobilized, and eventually led to the marked rise in the average effectiveness of Roman armies during the first century BC. However, these poorer recruits had little to return to in civilian life after their discharge, and the Senate, which continued to maintain that military service was the patriotic duty of all propertied Romans, refused to take responsibility for these men and provide them with some sort of livelihood. This encouraged a trend whereby legionaries became more loyal to popular commanders than they were to the State itself. The Roman army had ceased to be the entire State under arms, each class serving in accordance with its wealth so that men fought to preserve a community from which they benefited, and became something outside normal society. This was the change which allowed successive Roman generals to lead their armies against each other and Rome itself. Scipio Africanus could not even have dreamed of turning to the men who had served under him to bring armed force to bear against his opponents in the 180s.[6]

The rise of the professional army was a major factor in the Fall of the Republic. It is therefore important to understand to what extent the class of peasant farmers, which had traditionally provided the bulk of the legions, was really in decline during the second century BC and ask why this process occurred. The scale of the problem is now impossible to assess with any certainty, for our only evidence consists of occasional comments in our written sources and often suspect census figures. Archaeological evidence for this period is available for only a tiny fraction of rural Italy and although this sometimes suggests the survival of small farms throughout the period, we can never know whether this reflected general trends or the peculiar conditions of a small area. One view sees the falling numbers of peasant farmers as a direct consequence of the Second Punic War. For fifteen years Hannibal's army had marauded through Italy, burning or consuming crops, laying waste to fields and villages and killing the population. As a deliberate tactic, Roman commanders such as Fabius Maximus had laid waste to their own territory to deny the Punic army food and fodder. The devastation was particularly bad in the southern corner of Italy, where Hannibal's army had been confined for over thirteen years and which had been raided and thoroughly plundered by both sides.

When the Senate began to discharge soldiers and encourage a return to agriculture in the final years of the war, many of the owners of small properties lacked the wealth to restore their farms and begin to produce a viable crop once more. Most abandoned the countryside and migrated to the big cities, especially to Rome, where the profits of conquests were increasingly spent on lavish entertainments and public buildings. Their farms, along with large areas confiscated from the rebellious Italian communities and added to Rome's publicly owned land, were absorbed into large estates owned by the wealthy. Purchased with the profits of overseas expansion, these were worked by slaves captured during the same wars of conquest. Gradually these latifundia came to cover much of the most fertile land in Italy. Although there were fewer legions and *alae* in service in the second century these were recruited from the already reduced citizen and allied peasantry, and were now likely to spend even longer in distant service. Five to ten years on garrison duty in one of the Spanish provinces could well spell ruination for a small farmer whose land fell into neglect during his absence. In the long run this process swelled the urban poor, who were reliant on handouts and casual labour, frequently in debt and inclined to support any radical politician who offered them something better, whilst large parts of the countryside came to be worked by an almost exclusively servile population. Rioting in the city, disorder in the country and a widespread slave revolt were all to feature in the disturbances of the first century BC. The falling numbers of citizens eligible for military service set against the growing demand for long-term overseas garrisons eventually prompted fundamental change in the Roman army. In an extreme view, this process has been seen as a major factor not just in the end of the Republic, but in the later decline of the Roman Empire, and even in the poverty of southern Italy compared to the north still visible in the twentieth century AD.

Most of the longer-term claims for the impact of Hannibal's invasion have rightly been rejected. It is for instance highly questionable that it created factors prompting an inevitable collapse of the Roman Empire, more than six centuries later. Some have attempted to minimize the damage inflicted between 218 and 203, arguing that the literary accounts of widespread devastation are grossly exaggerated and even contradictory. In addition, the area of Italy which suffered most heavily from the depredations of both sides was the south, a region where the proportion of land owned by Roman citizens was relatively small. The consequences of the war should not as a result have had a major impact on the number of citizen farmers qualified for military service. In this view, the decline in the Roman peasantry was primarily a result of the increasing duration of legionary service resulting from overseas expansion in the second century BC. However, whilst it is probable that the extent of agrarian damage caused by the war in Italy is exaggerated by our sources, such exaggeration is entirely understandable and cannot be taken to mean that no significant hardship resulted. At least some areas farmed by Roman citizens had been directly affected by the campaigns against Hannibal and it must always be remembered that the decline in the free peasantry was also a problem for Rome's Latin and Italian allies. At least to some extent the Gracchi and later reformers attempted to relieve the plight of allied as well as citizen poor. It is more likely that a combination of the devastation caused by the Hannibalic invasion and the heavy demands of military service in the second century BC ruined many small farmers, and produced a shift in population away from the country to swell the urban poor. This was not universal. In some areas small farmers were able to survive and prosper for several centuries. Slave-worked latifundia were already in existence before the Romans intervened in Sicily, but the disturbances caused by the Hannibalic War and the wealth and slaves produced by subsequent conquests greatly encouraged their spread.[7]

The Punic Wars were not the sole cause of the major changes in Roman society in the mid to late Republic, but they were a highly important episode in Rome's history. During these conflicts the Romans mobilized massive human and economic resources to wage war with relentless determination. In doing so they were drawn into close involvement all around the shores of the Mediterranean, so that much of the fighting in the second century was a direct result of this contact. Rome was already an active imperialist, warfare an inseparable part of her political system, before the struggle with Carthage, but this produced a permanent increase in the scale and intensity of Roman war-making. The Romans became accustomed to maintaining a large army and governing and exploiting overseas provinces. The Romans, and most especially their élite, had profited from expansion for many years, but as the rate of expansion quickened, so the scale of the spoils massively increased. Rome was flooded with wealth, luxuries and slaves, as well as new ideas and cultural influences. Most of the problems which beset the Republic in the century before its end – increasingly fierce aristocratic competition; the rapidly escalating costs of a political career; the decline of the rural population and the dramatic increase of slavery, urban poverty and debt; the difficulties of recruitment which led to the creation of a professional army – were all directly or indirectly the consequences of imperial expansion. Ultimately the Republic failed to cope with these problems and a monarchy was created. Some would argue that the Republican system relied too heavily on outmoded institutions, perfectly adequate for a city state but utterly incapable of ruling a massive empire. The weakness of this view is that the institutions of the Principate remained for many years essentially those of a city state. Perhaps the Republican system in the second and early first centuries BC had simply become too inflexible to adapt as it had in the past to changing circumstances. Maybe the changes produced by Rome's rapid overseas expansion simply occurred too quickly for the state to deal with effectively. If this was so, then the Punic Wars had played a part, for they had undoubtedly accelerated Roman expansion.

The Punic Wars in Perspective

The world today would be a very different place if Carthage had won the struggle with Rome. The Romans would only have conceded defeat if their enemy had inflicted considerable real damage upon them; more, certainly, than they proved capable of doing. Defeat in such a large-scale conflict might have been enough to cause the collapse of Rome as a state. Roman expansion would have slowed for a very long time and perhaps never happened. The Graeco-Roman culture of the empire which covered much of Europe, North Africa and the Near East for more than 500 years had a profound influence on the subsequent development of the Western world in particular, and through this spread throughout most of the globe. A significant proportion of the world's countries now speak Latin-based languages, or languages heavily influenced by Latin, and use a version of the Latin alphabet. Many legal systems are based on Roman law. The existence of the Roman Empire, and the relative ease of travel it permitted, greatly facilitated the spread of Christianity and of course the creation of a Roman Catholic Church. Would any of this happened in the same way if the Romans had lost?

The Romans came close – we will never know how close – to defeat on very few occasions in either the First or Second Punic Wars, and never in the Third War. They did not lose because they refused to admit defeat in spite of enormous losses, and won through sheer determination and the willingness to expend massive resources in their war effort. The solidarity of all classes at Rome was remarkable, especially in comparison to other ancient city states, and, more often than not, their allies, Latin, Italian and overseas, were also inclined to remain loyal. The entire Roman state went to war, mobilizing an exceptionally high proportion of its manpower, marshalling all of its wealth and resources to pay, feed, clothe and equip its armies, and to construct great fleets of warships. Once (and for whatever reasons) the Romans came into direct conflict with Carthage they did everything necessary to achieve victory, grimly building new fleets or raising fresh legions to replace the ones they had lost, private individuals assisting when the State's finances ran low. The Romans took great pride in their ability to learn from their enemies, copying weaponry and tactics from successive opponents and often improving upon them. This characteristic was amply demonstrated in the Punic Wars by the speed with which Rome turned herself into a great naval power in the First War, or the steady improvement of her armies and generals during the Second.[8]

The Carthaginian war effort was never so wholehearted, and most of the State did not directly participate in the conflict until 149 when they were faced with the extinction of their city. This less determined approach to warfare was not because the Carthaginians remained at heart a nation of merchants, who viewed every enterprise in terms of profit and loss. It was the normal attitude towards warfare of every civilized state in the Mediterranean world. Only the Romans viewed every war as a life and death struggle, refusing to consider defeat whilst they had any means of carrying on the fight, and always pursuing total victory. The Carthaginians, and especially Hannibal, put the Romans under greater pressure than any other single foreign opponent. That they survived this ordeal confirmed their distinctive attitude towards warfare, until the changing conditions of late antiquity made it impossible to maintain. The Romans' relentless attitude to warfare was one of the most important factors in the creation of their Empire, combined with their remarkable talent for absorbing other peoples which gave it such stability. The same attitude to war tended to breed more conflict after an initial clash, and the differences between the Romans' and Carthaginians' expectation of how a beaten enemy should behave contributed in no small way to the renewal of war in 218 and 149.[9]

The historians of the twentieth century readily saw a parallel between the First and Second Punic Wars and the two World Wars of their own century. The struggle between Rome and Carthage was on an unprecedented scale and resulted in massive casualties just as the Great War shattered the European powers. The resentment of many on the losing side provoked the renewal of war and a wider, even more damaging conflict in both 218 BC and AD 1939. Some individual incidents seemed to have parallels between these conflicts separated in time by two millennia. In many respects the situation faced by Britain in the summer of AD 1940 was similar to that of Rome in late 216 BC. Both sides had suffered military disaster suddenly and unexpectedly, and it seemed only a matter of time before each would be overrun by the all-conquering victors. In each case the victors, intoxicated by the ease of their success, believed that all logic demanded that the other side admit defeat and come to a negotiated settlement. Yet Rome and Britain refused to seek peace and continued to fight, enduring further losses. Revisionists who have tried to argue that Hitler's Germany was incapable of launching a successful invasion across the English Channel in 1940 miss the point as certainly as those who debate whether or not Hannibal could have taken Rome in 216. These operations would in practice have been extremely difficult and perhaps impossible with the resources at the Germans' and Carthaginians' disposal. What is far more important is that both the Romans in 216 and the British in 1940 believed that a direct attack upon them was perfectly possible and imminent, posing a real threat to their very existence. In spite of this each preferred to fight on rather than accept defeat and persisted in this resolve in the face of continued pressure from the enemy. For the Romans as much as the British the period was to become their 'Finest Hour', remembered as a time of great unity when all classes stuck together and endured great hardship for the common good. Perhaps the biggest difference is that whilst this occurred in the last days of the British Empire, for the Romans it marked the beginning of their rise to World Empire.

Successes on the battlefield do not automatically bring victory in the wider conflict. Unless one side was overwhelmingly strong, it was rarely possible in the pre-nuclear age to inflict so much damage that an enemy was incapable of fighting on. Wars ended when one side lost its will to continue the struggle and capitulated. Breaking the collective willingness of an enemy population to fight on was the ultimate goal of the theories of Strategic Air Power developed in the 1920s and 1930s AD. When these were put into practice in the Second World War, civilian populations proved far more resilient than the advocates of aerial bombing had anticipated. The bombing of cities did not cause the rapid demoralization of the population, leading to rioting and civil disorder which would force governments to seek peace. Supporters of Independent Air Power argued that the failure was not through any flaw in the concept, but due to a lack of resources, and ultimately such theories reached their culmination in the development of the nuclear arsenal.

It is not always easy to discover which events will trigger the collapse of the collective fighting spirit of any state or people. In AD 1991 the United Nations waged a brief and highly successful campaign against Iraq, but this failed to result in the removal from power by his own people of Saddam Hussein, a prospect eagerly anticipated by politicians and much of the media in the West. In the same way, NATO operations in the Balkans later in the same decade failed to destroy the hold on power of the leaders of Serbia. Battlefield success did not produce the political results widely broadcast in the public debate, although this outcome came as little surprise to most military analysts. Military defeat did not persuade the population of a country to realize the inequalities and unfairness inherent in their political system – at least by Western standards – and turn against their oppressive leaders. Instead the threat from outside tended to bring far greater unity to each country. In our eyes the Roman system of government might seem deeply unfair, concentrating power in the hands of a tiny élite, whilst the system of alliances through which the city controlled Italy was surely oppressive and deeply resented by Latins and Italians. Hannibal may have believed this to be the case when he marched to Italy in 218, although it is difficult to know just how well he understood the peculiarities of the Roman system. Yet his appeal to Rome's allies to throw off the oppressor's yoke fell overwhelmingly on deaf ears. No Latins joined him and the bulk of the Italians also remained loyal. Fear of reprisals played a part, as perhaps did suspicion of Carthage's motives, but on the whole we are forced to conclude that most of the Italian communities felt that it was in their best interest to support Rome. In the same way, even the poorer classes at Rome felt a strong enough bond to the community to sacrifice their lives for it.

In the Introduction I stated that it was not my intention in this book to seek in the Punic Wars military lessons of direct relevance to modern warfare. Others are far better qualified to discuss modern strategy and tactics. The aim of this book has been to set the conflict between Rome and Carthage firmly within the context of warfare in the third and second centuries BC. If we are to learn from the past then history must first be understood on its own terms. One general point is worth emphasizing, namely that each society and culture tends to have a unique view of warfare which affects how they fight and as a result how they may be beaten. This can be seen in most periods of history, but the difference between two philosophies of war has rarely been as clearly illustrated as it was during the Punic Wars.

Notes to the Text

Introduction

1 For Cannae see chapter 8; Napoleon's belief that much could be learned from the study of ancient commanders, see D. Chandler, *The Campaigns of Napoleon* (London, 1966), pp. 137–139; for twentieth-century studies of the Punic Wars see B. Liddell Hart, *A Greater than Napoleon – Scipio Africanus* (Edinburgh, 1930), J. Fuller, *The Decisive Battles of the Western World* (London, 1954).

2 For relatively recent studies see T. Dorey & D. Dudley, *Rome against Carthage* (London, 1971), B. Caven, *The Punic Wars* (London, 1980), N. Bagnall, *The Punic Wars* (London, 1990) and Y. Le Bohec, *Histoire militaire des guerres puniques* (Paris, 1996) which cover the entire conflict; J. Lazenby, *Hannibal's War* (Warminster, 1978, reprinted with new preface: Oklahoma, 1998), and *The First Punic War* (London, 1996), J. Peddie, *Hannibal's War* (Stroud, 1997), and S. Lancel (trans. A. Nevill), *Hannibal* (Oxford, 1998) deal with individual wars, and in 1993 there was also a reprint of T. Dodge, *Hannibal* (1891); there is also the stimulating collection of papers in T. Cornell, B. Rankov & P. Sabin (edd.), *The Second Punic War: A Reappraisal*, British Institute of Classical Studies Supplement 67 (London, 1996). All of these works include bibliographies mentioning many more books and articles published within recent years on aspects of the subject.

3 Bagnall (1990) and Peddie (1997), both of whom were highly experienced soldiers, comment perceptively on some of the practical aspects of the campaign. Peddie pays more attention to the problems of supply than most other authors. For a general treatment of the differences between different cultures' concepts and practice of war, see J. Keegan, *A History of Warfare* (London, 1993).

4 Silenus and Sosylus, see Nepos, *Hannibal* 13. 3.

5 For Polybius see F. Walbank, *A Historical Commentary on Polybius 1* (Oxford, 1970), pp. 1–37.

6 See P. Walsh, *Livy* (Cambridge, 1961), and T. J. Luce, *Livy, the Composition of his History* (Princeton, 1977); Cynoscephalae, Polybius 18. 24. 8–9, Livy 34. 8. 13.

7 See Walbank 1 (1970), pp. 26–35; Polybius' criticism of the partisan nature of Philinus and Fabius Pictor, 1. 14–15.

Chapter 1

1 For a useful survey of the Mediterranean world in the third century BC see A. Toynbee, *Hannibal's Legacy. Vol. 1* (Oxford, 1965), pp. 20–83.

2 Origins of Carthage, see G. Picard & C. Picard, *Carthage* (rev. ed.: London, 1987), pp. 15–35, S. Lancel, *Carthage* (Oxford, 1995), pp. 1–34; Tarshish, Ezekiel 27. 12; Spain, Lancel (1995), pp. 9–14.

3 Sacrifice to Melquart, Polybius 31. 12; religion and culture, Picard & Picard (1987), pp. 35–50, Lancel (1995), pp. 193–256, esp. 245–56.

4 Picard & Picard (1987), pp. 56–124, Lancel (1995), pp. 78–102.

5 Exploration & colonization, see Picard & Picard (1987), pp. 91–100, Lancel (1995), pp. 100–109; the Neapolis of fourth-century Carthage, 141–2.

6 Lancel (1995), pp. 269–88; Agathocles, *Diodorus Siculus* 20. 8. 3–4.

7 Contrast Picard & Picard (1987), pp. 125–81 with the more up to date view in Lancel (1995), pp. 111–21.

8 Pyrrhus' lost manual, Plutarch, *Pyrrhus* 8; on Hellenistic warfare in general see F. Adcock, *The Greek and Macedonian Art of War* (Berkeley, 1957).

9 On ship construction and naval warfare see chapter 5; for Carthage's harbour see Lancel (1995), pp. 172–8, H. Hurst, 'Excavations at Carthage, 1977–8', *Antiquaries' Journal* 59 (1979), pp. 19–49.

10 *Lonchophoroi*, e.g. Polybius 3. 72. 3, 83. 3, 84. 14; for a discussion of the poor evidence for Punic armies see J. Lazenby, *Hannibal's War* (Warminster, 1978), pp. 14–16; for an interesting discussion of Gallic, Spanish and other tribal contingents in Hannibal's army see L. Rawlings, 'Celts, Spaniards, and Samnites: Warriors in a Soldiers' War', in T. Cornell, B. Rankov & P. Sabin, *The Second Punic War. A Reappraisal* British Institute of Classical Studies Supplement 67 (London, 1996), pp. 81–95. D. Head, *Armies of the Macedonian and Punic Wars* attempts to reconstruct Punic equipment and organization in some detail, but many of his conclusions are highly conjectural.

11 Exchange of troops in 218, Polybius 3. 33. 5–16. Note the difficulties in communicating with each other in the rebellious army during the Mercenary War, Polybius 1. 67. 3–13, 69. 9–13.

12 Marriage alliances between Punic aristocrats and Numidian royalty, e.g. Polybius 1. 78. 1–9, Livy 29. 23. 2–8; in Spain, DS 25. 12, Livy 24. 51. 7, Silius Italicus 3. 97, 106.

13 Autaritus' Gauls, Polybius 2. 7. 6–11.

14 500 Numidians, Livy 26. 38. 11–14; Libyans at Saguntum, Livy 21. 11. 8; Gauls at Tarentum, Polybius 8. 30. 1; *speirai* at Cannae, Polybius 3. 114. 4, cf. 6. 24. 5.

15 For war elephants in general see H. Scullard, *The Elephant in the Greek and Roman World* (London, 1974); Raphia, see Polybius 5. 84. 2–7.

16 See chapter 12.

17 A good recent survey of early Roman history is T. Cornell, *The Beginnings of Rome* (London, 1995).

18 On this period see Cornell (1995), pp. 345–68, & S. Oakley, 'The Roman Conquest of Italy', in J. Rich & G. Shipley, *War and Society in the Roman World* (London, 1993), pp. 9–37; refusal to negotiate with Pyrrhus, Plutarch, *Pyrrhus* 18–20.

19 On aristocratic funerals see Polybius 6. 53–4.

20 Factions dominate most modern accounts of the Punic Wars, e.g. B. Caven, *The Punic Wars* (London, 1980), pp. 20, 83–4, and to a lesser extent Lazenby (1978), pp. 4, 108. H. Scullard, *Roman politics 220–150 BC* (London, 1951) represents an extreme form of this view.

21 Polybius' famous description, Polybius 6. 11–19, 43–58, and F. Walbank, *A Historical*

Commentary on Polybius [3 vols] (Oxford, 1970), pp. 673–97, 724–746. For Roman politics in general see M. Gelzer, *The Roman Nobility* (London, 1968), M. Crawford, *The Roman Republic* (Glasgow, 1978), P. Brunt, *Social Conflicts in the Roman Republic* (London, 1978), pp. 1–73, F. Millar, 'The political character of the Classical Roman Republic', *Journal of Roman Studies* 74 (1984), pp. 1–19, and T. Wiseman (ed.), *Roman Political Life 90 BC–AD 69* (Exeter, 1985).

22 For a good introduction to the development of the Roman army see L. Keppie, *The Making of the Roman Army* (London, 1984), E. Gabba, *Republican Rome: The Army and Allies* (Berkeley, 1976), A. Goldsworthy, *Roman Warfare* (London, 2000), F. Adcock, *The Roman Art of War under the Republic* (Cambridge, 1960), and E. Rawson, 'The literary sources for the pre-Marian Roman Army', *Papers of the British School at Rome* 39 (1971), pp. 13–31.

23 Polybius 6. 19–42, and Walbank 1 (1970) pp. 697–723.

24 Polybius 11. 23. 1, 33. 1, and Walbank 2 (1970), p. 302. See also M. Bell, 'Tactical Reform in the Roman Republican Army', *Historia* 14 (1965), pp. 404–22.

25 On the find of a probable Roman *scutum* see W. Kimmig, 'Ein Keltenschild aus Aegypten', *Germania* 24 (1940), pp. 106–111. For Roman equipment in general see P. Connolly, *Greece and Rome at War* (London, 1981), pp. 129–42, and 'Pilum, gladius and pugio in the Late Republic', *Journal of Roman Military Equipment Studies* 8 (1997), pp. 41–57, and M. Bishop & J. Coulston, *Roman Military Equipment* (London, 1993), pp. 48–64.

26 Polybius 2. 33. 4 records an occasion in 224 when the *hastati* were given the *triarii*'s spears, indicating that the former normally carried another weapon, presumably the *pilum*. On the *pilum* see Bishop & Coulston (1993), pp. 48–50.

27 For the 'reform' of 211, see the unconvincing arguments in M. Samuels, 'The Reality of Cannae', *Militärgeschichtliche Mitteilungen* 47 (1990), pp. 7–31.

28 Cato's grandfather, Plutarch, *Cato* 1; on the saddle see P. Connolly, 'The Roman Saddle', in M. Dawson (ed.), *Roman Military Equipment: The Accoutrements of War*, BAR 336 (Oxford, 1987), pp. 7–27.

29 Sentries sleeping on guard, Polybius 6. 35. 6–37. 6, Livy 44. 33; punishments in general, Polybius 6. 37. 7–38. 4.

30 This decision-making process is implicit in our narrative accounts, and explicit in Vegetius 3. 1.

31 Telamon, Polybius 2. 24–31, esp. 27. 1–6.

32 E.g. Spurius Ligustinus mentioned in Livy 42. 34.

33 For the importance of *virtus* see N. Rosenstein, *Imperatores Victi* (Berkeley, 1990), pp. 114–51.

34 Space allocated to each legionary, Polybius 18. 30. 5–8, Vegetius 3. 14, 15, and discussion in A. Goldsworthy, *The Roman Army at War, 100 BC–AD 200* (Oxford, 1996), pp.179–80.

35 Roman armies ambushed, e.g. Polybius 2. 25, 3. 118, Livy 38. 40–1, & chapter 7. Livy noted that in 193 a consul sent out scouts even though he was marching in daylight, which implies that this was not normal, Livy 35. 4. For accidental encounters see Polybius 2. 27–8, 3. 61, 65, Livy 31. 33, Polybius 18. 19. For military intelligence in general see M. Austin & B. Rankov, *Exploratio* (London, 1995).

36 Delays before battle, see Polybius 3. 89–90, 110–113, 10. 38–9, 11. 21, 14. 8, Livy 34. 46, 38. 20, and esp. Livy 37. 38–9; armies camped near each other for long periods without fighting, see Polybius 1. 19, 57–8, Appian *Iberica* 11. 65; strategems to cover

withdrawal when in close contact with the enemy, Polybius 2. 25, 3. 68, 93–4, Livy 31. 38–9.

37 Forming up Roman armies, Polybius 3. 72, 113, 6. 31, Livy 34. 46, 40. 31, 40. 48, 41. 26; Punic armies also apparently using the processional method, Polybius 3. 113. 6, 11. 22; Macedonians at Cynoscephalae, Polybius 18. 22–5; confusion in deploying a Spanish army in haste in 195, Livy 35. 14; references to Roman tribunes being closely involved in deployment, Polybius 11. 22. 4, Livy 44. 36.

38 For the role of *optiones* see M. Speidel, *The Framework of an Imperial Legion. The fifth Annual Caerleon Lecture* (Cardiff, 1992), pp. 24–6.

39 For a detailed discussion of this issue see Goldsworthy (1996), pp. 138–40.

40 For a stylized account of the line system see Livy 8. 8. esp. 9–13. For a discussion of infantry combat in this period, see P. Sabin, 'The mechanics of battle in the Second Punic War', in Cornell, Rankov and Sabin (1996), pp. 59–79, esp. 64–73 and for the Roman tactical system see P. Sabin, 'The Multiple Line System in Republican Roman Armies', *Journal of Roman Studies* (forthcoming). For a detailed discussion on combat in a slightly later period see Goldsworthy (1996), pp. 171–247; on the role of the commander see Goldsworthy (1996), pp. 116–70.

41 See chapters 7 and 8.

Chapter 2

1 Thucydides 1, esp. 1. 23, 89–117.

2 Polybius 1. 7. 1–5. See F. Walbank, *A Historical Commentary on Polybius* 1 (Oxford, 1970), pp. 52–3 for a discussion of the chronology.

3 Polybius 1. 7. 6–13. Dionysius of Halicarnassus 20. 4 claims that the garrison was installed to defend the city against the Bruttians.

4 Appian, *Samnite History* 9. 3.

5 Polybius 1. 8. 3–9. 8. For the chronology of Hiero's career see Walbank 1 (1970), pp. 54–5. See *Diodorus Siculus* 22. 13 for an account of the action at the River Longanus.

6 Polybius 1. 10. 1–2; Hannibal's deception of Hiero, *Diodorus Siculus* 22. 13; inevitability of Carthaginian conquest of Sicily once they controlled Messana, Polybius 1. 10. 7–8, Zonaras 8. 8. For discussion of the war's causes see J. Lazenby, *The First Punic War* (London, 1996), pp. 31–42, B. Caven, *The Punic Wars* (London, 1980), pp. 8–16, Walbank 1 (1970), pp. 56–63.

7 Polybius 1. 10. 3–9.

8 Polybius 1. 11. 1–3. See also Walbank 1, p. 62, Lazenby (1996), p. 39. For a detailed discussion of the process involved see J. Rich, *Declaring war in the Roman Republic in the period of transmarine expansion* (Collection Latomus 149, Brussels, 1976).

9 The Philinus treaty, Polybius 3. 26. 2–5; Polybius' account of the three preserved treaties, 3. 22–26, cf. Livy 7. 27. 2, 9. 43. 26, *Periochae* 13, and *Diodorus Siculus* 16. 91. 1; Livy's 306 treaty, *Per.* 14. For discussion of these see Walbank 1 (1970), p. 337–56, Lazenby (1996), pp. 31–5; Caven (1980), pp. 15–16, and S. Lancel, *Carthage* (Paris, 1995), pp. 86–8, 362, both favour accepting Philinus' treaty. For a recent discussion of relations betweeen Rome and Carthage see R. Palmer, *Rome and Carthage at Peace. Historia Einzelschriften Heft. 113* (Stuttgart, 1997). On the incident at Tarentum see Livy *Per.* 14, Zonaras 8. 6, Orosius 4. 3. 1–2.

10 Dio 11. 1–4, Zonaras 8. 8.

11 For Defensive Imperialism see T. Mommsen, *The History of Rome* (trans. M. W. P. Dickson) (London, 1877–80), T. Frank, *Roman Imperialism* (New York, 1914), M. Holleaux, *Rome, la Grèce et les monarchies hellénistiques au IIIe siècle avant J.C. (273–205)* (Paris, 1921), E. Badian, *Roman Imperialism in the Late Republic* (Oxford, 1968), R. M. Errington, *The Dawn of Empire: Rome's Rise to World Power* (London, 1971).

12 For the economic motives for Roman imperialism see M. K. Hopkins, *Conquerors and Slaves* (Cambridge, 1978); the strongest argument for the Roman political and social systems encouraging aggression is W. V. Harris, *War and Imperialism in Republican Rome 327–70 BC* (Oxford, 1979), esp. pp. 9–104. For a more balanced view see J. Rich, 'Fear, greed and glory: the causes of Roman war-making in the middle Republic', in J. Rich & G. Shipley, *War and Society in the Roman World* (London, 1993), pp. 38–68, where he comments on the varying intensity of Roman war-making.

13 Harris (1979), pp. 183–5.

14 Polybius 1. 11. 3–11; the request for ships from the allies, Polybius 1. 20. 13–14. The story of C. Claudius, Dio 11. 5–10, Zonaras 8. 8–9.

15 See Lazenby (1996), pp. 43–6 for criticism of this tradition. The loss of the Carthaginian quinquereme, Polybius 1. 20. 15; Hanno's threat, Dio 11. 9, Zonaras 8. 9; Diodorus' account of the negotiations, 23. 1. 4.

16 Polybius 1. 11. 9–12. 4, 14. 1–8; on the defeat of the Roman cavalry, Zonaras 8. 9.

17 Polybius 1. 16. 1–11, Zonaras 8. 9. On the name Messala, see Pliny *Natural History* 35. 22.

18 Polybius 1. 16. 4–17. 1. Eutropius 2. 19. 2 and Orosius 4. 7. 3 claim that Hiero paid 200 talents.

Chapter 3

1 Mercenaries, Polybius 1. 17. 3–4; reduction in Roman army, 1. 17. 1–2; four legions again sent to Sicily, 1. 17. 6.

2 J. Roth, *The Logistics of the Roman Army at War* (Brill, 1999), p. 158, 171–2, 288, 316, 318.

3 General narrative, Polybius 1. 17. 6–13; the pickets outside the camp 1. 17. 11–12 and 6.37. 11. This institution is attested at the siege of Jerusalem in AD 70, Josephus, *Bellum Judaicum* 5. 482–3.

4 Caesar, *Bellum Gallicum* 2. 32, Cicero *De Officiis* 1. 35.

5 Polybius 1. 18. 1–7.

6 Polybius 1. 18. 8–19. 4; size of the Punic army, Polybius 1. 19. 2, *Diodorus Siculus* 23. 8. 1. The much later source of Orosius gives only 30 elephants, 1,500 cavalry and 30,000 infantry, 4. 7. 5.

7 Zonaras 8. 10; Polybius 1. 19. 6.

8 Polybius 1. 19. 7–11, *DS* 23. 8. 1, 9. 1, 7.

9 B. Caven, *The Punic Wars* (London, 1980), p. 25, Lazenby, *The First Punic War* (London, 1996), p. 58.

10 Zonaras 8. 10, Frontinus, *Strategemata* 2. 1. 4

11 Agrigentum, Polybius 1. 19. 13–15; Hiero supplying the Roman army, Polybius 1. 18. 11; extension of Roman war-aims, Polybius 1. 20. 1–2, and F. Walbank, *A Historical Commentary on Polybius* 1 (Oxford, 1970), p. 72, who cites Polybius' claim that the victory at Telamon in 225 BC encouraged the Senate to plan to expel the Celts entirely from Transpadine Gaul, 2. 31. 7.

12 Defections to Rome, *DS* 23. 4. 1; unsuccessful operations, *DS* 23. 3. 1 and 23. 4. 2. It is possible that these places were misidentified by Diodorus' excerpter, see Lazenby (1996) p. 53; Mytistratus, *DS* 23. 9. 2–3; Herbesus, *DS* 23. 8. 1; Camarina, *DS* 23. 9. 4; Enna *DS* 23. 9. 5.

13 Lipara a trap, Polybius 1. 21. 5–8, 8. 35. 9, Zonaras 8. 10, Livy *Per.* 17; Thermae, *DS* 23. 19. 1; the Gauls, Zonaras 8. 10, *DS* 23. 8. 3, Frontinus *Strat.* 3. 16. 3.

14 Thermae, Polybius 1. 24. 3–4, *DS* 23. 9. 4; annual changes in commanders, Zonaras 8. 16. The main drafts of reinforcements for the Punic armies in Sicily mentioned by Polybius were in 262, 1. 18. 8, and in 255 including 140 elephants, 1. 38. 2–3.

15 Polybius 1. 29. 1–10; Italian prisoners, Zonaras 8. 12; Kerkouane, Lancel (1995), pp. 268–9, 367.

16 Regulus' reluctance to take command, Dio 11. 20; his army, Polybius 1. 29. 9; First Legion, Polybius 1. 30. 11; Roman generalship, see A. Goldsworthy '"Instinctive Genius"; The Depiction of Caesar the general', in K. Welch and A. Powell (edd.), *Julius Caesar as Artful Reporter. The War Commentaries as Political Instruments* (Swansea, 1998), pp. 192–219.

17 Polybius 1. 30. 1–7; see Lazenby (1996), p. 100 for a discussion of the possible identity of Adys.

18 Roman officers spot the Carthaginian error, Polybius 1. 30. 9.

19 Polybius 1. 30. 10–14; dawn attack, Polybius 1. 30. 10; night attack, Zonaras 8. 13.

20 Use of Tunis as base, Polybius 1. 30. 15; desire to gain credit for ending war, 1. 31. 4–5; similar behaviour by other Roman commanders, e.g. Tiberius Sempronius Longus at Trebia in 218, Polybius 3. 70. 7, and Titus Quinctius Flamininus during the negotiations with Philip V of Macedonia in 198–197, Polybius 18. 11–12.

21 Polybius 1. 31. 1–8, Dio 11. 22–3.

22 Polybius 1. 32. 1–9; Xanthippus' arrival, *DS* 23. 16. 1; his competence, Polybius 1. 32. 7.

23 Polybius 1. 33. 1–6; see Lazenby (1996), p. 104 for a discussion of the possible site of the battle.

24 Polybius 1. 33. 9, see also Lazenby (1996), p. 104–5. For cases of more than three lines being formed by legions in the first-century BC, see Pharsalus, Caesar *Bellum Civile* 3. 89; examples of whole legions in reserve include Emporion in 195, Livy 34. 15, a victory over the Boii in 193, Livy 35. 5; examples from the Second Punic War include Numistro, Livy 27. 2, 12, and in Spain in 205, Livy 29. 2.

25 Polybius 1. 33. 8–34. 12.

26 For possible later service in Egypt see Lazenby (1996), p. 106, who mentions that Ptolemy III appointed a Xanthippus to a governorship in 245, Hieronymus *In Daniel* 11. 7–9; for the Regulus myth see Diodorus 23. 16. 1, *DS* 24. 12, and discussion in A. Pauly, G. Wissowa et al., *Real-encyclopädie der classischen Altertumswissenschaft* (Stuttgart, 1893–), Atilius (51), cols. 2088–92.

27 For Hamilcar's campaigns against the Numidians see Orosius 4. 9. 9. The chronology of Hanno's operations in Libya are uncertain, Polybius 1. 73. 1, 74. 7, *DS* 24. 10.

28 Polybius 1. 39. 7–40. 16. It does not really matter for our purposes whether Metellus fought the battle as a consul or proconsul. For a discussion of the relevant sources see Lazenby (1996), p. 120.

29 Casualties, Eutropius 2. 24, Orosius 4. 9. 15; elephants, Polybius 1. 38. 2, *DS* 23. 21, Zonaras 8. 14, Pliny *Natural History* 8. 16; Gauls, *DS* 23. 21.

30 Polybius 1. 41. 4–48. 11. Polybius gives the strength of the garrison as 10,000, 1. 42. 11, but Diodorus says that they consisted of only 7,000 infantry and 700 cavalry, *DS* 24. 1. However, he also says that a draft of 4,000 men was taken into the city by sea. The same passage gives the Roman strength.

31 Polybius 1. 56. 1–58. 9; Eryx, *DS* 24.8

Chapter 4

1 Polybius 1. 20. 6–14.

2 For the early history of Roman seapower see J. Thiel, *A history of Roman sea-power before the Second Punic War* (Amsterdam, 1954), pp. 3–59; the assumption that *classici* derived from *classis* or fleet see Thiel 1954), pp. 33–4, (J. Lazenby, *The First Punic War* (London, 1996), p. 63 takes a more cautious line); the defeat of the Roman squadron by the Tarentines, Livy *Per.* 12, Appian, *Samnite History* 7. 1. For a general survey of ancient naval warfare see W. Rogers, *Greek and Roman Naval Warfare* (Maryland, 1964), esp. pp. 266–305.

3 For the claims of Messala, see *Ineditum Vaticanum* 4.

4 T. Shaw (ed.) *The Trireme Project: Operational Experience 1987–90; Lessons Learnt. Oxbow Monograph 32* (Oxford, 1993); for a brief summary of the findings see L. Casson, *Ships and Seafaring in Ancient Times* (London, 1994), esp. pp. 60–77.

5 For the 'forty' see Casson (1971), pp. 50–51, 82–3; the 'thirties' see Athenaeus 5. 203c; also see Morrison (1996), pp. 1–40, and p. 309 for 'tens' as largest ships recorded as being used in battle; Carthaginians first to build 'fours', Aristotle, *Fragment* 600; Syracuse built first 'five', *Diodorus Siculus* 4. 41. 3.

6 See Casson (1971) pp. 84–5; Polybius 1. 20. 15.

7 J. S. Morrison (& J. F. Coates) *Greek and Roman Oared Warships* (Oxbow, 1996), pp. 259–60, 270–72, and attempted reconstruction, pp. 312–17; for the perceived weakness of the outrigger, Lazenby (1996), p. 65.

8 The Athlit ram, Casson, pp. 74, 90–91; the Marsala wreck, see L. Basch & H. Frost, 'Another Punic wreck in Sicily: its ram', *International Journal of Nautical Archaeology* 4 (1976), pp. 201–28 & H. Frost *et alii*, *Lilybaeum (Marsala) – The Punic Ship: Final Excavation Report. Notizie Degli Scavi di Antichita Supplemento al vol. 30, 1976* (Rome, 1981), pp. 267–70.

9 The dogfight analogy, e.g. Lazenby (1996), p. 95, Shaw (1993), p. 99; for the *diekplus*, Shaw (1993), pp. 99–104.

10 Innate conservatism of Romans, see Thiel (1954), pp. 66–7; 'five' as shorthand for 'warship' noted by W. W. Tarn, 'The Fleets of the First Punic War', *Journal of Hellenic Studies* 27 (1907), pp. 48–60, esp. pp. 59–60. F. Walbank, *A Historical Commentary on Polybius* 1 (Oxford, 1970), p. 74; Punic warship captured and used as model, Polybius 1. 20. 15; construction completed in sixty days, Pliny *Natural History* 16. 192, cf. Florus 1. 18. 7, Orosius 4. 7. 8.

11 H. Frost, 'The prefabricated Punic Warship' in H. Deviyner & E. Lipinski, *Studia Phoenica X: Punic Wars* (Leuven, 1989), pp. 127–135, esp. pp. 132–4; 'fives' never built in Italy before, Polybius 1. 20. 10.

12 For a discussion see Thiel (1954), pp. 73–8, Lazenby (1996), p. 65. For the census figures see P. Brunt, *Italian Manpower 225 BC – AD 14* (Oxford, 1971), p. 13, 32; for the Samnites see Zonaras 8. 11.

13 Treachery, Zonaras 8. 10; Asina, Pliny, *NH* 8. 169.

14 Polybius 1. 21. 9–11; garbled account of Mylae see Lazenby (1996), p. 67, Tarn (1907), p.51, Thiel (1954), pp.122–7.

15 Polybius 1. 22. 3–11; H. T. Wallinga, *The Boarding-Bridge of the Romans* (Gravenhage, 1956). See also Thiel (1954), pp. 101–28.

16 *DS* 23. 10. 1.

17 Polybius 1. 23. 1–10, Rogers (1964), pp. 276–7; the *corvi*, 1. 23. 9–10, Thiel (1954), p. 115.

18 *Corpus Inscriptionum Latinarum* 12. 2. 25, the commentary including Mommsen's reconstruction of the text.

19 Livy *Per.* 17.

20 Hannibal, Polybius 1. 24. 5–7; the Lipari Islands, Polybius 1. 25. 1–4, Zonaras 8. 12.

21 Polybius 1. 26. 7.

22 See Tarn (1907), pp. 46, 53; Thiel (1954), pp. 83–96, esp. 94.

23 As for instance in Thiel (1954), pp. 119–20, criticized by Lazenby (1996), pp. 87–8.

24 E.g. G. K. Tipps, 'The battle of Ecnomus', *Historia* 34 (1985).

25 Line 'thinner', Polybius 1. 27. 7.

26 Lazenby (1996), pp. 95–6.

27 Polybius 1. 26. 10–28. 14, Rogers (1964), pp. 278–91.

28 Polybius 1. 29. 1, see Thiel (1954), p. 117.

29 Zonaras 8. 14, Polybius 1. 36. 11.

30 Numbers, *DS* 23. 18. 1, Orosius 4. 9. 8, Eutropius 22. 3. For doubts about the numbers see Tarn (1907), p. 53, Thiel (1954), p. 94. On the *corvus* see Thiel (1954), pp. 235–6, Lazenby (1996), p. 112. Roman reliance on *bia*, Polybius 1. 37. 7–10.

31 Polybius 1. 38. 5–10.

32 Polybius 1. 39. 6.

33 Polybius 1. 39. 8, 15; Lilybaeum, 1. 41. 3–4; Hannibal, 1. 44. 1–7, 46. 1–3.

34 Polybius 1. 46. 4–47. 3.

35 Polybius 1. 47. 3–10.

36 Livy, *Per.* 19, Cicero, *de natura deorum* 2. 7, Florus 1. 19. 29, Suetonius *Tiberius* 2.

37 Drepana, Polybius 1. 49. 3–51. 12, Rogers (1964), pp. 296–9; the trial see N. Rosenstein, *Imperatores Victi* (Berkeley, 1990), pp. 35–6, 43, 79–80, 84–5, 184–5.

38 Polybius 1. 52. 4–54. 8, Zonaras 8. 15; the *lemboi*, Polybius 1. 53. 9.

39 Raiding of Africa, Zonaras 8. 16; census figures Brunt (1971), pp. 26–33; for 265–264 Eutropius 2. 18, 252–251 Livy *Per.* 18, 247–246 Livy *Per.* 19; Claudia see Livy *Per.* 19, Suetonius, *Tiberius* 2.3, Aulus Gellius, *Noctes Atticae* 10. 6.

40 Polybius 1. 59. 7–8.

41 Inability of smaller ships to damage a 'five' Polybius 15. 1. 3–2. 15, Livy 30. 25. 1–10; Morrison & Coates (1996), pp. 271–2, 285–91.

42 Livy *Per.* 19.

43 See Lazenby (1996), pp. 153–4.

44 Aegates Islands, Polybius 1. 59. 8–61. 8; losses *DS* 24. 11. 1–2, and Rogers (1964), pp. 301–3.

45 See Frost (1989), p. 128; dispute between Roman commanders, Valerius Maximus 2. 8. 2.

46 Polybius 1. 62. 1–2.

47 Note Polybius' comments on the higher quality of Roman marines out-balancing the Carthaginians' superior skills of seamanship, 6. 52. 8–9.

Chapter 5

1 *Diodorus Siculus* 24. 13. 1. Livy 21. 41. 6–7 implies that even so Hamilcar's soldiers were ransomed at 18 denarii a head.

2 T. Cornell, *The Beginnings of Rome* (London, 1995), pp. 188–9.

3 Polybius 1. 62. 1–9, 3. 27. 2–6. For a slightly different version see Zonaras 8. 17.

4 See J. Rich, 'The Origins of the Second Punic War', in T. Cornell, B. Rankov & P. Sabin, *The Second Punic War: A Reappraisal* (London, 1996), pp. 1–37, esp. pp. 23–4 with further references.

5 See G. Rickman, *The Corn Supply of Ancient Rome* (Oxford, 1980), pp. 12–13, 32–3, 37.

6 See J. Lazenby, *The First Punic War* (London, 1996), pp. 168–170 on the passivity of the Carthaginians during the war.

7 Zonaras 8. 16.

8 For office holding in the period see T. Broughton, *The Magistrates of the Roman Republic* (New York, 1951). In the two decades from 284 to 265, eleven of the consuls elected were holding the office for the second time. In 241–222 only seven men held office for a second time. On Caiatanus see Livy *Per.* 19, see also Lazenby (1996), pp. 137, 141.

9 G. Picard & C. Picard, *Carthage* (London, 1987), p. 194.

10 See N. Rosenstein, *Imperatores Victi* (Berkeley, 1990), pp. 35–6, 43, 79–80, 184–5, and Lazenby (1996), pp. 136–7.

11 Polybius' account of the Mercenary War, 1. 66.1–88. 7.

12 Polybius 1. 77. 5, 2. 7. 6–11.

13 Polybius 1. 83. 5–11; Appian *The Punic Wars* 5.

14 Polybius 1. 83. 2–4.

15 Polybius 1. 83. 11.

16 S. Dyson, *The Creation of the Roman Frontier* (Princeton, 1985), p. 246.

17 Polybius 1. 88. 8–12, 3. 28. 1–4.

18 See Dyson (1985), pp. 239–51.

19 Zonaras 8. 18.

20 *DS* 25. 10. 4, 19. 1.

21 Polybius 3. 13. 3–5.

22 See Picard & Picard (1987), pp. 202–203, 222–229.

23 Polybius criticizes Fabius Pictor for representing the Barcids as opposed by the majority of Carthage's élite, 3. 8. 1–11. Livy represents Hanno as leader of the faction opposed to the Barcids, e.g. 21. 3. 1–4. 1, 10. 1–11. 2. Zonaras 8. 17 claims Hamilcar went to Spain contrary to the wishes of the Punic leaders. *DS* 25. 8. 1 says Hamilcar won support of people by demagoguery and was voted an unlimited command in Spain. See also Nepos, *Hamilcar* 3.

24 Appian, *The Wars in Spain.* 5.

25 This seems to be the implication of Polybius' brief account, 2. 1. 5.

26 Contrast Picard & Picard (1987), pp. 209–29, with S. Lancel, *Carthage* (Oxford, 1995), pp. 376–80.

27 Embassy to Hamilcar, Dio 12. 48; Hasdrubal, Polybius 2. 13. 3–7, 3. 27. 9–10. For the presence of Roman traders see Dyson (1985), p. 180.

28 For an account of the campaigns in Cisalpine Gaul see Dyson (1985), pp. 26–34. Polybius' account of the Gallic Wars, 2. 14. 1–35. 10; Telamon, 2. 26. 1–31. 7; Flaminius' land bill, 2. 21. 7–9, his campaign 32. 1–33. 9.

29 Plutarch, Marcellus 6–8.

Chapter 6

1 Trade between Rome and Carthage, see R. Palmer, *Rome and Carthage at Peace* (1997), pp. 15–52. Guest friendship, Livy 27. 16. 5, 33. 45. 6.

2 Physical boundaries were imposed on both sides in the earlier treaties between Rome and Carthage, Polybius 3. 22. 4–7, 24. 4, 11; between Rome and Tarentum, Appian *Samnite History* 7, 79, between Carthage and Cyrene, Sallust *Bellum Jugurthinum* 2–10.

3 Treaty with Saguntum, Polybius 3. 30. 1–2; arbitration in Saguntum's internal dispute, 3. 15. 7.

4 Polybius 3.15.1–13, 17.1–11, Livy 21. 6.1–9. 2, 12.1–15. 2; Hannibal's wound, 21.7. 10.

5 The embassy, Polybius 3. 20. 6–21. 8, 33. 1–4, Livy 21. 18. 1–19. 5. On Fabius Buteo see Broughton, *The Magistrates of the Roman Republic* no. 116. F. Walbank, *A Historical Commentary on Polybius* 1 (Oxford, 1970), p. 334 on the probability of a conditional vote for war before the ambassadors left Rome. The brusqueness of Roman diplomacy, e.g. with Queen Teuta in 229, Polybius 2. 8. 6–13, with Antiochus IV in 168, Livy 45. 12.

6 Polybius 3. 9. 6–12. 7.

7 Polybius 3. 11. 5–8.

8 Polybius 3. 11. 5–8, Livy 21. 1. 4–5, Nepos, *Hannibal* 1. 2–6.

9 The best and most thorough recent discussion of the causes of the war is J. Rich, 'The origins of the Second Punic War', in T. Cornell, B. Rankov & P. Sabin (edd.), *The Second Punic War: A Reappraisal* (London, 1996), pp. 1–37. Rich cites around thirty major contributions on the subject.

10 See Rich (1996), pp. 14–18, esp. p. 17. Hamilcar's recruitment of captured enemy warriors, *Diodorus Siculus* 25. 10. 1; his response to the Roman envoys, Dio 12. 48.

11 On Hannibal's ambition see Livy 21. 5. 1–2.

12 See Rich (1996), p. 30.

13 On the Senate's plans and dispositions for 218, see Polybius 3. 40. 1–2, 41. 2, Livy 21. 17. 1–9.

14 Polybius 3. 40. 3–13, Livy 21. 25. 1–14.

15 Polybius 3. 40. 14, 41. 1–3, Livy 21. 26. 1–2.

16 For an incisive discussion of the naval situation see B. Rankov, 'The Second Punic War at Sea', in Cornell, Rankov and Sabin (1996), pp. 49–57, esp. pp. 52–4.

17 Polybius 3. 33. 17–18.

18 Polybius 3. 35. 1; the elephants, Appian, *The Hannibalic War* 1. 4.

19 A. D. Domínguez-Monedero, 'La campaña de Anibal contra los Vacceos, sus objectivos y su relación con el initio de la segunda guerra púnica', *Latomus* 45 (1986), pp. 241–58.

20 Livy 21. 21. 9.

21 Livy 22. 58. 3.

22 For the view that Hannibal's strategy was to break up Rome's confederation of allies, see J. Lazenby, 'Was Maharbal right?', in Cornell, Rankov & Sabin (1996), pp. 39–48, and J. Lazenby, *Hannibal's War* (Warminster, 1978), pp. 29–32, 85–6, 88–9.

23 Livy records the tradition that Hasdrubal had the young Hannibal summoned to Spain, implying that he had returned to Carthage at some earlier time. He implies that there were similar rumours about an unnatural relationship between Hannibal and Hasdrubal to the ones that had circulated concerning the latter and Hamilcar, Livy 21. 3. 1–6, cf. Nepos, *Hamilcar* 3. 1–2.

24 Polybius 3. 69. 12–13, 9. 22. 1–26, Livy 21. 4. 1–8.

25 Hannibal Monomachus, Polybius 9. 24. 4–8; Hannibal Barca's avarice, 9. 25. 1–26. 11.

26 Livy 21. 38. 6–9. For studies of the route see P. Connolly, *Greece and Rome at War* (London, 1981), pp. 153–66, Lazenby (1978), pp. 34–48, 275–7, S. Lancel, *Hannibal* (Oxford, 1998), pp. 57–80, and D. Proctor, *Hannibal's March in History* (Oxford, 1971) as a small sample of the existing literature.

27 Polybius 3. 35. 1–8, Livy 21. 22. 5–24. 1; distance to the Ebro, Polybius 3. 39. 6; crossing the Ebro in three columns, Livy 21. 23. 1.

28 Caven (1980), pp. 98–101.

29 Polybius 3. 35. 6–8, Livy 21. 23. 1–6; the Carpetani, Livy 21. 23. 4.

30 Polybius 3. 42. 1–4, Livy 21. 24. 2–5, 26. 6–27. 1. Importance of boundaries in tribal warfare, see Caesar, *Bellum Gallicum* 2. 17, 6. 23.

31 Polybius 3. 42. 5–43. 12, Livy 21. 27. 2–28. 4.

32 Polybius 3. 44. 4, 45. 6–12, Livy 21. 28. 5–12, also mentions an alternative version.

33 Polybius 3. 44. 3–13, Livy 21. 29. 1, 30. 1–31. 1.

34 Polybius 3. 41. 4–9, Livy 21. 26. 3–5.

35 Polybius 3. 45. 1–5, Livy 21. 29. 1–7.

36 See M. Austin and B. Rankov, *Exploratio* (London, 1995), esp. pp. 12–86 .

37 Polybius 3. 45. 5, 47. 1–5, Livy 21. 30. 1–31. 5.

38 Polybius 3. 49. 5–13, Livy 21. 31. 1–12.

39 Polybius 3. 50. 1–51. 13, Livy 21. 32. 6–33. 11.

40 Polybius 3. 52. 1–53. 10, Livy 21. 34. 1–35. 1.

41 Polybius 3. 54. 5–55. 9, Livy 21. 36. 1–37. 6; the story of the vinegar, 21. 37. 2–3; importance of wide-ranging knowledge for a commander, Polybius 9. 12. 1–20. 10; examples of ingenuity by other generals, e.g. Josephus, *Bellum Judaicum* 3. 271–81.

42 Times for the journey, Polybius 3. 56. 3. Earlier he mentions that it took nine days to reach the summit of the first pass, 3. 53. 9. Fifteen days certainly seems inadequate considering the number of days' rest Polybius mentions.

Chapter 7

1 Polybius 3. 56. 4, 3. 60. 5 for the army sizes. For the idea of leaving garrisons in southern France see J. Lazenby, *Hannibal's War* (Warminster, 1978), p. 34, fn. 9, citing G. Picard

& C. Picard *The Life and Death of Carthage* (1968, rev. ed. 1987), pp. 248, 250. Hasdrubal's attempt to march to Italy in 215, Livy 23. 27. 9. In 1812 Napoleon's army suffered huge attritional losses during the initial stages of the invasion of Russia, see D. Chandler, *The Campaigns of Napoleon* (London, 1966), pp. 780, 816.

2 Polybius 3. 60. 8–10. For a discussion of Hannibal's supply problems see J. Shean, 'Hannibal's mules: the logistical limitations of Hannibal's army and the battle of Cannae, 216 BC', *Historia* 45 (1996), pp. 159–187.

3 Polybius 3. 61. 1–12, Livy 21. 39. 3–10.

4 On the speeches and gladiatorial fight see Polybius 3., Livy 21. 40. 1–44. 9; the promise of citizenship 21. 45. 5–6. For a discussion of the single combats see L. Rawlings, 'Warriors in a soldier's war', in Cornell, Rankov & Sabin (1996), pp. 81–95, esp. p. 89.

5 Fluidity of cavalry combat, see Dio 56. 32, Tacitus *Annals* 6. 35. On the four-horned saddle see P. Connolly, 'The Roman Saddle', in M. Dawson (ed.), *Roman Military Equipment: The Accoutrements of War*, BAR 336 (Oxford, 1987), pp. 7–27.

6 Accounts of Ticinus see Polybius 3. 64. 1–65. 11 & 10. 3. 3–6, Livy 21. 45. 1–46. 10.

7 Polybius 3. 66. 1–8, Livy 21. 47. 1–8.

8 Polybius 3. 66. 9–68. 8, Livy 21. 48. 1–8.

9 Polybius 3. 68. 9–15, Livy 21. 51. 5–7. For a discussion see Lazenby (1978), pp. 55–6.

10 Polybius 3. 69. 1–14; his praise of Hannibal's decision not to fight, 69. 12–13; Livy 21. 48. 9–10, 52. 1–11.

11 Polybius 3. 70. 1–12, Livy 21. 53. 1–11.

12 C. Duffy, *Austerlitz* (London, 1977), p. 72.

13 Accounts of Trebia, see Polybius 3. 71. 1–74. 11; numbers 72. 2, 7–8, 11–13; elephants 72. 9, 74. 2. Livy 21. 54. 1–56. 8; numbers 55. 2–4; elephants 55. 2, 7–56. 1. Polybius 3. 74. 1 implies that Mago's troops were mainly Numidians. For a discussion see Lazenby (1978), pp. 55–58, P. Connolly, *Greece and Rome at War* (London, 1981), pp. 168–171, J. Kromayer & G. Veith, *Antike Schlachtfelder in Italien und Afrika* (Berlin, 1912), III. 1, pp. 47–99, and H. Delbrück (trans. W. Renfroe), *History of the Art of War. Volume 1: Warfare in Antiquity* (Nebraska, 1975), pp. 333–4.

14 This was the number of horsemen commanded by Gaius Centenius, Polybius 3. 86. 3, Livy 22. 8. 1.

15 The probably fictitious battle, Livy 21. 59. 1–9; Hannibal's disguises, Polybius 3. 78. 1–4, Livy 22. 1. 3.

16 Dispositions for the year, Polybius 3. 80. 1, 86. 1, Livy 22. 2. 1, 4.

17 On Flaminius' character, see Polybius 3. 80. 3–82. 8, Livy 21. 63. 1–15, 22. 3. 3–14.

18 Livy 21. 63. 5.

19 N. Rosenstein, *Imperatores Victi* (Berkeley, 1990), pp. 54–91.

20 Polybius 3. 78. 5–79. 12, Livy 22. 2. 1–3. 1. For the Porretta Pass see Lazenby (1978), pp. 60–61, fn. 20; for the Colline Pass see B. Caven, *The Punic Wars* (London, 1980), p. 119. Cato claimed that the bravest elephant in Hannibal's army was called the Syrian (Surus), Pliny *Natural History* 8. 5. 11.

21 The problem of supply, see Shean (1996), pp. 159–87, esp. 175–85.

22 Polybius 3. 80. 1–2, 82. 1–8, Livy 22. 3. 7–14.

23 On the possible battle sites see Lazenby (1978), pp. 62–4, Connolly (1981), pp. 172–5, and Kromayer & Veith (1912), pp. 148–93.

24 Livy 35. 4 mentions that in 193, the consul Merula took the precaution of sending out scouts even though he was marching in daylight, which implies that the practice was not normal.

25 Accounts of Trasimene, see Polybius 3. 9–85. 5, Livy 22. 4. 1–7. 5. Ovid mentions the date of the battle as *dies nefas, Fasti* 6. 767–8. Silius Italicus says that Flaminius wore a *crine Suevo* – Suebic scalp, clearly intended to mean Gallic, although the Suebi were a German people – as a crest, Silius Italicus, *Punica* 5. 132. For a discussion of the different versions of Flaminius' death see Rosenstein (1990), pp. 115–17.

26 Polybius 3. 86. 1–5, Livy 22. 8. 1.

27 Livy 22. 7. 6–14, 8. 2–4.

28 Polybius 3. 87. 6–9, Livy 22. 8. 5–7.

29 Plutarch, *Fabius Maximus* 1–4.

30 Livy 22. 9. 7–10. 10.

31 Livy 22.11.1–9; on the request to be allowed to ride a horse, Plutarch, *Fabius Maximus* 4.

32 Polybius 3. 86. 8–87. 5, Livy 22. 9. 1–5.

33 Polybius 3. 88. 1–90. 6, Livy 22. 12. 1–12. See P. Erdkamp, 'Polybius, Livy and the Fabian Strategy', *Ancient Society* 23 (1992), pp. 127–47, which argues convincingly that Livy grossly exaggerated the impact of Fabius' attempts to deprive Hannibal of food. For a discussion of the armies' possible routes during this campaign see Lazenby (1978), pp. 66–71, Connolly (1981), pp. 177–82. Plutarch mentions the military slang, 'kicking in the stomach', in *Lucullus* 11. 1.

34 Polybius 3. 90. 7–92. 10, Livy 22. 13. 1–15. 1.

35 Polybius 3. 93. 1–94. 6, Livy 22. 15. 2–18.

36 Fabius' nickname, Plutarch, *Fabius Maximus* 5; the election of Minucius and his subsequent defeat, Polybius 3. 100. 1–105. 11, Livy 22. 18. 5–10, 23. 1–30. 10.

Chapter 8

1 W. Heckmann, *Rommel's War in Africa* (London, 1981), p. 113; A. Beevor, *Stalingrad* (London, 1998), p. 297.

2 Polybius 3. 107. 8–15, Livy 22. 35. 1–36. 5. For modern views see J. Lazenby, *Hannibal's War* (Warminster, 1978), pp. 75–6, and F. Walbank, *A Historical Commentary on Polybius* 1 (Oxford, 1970), pp. 439–40, who support Polybius' figures; B. Caven, *The Punic Wars* (London, 1980), pp. 134–41, and P. Brunt, *Italian Manpower* (Oxford, 1971), p. 419 are amongst those who reject them.

3 Livy's claims of Varro's radical politics, 22. 25. 18–19, 34. 2–35. 4, 38. 6. See also R. Feig Vishnia, *State, Society and Popular Leaders in Mid Republican Rome 241–167 BC* (London, 1995), pp. 57–8.

4 Paullus' speech, Polybius 3. 108. 1–13; mood of the allies, Polybius 3. 107. 6; Livy's improbable version of a conversation between Fabius Maximus and Paullus, Livy 22. 38. 6–40. 4.

5 Polybius 3. 107. 1–7.

6 The Roman approach to Cannae, 3. 110. 1; Livy's version, 22. 40. 5–44. 1. For the battle site see Lazenby (1978), pp. 77–8, P. Connolly, *Greece and Rome at War* (London, 1981), p. 184, H. Delbrück (trans. W. Renfroe), *History of the Art of War. Volume 1: Warfare in Antiquity* (Nebraska, 1975), pp. 324–5 , and for a contrasting view see J. Kromayer & G. Veith, *Antike Schlachtfelder* (Berlin, 1903–31) III. 1, pp. 278–388, who place the battle south of the river, but a little nearer to the coast.

7 Polybius 3. 110. 2–11, Livy 22. 44. 1–3.

8 Near desertion of the Spanish, Livy 22. 40. 7–8, but see P. Erdkamp, 'Polybius, Livy and the Fabian Strategy', *Ancient Society* 23 (1992), pp. 127–47. For the conversation with Gisgo see Plutarch, *Fabius Maximus* 15. 2–3.

9 Polybius 3. 112. 1–5, Livy 22. 44. 4–45. 4. As Connolly (1981), p. 184 points out, the spur on which San Ferdinando di Púglia now lies stands out as the most obvious spot for Hannibal's camp.

10 Livy 22. 45. 5 claims that Varro did not consult Paullus. For the suggestion that Paullus was in fact in command see Connolly (1981), pp. 184–6.

11 At Metaurus, the consul G. Claudius Nero controlled the right, the praetor L. Porcius Licinus the centre and the other consul M. Livius Drusus Salinator the left, in spite of the fact that the battle was fought under his command, Livy 27. 98.

12 For the Roman deployment see Polybius 3. 113. 1–5, Livy 45. 5–8.

13 Aemilius Paullus sent the *triarii* to protect the baggage and begin construction of a camp and kept the rest of the army to cover them before Pydna, Livy 44. 37, and Merula ordered his *triarii* to guard the baggage when he encountered the Boii on the march in 193 BC, Livy 35. 4. However, in each case the commander had not planned to fight a battle. Lazenby (1978), p. 79 suggests that the 10,000 men consisted of one legion and its *ala*.

14 Hannibal's deployment see Polybius 3. 113. 6–114. 8, Livy 22. 46. 1–7.

15 Polybius 3. 115. 1–4, Livy 22. 47. 1–3; Paullus wounded, Livy 49. 1.

16 Livy 22. 47. 5.

17 Polybius 3. 115. 5–116. 4, Livy 22. 47. 4–10. For the use of Corps and Division sized columns by Napoleon's army and their inherent problems see J. Elting, *Swords Around a Throne* (London, 1988), pp. 536–7.

18 Livy claims that 500 Numidians pretended to desert, 22. 48. 2–4, but in Appian's version it is 500 Celtiberians who do so, *The Hannibalic War* 22.

19 Polybius 116. 5–8, Livy 22. 48. 1–6.

20 Polybius 116. 9–117. 12, Livy 22. 49. 1–18. For a discussion of the figures see Lazenby (1978), pp. 84–5. For a vivid attempt at depicting the final stages of the battle see V. Hanson, 'Cannae', in R. Cowley (ed.) *Experience of War* (1992). See also P. Sabin, 'The Mechanics of Battle in the Second Punic War', in Cornell, Rankov & Sabin (edd.), *The Second Punic War* (1996), pp. 59–79, esp. 67, which discusses the proportion of casualties usually suffered by each side in the battles of this period.

21 M. Middlebrook, *The First Day of the Somme* (1971), pp. 262–4.

22 Livy 22. 51. 5–9.

23 Polybius 3. 117. 4–5.

24 Livy 22. 52. 4, 7, 53. 1–54. 6.

25 Livy 22. 51. 1–4.

26 Field Marshal Sir Bernard Mongomery, *A History of Warfare* (London, 1968), p. 97. For the argument against Livy's judgement see Lazenby (1978), pp. 85–6 and 'Was Hannibal Right?', in T. Cornell, B. Rankov, and P. Sabin (edd.) *The Second Punic War: A Reappraisal*, British Institute of Classical Studies Supplement 67 (London, 1996), 39–48. The view is not new; Delbrück (1975), pp. 336–44 came to much the same conclusion.

27 Livy 22. 58. 1–9.

28 Revival of exchange system from First Punic War, Livy 22. 23. 6–8, Plutarch, *Fabius Maximus* 7; for Cincius Alimentus, Livy 21. 38. 3.

29 Hannibal fighting for honour and power, Livy 22. 58. 3.

30 Polybius 6. 58. 1–13, Livy 22. 58. 9–61. 10.

31 Postumius' disaster, Polybius 3. 118. 6, Livy 23. 24. 6–13.

32 Livy 22. 57. 10–12, 23. 14. 1–4.

33 N. Rosenstein, *Imperatores Victi* (Berkeley, 1990), pp. 139–40, Livy 22. 61. 14–5.

34 Livy 22. 56. 4–5, 57. 2–9, cf. Polybius 6. 56. 6–12.

35 Livy 26. 11. 6.

Chapter 9

1 For the desire of the poorer classes for change and the general loyalty of the aristocracies to Rome see Livy 23. 14. 7–12, 24. 13. 8, and esp. 24. 2. 8–11; examples of aristocratic leaders forcing a defection, 23. 30. 8, 24. 47. 6, and attempting to do so, 24. 13; aristocratic leaders claiming popular support, 24. 13. 2–3.

2 Defections, noting the exceptions in each area, Livy 22. 61. 11–13. Roman garrisons in Etruria, Livy 23. 5. 4, replaced 26. 28. 4–6; trouble anticipated at Arretium, 27. 21. 6–7, 22. 5.

3 The Bruttians' disappointment following their attack on Rhegium, Livy 24. 2. 1–11; appeals for protection from Roman raids, Livy 23. 42. 3 by Samnites, and 24. 12. 1–2, 25. 15. 1–3, 22. 15–16 by Campanians.

4 The deputation to Varro, Livy 23. 4. 1–6. 8; rebellion and the treaty with Hannibal, 23. 7. 1–3; Hannibal's occupation and the arrest of Decius Magius, 23. 7. 4–10. 13. Zonaras 9. 2. blames Hannibal for the bath house massacre.

5 Attempts at Naples, Livy 23. 1. 5–10, 14. 5, 15. 1–6; Nola, 23. 15. 7–17. 1.

6 Livy 23. 17. 7–18. 9, 19. 1–20. 3.

7 Battle of River Calor, Livy 24. 15. 1–16. 5; Beneventum 212, 25. 13. 3–14. 14; Bomilcar, Livy 23. 41. 10–12.

8 On legionary numbers in general see P. Brunt, *Italian Manpower* (Oxford, 1971), pp. 416–22. On the legions in 215–214 see J. Lazenby, *Hannibal's War* (Warminster, 1978), p. 95.

9 Livy 25. 20. 4.

10 Elections for 215, Livy 23. 24. 1–3, 31. 7–9, 12–14; for 214, 24. 7. 10–9. 3.

11 Capture of Casilinum, Livy 24. 19. 1–11; Arpi, 24. 45. 1–47. 11; desertions 23, 46. 6–7, 24. 47. 8, 11; co-operation between the consuls, 23. 39. 5–8, 24. 19. 3–9.

12 Lucius Bantius, Livy 23. 15. 7–16. 1, Plutarch *Marcellus* 10, cf. Plutarch *Fabius Maximus* 20.

13 Livy 23. 11. 7–13. 8.

14 Livy 24. 13. 1–5, 20. 9–15.

15 Polybius 8. 24. 125. 11, Livy 25. 7. 10–1(8)8. 10.

16 Polybius 8. 24. 4–34. 13, Livy 25. 8. 1–11. 20. Livy was uncertain whether to date this episode to 213 or 212, but the latter seems most likely, see Lazenby (1978), p. 110.

17 For a discussion of damage to crops, see V. Hanson, *Warfare and Agriculture in Classical Greece* (Berkeley, 1998), pp. 16, 30, 34–5, 50–52, 58–60, 106, 212–13, 219.

18 Earlier fighting around Tarentum, Livy 23. 46. 9–11, 25. 15. 1–3, 19. 1–20. 5, 26. 4. 1–10; single combats, 23. 46. 12–17. 8, 25. 18. 4–15.

19 Livy 26. 1. 2, defection of Campanians, 24. 47. 12–13.

20 Livy 26. 4. 3–10, see M. Samuels, 'The Reality of Cannae', *Militärgeschichtliche Mitteilungen* 47 (1990), pp. 7–29, esp. 11–15, who argues unconvincingly for a major reform.

21 Polybius 9. 3. 1–7. 10, Livy 26. 5. 1–6. 13.

22 Livy 26. 6. 14–17, 12. 1–16. 13.

23 Livy 27. 15. 4–16. 9, Plutarch *Fabius Maximus* 21, including the tradition involving Fabius' former mistress.

24 Livy 27. 16. 10–16.

25 Betrayal of Salapia, Livy 26. 38. 11–14; 1st Herdonea, Livy 25. 21. 1–10; 2nd Herdonea, 27. 1. 3–15; other battles employing whole legions in reserve, 27. 2. 1–12, 12. 7–17, 13. 11–14. 15. A clear example of an army forming in more than one set of *triplex acies* straight from the line of march came in 193, Livy 35. 4–5. At Emporion in 195 Cato kept an entire legion in reserve, but may have significantly outnumbered the enemy, Livy 34. 15. 3.

26 Trial of Fulvius, N. Rosenstein, *Imperatores Victi* (Berkeley, 1990), pp. 106–8, 120, 146, 188–9 and Livy 26. 2. 7–3. 12; death of Marcellus and Crispinus, Livy 27. 26. 7–27. 14, cf. Plutarch, *Marcellus* 29–30; attempt on Salapia, Livy 27. 28. 1–13.

27 Surrender of Lucanians and others, Livy 27. 15. 2–3; for African deserters fighting for the Romans in Spain see 28. 20. 1.

28 Scandal involving army contractors, Livy 25. 3. 8–4. 11; censors reduce equestrians, 27. 11. 15–16; Latin colonies, 27. 9. 7–10. 10.

29 Planned expedition in 216, Livy 23. 27. 9–12; actual march in 208, 27. 36. 1–4.

30 Livy 27. 39. 1–14, 43. 1–3; Licinus' legions under strength, 27. 39. 2.

31 Livy 27. 43. 4–46. 5.

32 Appian, *The Hannibalic War* 52.

33 Polybius 11. 1. 1–2. 11, Livy 27. 46. 6–49. 9; for the date of the battle and the tradition that Hasdrubal committed suicide, see Ovid, *Fasti* 6. 770; location of the battlefield see J. Kromayer and G. Veith, *Antike Schlactfelder in Italien und Afrika* (Berlin, 1913), III. 1, pp. 424–94; for one view of the improvements in Roman armies see J-P. Brisson, 'Les Mutations de la Seconde Guerre Punique', in J-P. Brisson, *Problèmes de la Guerre à Rome* (Paris, 1969), pp. 33–59.

34 Thanksgiving, Livy 27. 51. 8; the triumph, 28. 9. 2–20.

35 Livy 28. 46. 7–13, 29. 4. 6, 30. 18. 1–19. 6.

36 Hannibal's recall, Livy 30. 19. 12–20. 9.

Chapter 10

1 On Spain in general see S. Dyson, *The Creation of the Roman Frontier* (Princeton, 1985), pp. 174–84.

2 Polybius 3. 76. 1–13, Livy 21. 50. 1–51. 11. Polybius 3. 76. 8–9 claims that Hasdrubal knew of Hanno's defeat before he attacked, but Livy denies this, 21. 51. 1. Livy's account of the fighting after this is normally rejected under the assumption that he has mistaken a different version of the same events for later operations.

3 Polybius 3. 95. 2–96. 6, Livy 22. 19. 1–20. 3; the later raiding, Livy 22. 20. 4–21. 8.

4 Polybius 3. 97. 1–99. 9.

5 Livy 23. 26. 1–29. 17. For comparisons between Ibera and Cannae see J. Lazenby, *Hannibal's War* (Warminster, 1978) pp. 128–9, and B. Caven, *The Punic Wars* (London, 1980), pp. 140, 180.

6 Lazenby (1978), p. 129.

7 The Romans later tried to take advantage of this tendency amongst the Celtiberians, Livy 34. 19. 2–8.

8 Livy 25. 32. 1–39. 18; Marcius' rank see Cicero, *pro Balbo* 34, Valerius Maximus 2. 7. 15.

9 For military intelligence in the Republican period see M. Austin & B. Rankov, *Exploratio* (London, 1995), pp. 18–108.

10 Polybius 5. 108. 1–110. 11.

11 The treaty, Polybius 7. 9. 1–17; the negotiations and the capture of the envoys, Livy 23. 33. 1–24. 9.

12 Livy 23. 38. 8–10, 48. 3, 24. 10. 4, 40. 1–17.

13 *Supplementum Epigraphicum Graecum* 13. 382, Livy 26. 24. 1–25. 15.

14 For a discussion of the importance of booty see W. Harris, *War and Imperialism in Mid Republican Rome 327–70 BC* (Oxford, 1979), pp. 58–104.

15 For the Aetolians' reluctance to ally with Rome and delay over the treaty's ratification see Lazenby (1978), p. 116.

16 Echinous, Polybius 9. 41. 1–42. 4. For a narrative account with references to the sources see Lazenby (1978), pp. 161–7. For Hellenistic armies see F. Adcock, *The Greek and Macedonian Art of War* (Berkeley, 1962) and B. Bar Kochva, *The Seleucid Army* (Cambridge, 1976).

17 Attempted mediation, Livy 27. 30. 4–7; Mantineia, Polybius 11. 11. 1–18. 10; the Aetolians conclude peace with Philip V, Livy 29. 12. 1–4.

18 Livy 29. 12. 2–16.

19 Sicily, Livy 21. 49. 1–51. 4; Sardinia, Livy 23. 9–12, 34. 10–17, 40. 1–41. 9. For a discussion see S. Dyson, *The Creation of the Roman Frontier* (Princeton, 1985), pp. 251–4.

20 Polybius 7. 2. 1–8. 9, Livy 24. 4. 1–7. 9. Hiero sends aid, Polybius 3. 75. 7–8.

21 Livy 24. 27. 6–33. 8.

22 Polybius 8. 3. 1–7. 12, Livy 24. 33. 9–34. 16, Plutarch *Marcellus* 14–17.

23 Livy 24. 35. 1–39. 13.

24 Polybius 8. 37. 1–13, Livy 25. 23. 1–25. 13, Plutarch *Marcellus* 18.

25 Livy 25. 26. 1–15, 25. 27. 2–13.

26 Livy 25. 27. 6–7, 28. 1–31. 11, Plutarch *Marcellus* 19–20.

27 Livy 25. 40. 1–41. 7; Marcellus' ovation 26. 21. 1–13, Plutarch *Marcellus* 21–22.

28 Punic reinforcements, see Livy 26. 21. 14–17; Laevinus, Livy 26. 40. 1–15. Muttines appears on a later inscription from Delphi as Marcus Valerius Muttines along with his four sons, *Inscriptiones Graecae* 585, and he and one of the sons are mentioned as still serving with the army in 188 BC by Livy 38. 41. 12; Moericus, 26. 21. 10–13.

29 Livy 26. 40. 15–16

Chapter 11

1 Marcius as *propraetor senatui*, Livy 26. 2. 1–6; Nero, 26. 17. 1–2, Appian *The Wars in Spain*. 17; his campaign, Livy 26. 17. 2–16.

2 Scipio's appointment to the Spanish command, Livy 26. 18. 1–19. 9, and H. Scullard, *Scipio Africanus: Soldier and Politician* (London, 1970), p. 31; for interpretations based on factional politics see J. Lazenby, *Hannibal's War* (Warminster, 1978), p. 133 and B. Caven, *The Punic Wars* (London, 1980), pp. 191–2.

3 Scipio's character, Polybius 10. 2. 1–5. 10, and Scullard (1970), pp. 18–23, 27–32. On the virtues attributed to Scipio and later Roman commanders see S. Weinstock, *Divus Julius* (Oxford, 1971), *passim*, esp. pp. 35–6, 113, 136, 228, 224.

4 Scipio's forces, Polybius 10. 6. 7, 9. 6, Livy 26. 19. 10; for Punic dispositions contrast Polybius 10. 7. 5.

5 Seven-day march, Polybius 10. 9. 7; Scipio's speech, Polybius 10. 11. 5–8, Livy 26. 43. 2–8.

6 Polybius 10. 9. 8–10. 13, 12. 1–11, Livy 26. 44. 1–4.

7 Proximity of Punic armies, Polybius 10. 7. 5; Scipio's direction of the assault, Polybius 10. 13. 1–5.

8 On the difficulty of renewing an assault after a failure see Josephus, *Bellum Judaicum* 3. 280–88, 4. 30–53, 62–83, 6. 29–67, 131–148.

9 Polybius 10. 13. 6–15. 7, Livy 26. 44. 5–46. 10. See also A. Ribera, I Lacomba con M. Calvo Galvez, 'La primera evidencia arqueológica de la destrucción de Valentia por Pompeyo', *Journal of Roman Archaeology* 8 (1995), pp. 19–40 for evidence of Roman atrocities, although in this case committed during a civil war.

10 Polybius 10. 15. 8–17. 16, Livy 26. 47. 1–49. 10. For discussion of Roman plundering see A. Ziolkowski '*Urbs direpta*, or how the Romans sacked cities', in J. Rich and M. Shipley, *War and Society in the Roman World* (London, 1993), pp. 69–91, although not all his conclusions have been generally accepted.

11 E.g. Lazenby (1978), pp. 136–7, F. Walbank, *A Historical Commentary on Polybius* 2 (Oxford, 1970), pp. 192–6, Scullard (1970), pp. 39–67.

12 Polybius 10. 18. 1–19. 7, Livy 26. 49. 11–50. 14, cf. Plutarch, *Alexander* 21.

13 Polybius 10. 20. 1–8, Livy 26. 51. 3–14.

14 Polybius 10. 38. 7–10.

15 Battle and aftermath, Polybius 10. 39. 1–40. 12, Livy 27. 17. 1–20. 8; the mention of *calones* fighting, 27. 18. 12.

16 The defeat of Hanno, Livy 28. 1. 1–2. 12; the campaign in Baetica, 28. 1. 13–4. 4.

17 Polybius 11. 20. 1–9, Livy 28. 12. 10–13. 5.

18 Polybius 11. 21. 1–6, Livy 28. 13. 6–10.

19 Polybius 11. 21. 7–24. 9, Livy 28. 14. 1–15. 11.

20 For discussion of the location of the battle and Scipio's manoeuvre see Lazenby (1978), pp. 147–9, Walbank 2 (1970), pp. 296–304, and Scullard (1970), pp. 88–92.

21 Livy 28. 15. 12–16. 13.

22 Polybius 11. 25. 1–33. 6, Livy 28. 19. 1–29. 12, 31. 5–35. 12. See also S. Dyson, *The Creation of the Roman Frontier* (Princeton, 1985), pp. 184–7.

23 Polybius 11. 24. 1–4, Livy 28. 16. 11–12, 16. 14–18. 12, 35. 1–13.

Chapter 12

1 Livy 28. 38. 6–12, 40. 1–45. 10, Plutarch *Fabius Maximus* 25–26; rumour that Scipio would bring a bill before the People, 28. 45. 1.

2 Volunteers and contributions from allied communities, Livy 28. 45. 13–46. 1; size of army taken to Africa, 29. 25. 1–4. J. Lazenby, *Hannibal's War* (Warminster, 1978), p. 203 is reluctant to accept the large size of the legions claimed by Livy, but does not provide convincing arguments to justify his decision.

3 Laelius' expedition, Livy 29. 1. 14, 2. 7–5. 1; intensive training in Sicily, 29. 1. 2–14, 22. 1–5; criticism of Scipio's delay, Lazenby (1978), pp. 195–6; the supply of Scipio's expedition, see J. Roth, *The Logistics of the Roman Army at War* (Brill, 1999), pp. 161, 226.

4 Livy 29. 6. 1–9. 12.

5 Livy 29. 15. 4–21. 13, Plutarch *Cato the Elder* 3; different versions of the fate of Pleminius, Livy 29. 22. 7–10.

6 Livy 29. 24. 10–27. 5.

7 Livy 29. 27. 6–29. 3.

8 Livy 29. 29. 4–33. 10; Syphax's marriage to Sophonisba, 29. 23. 2–10. For a more detailed summary see Lazenby (1978), pp. 198–9, 202.

9 Livy 29. 34. 1–17; Livy's belief that there were two distinct actions involving commanders named Hanno, 29. 35. 1–2, cf. Lazenby (1978), pp. 205–6; Roman plundering 29. 35. 3–5; the parentage of the second Hanno see Livy 29. 34. 1, Dio 17. 65.

10 The siege and arrival of Syphax, Polybius 14. 1. 1–15, Livy 29. 35. 6–15; *castra Cornelia*, see Caesar, *Bellum Civile* 2. 24; the Numidian camp, Livy 30. 3. 1–10; centurions disguised as slaves, 30. 4. 1–3.

11 Polybius 14. 2. 1–6. 5, Livy 30. 4. 4–6. 9.

12 See Lazenby (1978), pp. 207–8, F. Walbank *A Historical Commentary on Polybius* 2 (Oxford, 1970), pp. 427–9.

13 Supplies of clothing, Livy 29. 36. 1–3.

14 Polybius 14. 6. 6–7. 9, Livy 30. 7. 1–13; for the possible locations of the battlefield see Lazenby (1978), pp. 208–9, Walbank 2, p. 447, H. Scullard, *Scipio Africanus: Soldier and Politician* (London, 1970), pp. 127–31.

15 Polybius 14. 8. 1–14, Livy 30. 8. 1–9. 1; the reasons for the Celtiberians' stubbornness, 30. 8. 8; war weariness of Libyan towns, Polybius 14. 9. 4–5.

16 Polybius 14. 9. 1–5, Livy 30. 9. 2; for a discussion of generals' *consilia* in a later period see Goldsworthy (1996), pp. 131–3.

17 Polybius 14. 9. 6–10. 1, Livy 30. 9. 3–9.

18 Polybius 14. 10. 2–12, Livy 30. 9. 10–1. 21; for a discussion see Lazenby (1978), pp. 209–11.

19 Livy 30. 11. 1–15. 14.

20 Livy 30. 16. 3–14.

21 Livy 30. 17. 1–14, 21. 11–23. 8; Polybius 15. 1. 2–4 states that the treaty was ratified by Rome.

22 Livy 30. 24. 5–12, Polybius 15. 1. 1.

23 Polybius 15. 1. 3–2. 15, Livy 30. 25. 1–10.

24 Brutality of the campaign, Polybius 15. 3. 14; the extension of Scipio's command, Livy 30. 1. 10–11; Caepio, 30. 24. 1–4; the consuls of 202, 30. 27. 1–5.

25 Polybius 15. 3. 4–5. 4, 5. 1–8. 14, Livy 30. 29. 1–10, cf. Frontinus, *Strategemata* 1. 1. 3, 6. 2. 1, 2.

26 Location of the battlefield see discussions in Lazenby (1978), p. 218, Walbank 2 (1970), pp. 445–51, Scullard (1970), pp. 142–55, 271–4, and J. Kromayer & G. Veith, *Antike Schlahtfelder in Italien und Afrika* (Berlin, 1912), III. 2 pp. 598–712.

27 Polybius 15. 9. 1–11. 12, Livy 30. 32. 1–33. 11, Appian, *Punic Wars* 40–41; the Macedonian 'legion', Livy 30. 26. 3, 33. 5.

28 Different officers speak to each of the Punic lines, Polybius 15. 11. 4–6, Livy 30. 33. 8–12.

29 Suggestion that Hannibal ordered his cavalry to flee and draw the Romans into pursuit, Lazenby (1978), p. 223.

30 Problematic passage in Polybius, 15. 13. 1; quotation of Homer, *Iliad* 4. 437, Polybius 15. 12. 9; description of Romans banging weapons against shields, 15. 12. 8.

31 Repeated charges, Livy 30. 34. 2; on the offensive use of shield see Livy 30. 34. 3, cf. Plutarch, *Caesar* 16, Tacitus, *Annals* 14. 36–7, *Agricola* 36; for the size and weight of Republican shields see M. Bishop & J. Coulston, *Roman Military Equipment* (London, 1993), pp. 58–9, P. Connolly, *Greece and Rome at War* (London, 1981), p. 131. Lazenby (1978), p. 224, and Walbank 2 (1970), p. 469 claim that the *principes* were not committed, but Polybius' text is ambiguous and their arguments rely on supposition.

32 The veterans' refusal to let fugitives into their ranks, Polybius 15. 13. 9–10.

33 Accounts of the battle, Polybius 15. 12. 1–16. 6, Livy 30. 33. 12–35. 11. Little or no useful detail is included in the heroic narrative of Appian, *Punic Wars* 40–47, or the brief account in Zonaras 9. 14. Appian gives Roman casualties as 2,500 plus more of Masinissa's men, *Punic Wars* 48.

34 Livy 30. 36. 1–11; the consul in 201, 30. 40. 7–41. 1; Scipio's *consilium* considers the destruction of Carthage, Livy 30. 36. 10–11.

35 Polybius 15. 18. 1–8, Livy 30. 37. 1–6.

36 Polybius 15. 19. 1–9, Livy 30. 37. 7–38. 5; Appian *Punic Wars* 54.

Chapter 13

1 Counting as pitched battles, Trebia, Trasimene, Cannae, Ibera, the River Calor, First and Second Herdonea, Baecula, Metaurus, Ilipa, the defeat of Mago, the Great Plains, and Zama.

2 On foraging and raiding see J. Roth, *The Logistics of the Roman Army at War* (Brill, 1999), pp. 117–55, 286–92; for a detailed discussion of raiding and crop destruction in Greek warfare see V. D. Hanson, *Warfare and agriculture in Classical Greece*, rev. ed. (California, 1998).

3 Role of sieges in propaganda, see J. Keegan, *A History of Warfare* (London, 1993), pp. 151–2.

4 For views on Hannibal's strategy see B. Caven, *The Punic Wars* (London, 1980), p. 141, J. F. Lazenby *Hannibal's War* (Warminster, 1978), pp. 85–6 and 'Was Maharbal Right?', in T. Cornell, B. Rankov and P. Sabin (edd.) *The Second Punic War: A Reappraisal*, British Institute of Classical Studies Supplement 67 (London, 1996), pp. 39–48, H. Delbrück *Warfare in Antiquity*, (trans. by W. J. Renfroe: Lincoln and New York, 1975), pp. 336–44, B. D. Hoyos 'Hannibal: What kind of genius?', *Greece and Rome* 30 (1983), pp.171–80, esp. pp.177–8, and S. Lancel, *Hannibal* (Oxford, 1997), pp. 109–11.

5 See S. Dyson, *The Creation of the Roman Frontier* (Princeton, 1985), pp. 186–98.

6 Dyson (1985), pp. 35–86, 87–125.

7 Livy 31. 1. 6–2. 4, 5. 16. 1. For discussion of other motives for the war, see F. Walbank, 'Polybius and Rome's Eastern Policy', *Journal of Roman Studies* 53 (1963) 1–13 (= *Collected Papers* (1988)), P. Derow, 'Polybius, Rome and the East', *JRS* 69 (1979) 1–15, Harris (1978), pp. 212–18.

8 Plutarch, *Aemilius Paullus* 19; for Hellenistic armies see also B. Bar Kochva, *The Seleucid Army* (Cambridge, 1976).

9 Recruitment of veterans from Scipio's army in 200, Livy 31. 14. 1–2.

10 Cynoscephalae, Polybius 18. 19. 1–33. 7, Livy 33. 6. 1–10. 10; Magnesia, Livy 38. 37–44, Appian, *Syrian Wars*, 30–36, Bar Kochva (1976), pp. 163–73; Pydna, Livy 44. 40–42, Plutarch, *Aemilius Paullus* 18–22.

11 Polybius 18. 44. 1–45. 12, Livy 33. 30. 1–11; concerns over discipline were reflected in Paullus' careful training of the army in Macedonia, Livy 44. 33–4, 36–40; the slaves, Plutarch, *Flamininus* 13.

12 Livy 37. 45.

13 R. Kallett-Marx, *Hegemony to Empire* (California, 1995), pp. 11–96.

14 For an introduction to this period see M. Crawford, *The Roman Republic* (London, 1978), pp. 49–83.

15 For Manlius Vulso see Livy 38. 44–50.

16 H. Scullard, *Scipio Africanus: Soldier and Politician* (London, 1970), pp. 210–44.

17 For the trial of the Scipiones see Livy 38. 50–56.

18 For Cato's career in general see A. E. Astin, *Cato the Censor* (Oxford, 1978); for Surus see Pliny *Natural History* 8. 5. 11.

19 For the black stone see Livy 29. 10. 4–11. 8, 29. 14. 5–14. The suppression of the Bacchic rites see Livy 39. 8–19, *Inscriptiones Latinae Selectae* 18 = *Corpus Inscriptionum Latinarum* 1. 2. 581.

20 Famously when Gaius Popilius Laenas browbeat Antiochus IV into submission, Livy 45. 12. On the growth of latifundia see K. Hopkins, *Conquerors and Slaves* (Cambridge, 1978).

21 For Hannibal's remaining in charge of the army, Nepos, *Hannibal* 7. 1–4, his turning the soldiers to agriculture, Aurelius Victor, *De Caesaribus* 37. 3, S. Lancel, *Carthage* (Oxford, 1995), pp. 277, 402, & (1997), pp. 180–185. His conflicts with other politicians and eventual exile, Livy 33. 45. 6–49. 8.

22 The wealth of Carthage, Lancel (1995), pp. 401–409; Punic spies, Zonaras 8. 11.

23 Livy 39. 51.

24 Livy 35.14.

Chapter 14

1 For criticism of the Roman behaviour see W. Harris, *War and Imperialism in Mid Republican Rome 327–70 BC* (Oxford, 1979), pp. 234–40.

2 Carthaginian politics after 201, Appian, *Punic Wars* 67–8, and G. Picard & C. Picard, *Carthage* (London, 1987), pp. 272–82; Ariston of Tyre, see Livy 34. 61. 1–6, 62. 6–7; Mago the Bruttian, Polybius 36. 5. 1. For a discussion of the motives for Roman warmaking in this period see J. Rich, 'Fear, greed and glory', in Rich & Shipley (edd.) *War* *and Society in the Roman World*, pp. 38–68, esp. p. 64.

3 Appian, *Punic Wars* 69, Plutarch, *Cato the Elder* 26–7, Livy *Per.* 47, and A. Astin, *Cato the Elder* (Oxford, 1978), pp. 125–30.

4 For the wars in Spain see S. Dyson, *The Creation of the Roman Frontier* (Princeton, 1985), pp. 199–218; Scipio Aemilianus in 151, Polybius 35. 4. 1–14; Galba, Appian, *Hispania*. 60.

5 For Flamininus see Polybius 18. 11. 1–12. 5.

6 For Masinissa's character see Polybius 36. 16. 1–12, Appian, *Punic Wars* 106. See Picard & Picard (1987), p. 272 for a useful comparison with the attitudes in modern times of former colonies to their old masters.

7 Appian, *Punic Wars* 67–9; Polybius 31. 21. 1–8 and for a discussion of the dating of this incident and others described by Livy see F. Walbank, *A Historical Commentary on Polybius* 3 (Oxford, 1970), pp. 489–91; see also B. Caven, *The Punic Wars* (1980), pp. 263–70, Picard & Picard (1987), pp. 279–90.

8 Appian, *Punic Wars* 70–73.

9 Appian, *Punic Wars* 74.

10 Polybius 36. 1. 1–6. 6, Appian, *Punic Wars* 75. The 'sixteen' captured from Perseus, Livy 45. 35.

11 Appian, *Punic Wars* 76–90. Cicero noted Censorinus' tendency towards Platonism, Cicero, *Acad.* 2. 32. 102.

12 Appian, *Punic Wars* 91–3.

Chapter 15

1 Appian, *Punic Wars* 95–6; for the archaeological evidence see S. Lancel, *Carthage* (1995), pp. 415–19, and 'L'enceinte périurbaine de Carthage lors de la troisième guerre punique', *Studia Phoenicia*, X: *Punic Wars*, pp. 251–78.

2 The Roman forces, Appian, *Punic Wars* 75, cf. P. Brunt, *Italian Manpower* (Oxford, 1971), p. 428 and Appendix 26, Appian, *Punic Wars* 93.

3 Appian, *Punic Wars* 97.

4 Appian, *Punic Wars* 98; it was common practice in the later Roman army to exploit the rivalry between different units and branches of the service, e.g. Caesar, *Bellum Gallicum* 1. 39–41, Josephus, *Bellum Judaicum* 5. 502–3, Tacitus *Hist.* 3. 24, 5. 16, *Inscriptiones Latinae Selectae* 5795.

5 Scipio's early life and character, Polybius 31. 25. 2–30. 3; actions in 151, Polybius 35. 4. 8–5. 2; in general see A. Astin, *Scipio Aemilianus* (Oxford, 1967), pp. 12–47.

6 Appian, *Punic Wars* 99.

7 Appian, *Punic Wars* 100.

8 Appian, *Punic Wars* 101–09. For the identification of Nepheris with the area of Djebel Zaghouan, see Lancel (1995), p. 419.

9 Appian, *Punic Wars* 110–11.

10 Appian, *Punic Wars* 112.

11 See B. Caven, *The Punic Wars* (London, 1980), pp. 282–3, Astin (1967), pp. 48–60 for first year of the war, 61–9 for Scipio's election.

12 Appian, *Punic Wars* 113–14.

13 Appian, *Punic Wars* 115–18.

14 Appian, *Punic Wars* 119–20; unfair distribution of supplies, Polybius 38. 8. 11.

15 Appian, *Punic Wars* 121–3, Lancel (1995), pp. 422–4.

16 E.g. Antonius Primus in AD 69, Tacitus, *Histories* 3. 17.

17 Appian, *Punic Wars* 124–6.

18 Appian, *Punic Wars* 127–30; for the archaeology of this area see Lancel (1995), pp. 156–72, 425–6.

19 Appian, *Punic Wars* 130–1; Polybius' portrayal of Hasdrubal 38. 7. 1–8. 15.

20 Appian, *Punic Wars* 132–5; on the survival of some remains from Punic Carthage see Lancel (1995), pp. 428–9.

21 Appian, *Punic Wars* 132.

22 For the later career of Scipio Aemilianus see Astin (1967), pp. 80–241; the capture of Numantia, Appian, *The Wars in Spain*. 90–91; rumours concerning his death, see Appian, *Bellum Civile* 1. 19–20, Astin (1967), p. 241.

23 The Elder Pliny rated Caesar as the greatest Roman commander because he had won more battles than anyone else, *Natural History* 7. 91–2, cf. Plutarch *Caesar* 15, Appian, *Bellum Civile* 2. 149–154.

24 Josephus, *Bellum Judaicum* 6. 403–8 for end of siege of Jerusalem.

25 On Roman involvement in Greece and the creation of the province of Macedonia see R. Kallet Marx, *Hegemony to Empire* (California, 1996), pp. 57–96.

Chapter 16

1 *Qui vincit non est victor nisi victus fatebur*, Ennius, *Fragment*. 31, 493.

2 P. Brunt, *Italian Manpower* (Oxford, 1971), pp. 422-34.

3 Trophies taken from temples after Cannae, Livy 22. 57. 10–11.

4 For logistics see J. Roth, *The Logistics of the Roman Army at War, 264 BC –AD 235* (Leiden, 1999).

5 For the change in the coinage see M. Crawford, 'War and finance', *Journal of Roman Studies* 54 (1964), pp. 29–32.

6 See L. Keppie, *The Making of the Roman Army* (London, 1984), E. Gabba, *Republican Rome: The Army and Allies* (Oxford, 1976), and R. Smith, *Service in the Post-Marian Roman Army* (Manchester, 1958) for the army in this period.

7 A. Toynbee, *Hannibal's Legacy. 2 vols.* (Oxford, 1965) represents the most forceful argument for the long-term impact of the Second Punic War. Brunt (1971) criticized this view and cast doubt on the extent of devastation during the Italian campaigns. A good and insightful survey of the debate is to be found in T. Cornell, 'Hannibal's Legacy: The effects of the Hannibalic War on Italy', in T. Cornell, B. Rankov & P. Sabin, *The Second Punic War: A Reappraisal* British Institute of Classical Studies Supplement 67 (London, 1996), pp. 97–117.

8 E.g. Sallust, *Bellum Catilinae* 51. 38.

9 For the dominance of commercial concerns in Punic thinking see B. Caven, *The Punic Wars* (London, 1980), *passim*, esp. pp. 291–4.

Chronology

The Roman consular year usually began in March and as a result the consuls remained in office for the first few months of the year after the date given here. There is some debate over to what extent the Roman calendar was at this period out of synchronization with the modern year. Numerals in brackets after a name denote whether the man had held the consulship before. Consuls who abdicated after a few days or whose election was declared invalid are not included here.

Date	Consuls	Events
264	Ap. Claudius Caudex M. Fulvius Flaccus	Outbreak of **First Punic War**; Roman expedition to relieve Messana.
263	M. Valerius Maximus Messala M. Otacilius Crassus	Hiero surrenders and allies Syracuse with Rome.
262	L. Postumius Megellus Q. Mamilius Vitullus	Siege of Agrigentum.
261	L. Valerius Flaccus T. Otacilius Crassus	Fall of Agrigentum; Punic naval squadrons raid Italian coast; Romans decide to build fleet.
260	Cn. Cornelius Scipio Asina C. Duilius	Scipio Asina taken prisoner at Lipara; Duilius wins sea battle off Mylae.
259	L. Cornelius Scipio C. Aquillius Florus	Fighting in Corsica and Sardinia as well as Sicily.
258	A. Atlius Caiatinus C. Sulpicius Paterculus	Romans win naval battle off Sulci.
257	C. Atilius Regulus Cn. Cornelius Blasio	Romans win naval battle off Tyndaris.
256	L. Manlius Vulso Longus M. Atilius Regulus – *suff.* (II)	Romans win naval battle off Ecnomus and invade Africa; Regulus defeats Punic army at Adys; peace negotiations fail.

255	Ser. Fulvius Paetinus Nobilior M. Aemilius Paullus	Regulus defeated by Xanthippus near Tunis; Roman fleet rescues survivors and defeats Punic navy off Hermaeum; heavy Roman losses in storm.
254	Cn. Cornelius Scipio Asina (II) A. Atilius Caiatinus (II)	Panormus captured.
253	Cn. Servilius Caepio C. Sempronius Blaesus	Roman fleet suffers in storm off Cape Palinurus.
252	C. Aurelius Cotta P. Servilius Geminus	Romans capture more towns in Sicily, including Lipara and Thermae.
251	L. Caecilius Metellus C. Furius Pacilus	Further fighting in Sicily; Carthaginians reinforce their army on the island.
250	C. Atilius Regulus (II) L. Manlius Vulso Longus (II)	Romans win battle outside Panormus and commence siege of Lilybaeum.
249	P. Claudius Pulcher L. Junius Pullus Dictator: A. Atilius Caiatinus *Mag. Equ*: Caecilius Metellus	Punic navy wins great victory off Drepana; Roman fleet suffers heavily in storm near Camarina; dictator sent to command in Sicily.
248	C. Aurelius Cotta (II) P. Servilius Geminus (II)	Sieges of Lilybaeum and Drepana continue.
247	L. Caecilius Metellus (II) N. Fabius Buteo	Sieges continue; Hamilcar Barca lands in Sicily.
246	M. Otacilius Crassus (II) M. Fabius Licinus	Continued low-intensity fighting in Sicily.
245	M. Fabius Buteo C. Atilius Balbus	Continued low-intensity fighting in Sicily.
244	A. Manlius Torquatus Atticus C. Sempronius Blaesus (II)	Hamilcar moves to Mt Eryx.
243	C. Fundanius Fundulus C. Sulpicius Galus	Continued fighting around Eryx.
242	C. Lutatius Catulus A. Postumius Albinus	New Roman fleet formed.
241	A. Manlius Torquatus Atticus (II) Q. Lutatius Cerco	Romans win decisive sea battle at the Aegates Islands; Carthage accepts peace; end of **First Punic War**.
240	C. Claudius Centho M. Sempronius Tuditanus	Outbreak of Mercenary War in Africa.
239	C. Mamilius Turrinus Q. Valerius Falto	

238	Ti. Sempronius Gracchus P. Valerius Falto	Rome annexes Sardinia and threatens Carthage with renewal of war.
237	L. Cornelius Lentulus Caudinius Q. Fulvius Flaccus	End of Mercenary War; Hamilcar Barca sent to Spain.
236	P. Cornelius Lentulus Caudinus C. Licinius Varus	Gallic raids on northern Italy.
235	T. Manlius Torquatus C. Atilius Balbus (II)	
234	L. Postumius Albinus Sp. Carvilius Maximus	
233	Q. Fabius Maximus M. Pomponius Matho	
232	M. Aemilius Lepidus M. Publicius Malleolus	The tribune C. Flaminius carries a bill to distribute the *ager Gallicus* to citizens.
231	M. Pomponius Matho C. Papirius Maso	
230	M. Aemilius Bardula M. Junius Pera	
229	L. Postumius Albinus (II) Cn. Fulvius Centumalus	Death of Hamilcar Barca; succeeded by his son-in-law Hasdrubal; First Illyrian War; Romans establish a protectorate on the Illyrian coast.
228	Sp. Carvilius Maximus (II) Q. Fabius Maximus (II)	
227	P. Valerius Flaccus M. Atilius Regulus	The praetor C. Flaminius probably the first governor of Rome's Sicilian province.
226	M. Valerius Messalla L. Apustius Fullo	
225	L. Aemilius Papus C. Atilius Regulus	Gallic invaders defeated at Telamon.
224	T. Manlius Torquatus (II) Q. Fulvius Flaccus (II)	
223	C. Flaminius P. Furius Philus	Flaminius wins victory over Insubres in Cisalpine Gaul.
222	M. Claudius Marcellus Cn. Cornelius Scipio Calvus	Insubres defeated at Clastidium and their capital, Mediolanum (Milan), captured.
221	P. Cornelius Scipio Asina M. Minucius Rufus	Hasdrubal assassinated and succeeded by Hannibal.
220	L. Veturius Philo C. Lutatius Catulus	Construction of *Via Flaminia*.

219	L. Aemilius Paullus M. Livius Salinator	Second Illyrian War; Siege and Fall of Saguntum.
218	P. Cornelius Scipio Ti. Sempronius Longus	Outbreak of **Second Punic War**; Hannibal's March to Italy; Romans defeated at Ticinus and Trebia; Cn. Scipio lands in Spain.
217	Cn. Servilius Geminus C. Flaminius (II) Dictator: Q. Fabius Maximus *Mag. Equ:* M. Minucius Rufus	Flaminius defeated at Lake Trasimene; Romans appoint Fabius Maximus dictator; Fabius avoids contact with Hannibal's army, but fails to prevent his escape from Campania; Minucius defeated in large skirmish; Cn. Scipio wins naval encounter off the River Ebro.
216	L. Aemilius Paullus (II) C. Terentius Varro Dictator: M. Junius Pera *Mag. Equ:* Ti. Sempronius Gracchus	Hannibal wins massive victory at Cannae; Capua and some other states defect; Cn. and P. Scipio defeat Hasdrubal Barca near the Ebro (Iber); Romans appoint dictator; continued fighting especially around Nola; Roman army massacred in Cisalpine Gaul.
215	Q. Fabius Maximus (III) Ti. Sempronius Gracchus	Further fighting around Nola; Hannibal takes Casilinum; Punic reinforcements arrive at Locri; death of Hiero; alliance between Hannibal and Philip V of Macedon; start of **First Macedonian War**.
214	Q. Fabius Maximus (IV) M. Claudius Marcellus (II)	Romans retake Casilinum; Gracchus defeats Hanno at River Calor; murder of Hieronymus and defection of Syracuse to Carthage; Marcellus begins to operate in Sicily; Laevinus defeats Macedonians at Apollonia; more fighting near Nola.
213	Q. Fabius Maximus the Younger Ti. Sempronius Gracchus (II)	Assault on Syracuse fails and Marcellus begins siege; Carthaginian army lands in Sicily.
212	Ap. Claudius Pulcher Q. Fulvius Flaccus (III)	Hannibal captures Tarentum; Romans start siege of Capua; Hanno defeated at Beneventum; Gracchus killed; Hannibal wins victory at Herdonea; in Sicily Marcellus eventually captures Syracuse.
211	P. Sulpicius Galba Maximus Cn. Fulvius Centumalus Maximus	Hannibal marches on Rome, but fails to prevent the fall of Capua; P. and Cn. Scipio defeated and killed in Spain; alliance between Rome and Aetolian League.
210	M. Valerius Laevinus M. Claudius Marcellus (III)	Hannibal wins second victory at Herdonea; Scipio Africanus appointed to Spanish command; Lilybaeum captured by Romans;

		mixed fortunes in Greece; Romans raid African coast.
209	Q. Fabius Maximus (V) Q. Fulvius Flaccus (IV)	Tarentum recaptured by Fabius; Scipio takes New Carthage; further fighting in Greece.
208	T. Quinctius Crispinus M. Claudius Marcellus (IV)	Both consuls killed in ambush; further Roman raids on African coast; Scipio wins battle of Baecula, but Hasdrubal Barca still leaves Spain.
207	C. Claudius Nero M. Livius Salinator (II)	Hasdrubal Barca invades Italy, but defeated at Metaurus; Philip V's allies win victory at Mantineia; more Roman raids on African coast.
206	L. Veturius Philo Q. Caecilius Metellus	Aetolians make peace with Philip V; Scipio wins decisive victory at Ilipa and later suppresses Caecilius Metellus rebellion by Spanish tribes.
205	P. Cornelius Scipio P. Licinius Crassus Dives	End of **First Macedonian War**; Scipio prepares invasion of Africa; more Roman raids on African coast; Locri captured and Pleminius scandal; Mago invades Italy.
204	M. Cornelius Cethegus P. Sempronius Tuditanus	Invasion of Africa.
203	Cn. Servilius Caepio C. Servilius Geminus	Scipio destroys enemy winter camps and wins victory at Great Plains; Hannibal and Mago recalled.
202	Ti. Claudius Nero M. Servilius Pulex Geminus	Scipio defeats Hannibal at Zama.
201	Cn. Cornelius Lentulus P. Aelius Paetus	Peace formally concluded; end of **Second Punic War**.
200	P. Sulpicius Galba Maximus (II) C. Aurelius Cotta	Start of **Second Macedonian War;** heavy fighting in Cisalpine Gaul.
199	L. Cornelius Lentulus P. Villius Tappulus	
198	T. Quinctius Flamininus Sex. Aelius Paetus Catus	
197	C. Cornelius Cethegus Q. Minucius Rufus	Cethegus wins major victory over Insubres; Flamininus defeats Philip V at Cynoscephalae and ends **Second Macedonian War;** rebellion in Spain.
196	L. Furius Pupureo M. Claudius Marcellus	Marcellus defeats Insubres; Hannibal elected suffete.

195	L. Valerius Flaccus M. Porcius Cato	Hannibal exiled; Cato campaigns in Spain, winning a major battle at Emporion.
194	P. Cornelius Scipio (II) Ti. Sempronius Longus	Victory over Lusitanian tribes, but war continues.
193	L. Cornelius Merula Q. Minucius Thermus	
192	L. Quinctius Flamininus Cn. Domitius Ahenobarbus	Beginning of **Syrian War** with Antiochus III.
191	P. Cornelius Scipio Nasica M. Acilius Glabrio	Antiochus III defeated by Romans at Thermopylae; Scipio defeats Boii in Cisalpine Gaul.
190	L. Cornelius Scipio C. Laelius	Seleucid fleet led by Hannibal defeated.
189	Cn. Manlius Vulso M. Furius Nobilior	Antiochus III defeated by L. Scipio at Magnesia, brings the **Syrian War** to an end; Vulso attacks the Galatians.
188	M. Valerius Messalla C. Livius Salinator	
187	M. Aemilius Lepidus C. Flaminius	Beginning of attacks on Scipios; *Via Aemilia* and *Via Flaminia* constructed in northern Italy.
186	Sp. Postumius Albinus Q. Marcius Philippus	Philippus defeated by Ligurians.
185	Ap. Claudius Pulcher M. Sempronius Tuditanus	
184	P. Claudius Pulcher L. Porcius Licinus	Exile of Scipio Africanus; Cato's censorship.
183	Q. Fabius Labeo M. Claudius Marcellus	Death of Scipio Africanus.
182	L. Aemilius Paullus Cn. Baebius Tamphilus	
181	P. Cornelius Cethegus M. Baebius Tamphilus	Major rebellion by Celtiberian tribes.
180	A. Postumius Albinus Luscus C. Calpurnius Piso	
179	L. Manlius Acidinus Fulvianus Q. Furius Flaccus	Celtiberians defeated.
178	A. Manlius Vulso M. Junius Brutus	

177 C. Claudius Pulcher
Ti. Sempronius Gracchus

176 Cn. Cornelius Scipio Hispallus
Q. Petillius Spurinus

175 M. Aemilius Lepidus (II)
P. Murcius Scaevola

174 Sp. Postumius Albinus Paullulus
Q. Murcius Scaevola

173 L. Postumius Albinus
M. Popillius Laenas

172 P. Aelius Ligus
C. Popillius Laenas

Both consuls plebeian for the first time; start of **Third Macedonian War**.

171 P. Licinius Crassus
C. Cassius Longinus

170 A. Atilius Serranus
A. Hostilius Mancinus

169 Cn. Sevilius Caepio
Q. Marcius Philippus (II)

168 L. Aemilius Paullus (II)
C. Licinius Crassus

167 Q. Aelius Paetus
M. Junius Pennus

Perseus defeated at Pydna, ending the **Third Macedonian War**; Kingdom of Macedon dissolved.

166 C. Sulpicius Gallus
M. Claudius Marcellus

165 T. Manlius Torquatus
Cn. Octavius

164 A. Manlius Torquatus
Q. Cassius Longinus

163 Ti. Sempronius Gracchus (II)
M. Iuventius Thalna

162 P. Cornelius Lentulus
Cn. Domitius Ahenobarbus

161 M. Valerius Messalla
C. Fannius Strabo

160 M. Cornelius Cethegus
L. Anicius Gallus

159 Cn. Cornelius Dolabella
M. Furius Nobilior

158	M. Aemilius Lepidus C. Popillius Laenas (II)	
157	Sex. Julius Caesar L. Aurelius Orestes	
156	L. Cornelius Lentulus Lupus C. Marcius Figulus	
155	P. Cornelius Scipio Nasica M. Claudius Marcellus (II)	
154	L. Postumius Albinus M. Acilius Glabrio – *suff.*	Victory over Ligurians; major war begins in Lusitania.
153	Q. Fulvius Nobilior T. Annius Luscus	Major rebellion by Celtiberians.
152	L. Valerius Flaccus M. Claudius Marcellus (III)	
151	A. Postumius Albinus L. Licinius Lucullus	Carthage declares war on Masinissa.
150	T. Quinctius Flamininus M. Acilius Balbus	
149	L. Marcius Censorinus M. Manilius	Start of **Third Punic War**; campaign begins with Roman failures; Andriscus invades Macedonia.
148	Sp. Postumius Albinus Magnus L. Calpurnius Piso Caesoninus	Poor performance of Roman army in Africa continues.
147	P. Cornelius Scipio Aemilianus C. Livius Drusus	Scipio given African command and tightens siege of Carthage.
146	Cn. Cornelius Lentulus L. Mummius	Capture and destruction of Carthage; end of **Third Punic War.**

The Republican Political System

The Magistrates

CENSORS

Two hold office for five years. Role: to carry out the census, the revision of the roll of citizens, also review membership of the senate, admit and expel senators.

CONSULS

Two a year – senior executive officers of the state. Role: to preside over senate and assemblies when in Rome, govern provinces and lead armies abroad to fight all major wars.

PRAETORS

Initially one (four a year from 227; six a year from 197 with need to organize Spanish provinces). Role: primarily judicial and to govern provinces lead armies not led by the consuls.

AEDILES

Four a year (two curule, two plebeian) Role: municipal administration, organization of corn supplies and festivals etc.

TRIBUNES OF THE PLEBS

Ten a year. No patrician allowed to hold the office. Role: to preside over *concilium plebis*.

QUAESTORS

Number gradually rises to ten a year. Role: financial administration at Rome and in the provinces.

The Senate

Membership around 300, regulated by the censors. Members had to be from the 18 senior equestrian centuries – therefore property of at least 400,000 HS. (one HS=100 sesterces, the silver coin that was the basic currency before the introduction of the denarius during the Second Punic War) They had little formal power, but were there to advise the magistrates, especially the consuls. Also received foreign embassies. Considerable prestige from the *auctoritas* of its ex-magistrates and exercised much power, influence because of its permanence.

The Assemblies

1 CONCILIUM PLEBIS

Only plebeians allowed to attend – divided into 35 tribes (4 urban, 31 rural) – membership based on ancestry – presided over by a Tribune of the plebs.

FUNCTION (a) Election of the ten tribunes of the plebs and the plebeian aediles+ special commissioners. (b) Passing Legislation.

2 COMITIA TRIBUTA

Made up of citizens including patricians – divided into 35 tribes (4 urban, 31 rural). Membership based on ancestry. Presided over by a consul, praetor or curule aedile.

FUNCTION (a) Election of curule aediles, quaestors, + special commissioners. (b) Passing Legislation.

3 COMITIA CENTURIATA

Made up of citizens – divided into 193 voting centuries. Originally derived from military organization of citizen militia. Membership of the group was based on possession of a standard of equipment. Eighteen equestrian cavalry centuries at the top (*equites equo publico* – able to claim a horse paid for by the state). Had come to be based on property qualification. Those better equipped wealthier voted first. Also had fewer members in their centuries – therefore had a disproportionate influence on voting. Presided over by a consul or praetor.

FUNCTION (a) Election of consuls, praetors and censors. (b) Declarations of War and ratification of Peace Treaties. Some legislation.

The Consular Army

THE CONSULAR ARMY

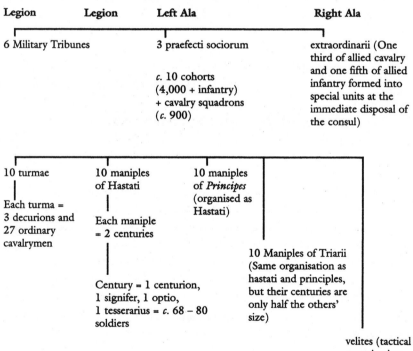

Legion	Legion	Left Ala	Right Ala
6 Military Tribunes		3 praefecti sociorum	extraordinarii (One third of allied cavalry and one fifth of allied infantry formed into special units at the immediate disposal of the consul)
		c. 10 cohorts (4,000 + infantry) + cavalry squadrons (c. 900)	

10 turmae

Each turma = 3 decurions and 27 ordinary cavalrymen

10 maniples of Hastati

Each maniple = 2 centuries

Century = 1 centurion, 1 signifer, 1 optio, 1 tesserarius = c. 68 – 80 soldiers

10 maniples of *Principes* (organised as Hastati)

10 Maniples of Triarii (Same organisation as hastati and principles, but their centuries are only half the others' size)

velites (tactical organization unknown, but probably attached to maniples for administrative purposes)

Index